WINCH, Robert Francis. Familial organization: a quest for determinants, with the collaboration of Rae Lesser Blumberg and others. Free Press, 1978 (c1977). 340p bibl index 77-2434. 13.95 ISBN 0-02-935340-8. C.I.P.

A structural-functional approach to the study of the family, incorporating social psychological exchange theory. It consists primarily of applications of basic sociological and social psychological theory. The book looks carefully at the way family organization varies with function, examines the effects of changes in the mode of subsistence on family organization, and seeks to develop a set of family system determinants. A hypothesized model, labeled as a materialist-evolutionary approach to the explanation of the structure and functioning of the family, is developed and tested, using George P. Murdock's *Ethnographic atlas* (1967). This is a significant extension of Winch's highly regarded work in this field. It is well indexed and has a useful reference section. Upper-division and graduate level.

LARRY A. JACKSON LIBRARY
Lander College
Greenwood, S. C. 29646

FAMILIAL
ORGANIZATION

FAMILIAL ORGANIZATION

A Quest for Determinants

by Robert F. Winch

with the collaboration of
Rae Lesser Blumberg
María-Pilar García
Margaret T. Gordon
Gay C. Kitson

221014

THE FREE PRESS
A Division of Macmillan Publishing Co., Inc.
NEW YORK

Collier Macmillan Publishers
LONDON

LARRY A. JACKSON LIBRARY
Lander College
Greenwood, S. C. 29646

Copyright © 1977 by The Free Press
A Division of Macmillan Publishing Co., Inc.

All rights reserved. No part of this book may be reproduced or transmitted in any
form or by any means, electronic or mechanical, including photocopying, recording,
or by any information storage and retrieval system, without permission in writing
from the Publisher.

The Free Press
A Division of Macmillan Publishing Co., Inc.
866 Third Avenue, New York, N.Y. 10022

Collier Macmillan Canada, Ltd.

Library of Congress Catalog Card Number: 77-2434

Printed in the United States of America

printing number

1 2 3 4 5 6 7 8 9 10

Library of Congress Cataloging in Publication Data

Winch, Robert Francis, 1911-1977
    Familial organization.

    Includes bibliographies and index.
    1. Family--United States. I. Title.
HQ536.W56   301.42'0973   77-2434
ISBN 0-02-935340-8

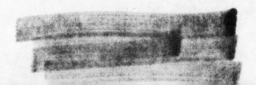

To Martie

Contents

List of Tables

List of Figures

Preface

This book seeks to extend the scope of a theory I first stated in the second edition of *The Modern Family* (1963: Chap. 1). The theory asserts that the unit of sociological analysis is the social system and that the critical dimensions of sociological analysis are structure, function, and influence. It is to be expected that societies will be distributed along these three systemic dimensions and that in complex societies important subsocietal categories (for example, the socioeconomic and ethnic) will also be found to vary in these respects.

The extension of the theory makes its evolutionary basis more explicit and views the economy as salient. It anticipates that the way in which other subsocietal systems, including the family, are organized will be affected by the way in which people make their living—that is, by the mode(s) of subsistence and the related technology. Although there is evidence that the polity, the church, the school, and the family *can* have impact on the economy, I see no reason to challenge the seeming consensus that the economy is the major source of social dynamics.

Some of the support for this theory comes from the ideas and empirical work of other scholars (see especially Chap. 5). There are, however, four original studies that are important in the development of the theory. In the early 1960s Scott Greer and I collaborated on two studies (see Chap. 2) of voluntary associations (his topic) and the family (my interest). I wish to express my warm appreciation to Professor Greer for our long friendship and for the intellectual stimulation that I have derived from him. As this pair of projects developed, Rae Lesser Blumberg, who had been one of our research assistants, demonstrated such competence and zeal that she soon became an associate. By the time of our first publication from these data she was a co-author. These studies explore correlates of familial structure and functioning in two sample surveys. The third study (Chap.

3) looks into conditions under which American families exert much or little influence on their (college student) sons. Margaret T. Gordon joined that project after the data were gathered and contributed to the analysis and the writing of the resulting monograph. The fourth study (Chap. 4) relates size of familial structure in preindustrial societies to the basic modes of subsistence in those societies. This study is an expansion of an analysis Rae Blumberg carried out in her doctoral dissertation. As can be seen, some of the chapters in this book are based in part on prior co-authored papers, referred to in the bibliography. I have revised, recombined, and reinterpreted some of these materials. Accordingly, the final versions do not necessarily represent the views of their co-authors. I wish to pay tribute to the high quality of the contributions made by Professors Greer, Blumberg, and Gordon and to express my earnest thanks for the great help they have provided.

Along the way a number of other people have contributed greatly to the collection and analysis of our data. Among those who aided in getting the initial study under way were Muriel Adler, Ineke Cunningham, Henry Ettman, Claire Gilbert, David Kaufman, and Susan Weiss. Harry Sharp, director of the Wisconsin Poll, was very helpful in making available to us resources for the statewide survey in Wisconsin. Joyce Sween participated in the construction of indexes and did a good deal of our programming. Valuable programming skills were provided subsequently by Dick Schreckengost, Stepan Nazar, Richard Hay, Jr., and Michael Hennessy.

The studies undertaken by Professor Greer and me were initially part of a program under the auspices of Human Sciences Research, Incorporated, where Peter G. Nordlie and S. D. Vestermark, Jr., were helpful in a wide variety of ways. Considerable assistance was provided through a planning grant by the National Institute of Mental Health (MH-16977) and the understanding cooperation of Lorraine Torres and David Pearl. Aid also came from the National Institute for Child Health and Development through the Cross-National Research Project, directed by Marvin B. Sussman. Special thanks are also due the John Simon Guggenheim Memorial Foundation for a second fellowship that freed my time for a year and enabled me to prepare the first draft of this book.

A delightful setting and hospitality during my Guggenheim fellowship were provided by the University of Hawaii, to which I should like to offer my special thanks to their Department of Sociology and its chairman, Edmund Volkart, and also to Margaret Schwertfeger, who was resourceful in locating library materials, and to Freda Hellinger for capable typing service. I am appreciative also of the typing service provided by Carel Rynak at Northwestern University.

I was the beneficiary of two critiques of the entire manuscript—one by Rae Blumberg, who had been associated with many aspects of the work, and the other by Gay C. Kitson, who brought a fresh perspective to the task. Because I fell ill, Professor Kitson also participated in an extensive reworking of Chapter 2 and has seen the book to press for me. Although neither Professor Blumberg nor Professor Kitson is responsible for the book's remaining faults, I am most appreciative of their detailed and constructive criticisms and assistance.

The foregoing paragraphs have underscored the point that many hands and minds have contributed to this book. Not all features of the book are collective products, however, nor can I be sure that there would be consensus among us on all the points the book raises. For this reason I am following a procedure that I hope will be understood by the reader and not prove irritating. Where I believe I am referring to an activity of a collaborative nature or stating an opinion I think we agree upon, I shall use the plural personal pronoun—we, our, us. But where the activity is mine alone or I feel there might be dissensus, I use the singular pronoun—I, my, me.

R. F. W.
Highland Park, Illinois

February, 1977

FAMILIAL
ORGANIZATION

Chapter 1

Introduction

Robert F. Winch

"Family" is a word that may refer to a group of two people—husband and wife, say, or mother and infant—or of hundreds—as in the case of clans. Activities of the family may consist of little more than providing company and giving solace, as among the kibbutzim of Israel, or they may embrace virtually all of society's interaction, as among traditional agrarian Chinese. A father may be unable to get his son to move a lawn mower, or he may determine the boy's occupation and life chances for all the latter's adult years.[1]

In this book my associates and I aspire to specify the major determinants of the structure, functions, and influence of that form of social organization we call the family—why the family tends to be extended, functional, and powerful among sedentary agricultural tribes and Jewish entrepreneurs whereas it tends to be to be small among hunting bands and both small and low in functionality among suburban WASPs.

Sociological Theory of This Book

Our theoretical stance in studying the family relies primarily on sociology, secondarily on social psychology. We shall also make use of studies done by ethnographic anthropologists. Generalizations across societies—whether tribal, industrial, or both—are sociological propositions, we contend, although we realize that others may prefer to speak of them as being part of social, or cultural, anthropology.

Based in part on Winch (1971, Part I) and Winch (1972).

1

I propose that the subject matter of sociology is the analysis of social systems —their origins, structures, functions, the conditions under which and the directions toward which they change, and the circumstances of their disappearance. Let us conceive of a social system as a set of differentiated social positions whose incumbents interact interpositionally with respect to some one or more activities (or tasks). When our attention is upon the system as a set of inter-related positions, we are attending to its structure; when we are looking at the common activities and their consequences, we are attending to its functions. When we investigate the degree to which an individual's behavior is governed by his/her responsibilities to the system, we are concerned with the system's influence.

Having proposed that the major concepts for the analysis of the family be structure, function, and influence, I am obliged to relate these concepts to each other and to indicate how they may be used. I view structure and function, singly and jointly, as criteria that may define the family (or, as I shall now say, the familial system). Later in this book we shall be considering relationships between structure and function as well as between each of them and influence. Since the familial system and, indeed, the societal system are not viewed as closed, however, we shall also expect, and develop theory for, change in the familial system coming from both outside and inside.

From the foregoing analytical viewpoint, when does a set of human beings constitute a familial system? As implied above, there are three possibilities.

1. One option is that to qualify as a familial system that set of individuals must present differentiated positions, the relations among which bear designations of kinship. For example, a man, a woman, and their child bearing the designations of husband-father, wife-mother, and offspring would be recognized as a complete nuclear family. Of course this is a *structural* definition, and it leads to a quest for information that answers such questions as to the makeup of the modal family of a society or of a subsocietal category (e.g., whether female-headed families are overrepresented among white, as well as black, residents of central cities in the United States).

2. One can impose the requirement that to qualify as a familial system a social group must be engaged in one or more activities we recognize as familial— for example, sexual gratification, reproduction, child rearing. Of course this is a *functional* definition. A consequence of the functional definition is that it brings within scrutiny social systems not otherwise thought to be within the field of the family—for example, the family of the hippie commune.

3. One can impose *both structural and functional* requirements. Presumably the notion of a full-blown familial system would require both criteria. From such a formulation it can be seen that *partial* fulfillment of the dual criteria can be interpreted as suggesting a nuclear family at the beginning or at the end of its familial cycle, or perhaps a transitional familial type. Let us conceive of a set consisting of all combinations of living human beings. Then one pair of subsets would consist of those combinations that comply with the structural definition

of familial systems (A) and those that do not ($\overline{\text{A}}$). A second pair of subsets would consist of those that comply with the functional definition of familial systems (B) and those that do not ($\overline{\text{B}}$). The intersecting subset AB would consist of those groups that qualify as families both structurally and functionally. Of considerable interest, however, both from the standpoint of theory and of social action would be those in two of the other subsets $\overline{\text{A}}$B and A$\overline{\text{B}}$. If it should be true that function precedes structure, then subset $\overline{\text{A}}$B would be interpretable as a nascent familial system. If it should be true that absence of function precedes dissolution of the system, then subset A$\overline{\text{B}}$ would be interpretable as true familial disorganization. Of course, subset $\overline{\text{A}}\overline{\text{B}}$ consists of cases that are irrelevant to our interest.

What are the functions of families, of societies, and of other social systems? It seems useful to postulate a set of functions that appear to be necessary for a society to continue in being. Some call these functions societal requisites; I speak of them as basic societal functions. This means that I postulate that the functions I am about to specify are individually necessary and jointly sufficient for the survival of a human society (or social system). The carrying out of each of these functions necessitates some social organization (or structure), and the family is one of these organizations. With such a set of functions one problematic issue of interest to us as students of the family concerns the degree to which the family fulfills the entire set of society-serving activities and hence is important to the societal system. Then it is also useful to look to the familial system to infer such additional functions as may be implied by its structure and its basic societal function.

Various writers have proposed lists of basic societal functions. For example, I have proposed that for a society to carry on indefinitely, provision must exist for each of the following activities:

1. replacement of members lost through death or emigration, generally through sexual reproduction (*replacement function*)
2. production and distribution of goods and services (*economic function*)
3. accommodation of conflicting interests, resolution of disputes, and protection from violence (*political function*)
4. maintenance of sense of purpose and provision of answers to unanswerable questions (*religious function*)
5. training of new recruits to assume adult roles (*socializing-educational function*)[2]

Are these five functions equal in importance? In the sense that all five are assumed to be necessary for the continuation of a social system they are. At any given moment and in any specific context, however, one or another may be of overriding significance. Since we become hungry every day but reproduce only by generations, it is clear that the needs that give rise to these functions vary greatly in the frequency with which they importune mankind. In this sense, as many writers have insisted, the economic function has chronic and perhaps foremost significance. The way in which various peoples make their living keeps recurring in our deliberations about how the family is organized and, indeed, this consideration provides a point of departure for the model of familial organization proposed in Chapter 6 below. But it should be borne in mind that for one fleeing from hostile terrain to the haven of his protective kin, the political function is—momentarily, at least—of transcendent importance. And for the bereaved, religion—again, for the time being—may outweigh any other function.

Because the nuclear family has usually been the only social structure that could legitimately fulfill the function of replacement, normally it has also had the *parental function* of *nurturing and controlling* the child. Because the family has been the social structure through which children normally enter the society, the family has borne the *position-conferring function*. It sometimes fulfills this function for other members as well—for example, wives in situations of economic dependency. Because interaction in the family is typically primary in Cooley's (1909) sense of being intimate and face-to-face, the family has frequently borne the function of *emotional gratification*. That is, the family provides an emotional haven for the assuaging of personal tragedies and the dressing of psychic wounds and it provides a responsive audience for the sharing of personal triumphs and joys.[3]

I have postulated five functions as necessary for societies to survive. Of these the function of replacement is generally fulfilled within the familial system. The degree to which one or more of the other four basic societal functions are carried out by the family varies greatly from one society to another. Among the peasantry of prerevolutionary China, the family was a unit of production and it conducted religious services centering around the worship of dead ancestors; in the Israeli kibbutz described by Spiro (1956) the family fulfills neither of these functions. Furthermore, within complex societies there is functional variation among subsocietal categories, especially those linked with socioeconomic status and with ethnicity. An example of such intrasocietal variation comes from one of our studies (see Chap. 2 below) wherein Jews in an upper-middle-class suburb reported a history of more involvement in family businesses than did Catholics or Protestants. Finally, I have postulated two functions—parental and position-conferring—as corollaries of the family's function of replacement, and one—emotional gratification—as a corollary of its small and intimate structure.

With this much conceptual development I turn to a way of making empirical use of the structural and functional criteria for defining familial systems. This begins by asking a respondent to name his/her kin, which results in a slate of candidates for membership in the respondent's familial system. Selection into membership, however, is a decision of the analyst, who would require that each nominee be shown to be participating with the respondent in some activity subsumable under one or more of the functions mentioned above. Presumably (usually?) the respondent's spouse is involved with the respondent in procreation. A brother or sister's husband or some other relative may be involved with the respondent in mutual defense (political function); a woman and her mother may be involved in cultivating a garden (economic function); and so on.

To extend this notion, let us assume that we are investigating the familial system in a hitherto unknown society, but that for some reason we know enough of its language to do some interviews. Somehow we are able to identify and obtain the cooperation of a representative set of respondents. Our initial questions ask with whom they engage in various sorts of activities we can classify as subsumable under one or another of the foregoing functions.[4] Then the respondents should be asked to identify all living relatives and the nature of the kin tie to each other. Cross-tabulation of each respondent's functional activities and that respondent's co-actors would enable us to draw functional limits on the familial system and kin limits on the functions.

Now it can be seen that operationally our definition of a familial system is structural-functional in the following way:

1. Ego reports whom he/she recognizes as kinsman (structural criterion).
2. Ego reports with whom he/she engages in activities the analyst interprets as functional (with respect to some set of functional categories such as those proposed above).
3. The analyst then reduces ego's nominations of the members of his/her familial system by eliminating those not mentioned in step 2.
4. To those ego names in step 2 the analyst may add some individuals to ego's familial system—even though they are not related by blood, marriage, or adoption—on the basis of fictive kinship plus their participation with ego in functional activities. We shall return to this theme in a later chapter when we consider Stack's (1974) description of mother-headed households.

Among numerous others, Hempel (1959) and Turner (1974) have emphasized that, depending on how it is carried out, functional analysis may be vulnerable to such criticisms as being teleological, tautological, and nonempirical. I believe that the theorizing of this book avoids the hazards of which they warn. And on the positive side it should be noted that functional analysis sensitizes author and reader to a roster of important task-oriented activities around which important structures of societies are organized. In so doing, this mode of analysis makes empirically problematic the relation of the subsocietal system of interest —the family—to other subsocietal systems and to societal systems both across societies and through time.

Among other critics of a structural-functional sociology are the Lenskis (1974), who point out that this mode of analysis fails to deal with conflict and change, and propose to substitute an approach they call ecological-evolutionary. Just how vulnerable structural-functional theory is to these latter charges depends, it seems to me, on the particular theorist one has in mind. The Lenskis are referring to Talcott Parsons. Without seeking to diminish Parsons' contributions, I should propose that he is not the only writer whose work merits our attention. A theorist who sought to integrate the concepts of function and change was Ogburn, one of whose best known books was entitled *Social Change* (1922).

It is my view that although there is nothing inherent in structural-functional sociology to preclude the analysis of change and conflict, it is desirable to supplement the theory in the direction the Lenskis propose. Indeed, in one passage they label their own orientation as "structural-functional-ecological-evolutionary" (Lenski and Lenski, 1974:24). It is my view, however, that the term "ecological" does not quite capture the meaning that is most important. In line with Sumner's comment that the first task of life is to make a living, we shall be looking at the ways in which peoples organize the economy, the environment from which they wrest a living, their mode of subsistence, the technology with which they exploit the environment, and the ways in which they organize to produce a living and to divide the fruits of production, including the resulting systems of inequality.

An assumption of this book is that certain categories of activities must be carried out for social systems to survive and that these activities reward some members of those systems, although simultaneously those activities may not only fail to reward but may even punish other members of the systems. Part of the structural-functional analysis involves noting how responsibility for important functions, especially basic societal functions, passes from some concrete structures to others and what are the consequences of such changes. Ogburn (1929) was an innovator and contributor to this type of analysis. He explained the contemporaneous American family as a resultant of the loss of functions to other structures in American society—especially the economy and the school. By making problematic the structural location of specified functions, he devised a strategy for the analysis of social change and social institutions.

Important changes in the mode of subsistence, frequently occasioned by technical innovation, tend to be followed by changes in the economy and then in the family and other subsocietal systems. Although changes in other systems can have impact on the economy, it seems that significant societal changes originate more often in the economy and that their consequences then tend to radiate into other subsocietal systems.

In the sense that we look to the way of making a living for the major innovations, the resulting theory may be called "materialist." In the sense that we are interested in following societies from simple to more complex degrees of organization, it may be called "evolutionary." Thus the effort to account for any particular familial pattern—its structure, functioning, and influence—will be based on an orientation that is materialist and evolutionary.

Social Psychological Theory of This Book

The viewpoint of social psychology leads to the consideration of the family as a set of interacting individuals. This suggests such questions as the following. Why do individuals participate in the family? Why do people marry? Why do they choose the particular spouses they do? Why do they remain married? Why do parents suffer through the frustrations of parenthood? Why do children put up with the authoritarian intolerance of parents? Why do adult offspring provide support—emotional and financial—to aged and dependent parents?

The usual answers to most questions of this type are cultural, that is, people learn that it is "right" to marry, to become faithful spouses and "good" parents, to exhibit filial solicitude, and so on. Then why do some fail to conform to such expectations?

That variety of social psychological theory known as exchange theory (Thibaut and Kelley, 1959; Homans, 1961, 1974; Blau, 1964) is relevant to such questions. It enables one to account for the continued participation of an actor in—or withdrawal from—a social system on the basis of the gratification the actor derives and/or expects to derive from the system and the perceived opportunities for equal or greater gratification from membership in some other social system.

Two examples come to mind. First, let us assume a society in which mate selection is voluntary (rather than arranged) and is based on mutual attraction. Let us assume further that there are two men, A and B, and one woman, C, in the same field of eligibles. Why does A find C attractive whereas B finds her a bore? Our theory implies that A has received more gratification from his relationship with C and anticipates more than does B. Furthermore, it implies that what is popularly known as love can be stated as an emotional state linked to a perceived history and expectation on the part of the lover that the person loved has been and will continue to be a source of gratification. This variant of exchange theory has come to be known as the theory of complementary needs in mate selection (Winch, 1958).

Another example concerns Mr. X and Mr. Y, who are, respectively, lower-status and upper-status fathers of adolescent boys. Let us assume both fathers are concerned lest their sons' friends persuade the sons to drop out of school rather than to pursue their studies. Mr. X has consistently offered poor advice and has been a failure in business; Mr. Y has the opposite record. In a later chapter we shall develop the hypothesis suggested by these "facts" as to which father would be likely to have the greater influence with his son.

The latter example enables us to link our two basic theories. Membership in a social system, our theory suggests, exposes one to the behavior of incumbents of various positions in the system, and thus structure can be viewed psychologically as a set of models whose behaviors a neophyte can observe and learn. The functions of a social system are generally viewed as system-serving, but it also seems useful to look upon social systems as rewarding some of their members and therefore as having functions that are individual-serving. In our last example the theory might be phrased that family and peer group are competing for the boys' acceptance of their position-conferring (or status-conferring) function. Thus function may be conceptualized as both system-serving and individual-serving, and this Janus-faced aspect of function may be added to the model-position formulation as a second conceptual link between our structural-functional sociology and our social psychological exchange theory (Winch, 1962, 1970; Winch and Gordon, 1974).[5]

Plan of This Book

In the foregoing pages I have tried to outline the nature of the general theory —sociological and social psychological—that underlies our work. Applications of these somewhat abstract formulations appear in the chapters that follow and that constitute the bulk of the book. Our own studies are reported in Chapters 2 to 4. When they were undertaken, they were not conceived as integral parts of a master plan. Rather, each was seen as a self-contained study; each had its own problem, data, and technique of analysis. In retrospect, however, I now see that a common theory has stimulated them and is informed by them. Indeed, the purpose of this book is to explicate that theory, develop it into a model, test and then refine the model. Of course, if the interrelations of these studies had been evident to me when they were planned, it would have been possible to make them more interlocking and mutually illuminating.

The history of these studies may be divided into two major phases. With Scott Greer and Rae Lesser Blumberg as my principal associates, I began in the early 1960s an effort to measure familial structure and functionality—first in a suburban and then in a statewide sample, both in the United States. Success in this quest led us to search for correlates of a summary variable of familial complexity we came to call isolation-extended-familism. Two of the more promising predictors of extended familism turned out to be ethnicity and migratory status. These findings led us to conclude that several types of American family could be distinguished (Chap. 2). In Chapter 3 we report on a study seeking to relate the family's influence over sons to its structure and functioning. Here we invoke our parallel social psychological theory.

While our group was at work exploring and operationalizing structure and functioning of American families, two especially seminal works on the family were published: Nimkoff and Middleton (1960) and Goode (1963). Both works related the complexity of familial structure to the complexity of societies, but they seemed to come to contrary conclusions as to the way in which these variables were related. We were stimulated to reconcile these seemingly contradictory findings with the outcome as shown in Chapter 4. In the sense that this work led us to intersocietal comparisons[6] and the use of Murdock's Ethnographic Atlas, this enterprise constituted a bridge between the earlier stages of our work, which sought to operationalize and find correlates of American familial organization, and the more recent undertakings, which are reported in Chapters 6 to 10.

The second phase of our undertaking began with a search for a comprehensive theory of familial organization. Most of the evidence of variation in familial organization appears in the ethnographic literature, and it is not surprising that most of the theorizing on this score has been published by ethnologists (Chap. 5).

Our formulation proposes a large number of influences that shape the organization of the family. These include factors pertaining to the economic function—the environment and the technology by means of which a society produces its subsistence and wealth, the nature of work and the division of labor, the presence and ownership of surplus, and the control of the means of production. Our formulation also attends to the socializing-educational function—the way people are socialized into various adult roles—and the political function, including levels of administration and dimensions of inequality. We have not yet worked the religious function into our model although we have made one foray with a religious variable (Blumberg, Carns, and Winch, 1970). Our theory as to how these factors are related to each other is presented in Chapter 6. To the extent that it is possible to do so, we have operationalized our model with data from the Ethnographic Atlas and have undertaken an empirical check on our formulation in Chapter 7.

The mother-headed household is the focus of interest in the next two chapters. In Chapter 8 Blumberg and Garcia use data of the U.S. Census to show that when income is controlled the correlation of mother-headed households with race disappears; they also relate the separate households of women in polygynous societies to the economic functionality of those women. In Chapter 9 I use ethnographies from the Caribbean, Latin America, and the United States to challenge the existence of a pattern of a mother-child family.

In the final chapter we seek to revise and to improve our formulation on the basis of the wisdom distilled from our empirical undertakings. We cannot be sure whether Chapter 10 merely tolls the knell of phase 2 of our project or heralds a new and productive stage 3; we can only hope.

Notes

1. There are some, however, who use "family" to refer either to a set of a father, a mother, and their minor children or to related persons occupying a common dwelling unit. When family is so used, other relatives are frequently referred to as "kin." (See, e.g., Goody, 1971: 83; Farber, 1976.)

2. Elsewhere (Winch, 1971), I have discussed the family's fulfillment of the basic societal functions: replacement, Chapter 7; economic and political, Chapter 4; religious and socializing-educational, Chapter 5. It is my opinion that a large part of the confusion appearing in the literature about the difficulty in distinguishing between nuclear and extended familial systems results from failing to make the distinction between structure and function in some such fashion as appears above. (Cf., e.g., Yorburg, 1975; Hendrix, 1975; Anderson, 1971.)

3. More extended discussions of the family's derived functions appear in Winch, 1971, as follows: parental, Chapters 13–17; position-conferring, Chapter 8; and emotional gratification, Chapter 9. Related to the position-conferring function with its implications about status and property is the transferring of property and rights from one generation to the next. Writing in the context of Barbadian society, Greenfield (1966: 99) remarks that "one of the primary motivations for legal marriage appears to be the desire to insure the property rights of the conjugal partner and children."

4. In operationalizing functions we should note the contribution of Freed and

Freed (1971) who have created a profile test to use in any society in which each respondent is asked to whom he/she gives and from whom he/she receives: influence, instruction, help, sympathy.

5. Adam Smith's (1814 [1776]) notion of the "invisible hand" is an early formulation of how individually oriented and collectively oriented theories may be interrelated. For a writer who seems unhappy at such attempts at integration see Ekeh (1974).

6. Simultaneously, there were other influences stimulating me to an intersocietal perspective. At the 1966 meeting of the International Sociological Association in Evian, France, Reuben Hill, then chairman of the Committee on Family Research, appointed me to a subcommittee under the chairmanship of Marvin Sussman to plan an intersocietal study. At that time also intersocietal studies were being stimulated at Northwestern University by the Council on Intersocietal Studies, of which Richard D. Schwartz was serving as director.

Chapter 2

Types of American Families: An Unsatisfactory Classification

Robert F. Winch
Gay C. Kitson

In our opinion Goode's *World Revolution and Family Patterns* (1963) is the best sociological analysis of the family. The accolade does not commit us, however, to concur with each of the many conclusions and opinions of that richly interesting book. In that monograph Goode concluded that as traditional societies became modernized, their diverse familial systems were converging on what he called the conjugal family—that is, a nuclear family in interaction with kinsmen. He noted the diversity in traditional familial systems—patrilineal or matrilineal or other, polygamous or monogamous, extended or not—and saw a single pattern emerging. Goode's ingenious analysis of intransigent data raises two questions that will constitute the problems of the present chapter and Chapter 4:

1. Is it true that a single pattern of familial organization is emerging, or is there evidence of a plurality of patterns? The present chapter will present

Based in part on Winch, Greer, and Blumberg (1967), Winch and Greer (1968), Winch, Greer, Blumberg, and Sween (1969), Winch (1974a), and Winch (1976).

evidence concerning a variety of patterns which are visible in the contemporary United States and suggest some reasons for their existence.

2. In general, what are the conditions that give rise to the nuclear family system? From a welter of contradictory findings it now seems tenable to conclude that there is a tendency for a familial pattern to be related to the complexity of the society in which it exists. The relation between the complexity of the family and that of society is the topic of Chapter 4.

As we begin our review of the literature, we note that over the past couple of generations there have been three somewhat contradictory views as to the nature of the American family and the process by which it was getting to wherever it was going.

Writers Representing the American Family as Both Isolated and Nuclear

In the 1930s and 1940s leading scholars were writing confidently that the American family was nuclear and isolated. The phrase "isolated nuclear family" seems to have been launched into social science by Talcott Parson's essay of 1943. Among others expressing the view that the American family is characteristically of the isolated nuclear form were Carle C. Zimmerman (1947) and Louis Wirth (1938).

The locus of power, authority, and influence was the focus of Zimmerman's analysis of the family (1947). As he viewed the classical Athenian and Roman and the modern Western civilizations, he found that he could distinguish three types of familial organizations. "Atomistic" is the rubric Zimmerman applied to the type exerting the least control over the behavior of its members.[1] He found the American family to have been generally atomistic since early in the nineteenth century. Zimmerman added a note of Spenglerian inevitability by his claim that the isolated ("atomistic") nuclear family was a concomitant of the late or decadent stage of great civilizations.

Wirth's view of the urban family was a corollary of his view of the urban way of life (1938). To him, social relationships in the city were impersonal, superficial, transitory, segmental, anonymous, and even anomic. In the city, he said, the bonds of kinship were weak, and the individual members were thus free "from the large kinship group characteristic of the country . . . [to] pursue their own diverging interests in their vocational, educational, religious, recreational, and political life" (p. 21).

In a later work, Parsons speaks of the American family as "an open, multilineal, conjugal system . . . made up exclusively of interlocking conjugal families" (1949: 174, 175, 180). The fact that this system lacks "any structural bias in favor of solidarity with the ascendant and descendant families in any one line of descent has enormously increased the structural isolation of the individual conjugal family." Also relevant is his observation that the American "isolated nuclear family" has become almost completely functionless on the macroscopic level and, for its members, retains only the functions of the socialization of children and the stabilization of adult personalities (Parsons and Bales, 1955: 16-17).

Somewhat different versions of the same theme came from Ogburn and from Burgess and Locke. Ogburn (1929) presented survey data to show that the instrumental functionality of the American family was declining; of those functions he attributed to the family, he concluded that only what he called the "affectional function" was flourishing. Burgess and Locke (1945) captured a similar notion in the title of their textbook: *The Family: From Institution to Companionship.*

Writers Representing the American Family as
Participating Actively in a Kin Network

The literature just reviewed portrayed the American family as limited in function, weak in influence, nuclear in form, and isolated from kinsmen. There followed a spate of studies purporting to challenge some of these formulations. Dotson (1951) found that among the urban working class there was little participation in voluntary organizations but that family and kinship provided companionship and recreation. Greer (1956, 1958) reported that about three quarters of his Los Angeles respondents were visiting kinsmen at least as often as once a month, and he concluded that the interaction of urban residents with their kinsmen constituted "the most important social relations for all types of urban populations." Litwak (1960) wrote that about one third of his sample of Buffalo housewives reported having received visits from kinsmen as often as once a week, and he went on to posit what he called the "modified extended family," which he said

> differs from the "classical extended" family in that it does not demand geographical propinquity, occupational involvement, or nepotism, nor does it have an hierarchical authority structure. On the other hand, it differs from the isolated nuclear family structure in that it does provide significant and continuing aid to the nuclear family. The modified extended family consists of a series of nuclear families bound together on an equalitarian basis, with a strong emphasis on these extended family bonds as an end value (p. 10).

It is difficult to tell from Litwak's writing just how widespread he believes the modified extended family to be in American society and whether or not he believes it to be concentrated in specific socioeconomic strata, occupations, or other categories, and thus far he has not presented data on this point.

Sussman (1954, 1959) found that the overwhelming majority of urban families he studied engaged in some form of mutual aid with their parents and that the maintenance of intergenerational continuity was greater when marriages were culturally homogamous. The Detroit Area Study of the University of Michigan Survey Research Center (1956: Chaps. 4 and 5) discovered that only 11 percent of the families in their Detroit sample had no households of kin in that metropolitan area. The authors stated that most respondents reported having engaged in some mutual aid with relatives, and they concluded: "The 'typical' Detroiter is very much a member of an extended family group. . . . There is little doubt that the kin group is continuing to play an important part in the metropolitan family."

Aiken (1964) reported that spatial and genealogical proximity are positively correlated with interaction with kin. In his Detroit sample he found that 85 percent of all visits were with primary (nuclear) relatives, and 90 percent were either with primary relatives or with secondary (extended) kin in the same neighborhood (pp. 81-82). "The effective kinship unit in American urban centers appears, in general, to encompass only households across two generations, and it consists largely of parent-child and sibling relationships" (pp. 79-80). Aiken found the following conditions to be conducive to a high level of interaction with kin: the household of the respondent's kin contains a nuclear relative of the respondent, that relative is female and related to the wife in the respondent's household, there exists a connecting relative in the kinship unit (especially the wife's mother), the responding unit is early in the family cycle and is of blue-collar and middle educational status (pp. 274-275). Social categories registering the highest percentages with no household of kin in the Detroit area—and in that sense isolated—were as follows (pp. 101-102):

Head of household has:
  white-collar occupation, 19%
  income of $10,000 (1955 dollars) or more, 25%
  education beyond high school, 28%
Both husband and wife are migrants, 20%

Leichter and Mitchell (1967) studied kinship among clients of the Jewish Family Service of New York City. These were largely native-born adults whose parents had migrated from Eastern Europe. From separate genealogies obtained from husbands and wives of 10 couples, the average number of kin recognized per couple was 241, of whom about 20 percent were deceased, and well over half of whom were seen regularly at big family gatherings. The expectation is for a considerable amount of interaction with kin. About half of the wives talk with at least one kinsman by telephone every day. No one in the study was without at least one household of kin in New York City, and over half had at least one such household within walking distance. About an eighth had a household of kin living in their own buildings. One such arrangement involved a parental couple who lived in an apartment beside the apartment of their married daughter. They had broken through the wall in order to provide easy access to each other's quarters. About 95 percent of the families had received services and/or monetary aid from kin, and about the same proportion said they had given such aid. "Kin are obligated to give assistance if it is necessary; they also have a right to give it" (p. 123). According to their norms, one can trust relatives and get love from them; moreover, it is selfish to cut oneself off from one's relatives. With such large kin networks there is a problem in drawing kin boundaries. For social occasions this raises excruciating problems. No matter what you do, one respondent said, "you insult somebody anyhow."

Where aid is in the form of money, the flow has usually been reported from the older to the younger generation and of a relatively brief duration, as in a temporary crisis or in assisting a newly married offspring in getting established (Sussman, 1953; see also Sharp and Axelrod, 1956). In the literature on the aged, however, a reverse flow is portrayed (Rosow, 1967; Shanas et al., 1968). It is with the latter evidence in mind that Schnaiberg and Goldenberg (1975) have argued that sociologists have largely overlooked the instrumental functionality of offspring to parents, especially among lower working classes. Aid from younger to older generations, however, was not in the evidence adduced by the revisionists.

Finally, Adams (1968) studied approximately eight hundred young and middle-aged white adults in Greensboro, North Carolina. Aside from declaring that his respondents were all white, Adams gave no information concerning their religio-ethnic characteristics. The location of his study suggests that his sample was more heavily weighted with native-born Protestants of British ancestry than would be generally the case with urban samples in this country. He found that the interactions of these respondents with kin were dominated by their involvement with parents. This interaction, he said, provided intimate communication, concern for each other's welfare, and mutual aid even when affectional ties were weak. Relationships among adult siblings, on the other hand, are characterized by the terms "interest" and "comparison," by which Adams appears to mean that the sibling represents primarily a point of reference or pacemaker in the mobility race and that mutual aid and companionship are not very important. Cousins and other relatives he found to be functionally irrelevant. Adams reported that upward mobility does not restrict interaction with parents. In his data the mother-daughter bond is strong, and females and aged serve as foci of kin affairs.

These findings have been interpreted as more or less direct refutation of the earlier formulations of Zimmerman, Wirth, and Parsons. Perhaps the most emphatic statement comes from one sociologist quoting another as saying, "The isolated nuclear family is a myth. This has already been conclusively demonstrated. It does not merit any further attention of the field, and I, for one, refuse to waste any more time even discussing it" (Rosow, 1965: 341).

Although the tone of these revisionistic writers of the 1950s suggested their conviction that they had soundly refuted the writers of the 1940s and had demonstrated the errors of the earlier writers, it turns out, as we shall see, that as far as Parsons and Zimmerman are concerned, the revisionists did not really join issues with them.

Writers Representing the American Family
as Having Long Been Nuclear

In 1963 Goode seemed to write a Q.E.D. to this discussion by claiming that around the world as societies developed, their familial systems—no matter what their traditional form—seemed to be converging on a conjugal system involving interaction with kinsmen, or what writers of the 1950s had been claiming was the American pattern. In this same volume Goode asserted that in Western Europe and North America the family had been nuclear[2] for a long time—ante-dating the onset of the industrial revolution—and he spoke of the extended family as "the classical family of Western nostalgia," a phrase he had also used in his earlier work on divorce (1956:4). (For more on the long-standing nature of the nuclear family, see Bane, 1976, and Chapter 5 below.)

Thus the three views of the past two generations may be summarized as: (1) an allegation that the American family was becoming isolated and nuclear; (2) a denial that it was isolated; and (3) a further allegation that it had long been nuclear and this state was, therefore, not a recent development.

We shall try to show in the following pages that we have in the United States both isolated and non-isolated nuclear families and both nuclear and extended families. From the assertion that we have a plurality of familial types, it follows that we must disagree in part with all of the foregoing points of view. In our cloudy crystal ball it appears that we have and shall continue to have familistic pluralism rather than monism.

Difficulties Involved in Testing the Formulations of the Earlier Writers

How can it happen, one might ask, that in a relatively short time—a decade or two at the most—opinion can shift from one belief to its polar opposite about a state of affairs that exists under our eyes: the nature of the family in American cities? Where such radical shifts occur, one inference is that there may be poor science.

As we try to assess the American family in the light of the conflicting views portrayed above, it becomes advisable to state as clearly as possible what the issues are—what was claimed by the earlier writers and the nature of the evidence viewed as refutation.

Since the range over which Zimmerman seeks to generalize is the complete sweep of Western civilization starting with the Greeks of Homeric times, his standard of a strong family system comes from early Athens and early Rome, and his data are historical. Zimmerman asserts that from the founding of America as a white society its family has been atomistic, except for the highland clans of the Appalachian and Ozark mountains. It is clear that the authors of the more recent studies have made no effort to compare their observations with such historically remote forms. Hence the recent studies have not joined issues with Zimmerman.

To Wirth the city was a lonely, if fascinating, scene. The urbanite was cut off not only from kinsmen, but from diffuse social contact generally.[3] (Both Parsons and Goode, n.d., saw the small and minimally functional American family as being consistent with the demands of the urban-industrial society the United States had become.) It should be noted that these formulations appeared in a literature that had been presenting urban life as ideal-typically opposite from rural or tribal life. Illustrations of such pairs of terms are folk-urban, *gemeinschaft-gesellschaft,* sacred-secular, and diffuseness-specificity.

If we were to interpret the ideal type as a proposition about reality, we might hypothesize that:

1. All rural (or tribal) residents live in households of extended families and have warm, diffuse relationships with all their kinsmen.
2. No urban resident lives in a household with any extended kinsman or has a warm, diffuse relationship with any of his kinsmen.

Given this extreme phrasing, a single negative case would suffice to falsify either hypothesis. We know of course that ideal types are intended to be exaggerations of reality, but it seems possible that some of the critics of the notion that the American familial pattern was isolated and nuclear reified the ideal type and had in mind such a hypothesis as (2) when giving expression to their refutation. After all this has been remarked, however, it is necessary to conclude that Wirth's manner of thought and style of writing were such as to produce virtually no operationalizable and hence falsifiable propositions.

Perhaps another source of the opinion that the American family is nuclear and isolated is the nature of the data on the family supplied by the U.S. Bureau of the Census. The Bureau uses the household as its unit of observation. Thus, the "family" reported by the Census consists of related persons sharing a dwelling unit. Although we know from ethnographic accounts that some American familial patterns transcend households (e.g., Leichter and Mitchell, 1967; Ianni, 1972), still no intimation of that emerges from census reports.

The paragraph quoting Parsons' views in a previous section of this chapter shows his reasoning that the American kinship system produces the isolated nuclear family, but that passage does not provide defining characteristics that would make possible some estimation as to the prevalence of such a familial form. Elsewhere Parsons has provided more operational language. Commenting that the isolation of the nuclear family does *not* imply a break in the relations of the spouses with their families of orientation, Parsons explains that to him this isolation does mean that (1) the nuclear family "normally" has its own household "not shared with members of the family of orientation of either spouse" and (2) that typically the household is economically independent of any other household (Parsons and Bales, 1955: 10-11).

What evidence can be marshalled to show whether or not American families are isolated in the sense that Parsons uses this term? The statistic relevant to Parsons' condition (1) above is the percentage of married couples who have their own households and have no relatives other than their children in the household. According to the U.S. Bureau of the Census (1972a: Table 1, p. 3), 98.5 percent of all married couples had their own households in 1972, and in 1970 not more than one household in seven contained relatives other than their own children (1972b: Table 54, p. 278). For an overwhelming majority of the American population, then, Parsons' condition (1) is empirically confirmed.

Parsons' condition (2) concerns the economic independence of the household.

Data from the University of Michigan national panel survey of economic progress among 5,000 families indicate that the majority of American families are economically independent. While there are variations by income levels, Baerwaldt and Morgan (1973: 207) demonstrate that on the average only 1 to 2 percent of the total family income is contributed to dependents outside the nuclear family. Those in families with a middle-aged head and those at the highest income levels contribute the most to outside dependents. Young families and those with an aged head are the most likely to receive help. Several local studies suggest that a greater proportion of families give financial aid to and receive aid from relatives. Using urban samples, Sussman (1959) and Hill (1970) indicate that a majority of their respondents reported giving and/or receiving financial aid to or from kinsmen. It appears, however, that a family was listed as receiving financial aid from a kinsman if this had happened only once. Although it is possible that some may interpret such data as refuting Parsons' position with respect to his condition (2), it seems evident that the Sussman and Hill data are not directly relevant since Parsons is apparently referring to an enduring state of affairs rather than to nonrecurring financial aid given in an emergency. For the majority of the population, therefore, Parsons' second criterion, that of economic independence of related nuclear households, seems to be supported. As Baerwaldt and Morgan conclude (1973: 207-208) after also reviewing some limited data on nonfinancial family help: "the pattern of giving and receiving time and money between families is a small and probably irregular form of transfer income in this society."

Concerning Parsons' views on the isolated nuclear family, then, it appears that the revisionists have not contested his assertions about the American family system being open, multilineal, and conjugal. It turns out that by "isolated" Parsons does not mean cut off from contact; indeed, we have noted above about his writing of the American familial system consisting of "interlocking conjugal families." With respect to Parsons' two operational criteria for the isolated nuclear family, it develops that his first criterion—separate households—is clearly substantiated, and, in support of his second criterion, the vast majority of households are economically independent—and finally, that the data of the revisionists do not bear directly on either of these two criteria.

In summary, the formulations of Zimmerman and Wirth are not researchable with respect to whether or not the American nuclear family is isolated. Parsons has suggested two criteria for isolation, but it is possible to allege, as Litwak has done, that a family could be isolated by Parsons' two criteria and still not "really" be isolated. We shall examine data in the following section on Goode's assertion that the American family has long been nuclear.

Some National Data on the Structure of
Domestic Families

The United States took its first census in 1790. At that time the mean household contained nearly six persons (5.7). By 1900, it was 4.6, 3.4 in 1950, 3.1

in 1970, and 2.9 in 1975 (Winch, 1974b: 480; U.S. Bureau of the Census, 1976b: 39). Yet this change in number of persons reflects no alteration in familial positions (husband-father, wife-mother, offspring-sibling, and so on). The reason is that neither at the beginning nor at the end of the interval did the modal household contain any relative outside the nuclear family (grandparent, uncle, and others). Virtually all of the decrease in size of household can be attributed to a reduction by two and a half in the number of children in the average household at any one time (Winch, 1974b: 480). According to official statistics, it thus appears that the average domestic American family has been nuclear ever since 1790. Therefore, there is evidence in favor of Goode's assertion that the nuclear family is not a recent development.

What can the data of the U.S. Bureau of the Census tell us about the contemporary American family? First, we must notice that when the Census Bureau uses the term "family," it is referring to two or more persons related by blood, marriage, or adoption who are residing together. Since common residence is a characteristic of some but not all familial systems, we cannot accept the Census Bureau's definition of family as our own. This is a point that will be developed later in this book. For the moment, however, we shall use the term "domestic family" to refer to related persons who share a dwelling unit, that is, to what the Bureau calls "family."

Approximately 90 percent of the population of the United States lives in domestic families. For March 1975 it was estimated that 190,471,000 persons lived in 55,712,000 domestic families with an average of 3.42 persons per family (see Table 2-1). Of the roughly 56 million domestic families estimated to exist at that time, 84 percent were of the husband-wife type, less than 3 percent were families with other male heads, and 13 percent were headed by women. Among blacks a little over a third of all domestic families are female-headed, and in central cities this proportion rises to 39 percent.

Although the data of the census cannot enlighten us about familial systems that transcend dwelling units, they do provide insights into several types of extended domestic families. One of these is the domestic family that includes a subfamily. The bureau employs the concept of a "subfamily," defined as "a married couple with or without children, or one parent with one or more own single children under 18 years of age, living in a household and related to, but not including, the head of the household or his wife" (U.S. Bureau of the Census, 1976a: 90). From this definition it follows that the total domestic family of which the subfamily is a part constitutes some sort of extended family. (By our definition, an extended family is a social system consisting of two or more familial positions, at least one dyad of which is not a nuclear dyad.) For March 1975 it is reported that there were 1,349,000 subfamilies comprising 3,477,000 persons. When we relate the number of subfamilies to the number of families shown in Table 2-1, we conclude that about 2 percent of all domestic families include subfamilies and therefore may be considered extended.

In Table 2-2 it can be seen that about 54 percent of all persons living in domestic families are either heads of families or wives of heads. (It is the prac-

TABLE 2-1. Distribution of Persons in Families and of Domestic Families in the United States, by Type of Domestic Family Used by U.S. Bureau of the Census and by Race: March 1975

Type of Domestic Family	Persons N (in thousands)	%	Families N (in thousands)	%
Total	190,471	100.0	55,712	100.0
Husband-wife families	162,856	85.5	46,971	84.3
Other families with male head	4,371	2.3	1,499	2.7
Families with female head	23,245	12.2	7,242	13.0
White families	166,111	100.0	49,451	100.0
Husband-wife families	147,021	88.5	42,969	86.9
Other families with male head	3,611	2.2	1,270	2.6
Families with female head	15,480	9.3	5,212	10.5
Black families	21,440	100.0	5,498	100.0
Husband-wife families	13,250	61.8	3,346	60.9
Other families with male head	706	3.3	212	3.8
Families with female head	7,485	34.9	1,940	35.3

Source: U.S. Bureau of the Census. Current Population Reports, Series P-20, No. 291, February 1976. "Household and Family Characteristics: March 1975." Especially Tables 1 and 7.

tice of the Census Bureau to regard the husband as the head of a husband-wife domestic family.) Forty-two percent of the persons living in families are the "own" children of heads. The remainder of persons living in families—about 4 percent—are other relatives. Of these we have seen that approximately 2 percent consist of subfamilies. This leaves another 2 percent that constitute still other forms of the extended family; for example, a nuclear family plus the widowed mother of the husband or wife, or a nuclear family and the unmarried brother of the head of the household, and so forth. Looking at all "other relatives" we see this gives an average of about 1 "other relative" for every 7 families. The incidence of "other relatives" varies considerably, however, depending on the type of family. On the average "other relatives" appear in only about 1 in every 12 families of the husband-wife type. In families with "other male heads," however, the number of "other relatives" is equivalent to about 7 for every 8 such families. Among female-headed families there is an "other relative" in nearly half of the families on the average, and this figure rises to about 7 out of 10 among black, female-headed families.

The likelihood that a person age 14 or over will be a member of a subfamily as distinct from an "other relative" living in a domestic family varies across the

TABLE 2-2. Percentage Distribution of Persons Living with Domestic Families in the United States, by Relation to Head of Family and by Type of Domestic Family Used by U.S. Bureau of the Census: March 1975

Relation to Head of Family	Total	Type of Domestic Family			Black Families with Female Heads
		Husband-Wife Families	Families with Other Male Heads	Families with Female Heads	
All persons	100.0	100.0	100.0	100.0	100.0
Male heads	25.4	28.8	34.3	—	—
Wives of heads and female heads	28.5	28.8	—	31.1	25.9
Own children *(all ages)*	41.7	40.0	36.3	55.7	57.3
25 and over	2.1	1.3	7.3	6.8	3.7
18–24	6.7	6.3	8.6	9.2	8.8
12–17	12.4	11.9	11.6	15.6	16.5
6–11	11.0	10.8	5.9	14.0	16.6
3–5	5.1	5.1	1.8	6.2	7.0
0–2	4.4	4.6	1.2	3.9	4.7
Other relatives	4.4	2.4	29.4	13.2	16.8
Mean number of persons per family	3.42	3.47	2.92	3.21	3.86
Mean number of own children per family	1.43	1.38	1.06	1.79	2.21
Mean number of own children under 18	1.13	1.12	0.60	1.27	1.73
Mean number of other relatives per family	0.15	0.08	0.86	0.42	0.65

Source: U.S. Bureau of the Census. Current Population Reports, Series P-20, No. 291, Feburary 1976. "Household and Family Characteristics: March 1975." Especially Tables 1 and 7.

life cycle. Appendix Table F-1, based on figures from the 1970 Census, displays the percent of subfamily members and the mean number of all relatives of the head living in domestic families by age, sex, and race. Males at all ages are more likely than females to be members (including being the heads) of subfamilies. As a percentage of all relatives of the head living in domestic families, subfamilies are most likely at ages 25 to 34 for both races and sexes. The mean number of other relatives present in domestic families also varies by age. Black and white females between the ages of 14 and 24, and 45 and over are more likely than males of either race to be present as other relatives in domestic families. The pattern of blacks being more likely than whites to be present in domestic families as "other relatives" holds up even within the different age categories.

The mean number of other relatives present in domestic families further varies by family income (see Appendix Table F-2). For the total population in 1970 there are relatively small differences in the mean number of other relatives by 1969 income, although they are somewhat more likely to be present when family income is low or high. However, when the data are broken down by type of domestic family and race, some interesting differences appear. First, among white, husband-wife families there are again relatively small differences by income in the mean number of other relatives present with the most other relatives present at the highest income levels reported—$15,000 and above. Second, black, husband-wife families at all income levels report more relatives of the head present than do white, husband-wife families—with the highest proportion present when income is $15,000 or more. A third point is that while blacks at all income levels in husband-wife and female-headed families have more other relatives present than do whites, both black and white families headed by females have substantially more other relatives of the head present than do husband-wife families of either race. Black, female-headed families have the most other relatives present.

Returning to Table 2-2, one other feature of note concerns the distribution of children by ages. A little over 20 percent of all persons in husband-wife domestic families are children under the age of 12. In families with "other male heads," however, they constitute less that 9 percent of all members; in black, female-headed families, on the other hand, they comprise slightly over 28 percent. This pattern is due in part to the fact that divorced mothers are more likely than divorced fathers to obtain custody of young children, who are often not consulted by the court concerning with whom they would like to live.

The evidence in Table 2-1 that 15 percent of all domestic families are not of the husband-wife variety raises the question as to the extent to which children in the United States are living in families that do not include both parents. From Table 2-3 we learn:

1. Four out of every five children under 18 in the United States live with both parents (80.0%).
2. Roughly 1 child in 6 (15.8%) lives with the mother only.
3. Slightly more than 1 child in 100 (1.2%) lives with the father only.

TABLE 2-3. Percentages of the 67 Million Persons Under 18 Years of Age in the United States Living With One or Both Parents, By Race: March 1976

Living Arrangement	Total	White	Black
Total	100.0	100.0	100.0
In families	99.3	99.4	99.0
Living with both parents	80.0	85.1	49.6
Living with mother only	15.8	11.8	40.1
Living with father only	1.2	1.2	1.5
Living with neither parent	2.3	1.3	7.8
Not in families	0.7	0.6	1.0

Source: U.S. Bureau of the Census. Current Population Reports, Series P-20, No. 306, January, 1977. "Marital Status and Living Arrangements: March 1976," Table 4.

4. By combining the percentages in points 1 and 2, we see that 19 children out of every 20 (95.8%) live with their mothers, whether their fathers are present or absent.
5. By comparing the percentages in points 2 and 3, we note that a child living with only one parent is 12 times more likely to live with the mother than with the father.

Table 2-3 reveals, moreover, that the pattern for blacks differs in interesting ways from that for whites:

6. About half (49.6%) of the black children live with both parents.
7. Two in five (40.1%) of the black children live with their mothers only.
8. The proportion living with fathers only is just slightly higher than among whites (1.5% for blacks and 1.2% for whites).
9. The combination of percentages in points 6 and 7 shows that about 9 out of every 10 black children (89.7%) live with their mothers, irrespective of their fathers' residence.
10. By considering points 7 and 8, we find that a black child living with only one parent is over 26 times as likely to be living with the mother.

And finally:

11. Black children are over 4 times as likely as white children not to be living with either parent (8.8% for blacks and 1.9% for whites).

In view of the importance of marriage to the founding of what the Bureau of the Census calls "families" (and what we call "domestic families"), it is of interest to take note of statistics on marriage in the United States. Table 2-4 shows the percentage marital distribution of the entire adult population (age 20 and over) of the United States. Included also is the distribution for the age range 45-54 years. This category was selected because (1) by age 45 just about everyone who will ever marry has done so, and (2) this age group is young enough to

TABLE 2-4. Percentage Distribution of the Marital Status of the Adult Population (20 and Over) and of Age 45-54 in the United States, by Sex and Race: March 1976

Subject	All Races 20 & over	All Races 45-54	White 20 & over	White 45-54	Black 20 & over	Black 45-54
Male	100.0	100.0	100.0	100.0	100.0	100.0
Single	16.9	5.6	16.1	5.3	22.8	8.1
Married, Wife present	73.1	84.5	75.0	86.7	56.4	62.3
Married, Wife absent	3.0	3.2	2.2	2.1	10.0	14.8
Separated	2.1	2.3	1.4	1.3	8.7	13.1
Other	0.9	0.9	0.8	0.8	1.3	1.7
Widowed	2.7	1.5	2.6	1.2	4.5	4.1
Divorced	4.3	5.2	4.1	4.7	6.3	10.7
Female	100.0	100.0	100.0	100.0	100.0	100.0
Single	11.4	4.4	10.4	4.2	18.6	6.3
Married, Husband present	64.7	77.3	7.2	80.0	43.4	52.6
Married, Husband absent	4.1	4.0	2.9	2.6	14.0	16.2
Separated	3.2	3.1	2.2	1.8	12.4	14.3
In armed forces	0.1	–	0.1	–	0.1	0.1
Other	0.8	0.9	0.7	0.8	1.5	1.7
Widowed	13.8	7.2	13.7	6.5	15.6	13.9
Divorced	6.0	7.1	5.8	6.7	8.4	11.0

Source: Same as that of Table 2-3 above: Table 1.

avoid showing the large male-female differences in mortality that occur among the aged. From Table 2-4 we learn:

12. That about 19 out of every 20 people of both sexes who survive to age 45 either are or have been married.
13. For those 45 to 54, in the two racial and two gender categories considered, the category with the lowest proportion of ever married is black males (91.9%).
14. Among those who have been married by age 45, the race-sex category showing the highest percentage not living with spouse is black females (41.1%).

In conclusion, data from the U.S. Bureau of the Census support the common beliefs that the great majority of domestic families are of the husband-wife type, that nearly as great a majority of children live with both of their parents, and that almost all adults marry. But it is also seen that about a seventh of all domestic families are not of the husband-wife type and that about 2 percent include subfamilies, with another 2 percent consisting of other forms of the extended family. Further, the likelihood that a family will be extended varies by type of domestic family, race, and income. Finally about a sixth of all American children live with their mothers and their fathers are absent from their homes and 1 percent live with their fathers with their mothers absent from the home.

When we cross-tabulate the Census Bureau's types of domestic families—husband-wife, other male-head, or female-head families—with presence or absence of other relatives, it follows that there are six types of domestic families. Again let us note that these data refer to domestic families only and leave us uninformed about familial systems that transcend single households.

Our Own Studies of the Familial System in the United States

The survey of literature with which this chapter began pointed up a dispute over the question as to whether the American family was or was not of the isolated nuclear type. We saw that the literature was inconclusive. In the next section we took note of the kind of information about the American family that is available in census reports. Although the Bureau of the Census gathers a great deal of data about American families and much of the resulting information is of interest, the fact that the Bureau of the Census uses the dwelling unit as its unit of reporting and of analysis renders census reports mute on the issue. Accordingly, we turn to two of our own studies which address this issue.

In the early 1960s Robert Winch, Scott Greer, and Rae Lesser Blumberg undertook a study for the purpose of scrutinizing the potentiality of familial systems as social resources under a condition of disaster. It was our idea that one kind of information that would be important was the degree to which there existed what we called "extended familism," that is, the degree to which familial systems transcended the nuclear family. Operationally, we reasoned this should mean that to the extent that such a phenomenon existed, there should be not only some recognition of kin beyond the nuclear family but also interaction with those kin, some exchange of goods and services with them, and some sense of trust. Also it was of interest to try to identify some predictors of extended familism—variables of some degree of visibility that would allow us to predict in which segments of American society extended familism would be relatively widespread and in which segments it would be relatively absent.

At that time Leichter and Mitchell were engaged in their study of kinship among clients of the Jewish Family Service in New York City. Hope Leichter had told the senior author that they were finding kin networks of extraordinary magnitude among these Jewish informants. Since their results seemed to indicate that Jews were likely to exhibit much more extended familism than would gentiles, we decided to stratify our sample on the basis of Jewish–non-Jewish ethnicity. (Their monograph was published in 1967.)

Ethnicity and Extended Familism in an Upper-Middle-Class Suburb

At the outset we did not have a theory as to why Jews should be more familistic than non-Jews but, as we reflected on the matter, a set of hypotheses emerged. On the basis of the Leichter-Mitchell study, we hypothesized that Jewish ethnicity would be associated with extended familism. The explanation we developed involved two intervening variables: occupation and migration. The hypothesized process is as follows:

1. Ethnicity, which implies differential life chances, results in occupational concentration.
2. The resulting differences in occupational concentration lead to differences in migration.
3. Migration lowers the probability that an individual will have households of kinsmen living nearby and thus lowers the probability of the individual's interacting with kinsmen.

For our purposes it seemed useful to think of religious affiliation as pertaining more to ethnicity than to religion, since our interest was more in subculture and differential life chances than in theology. In particular, it was proposed that the Jewish ethnic category had tended to concentrate in certain categories of urban occupations, most notably as small merchants and free professionals. The large corporate bureaucracies have not traditionally courted Jews to become employees, but have been most receptive to white Protestants whose origins are in the United Kingdom and northwestern Europe. Catholics have been more acceptable to these organizations than Jews, but less so than the WASPs. And our interpretation ran that because of discrimination Jews tended to collect in the kinds of occupations just characterized, that these occupations were of the type to reward one's remaining in the city of one's birth and to discourage spatial mobility, that because of this Jews tended to live with many more of their relatives nearby than did either Catholics or especially Protestants, and thus that extended familism had been a consequence of this chain of circumstances.

As we began this study in the early 1960s, there was evidence that the Jews had a different occupational pattern from non-Jews in the United States. One source was the Anti-Defamation League, which had published a number of studies, including *Some of My Best Friends* . . . (Epstein and Forster, 1962: Chaps. 13–16, especially pp. 207, 225). In this study it is reported that discriminatory employment patterns and a resulting ethnic folklore had led Jews to concentrate in self-employment—for example, as proprietors and self-employed professionals and salespeople, in businesses controlled by fellow Jews, and in government service. Bogue (1959: Table 23-12, p. 703) had shown that there were higher proportions of Jews than of any other religion in the managerial-official-proprietary and sales categories and that Jews were near the top in the professional-technical category.

It seems clear that Jews have remained involved in family capitalism to a much greater extent than have non-Jews. Family capitalism calls for a certain degree of kinship solidarity and it probably inhibits geographic mobility. Non-Jews, on the other hand, have participated in the larger American shift to corporate capitalism, where ownership is separated from control and the pains of frequent bureaucratic transfers are mitigated by the corporation's replacement of the clan as the "protective community." In sum, Joe Cohen's son is more likely to work for Cohen and Son and stay put, whereas Joe Smith's son is more likely to work for World-Wide Widgets and get transferred. We argued that this hypothesized process had consequences for the number of kin each was likely to find in his vicinity.

The Sample. We had not formulated our three-stage hypothesis as we began gathering data and only later realized that we lacked occupational information. This necessitated call-backs and resulted in a reduced sample. First we shall discuss the initial sample, and then the reduced sample.

The sampling unit was the household. The interviewee was the wife of the head of household. The sample was designed to have equal numbers of Jewish and non-Jewish households. The initial interviews were conducted in 1962 and 1963 in an upper-middle-class suburb of Chicago. The Jewish subsample differed from the non-Jewish in that the former was a bit younger on the average had a bit less education and income, and appeared to be more upwardly mobile than the non-Jewish.

Call-back interviews were carried out on 243 households—that is, 79 percent of the original 307. Of 10 items of comparison the call-back subsample differed significantly from the uncontacted subsample on only one: the responding households had on the average a significantly higher income. The following analysis is based on these 243 cases.

Measures of Extended Familism. Respondents were shown a card listing numerous categories of affinal and consanguineal relatives. For each category they were asked how many households of kin they had in the metropolitan area, and for each such household they were asked a few questions, beginning with the name of the connecting relative. From the resulting data we have constructed four indexes of extended familism. These we have called extensity of presence, intensity of presence, interaction, and functionality. Each respondent's *extensity of presence* is given by the total number of such households. For *intensity of presence* relatives are classified into those who were in the respondent's and her husband's families of orientation (characterized as nuclear) and others (characterized as extended). *Interaction* refers to the number of households of kin in the area with which some member of the respondent's household has interacted as often as at least once a month. The score on *functionality* consists of the number of times the respondent says "relative" when asked about the most frequent source with respect to a number of questions about giving and receiving aid, services, loans, and so forth. The questionnaire items used for this analysis appear in Appendix A.

Ethnicity, Occupation, Migration. The independent variable is ethnicity, classified as Protestant, Catholic, and Jewish. For our purposes an ethnic category is an aggregate of people sharing and participating in a common culture or subculture. As noted above, since our interest is in culture rather than in attitudes toward or beliefs about a supernatural being, we speak of this variable as ethnicity rather than as religious affiliation.[4]

Occupation is measured by classifying the jobs of the heads of households as entrepreneurial or bureaucratic. A person was placed in the entrepreneurial category if he had a share in a family business, was a free professional, and/or derived his income largely or entirely from commissions or profits rather than salary. Otherwise he was classified as bureaucratic.

A person was classified as a nonmigrant if he or she had been born in the Chicago metropolitan area or had been brought to the area by his parents before becoming 18 years old.

Hypotheses. Our hypotheses relate ethnicity to familism and seek to interpret that relationship through occupation and migration.

H_1: Ethnicity is associated with extended familism in that Jews are most familistic, Protestants least, and Catholics intermediate.

H_2: Ethnicity is associated with occupation in that Jews are more entrepreneurial, non-Jews more bureaucratic.

H_3: Occupation is associated with migration in that spouses in bureaucratic occupations are more likely to be migrants than those in entrepreneurial.

H_4: Migration is associated with familism in that migrants show less extended familism than nonmigrants.

H_5: The association of ethnicity with extended familism is explained by occupation and migration in that when these intervening variables are controlled, the association becomes zero.

Results. Table 2-5 shows the relationship between ethnicity, as indexed by religious affiliation, and our four measures of extended familism. The gammas support H_1. On all four measures the Jews show the greatest familism, the Protestants least. The gammas are quite high for the first three measures of extended familism—extensity and intensity of presence of kin and interaction with kin—and substantially lower for the functionality of kin. The top panel (on extensity) shows that whereas 97 percent of the Jews have relatives in the area and over 70 percent have 15 percent or more households of kin, 30 percent of the Protestants had no kin at all in the metropolitan area.

Ethnicity is correlated with occupational category when occupations are classified as being either entrepreneurial or bureaucratic, thereby supporting H_2 (see Appendix Table F-3). There is a higher proportion of Jews in entrepreneurial occupations than is the situation with Catholics or Protestants. The magnitude of the association, however, is not nearly as high as was anticipated.[5]

As H_3 proposes, bureaucratic occupations involve more geographic mobility than do entrepreneurial occupations (see Appendix Table F-4). The proportion of couples with both spouses migrant is higher among bureaucratic than among entrepreneurial occupations. Again, however, the magnitude of the association is surprisingly low.

Because we were not confident in classifying occupations as entrepreneurial or bureaucratic, we tried another way of getting at a similar result. We had one question as to whether the head of the house was at the time of the survey involved in a family business, and another as to whether or not he ever had been.

TABLE 2-5. Percentage Distribution of Ethnic Categories of Suburban Respondents by Level of Each of Four Measures of Extended Familism

Measure of Extended Familism	Ethnicity						Total		Gamma
	Jewish		Catholic		Protestant				
	N	%	N	%	N	%	N	%	
Extensity of presence (number of households of kin in metropolitan area):									
None	3	2.7	7	12.3	22	30.1	32	13.3	.77*
1–14	28	25.5	35	61.4	45	61.6	108	45.0	
15+	79	71.8	15	26.3	6	8.2	100	41.7	
Intensity of presence (classification of kin in area):									
None	3	2.7	7	12.3	22	30.1	32	13.3	.66*
Some	44	40.0	37	64.9	42	57.5	123	51.3	
Both have nuclear and extended	63	57.3	13	22.8	9	12.3	85	35.4	
Interaction (number of households of kin interacted with regularly):									
None	3	2.7	8	14.0	24	32.9	35	14.6	.75*
1–5	34	30.9	33	57.9	44	60.3	111	46.2	
6+	73	66.4	16	28.1	5	6.8	94	39.2	
Functionality (of interaction with households of kin):									
Low (0–5)	44	40.0	27	47.4	47	64.4	118	49.2	.33*
High (6+)	66	60.0	30	52.6	26	35.6	122	50.8	
Number of cases	110		57		73				

*Significant at the .001 level.

Family businesses may be considered almost pure examples of entrepreneurship. Of course, since not all businesses are organized on a familial basis, the affirmative category does not necessarily include all who have ever been engaged in entrepreneurial occupations. It turned out that the proportion of heads of households currently in family businesses was too small for effective analysis, but the proportion ever so engaged was satisfactorily large.

Appendix Tables F-5 and F-6 show the results of the question on family business. As in Appendix Tables F-3 and F-4, veterans of family businesses are more likely to be Jewish than Catholic or Protestant, and they are less likely to be geographically mobile than those without this experience. The magnitudes of the gammas are very similar to those in Appendix Tables F-3 and F-4.

Appendix Table F-7 reports on H_4—the relationship between migratory status and the four measures of extended familism. The table reveals that migratory status is highly correlated with the first three measures, which involve the extensity and intensity of the presence of kin as well as interaction with kin. The correlation with functionality is moderate.

Given the remarkable similarity between the distributions in Table 2-5 (ethnicity and familism) and Appendix Table F-7 (migration and familism), the question naturally arises as to whether ethnicity and migratory status may be different measures of the same underlying variable. Appendix Table F-8 measures the association between ethnicity and migratory status and reveals that these two variables are correlated, but the magnitude of the association is not high enough to warrant the conclusion that they are indicators of the same underlying variable.

Before proceeding to the results of partialing, it is of some interest to investigate the one remaining bivariate relationship among our four variables. Appendix Table F-9 gives the bivariate distribution of occupational classification— entrepreneurial versus bureaucratic—and extended familism. The pattern of correlations is very similar to those in Table 2-5 (ethnicity and familism) and Appendix Table F-7 (migration and familism) except that the magnitudes of the gammas are appreciably lower. Even so, it is clear that with migratory status and ethnicity uncontrolled, entrepreneurial households are more familistic than are bureaucratic households.

According to H_5, occupational concentration and differential migration should account for the correlation between ethnicity and extended familism. We now have the data to test this hypothesis. Table 2-6 recapitulates the four gammas between ethnicity and extended familism that appear in Table 2-5. It also shows the four corresponding partial gammas with occupational classification (entrepreneurial vs. bureaucratic) and migratory status held constant. If our hypothesis is to prove correct, then the four partial correlations shown in the right column should all be approximately zero. It is clear that such is far from the case. Rather, we find that controlling for occupational classification and migratory status leaves the correlations between ethnicity and familism substantially unchanged.

TABLE 2-6. Summary of Correlations (Gammas) between Ethnicity and Four Measures of Extended Familism: Zero-Order and Partial with Occupation and Migratory Status Controlled

Measure of Extended Familism	Zero-Order	Partial
Extensity	.77	.76
Intensity	.66	.61
Interaction	.75	.72
Functionality	.33	.23

TABLE 2-7. Percentage Distribution of Ethnic Categories to Question of Trust*

Responses to Question on Entrusting Child's Care	Ethnicity			
	Jewish	Catholic	Protestant	Total
Relatives of wife	73.0	47.8	31.0	58.1
Relatives of husband	12.4	30.4	17.2	17.0
Friend or agency	5.8	8.7	19.0	9.5
No one in metropolitan area	8.8	13.0	32.8	15.4
Number of cases	137	46	58	241

*Gamma (.52) significant at the .01 level.

The reasoning that led us to propose the foregoing hypotheses can also suggest attitudinal predictions, namely that differences in ethnicity and migration would correlate with degree of trust in the extended family. For a question that would tap the variable of trust as well as could be done in a nonstressful situation, we adapted a questionnaire item from the study of Jewish kinship by Leichter and Mitchell (1967):

> If something happened to you and your husband, whom in the Chicago area would you want to see raising your children?

For this analysis the number of respondents is reduced because not all of them had dependent children. Roughly 3 out of 5 reported they would like to have relatives of the wife raise their children; 1 in 6 said relatives of the husband; 1 in 7 said no one in the metropolitan area; and 1 in 10 mentioned an agency or a friend (see Table 2-7).

As the previous findings suggest, ethnicity and migration are predictive of family-type responses to this question of trust. Seventeen out of every 20 Jewish respondents would want kinsmen to rear their children and nearly 3 out of 4 Jewish respondent would opt for relatives of the wife. For Protestants the proportion of kin responses was less than half, and less than 1 out of 3 chose the wife's relatives. Although more wives in all three ethnic categories chose their

TABLE 2-8. Percentage Distribution of Migratory Statuses to Question of Trust*

Responses to Question on Entrusting Child's Care	Both	Migrant Spouse		Total
		One	Neither	
Relatives of wife	16.7	40.5	72.7	57.0
Relatives of husband	3.3	33.3	17.4	18.7
Friend or agency	16.7	11.9	5.0	8.3
No one in metropolitan area	63.3	14.3	5.0	16.1
Number of cases	30	42	121	193

*Gamma (−.69) significant at the .01 level.

own kin than chose their husbands', the proportion nominating husbands' relatives was highest among the Catholics—3 out of 10.

The variable of migration is also correlated with kin responses. Where neither spouse is a migrant, 9 out of 10 responses are for kin to raise their children and 3 out of 4 for wife's kin. Where one or both are migrants, one half are kin responses and less than one third are for wife's relatives (see Table 2-8).

Other findings of some interest that emerge from this set of tables are as follows:

1. Half of the Jews, but only a third of the Protestants, are entrepreneurial see (Appendix Table F-3).
2. Not only are Jews more entrepreneurial, less migratory, and more familistic than either Catholics or Protestants, but when migratory, it appears they are much more likely to live in the spouse's home community; only one fifteenth of the Jews were in the both-migrant category as contrasted with one third of the Protestants (see Appendix Table F-8).
3. Appendix Table F-3 shows that there are 101 entrepreneurs: 53 Jews, 25 Catholics, and 23 Protestants. In this category there is a strong presumption of the individual's freedom to choose his location although there is usually an apparent advantage to remaining in one's native community, especially if the kin group if functional. We find that 6 of the 23 Protestant couples live where both spouses are migrants, but this is the case with only 1 household out of the 53 Jewish cases. Even when the Jews are bureaucrats, their proportion of migrants is low (19 out of 57 households, or one third) compared with that of the Protestants (33 out of 50, or two thirds).

In these findings the Catholic subsample falls between the Protestants and the Jews.

With the exception of those pertaining to trust, Appendix Table F-10 summarizes all of the zero-order correlations that have been reported above.

Interpretation. The foregoing results have shown that in this sample Jews have many more relatives in the metropolitan area than have either Catholics or Protestants who share the same migratory and occupational characteristics. How is the luxuriant kin network of the Jews to be explained?[6]

Our proposed explanation has two foci for further investigation: history and ecology. Most of the Jews in this sample had their origins in Eastern Europe. Most of the Catholics and Protestants in this sample had ancestors who migrated from northern and western Europe. Modal years for migrants from Poland, the Baltic states, and what was then Russia were in the first quarter of the twentieth century whereas modal years for migrants from Great Britain, Ireland, Scandinavia, and Germany were in the latter half of the nineteenth century (U.S. Bureau of the Census, 1960: 56-57). Consistent with these observations is the fact that the average Catholic or Protestant family in our sample has had antecedents in the United States at least a couple of generations longer than the average Jewish family. The Christian ethnic groups thus arrived early enough to have participated in the two great movements of the American population: the westward expansion of the past two centuries and the exploding urbanization of this century. Both of these movements have tended to redistribute the population, and thus to reduce the probability that any given "early settler" Christian family would have a large concentration of kin in its locality. Arriving after the closing of the frontier in 1890, the Jews concentrated in a small number of port-of-entry cities.

Our historical interpretation leads to an ecological one. Jews in the United States are concentrated in relatively few places. These are large metropolitan areas, and Chicago is one of them, it ranks fourth in the country with respect to the size of its Jewish population.

Around the time of this study over 60 percent of all United States Jews lived in the New York, Los Angeles, Philadelphia, or Chicago areas (see Appendix Table F-11). Actually, 60 percent is an underestimate because the New York figures exclude the Connecticut and New Jersey communities that are normally included in the New York metropolitan area and contain many Jews. Similarly, the Philadelphia and Chicago figures exclude the New Jersey and Indiana communities that are usually considered part of their respective standard metropolitan areas. The New York data suffer from the additional handicap of being several years older than the rest of the data.

To emphasize, the New York data, which show over 40 percent of all American Jews living in New York City and three suburban New York State counties as of 1962, are gross underestimates of the true state of ethnic concentration. Little wonder that studies of New York Jews' kinship networks reveal even larger numbers of local relatives than our Chicago findings: as noted above, in the Leichter-Mitchell study some respondents were able to name astonishing numbers of kin, running literally into the hundreds.

To put the data on geographic concentration of Jews in national perspective, Appendix Table F-12 shows that nearly 90 percent of the U.S. Jews lived in

10 states, which contained less than half of the total U.S. population. The 10 most populous states contained about 55 percent of all Americans but nearly 87 percent of American Jews.

The above figures offer a convincing background for certain aspects of the observed Jewish extended familism in a Chicago suburb. The high ecological concentration makes understandable the larger local kin networks of the Jews in the sample. It provides a possible alternate explanation for the fact that the Jews were considerably more likely to be natives of the metropolitan area than were the Christians. Thus both the larger kin enclaves and the higher proportion of nonmigrants observed among Jews are attributed to the fact that the study was conducted in Chicago, not Cedar Rapids.[7] Finally, the fact of ecological concentration can be invoked to explain the finding that Jewish migrant couples have more extended familism than do Christian migrant couples. For these reasons the Jewish couple moving to Chicago from the Bronx is more likely to have kin already resident in the Windy City than is the Protestant couple arriving from a small town.

As a cautionary concluding note, whereas ecological concentration may constitute a plausible explanation for the size and density of the local kin of an ethnic category that finds Chicago one of its principal "natural habitats," it cannot explain elements of extended familism involving the salience and strength of the kinship bond. Our query about trust suggests that these aspects of familism, too, vary by ethnicity. It may be that members of ethnic groups who have experienced a history of being discriminated against are even more likely than others to feel that relatives are the only people who can be trusted. Ecological concentration marks a waystation, not the destination, on the road to a theoretical explanation. See Mindel and Habenstein (1976: Chap. 17) for a recent formulation on ethnicity and the family and the same source (Chap. 15) on the Jewish family.

Our Statewide Sample

It will be realized that we designed our suburban study to be homogeneous with respect to two variables that are frequently correlated with sociological phenomena—socioeconomic status and urban-rural residence. A year of so after we finished gathering data for the suburban study, but before we had finished our analysis, an opportunity arose to replicate that survey in an abridged form with a statewide sample in Wisconsin.[8] (The questionnaire items used appear in Appendix B.) Although this sample offered a much broader range with respect to socioeconomic status and urban-rural residence, it lacked the full ethnic spectrum represented in the United States. In particular, it had too few Jews and blacks to permit their being used as statistical categories.

We developed two indicators of socioeconomic status: family income, divided into five categories, and education of male head of family, divided into four levels. With respect to monotonic relationships with family income, three of the four measures of familism[9] yielded nonsignificant gammas. The one significant relationship ($G = -.15$) occurred with respect to intensity: 20 percent of those in the highest income category reported no local kin as contrasted with 8 percent in the lowest; 12 percent in the highest income category reported having households both of nuclear and of extended kin in the local community as contrasted with 27 percent of the poorest. Only by this one out of the four indicators of extended familism did there prove to be a significant trend for the poorer respondents to give more familistic responses.[10] (See Appendix Table F-13.)

When we look at our other socioeconomic index—number of years of education of the head of the family—again we do not see evidence of a consistent relationship with extended familism. All four gammas are statistically significant, but they do not agree with respect to sign. Three are negative, one is positive. For extensity, intensity, and functionality we find that among the families with the more highly educated heads there is a higher proportion having no households of kin in the local community. With respect to interaction, however, there is a reversal, and the families of the more educated heads interact a bit more with their kin. All of these relationships are quite small, however (see Table 2-9).

The lack of a precisely specified, clearly observable, and consensually meaningful standard of either isolation or nonisolation has made it difficult to test the formulation of Wirth and Parsons that the American nuclear urban family is isolated.[11] The same difficulty appears in the writings of the revisionists who deny that isolation. To remedy this unsatisfactory state of affairs, let us compare the family in urban Wisconsin with the family in rural parts of that state. If Wirth and Parsons are correct, we should expect to find a greater proportion of isolated families in urban areas than in rural. Whether or not the revisionists would deny this is not evident from their writings.

To get the purest possible measure of urbanism, we classify Milwaukee, Madison, Wauwatosa, and West Allis as urban; our rural category consists of all unincorporated territory not in any Standard Metropolitan Statistical Area (SMSA). The remaining area is labeled "other" and is regarded as of intermediate urbanism-ruralism.

Although the percentages in the first row of each of the four panels in Table 2-10 suggest a slight urban-rural gradient whereby respondents in metropolitan areas are more isolated than in rural areas, this tendency in the top two panels is not statistically significant. For the top panel, for example, the chi-square statistic corresponds to a chance probability between .5 and .7. It follows, then, that neither extensity nor intensity—nor, thereby, isolation of domestic family—correlates significantly with urbanism-ruralism. Yet the other two measures of extended familism—interaction and functionality—are significantly and monotonically related to urbanism-ruralism with ruralism at the more familistic end. We conclude, therefore, that although there is little variation in the number of households of kin or in degree of isolation from kin as we move from the country through the small towns and suburbs to the city, there is a decrease in both interaction and functionality. To state it more fully, on the average, rural households interact more with their kin than do urban households, and this interaction tends to be more functional. When socioeconomic status is used as

TABLE 2-9. Percentage Distribution of Wisconsin Respondents by Education of Male Head of Family and by Level of Extended Familism for Four Measures of Extended Familism

Measure and Level of Extended Familism	Years of Education of Male Head of Family					
	0-8 N = 143	9-11 N = 95	12 N = 149	13+ N = 123	Total N = 510	Gamma
Extensity of presence						
None	5.6	10.5	11.4	29.3	13.9	-.18**
Some	51.0	44.2	44.3	36.6	44.3	
High	43.4	45.3	44.3	34.1	41.8	
Intensity of presence						
None	5.6	10.5	11.4	29.3	13.9	-.26**
Some	69.2	64.2	63.1	56.1	63.3	
High	25.2	25.3	25.5	14.6	22.7	
Interaction						
None	8.4	6.3	6.7	8.9	7.6	.13*
Some	60.1	45.3	37.6	47.2	47.6	
High	31.5	48.4	55.7	43.9	44.7	
Functionality						
None	8.4	14.7	10.7	19.5	12.9	-.14*
Some	52.4	48.4	59.1	49.6	52.9	
High	39.2	36.8	30.2	30.9	34.1	

*Significant at the .05 level.
**Significant at the .01 level.

TABLE 2-10. Percentage Distribution of Wisconsin Respondents by Ecological Type and by Level of Extended Familism, for Four Measures of Extended Familism

Measure and Level of Extended Familism	Metropolitan	Other	Rural	Total	Gamma
			Ecology[a]		
Extensity of presence	N = 115	N = 286	N = 112	N = 513	
None	17.4	14.0	10.7	14.0	.10
Some	40.0	48.6	38.4	44.4	
High	42.6	37.4	50.9	41.5	
Intensity of presence	N = 115	N = 286	N = 112	N = 513	
None	17.4	14.0	10.7	14.0	.09
Some	60.9	64.0	64.3	63.4	
High	21.7	22.0	25.0	22.6	
Interaction	N = 115	N = 286	N = 112	N = 513	
None	7.8	7.7	7.1	7.6	.20*
Some	55.7	49.7	35.7	48.0	
High	36.5	42.7	57.1	44.4	
Functionality	N = 115	N = 286	N = 112	N = 513	
None	20.0	12.6	7.1	13.1	30*
Some	59.1	52.8	47.3	53.0	
High	20.9	34.6	45.5	33.9	

[a]The three ecological types are:
Metropolitan: Milwaukee, Madison, West Allis, and Wauwatosa
Rural: unincorporated territory outside any SMSA
Other: residual territory-small cities, suburbs, etc.
*Significant at the .01 level.

TABLE 2-11. Percentage Distribution of Categories of Intensity of Presence of Kin by Migratory Status*

Migratory Status of Spouses	Intensity of Presence			
	None N = 71	*Some* N = 317	*High* N = 116	*Total* N = 504
Both migrants	94.4	43.8	20.7	45.6
One migrant	2.8	36.0	29.3	29.8
Neither migrant	2.8	20.2	50.0	24.6

*Gamma (.67) significant at the .01 level.

a control variable, the correlations between the rural-urban dimension and extended familism (as measured by interaction and functionality) remain generally unaffected.[12]

When migratory status was used as a control variable, the correlations between ecology and two measures of familism disappeared where neither spouse was a migrant but held up otherwise. In other words, in couples where one or both spouses are migrants, there is more interaction and more functional interaction with kin among rural families than among urban. An understanding of how migratory status is associated with extended familism can be obtained from Table 2-11 where it is seen that 94 percent of the isolated nuclear domestic families involve couples, both of whom are migrants.

Extended Familism and Ethnicity

In the suburban study we regarded the classification of respondents into Jewish and non-Jewish as a dimension of ethnicity rather than of religion, because we were interested in values and behavior pertaining to the family rather than in theology. In the Wisconsin study the same reasoning led us to look for what we thought of as ethnicity in our data on religious affiliation. Two large denominations, accounting for slightly more than two thirds of the sample, were Roman Catholic and Lutheran.

We were intrigued to see whether, with our highly familistic Jews absent from the analysis, we should still find that ethnicity correlated with extended familism. Appendix Table F-14 shows a pattern that is similar to, but markedly weaker than, that found in the suburban study—the interaction and two presence measures producing larger gammas than functionality. With respect to extensity and intensity of presence, Catholics are most familistic, Lutherans intermediate, and other Protestants least. In the case of interaction, Lutherans are a bit more familistic than Catholics, and the gamma would be larger (-.23) if these two categories had been reversed.

When the two indexes of socioeconomic status are employed as control variables, it is found that at the high level of SES all six correlations between ethnicity and the three measures of extended familism (with which it correlated significantly) remained significant and in the same direction. At the lower socioeconomic level, however, the four following correlations became nonsignificant: with income as the index, the correlations with interaction and extensity;[13] with education as the index, the correlations with interaction and intensity. These results indicate that the order of ethnic categories with respect to extended familism—Catholics most familistic, Lutherans intermediate, and other Protestants least familistic—is operative at the upper socioeconomic level, but at the lower level, especially with respect to interaction, there is some tendency for ethnic differences to wash out.

When migratory status is introduced as a control variable, the correlation between ethnicity and extended familism remains for the "both migrant" category but disappears for the other two migratory statuses. When one or both spouses are nonmigrants, the data indicate that Catholics and Lutherans are not significantly more familistic than other Protestants.

Since both socioeconomic status and migratory status affect the correlation between ethnicity and extended familism, it is of interest to see what happens when they are introduced simultaneously as control variables. The result is that most of the correlations between ethnicity and extended familism shrink to nonsignificance. Of the 36 gammas computed, only six remained significant.[14] Of these six, three combined the both-migrant status with high socioeconomic status; of the other three, two combined the both-migrant and low socioeconomic statuses, and the sixth combined one spouse migrant with high SES.

From the foregoing findings it should follow that the correlations between the three categories of ethnicity and the three measures of extended familism with which it correlates significantly are higher in metropolitan areas, where the proportion of migrants and the average SES are relatively high, than in rural areas, where they are low. As Appendix Table F-15 indicates, such a relationship is supported by the data, which also show the relationship in small towns and suburbs (the "other" ecological level) to be much like that in metropolitan areas.

Taking into account that there is an ethnic gradient of migration such that the proportion of migrants is lowest among Catholics and highest among other Protestants,[15] these results seem to indicate that for the most part the correlation between ethnicity and extended familism prevails where both spouses are migrants and their socioeconomic status is relatively high, and that this familism consists in interacting with more households of kin and, to some extent, having more households of kin with which to interact. In other words, when neither spouse is a migrant, there is no significant difference among ethnic categories with respect to extended familism, but when both spouses are migrants, the correlation of ethnicity with familism prevails.

We may summarize the Wisconsin study as follows:

1. All four of our somewhat diverse indicators of extended familism show the overwhelming majority of our respondents to be involved with kin and

therefore to be nonisolated. This is true with even the least familistic sub-categories of our respondents. Degree of isolation for the state, blacks and Jews excluded, is estimated at 14 percent; for white Protestants, 22 percent.

2. Ruralism correlates significantly with extended familism as indexed by functionality and interaction, but there is little difference between rural and urban couples in the number of households of kin or the degree of kinship of these households.

3. The ruralism-familism correlation is not related to socioeconomic status, but it is to migratory status; that is, the correlation stands up where one or both spouses are migrants and disappears where neither is a migrant. Stated differently, nonmigrant urban couples are as familistic, on the average, as nonmigrant rural couples, but migrant urban couples are less familistic than migrant rural couples.

4. Ethnicity—represented here as Catholic, Lutheran, and other Protestants—correlates significantly with extended familism in that Catholics and Lutherans are more familistic than other Protestants with respect to extensity, intensity, and interaction, but there is little difference among ethnic categories with respect to functionality.

5. With respect to our control variables, the ethnicity-familism correlation tends to hold up for migratory couples of relatively high socioeconomic status and those in urban areas; conversely, there is little correlation between ethnicity and familism in couples of low SES where one or both spouses are nonmigrants, and in rural areas.

6. Nonmigration is strongly associated with the maintenance of extended kin networks. Perhaps the rural and, to a less extent, small-town and suburban areas are more conducive, culturally or ecologically, to using whatever kin system is present.

Isolation-Extended Familism as a Dimension of Familial Organization

Our analysis so far leads to the conclusion that we may distinguish two empirical types on a continuum of isolation-extended familism as follows:

1. An isolated nuclear family. From the suburban and Wisconsin data tables we might estimate that around 15 percent of husband-wife domestic families or 13 percent of all domestic families in the country are isolated as we have operationalized this term.[16] It will be recalled, however, that our operationalization refers to an absence of any *local* household of kin.

2. A nuclear family embedded in a network of extended kin. Given that husband-wife families are reported to constitute about 85 percent of all U.S. domestic families (Table 2-1) and that we estimate from our Wisconsin sample (Appendix Table F-13) that about 85 percent of domestic families are embedded (not isolated), we offer the guess that about 70 to 75 percent of all U.S. domestic husband-wife families are of the embedded nuclear type.

Obviously the foregoing quantitative guesses are based not only upon data from one limited region of the country but upon a brief time span as well, and hence the data are subject to error. Moreover, the criterion for isolation is the reported absence of any households of kin in the local area. The degree of isolation will vary with the criterion used. Indeed in an era of long-distance telephone calls and jet airplane travel, family help may be as close as the telephone or the airport even when there are no kin in the local area. In fact when we used interaction with any household of kin by any means within the previous month (rather than presence of kin in the area), the proportion isolated was lowered from about 14 percent to about 7 percent.

Since we have postulated a dimension of isolation-extended familism and have proposed that two types may be located along this dimension, it becomes necessary to discuss the substance of that variable. We may begin by remarking that nuclear families that have no kin and/or are not in touch with such kin as they may have are at the low (or zero) end of such a continuum. What about nuclear families that are in touch with kin with some frequency? As far as functionality is concerned, it appears from the various studies that typically such interaction involves visiting and occasional mutual aid, but hardly adds up to what we think of as true extended familism. Rather, we submit, that term denotes the existence of substantial instrumental activity among a set of persons who are related to each other outside their nuclear families. A pair of examples will be useful for the purpose of illustrating in virtually ideal-typical fashion the extreme values along this continuum. The family in the kibbutz described by Spiro (1956) was minimally functional, indeed so slightly functional that some writers expressed doubt that the family existed in that setting. There were married couples, and they procreated. Thereby they satisfied our minimum criterion of a family. As family members they did not have responsibility for rearing or training children, for working together as economic, political, or other instrumentally functional units. At the high end of the scale of familial functionality on the other hand is the family of traditional China, wherein the family served as an economic unit (producing and distributing goods and services), a political unit (settling disputes and affording protection), socializing unit (training its young), and religious unit (worshiping ancestors). What we mean by the dimension of extended familism, then, is the degree to which a set of individuals who are all related to each other and include at least one non-nuclear dyad carry out collectively a set of instrumentally important activities.

By this definition it is clear that the isolated nuclear family should be very low on extended familism. But what about the nuclear family embedded in a network of kin? The critical element is the importance of any activities carried out by a familial collectivity. Parsons has proposed, and there seems to be a good deal of evidence from studies to support his view, that the American pattern is one of interaction between nuclear households that may include some exchange of more or less trivial goods and services, such as the lending of tools, babysitting, and so forth. To the extent that this is true, kinsmen tend to provide some mutual aid for each other, some occasional assistance, especially at times of crisis (and when one needs a plumber's friend or a babysitter the help may be invaluable); and do visit with each other on a recreational basis. But, generally the important work of life is done in other social systems and with other sets of people. It should be emphasized, however, that the data on this question are fragmentary and that just how much true extended familism exists in the United States remains to be determined.

Extended Familism in the United States

Now let us begin to weave together some of the strands of evidence that point to various conditions under which extended familism occurs in the United States. First let us recall that from a structural point of view the Census Bureau shows that at a minimum 2 percent of domestic families are extended since they contain subfamilies. Just how many more family units contain "other relatives" is difficult to ascertain. If we distribute the 4,834,000 other relatives who are not members of subfamilies 1 to a family, 8.7 percent of all domestic families would have 1 "other relative." If we further assume that these families do not also contain subfamilies, the maximum possible percent of domestic families that could contain some non-nuclear dyad would be 11.1 percent (8.7% containing other relatives + 2.4% containing subfamilies). Therefore the minimum and maximum figures for domestic families which are extended would be 2.4 percent and 11.1 percent.

We have demonstrated that being at least part of a network of kin, and perhaps of a true extended family, tends to be more likely (1) among Jews or Catholics rather than WASPs, (2) among nonmigrants, (3) in the middle and working classes rather than in the upper-middle class, and (4) when the family head is employed in an entrepreneurial rather than a bureaucratic occupation. Are there any other conditions under which a network of kin or extended familism is likely? Although we cannot be very precise about the characteristics of the kin networks, ethnographies, census, and survey data, as well as biographical accounts all provide some additional hints.

We have noted that the Census Bureau shows about 1 of 8 domestic families (13.0%) to be female-headed and 1 of 37 (2.7%) to be male-headed. Three in five of these female heads of household have at least one of their own offspring under the age of 18 in the home and about one quarter have at least one "own" child under the age of 6. For other male-headed households, a third have at least one of their own children under age 18 at home and about 1 in 14 (7%) have a child under the age of 6 (U.S. Bureau of the Census, 1976a: 7-8). If these domestic units are isolated from kin, there is the question as to how the woman or man can both care for one or more small children and still perform as a provider for the household.

Let us use the term "single-headed family" to refer to domestic families other than husband-wife families, that is, to those designated by the Census Bureau either as having an "other male head" or as having a "female head."

Then one cue the Census Bureau gives us about the support of dependent children is that single-headed families are much more likely than husband-wife families to include some "other relative." In the case of husband-wife families there is only 1 other relative for about every 12 domestic families. In the case of other male-headed households there is 1 other relative for about every 1.2 families. In female-headed domestic families there is 1 for every 2.4, for black female-headed 1 for every 1.5.

Sharing the important functional task of rearing the child of a relative is, as we have suggested, probably an indicator of extended familism. As will be discussed more fully in Chapter 9, such child-care arrangements may also involve several domestic households. Stack (1974), for example, reports that 20 to 35 percent of the low income black children she studied in a midwestern community were cared for by adult female kin other than their biological mothers. These data serve as a reminder, then, that extended familism may go beyond the boundaries of the domestic family, at least among low income blacks.

Indicators of extended familism among other ethnic groups include census data from 1970 which illustrate that families of Spanish heritage are more likely than whites but less likely than blacks to have other relatives present in the domestic family. For those of Spanish heritage, there is a mean of .25 other relatives present per family versus .43 for blacks and .13 for whites (U.S. Bureau of the Census, 1973a: Table 206). A survey of school desegregation in Riverside, California, reinforces the points that the presence of other relatives in the domestic family varies by ethnicity, often occurs under conditions of poverty, but illustrates that this pattern is not simply most prevalent among single-headed families. Of the three ethnic groups studied, the heads of the Mexican-American families had the lowest educational and occupational status. The percent of single-headed households among the Mexican-Americans was similar to that of the Anglos (5% vs. 4% for the Anglos) compared to 15 percent for the blacks. The Mexican-American domestic families, however, were the most likely of the three groups to be extended (Appendix Table F–16).[17]

A large familial system has also been described by Campisi (1948), Gans (1962), Lopreato (1970), and Ianni (1972) among the Italian Americans. As we have seen, a somewhat similar system among Jewish Americans has been reported by Leichter and Mitchell (1967). Such groups are Catholic or Jewish, not WASP. However, large systems have been reported among rich and successful WASPs as well (e.g., accounts of upper-upper-class families by Warner and Lunt, 1941, and a study of the Du Pont family by Chandler and Salsbury, 1971. See also Domhoff, 1967; Zeitlin, 1974). Being both Jewish and rich are characteristics of families studied by Birmingham (1967) and being both Catholic and rich characterizes families Corry (1977) has examined.

Successful families frequently have an early period when they make use of kinship to organize their economic activities. It appears that such activities usually involve a small number of participants, some division of labor, and a risk that the collective enterprise would be harmed if one or more of the participants should cheat or betray the others as, for example, through divulging information to outsiders. It appears that this emphasis on trust is the one advantage a kin-linked organization can offer over other types. As such enterprises become successful, they grow, and as they grow, they develop an increased demand for managerial and technical skills the family can no longer provide. At this point universalistic criteria for recruitment become more important than particularistic, and if the enterprise is to continue to develop, it frequently must convert from a family business to a public corporation. (See Chandler and Salsbury, 1971, for a discussion of how Pierre Du Pont handled this problem.)

One of the more revealing accounts of how a successful family makes use of kinship appears in a history of a family that is not American—the Rothschilds (Corti, 1928a, 1928b). Meyer Amschel Rothschild (1774–1855), the founder of the banking dynasty, instructed his children not to marry outside the Jewish faith and urged his sons to marry their cousins. The children appear to have followed his exhortation with the consequence that in the male line the Rothschilds were quite inbred and the banking firm remained under their close control. On the female side, however, there was considerable exogamy, even with Christians, and the mating of the women seemed designed to raise the social standing of the family, especially through marriages to nobility.

Meyer Amschel involved his sons in the business at an early age. When the oldest daughter was married, the son-in-law was not employed in the business, but when the oldest son married, the daughter-in-law was given a post. No daughter or child-in-law had any right to see the company's books. In his will Meyer Amschel made a settlement on his widow and daughters with the understanding that neither the daughters nor their husbands would make any subsequent claim on the family fortune. He divided the business equally among his five sons, who established successful branches of the Frankfurt Rothschild enterprises in London, Paris, Vienna, and Naples.

It is not clear to what extent the Rothschild model can be applied to successful American families. Birmingham's account of rich Jewish-American families sounds quite similar; see, for example, his report on the Seligmans. Moreover, there are accounts of the importance of the extended family in early American history. Greven (1970) states that through the seventeenth century in Andover, Massachusetts, the familial pattern was patriarchal and that the basis of the patriarch's control, especially over his sons, lay in determining when the sons might acquire property, especially land. Hall (1974) is more concerned with families in commerce and asserts that:

> up to the end of the eighteenth century, family structure was genuinely patriarchal, organized around the father who, as head of the household, head of the family business, and agent of the state and church for the implementation of social policy, controlled the actions of those under him and could extend or deny autonomy for his sons at will.

What we are proposing, then, is that in the United States in addition to the other circumstances outlined above some extended families exist—in unknown number—organized around great fortunes (e.g., the Rockefellers or Fords) or family enterprise, which may or may not involve great wealth, the latter possibility exemplified by a couple of brothers running a neighborhood store.

What kind of order can we make of these seemingly quite disparate conditions under which extended familism seems to occur? We have discussed census data indicating that some domestic families are extended and presented other more fragmentary evidence concerning extra domestic household extended familism.

Conditions Under Which Extended Familism Occurs

Tentatively, we suggest the following hypotheses to account for the presence of extended familism in the United States:

1. Extended familism is likely to occur under conditions in which it is functional to the familial system to share resources. Such conditions include:
   (a) when resources are scarce as in conditions of poverty.
   (b) when an ethnic group—such as Catholics, Italian Americans, Jews, blacks, Mexican Americans, and so forth—is discriminated against. Such discrimination may range from minor slights to actual physical threat.
   (c) when a familial system is incomplete, as in, for example, the situation of the single parent family or that of an aged relative who needs assistance.
2. Extended familism is also likely to occur under conditions in which it is functional to the familial system to protect and derive benefit from its combined resources. Such conditions include:
   (a) a family-owned business whether it be a small father and son store or the Carter family peanut warehouse.
   (b) great wealth—families such as the Rockefellers, Du Ponts, or Mellons.
3. These conditions may also be combined so that, for example, members of an ethnic group that is discriminated against may be even more likely than others who experience less discrimination to have strong ties to the extended family under conditions of poverty, when the familial system is incomplete, when a business is family owned, or when there is great wealth.

A Schematic Diagram

In Chapter 1, procedures were outlined for investigating the familial system in an unknown society. The researcher, it was suggested, would explore with ego whom he or she considered kin and their relationship to him or her. This would provide data with which to analyze that society's familial structure. One would also determine with whom ego engaged in important instrumental activities. By comparing ego's nominees for inclusion in the familial structure and instrumental network, it would be possible to ascertain the degree to which ego's family in this unknown society was extended and highly functional. Through aggregation of individual responses on structure and function of the family system, a distribution of family types for the society would be developed. We have used this scheme for analyzing familial patterns in the suburban and statewide surveys and shall continue using it as we conclude our analysis of familial patterns in the United States.

In this chapter we have discussed a great deal of information about American familial structure but, as we have noted, it pertains only to domestic families. We can, however, make use of these data to create a scale of familial structure involving two subscales. The first consists of the Census Bureau's categories of domestic families: husband-wife, other male-headed, and female-headed families. The second is the absence or presence of an "other relative" in the household. This scale enables us to determine whether the domestic family is extended. We have no way of determining the structure of extended families that go beyond the single household.

As concerns function, we have no information about the degree of functionality of domestic families, whether extended or not. Logic would suggest, however, that providing care for an aged relative or food and lodging for an unemployed son and his family are instrumental activities.[18] Furthermore, as we have noted, we know little about the ties of domestic families—whether extended or not—with kin outside of the household.

We know more, however, about the extra-household extended kin network. We have found, using survey data, that about 1 in 7 American families appears to be isolated. It thus seems to follow that for such families the extended kin network has no functionality whatsoever. This leaves 6 of 7 families which are embedded in kin networks. Information suggests that interaction among kin for the most part provides recreational and emotional support. However where certain other types of activities occur—such as involvement in child care and common economic activities—it follows that true extended familism exists as we conceive that term.

This reasoning leads to a scale of functionality of the kin network with three categories: isolated, meaning zero functionality; involved in a kin network, meaning largely expressive functionality; and extended familism by which we refer to the presence of instrumental activities as a common endeavor. Expressive functions may also be performed but they are not a necessary condition of extended familism. Kin members could loath one another but still be tied together instrumentally.

The schema that we have just outlined is presented in Table 2-12. In it we have arrayed what data we have for American families to try as far as possible to fill the cells, but for the most part we can only make guesses about the values of the marginals—and hence the subtitle of this chapter, "an unsatisfactory classification."

The purpose of this chapter has been to try to figure out what our family patterns have been in the recent past and what they are at present; it is not

TABLE 2-12. Schematic Diagram for Structural Analysis of Domestic Families and Functional Analysis of Their Kin Networks

Structure of Domestic Family		Functionality of Kin Network *Percent*			
Type of Family	*Relative other than own child in home?[a]*	Isolated: No Function	Embedded: Expressive	Extended: Instrumental & Perhaps Expressive	Total
Husband-Wife	Total	12	(. . . . . 72 . . . .)		84.3
	Absent	?	?	?	?
	Present	?	?	?	?
"Other Male Head"	Total	?	?	?	2.7
	Absent	?	?	?	?
	Present	?	?	?	?
Female Head	Total	?	?	?	13.0
	Absent	?	?	?	?
	Present	?	?	?	?
Total	Total	?	?	?	100
	Absent	?	?	?	(88.9–97.6)
	Present	?	?	?	(2.4–11.1)

[a]The "present" category designates the percentage of domestic families that include some relative other than husband, wife, and their offspring. Hence this percentage includes those containing subfamilies. The presence of an "other relative" who is not part of a subfamily also results in there being 2 or more familial positions at least one of which is a non-nuclear dyad and thus, by our definition, creates another type of extended domestic family.

intended as a projection of the future. We do know that marriages and births are going down whereas divorces and unmarried cohabitating continue to rise (Glick, 1975; U.S. Bureau of the Census, 1977). It is uncertain how long these trends will or can continue at the present rates. They undoubtedly do have an impact on contacts with and dependence on kin. For example, Spicer and Hampe (1975) and Anspach (1976) report that after divorce, contacts with the former spouse's family often become attenuated. At the same time, we have seen that single parent domestic families seem to rely more on members of the extended, presumably consanguineal, family than do husband-wife couples as indicated by the presence of more "other relatives" in the household. Such living arrangements often seem designed to provide aid and support for child care. If the birth rate continues to go down even if the divorce rate remains high, this reason for reliance on the extended family may decline in importance.

There seem to be few data available on contacts with kin among cohabitaters. We might predict that cohabitating would produce fewer contacts by the couple with kin to the extent to which the couple feels uncomfortable revealing their living arrangements to their relatives; alternatively kin contacts might also be reduced if relatives are unaccepting of the arrangement.

Another trend with possible consequences for contacts with relatives is the increasing proportion of the population that is aged. As we have seen, along with single parent families, the aged are among the more likely categories to be living with other relatives. As the proportion of the aged population increases, this might suggest a shift in the age composition (from young to old) and structure (from subfamilies to more "other relatives") of domestic extended families but not necessarily a decline in their numbers.

Summary and Conclusions

Zimmerman claimed the American family was "atomistic." By this he meant that it was isolated and functionless. By isolated he meant little functional interaction with kinsmen. Ogburn seemed to assume the American family was nuclear; he did not speculate on its connections with kin. He said it was losing all functions but the affectional. Wirth said the process of urbanization was detaching individuals from familial influence. Parsons used the phrase "isolated nuclear family," which seemed to summarize the observations of Zimmerman, Ogburn, and Wirth, and of Burgess and Locke. For a time the sociological community seemed to believe that the pattern of the American family was isolated as well as nuclear.

Actually, as we have seen, Parsons did not mean that the American family was isolated in the literal way it was interpreted. The revisionists of the 1950s showed that for their urban samples most domestic families had kin, were in contact with these kin, that interaction with kin was a major form of recreation (especially in the lower social strata), and that a high proportion of households reported giving and/or receiving emergency aid from kinsmen. The revisionists seemed to interpret such data as demolishing the Parsonian stance about the American family.

We have seen that what Parsons meant by isolated was that the nuclear family should have its own dwelling unit (which the census data confirm for the American population), and that it be economically independent of kin (which data from the University of Michigan 5,000 family survey support). Goode maintained that the American family had been nuclear since before the industrial revolution.

Parsons and Goode theorized that the nuclear system was consistent with the demands of the economy in an industrialized-urbanized society, which required individuals as units of labor, that individuals be hired and promoted on the basis of universalistic rather than particularistic criteria, and that the employees be sufficiently detached from the familial system to be spatially and socially mobile.

Over the period of nearly two centuries that the United States has been taking censuses, the data on composition and mean size of household show that the modal domestic family has been nuclear throughout the period, supporting Goode's contention, and that although there has been a decline in the size of the average household, that decline has been mostly in the number of children and to a much smaller extent in the number of unrelated persons (presumably servants and roomers or boarders).

Having concluded that the spokesmen of the three schools of thought were talking past each other, we made use of our variable of isolation-extended-familism with its four indexes. With our criterion of isolation (absence of any household of kin in the community of residence) we found that only a small minority of domestic families was isolated (13% in the suburban sample and 14% in the Wisconsin sample).[19] We also found some of the social characteristics of isolated families: upper middle class, suburban, Protestant, in bureaucratic occupations, and migratory. These social characteristics make it easier for this group to be mobile. Their isolation seems to be the result of the fact that they have migrated from their kinsmen. Among domestic families with these characteristics, the incidence of isolated families runs in the range of 20 to 25 percent. These observations require two qualifications:

1. There are other ways of defining isolation. If the criterion had been the number of relatives who might be expected to aid in an emergency, perhaps the percentage of isolated domestic families would be less; but, on the other hand, it might be greater.

2. These data lead to the conclusion that around 72 percent of all domestic families include married couples and are embedded in networks of local kin; around 13 percent include married couples and are isolated in the sense of not having local kin; and about 12 percent are female-headed, a topic on which we shall have more to say in Chapters 8 and 9. In addition, there are a little over 2 percent of domestic families that are other male-headed, that is, without resident wives-mothers.

In our suburban study we hypothesized that ethnicity would predict extended familism and that it would do so through the intervening variables of occupational and migratory status. On the basis of our sample of upper-middle-class suburban households we found that although ethnicity and migration were both good predictors of familism, the process did not work in the manner hypothesized. Our index of ethnicity was affiliation with one of the three major religious traditions in the United States: Protestant, Catholic, Jewish.

We have suggested several conditions under which extended familism is likely to occur. The first is under conditions of disadvantage in which it is functional to share scarce resources and/or to band together for mutual protection. The second is under conditions of advantage—when it is functional for the family to protect and benefit from abundant resources. It follows then that for the majority of the population that lives in neither great plenty nor deprivation, the "costs" involved in extended familism outweigh the potential rewards.

A conclusion we draw from our schema (Table 2-12) and its many empty cells is that despite sometimes heated discussions by several generations of social scientists about isolation-extended familism, much more information is needed about American kinship structure before any definitive statements can be made about its forms. Thus, it would appear that there is and always has been a plurality of types of American families.

Notes

1. Zimmerman's other two types are the "trustee" and the "domestic." The former is the type of "maximum strength," having power of controlling the life and death of its members. The latter is the type of "medium strength," viewed by Zimmerman as the most common type in the world (Zimmerman, 1947).

2. Actually, Goode's term was conjugal, by which he meant that the familial system was nuclear but not isolated from kin.

3. In an analysis of Wirth's views on the urban way of life Gans (1968:35) states that Wirth's formulation "applies only—and not too accurately—to the residents of the inner city." Three of the five types of inner-city residents—the cosmopolites, the unmarried or childless, and members of ethnic groups—have social ties and contacts that "detach" them from their neighborhoods and therefore from the negative effects of the urban way of life as well. The two groups that Gans does consider to be effected are the deprived (the poor and those who are otherwise socially or physically handicapped) and the trapped or downwardly mobile. For the remainder of the urban and suburban population, social relationships are quasi-primary—"interaction is more intimate than a secondary contact but more guarded than a primary one" (p. 40). Gans' reformulation, however, still suggests that on a continuum of isolation-extended-familism, the majority of families live lives closer to the isolated end.

4. In the same way that we use the term "ethnic category" to refer to each of the three sets of religious affiliations, Lenski (1963) speaks of a "socio-religious group." He maintains that these groups have both associational and communal aspects, that the Catholics are associationally strong (as evidenced by a high proportion attending mass regularly), that the Jews are strong communally

(through being highly endogamous and having most of their friends among the Jews), and that the Protestants are not especially strong in either regard.

5. Lenski (1963: 216) reports a similar pattern in percent of respondents visiting relatives weekly: Jews, 75; Catholics, 56; Protestants, 49. (In some of his other findings, however, he finds Catholics even more familistic than Jews.)

6. It appears that Lenski (1963: 247) might reverse the question and ask: Why is the familial system of the Protestants so restricted? His answer has to do with religion itself. He interprets evidence from his study and from others as indicating "that the Protestant churches have long been, and continue to be, a force in society weakening the bonds of the extended family (and perhaps of the immediate family as well) and simultaneously stimulating the formation of, and participation in, voluntary associations." A replication of Lenski's study (Schuman, 1971) failed for the most part to reproduce Lenski's findings with respect to work and attitudes toward work. The published report of the replication, however, does not touch on variables pertaining to extended familism or any of the other variables involved in the present chapter.

7. Nor in Detroit, where Lenski gathered his data.

8. This survey is based upon a multistage area probability sample design that gives each housing unit in the state an equal chance of being selected for interviewing. The procedure begins with a sample of the state's counties and moves to a sample of U.S. Census enumeration districts within counties. From the enumeration district is made a sample of chunks (geographical areas containing approximately 30 housing units each). From each chunk is drawn a sampling segment (a small geographical area containing approximately four housing units). This procedure identifies for the interviewer the housing unit within which he or she is to make the call. Finally, there is a random procedure for selecting the person to be interviewed among the persons in the household who have passed their twenty-first birthdays. In the two largest cities of Wisconsin—Milwaukee and Madison—a somewhat different procedure is followed: a sample of addresses is drawn from the annually revised city directory, and coverage of addresses not appearing in the directories is obtained through the use of area samples of city blocks. No substitutions are permitted for sample housing units or for respondents. Four or more calls are made by the interviewers, if necessary, in order to interview the randomly specified respondent. A sample of 702 people was interviewed—322 men and 380 women. As of 1960, about 48 percent of the population of Wisconsin over the age of 19 was male; in the sample the proportion of males was 46 percent. We wish to thank Harry Sharp, director, and the Wisconsin Sample Survey Laboratory, for making these data available to us.

Because of our interest in having data comparable with those from the suburban study, especially with respect to the opportunity of a household to engage in familistic behavior, we based our statewide sample on married couples. (It is reasonable to assume that the number of households of kin available to a married couple is different from the number available to a single person.) Accordingly, we eliminated from the sample all respondents who were not either married male heads of households or wives of heads. As in the suburban study, we were also interested in the religious affiliation of respondents.

Because they represented categories too differentiated from others to be combined with them and too small for separate analysis, Jews and eastern rite Catholics were omitted. The number of nonwhites was also too small for statistical analysis. After these exclusions were made, the sample of 702 shrank to 513. Of these, there was an absence of information with respect to migratory status on nine individuals and with respect to religious affiliation on one.

9. Minor changes in the operational definitions of the categories of the indicators were introduced. Details may be seen through comparing the section above entitled "Measures of Extended Familism" (pertaining to the suburban study) with the footnote explanation of Appendix Table F-13 (pertaining to the Wisconsin study).

10. By the criterion of the chi-square statistic all of the measures of extended familism except functionality are related to income in a nonrandom manner (having values of the chi-square statistic corresponding to probabilities under .05), but the bivariate distributions defy any parsimonious interpretation.

11. Parsons' condition (1)—separate households—is precisely specified and clearly observable, but its meaning is simply that America has a nuclear family system or, more precisely, a nuclear family residential system. There is nothing about the concept of the nuclear family system that indicates the degree to which related nuclear families may be isolated from each other. Parsons' condition (2)—economic independence—is both precisely specifiable and clearly observable, but its meaning, like that of Parsons' condition (1), has been challenged by Litwak in the latter's formulation of the "modified extended family."

12. As in the suburban study, a person was classed as a nonmigrant if he or she had been born in the community where interviewed or if brought there before turning age 18. Migratory status was trichotomized: both migrants, one spouse migrant, and neither spouse migrant. Migratory status is correlated with education of the head of the family in that in 59 percent of the families whose heads had 13 or more years of education, both spouses were migrants to the community, whereas 41 percent of the couples were migratory in families whose heads had not gone beyond high school. When the education-familism gammas were run within categories of migratory status, significant gammas resulted for extensity and intensity only in the both-migrant category, in intensity only in neither-migrant, and in functionality in no category.

13. This correlation was marginal, however, the pattern of association being the same and the gamma being just slightly below that required for the .05 level of significance.

14. The 36 gammas represent three indexes of extended familism (extensity, intensity, interaction), three levels of migration, two indexes of socioeconomic status, each at two levels, and $3 \times 3 \times 2 \times 2 = 36$.

15. Gamma = .21, significant at the .01 level.

16. In the Detroit Area Study mentioned on page 13 above, the percentage of isolated families was 11.

17. Williams (1976) has reported that Mexican-American migrant workers also live in a network of extra-household kin relations similar to the one Stack (1974) has described for low income blacks.

18. For discussion of young, white, working-class couples forced by economic circumstances to move in with one or the other set of parents, see Rubin (1976).

19. See n. 16 above.

Chapter 3

Familial Structure and Function as Influence

Robert F. Winch
Margaret T. Gordon

On the opening page of this book we announced that structure, function, and influence were aspects of familial organization we aspired to explain. In Chapter 2 we dealt with familial structure and function. In the present chapter we look to familial structure and functioning to explain variation in familial influence.

In our view the task of social psychology from the standpoint of a sociologist is to explain individual behavior as a consequence of the structures and functioning of social systems. Unless one is a hermit or a feral man, one belongs to and participates in at least one social system. Unless one is in a very primitive society or in what has come to be called a total institution (Goffman, 1961), one participates in more than one social system. Involvement in two or more social systems renders problematic their relative influence on one's behavior.

Our Study

We begin with the common observation that early learning occurs largely in the family and with the common question as to why some parents influence their children more than other parents do. Thus, we regard the family as primary

Adapted by permission of the publisher from *Familial Structure and Function as Influence* by Robert F. Winch and Margaret T. Gordon. Lexington, Mass.: Lexington Books, D. C. Heath and Company (1974). Reprinted by permission of the publisher.

in the sense of being the earliest source of influence; we are content to let the data record whether or not we are correct in our surmise that it is also the most important source of influence.

In connection with the influence of parents and of the family in general, there arises the complementary question as to what are the other important sources of influence on those children. More sociologically, which alternate social system(s) substitute for the family when the family exerts relatively little influence? Peers come to mind as a source of influence, but generally it seems they tend not to be organized into social systems with differentiated positions. Groups and networks seem more apt terms to characterize their interaction. Would it be possible to study peers in social systems? Our solution was to create a design such that every research subject (S) was a member of a college fraternity (a social system of peers) as well as a son in a familial system in which there were both a resident father and mother.

The research task we set for ourselves, then, was to see if we could predict the conditions under which the family would have more or less influence on the son, and to see whether the fraternity became the source of influence when the family was relatively uninfluential.

The theory from which our hypotheses emerge asserts that the structure and the functioning of a social system are the critical determinants of that system's influence (see Figure 3-1). Our initial structural hypothesis is that a social system will exert its influence by presenting its members with one or more suitable models. Originally we had hoped to vary familial structure by having half of our Ss with, and half without, fathers. Fortunately for our Ss, but unfortunately for our research design, we were unable to get nearly enough Ss without fathers. Therefore, we recast our structural hypothesis to the effect that a social system that presents its members with two suitable models will have more influence than a system that presents just one model. Accordingly, we sought to vary the familial structure by getting half of our Ss with and half without another suitable role-model—an older brother. We predicted that families with two suitable models—older brother as well as father—would influence their sons more than would families with only the single model of father.

We also hypothesized that function, conceived in the Janus-faced fashion,[1] would result in reward and hence in influence. We decided to study the function of status-conferring. As it pertained to the family, status-conferring was measured by our index of socioeconomic status (SES) relative to intrafraternity standards.[2] We predicted that families of high SES would be more influential with their sons than would families of low SES. Furthermore, we formulated what we called a "vacuum theory" of peer influence—that is that the influence of peers would be reported only in situations where the influence of families was reported to be relatively slight. Hence it was predicted that the influence of fraternities would be correlated with low familial SES.

No effort was made to vary the structure of the fraternities studied. In a sense, however, we did vary the S's position in the fraternity by dichotomizing the members of each fraternity on the basis of the duration of membership.

Figure 3-1 Identification (Influence) Stated as an Outcome of Structure and Function*

The following diagram relates social structure and social function to identification:

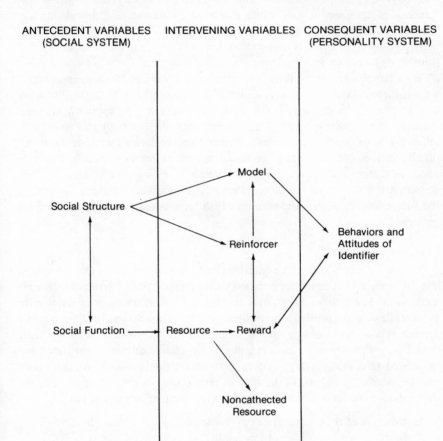

ANTECEDENT VARIABLES (SOCIAL SYSTEM)　　INTERVENING VARIABLES　　CONSEQUENT VARIABLES (PERSONALITY SYSTEM)

Social Structure

Social Function → Resource → Reward

Model

Reinforcer

Behaviors and Attitudes of Identifier

Noncathected Resource

*Three previous versions of this paradigm have been published with the first being in Winch (1962:147). The present version differs from that in addition of the reinforcer. The second version appeared in Winch (1970:581). Unfortunately that figure as well as the text generally contained errors, and that presentation should be regarded only as containing a rough statement of the author's intention. The third was in Winch and Gordon (1974:26).

Previous work among whites had shown the functionality of extended kin networks to vary with affiliation with one of the three major religious categories of the United States (see Chap. 2 above; see also Winch, 1962: 122). (Because, as noted previously, we were more interested in the cultural than in the theological properties of these categories, we have called this variable "ethnicity.") The rank order of the functionality of kin networks from high to low was: Jewish, Catholic, Protestant. This led us to expect that there might be differences in influence among white Protestant, Catholic, and Jewish nuclear families. Because of the unique history of blacks as a slave people and as an underprivileged minority, it seemed also that their family might be an interesting fourth category.

Both families and fraternities—at least through the mid-1960s when our data were gathered—tended to be ethnically homogeneous. Because fraternities were easy to identify by ethnicity and because they were easy to approach, we used them as our sampling units. Unlike fraternities, college campuses were both ethnically homogeneous and heterogeneous. Being undecided whether the effect of ethnicity would be more pronounced among Ss on an ethnically homogeneous or heterogeneous campus, we decided to include both. This decision necessitated doing the study on an ethnically homogeneous campus for each of the four ethnic categories and then on a fifth campus that was ethnically heterogeneous.[3]

Our Procedure

To test our ideas about the conditions under which the family exerts more or less influence on offspring, we gathered written responses to a series of questionnaires from 314 male undergraduate students who were members of fraternities at five colleges in the northeastern quadrant of the United States. The Ss responded to four sets of questions pertaining to individuals with whom they identified, from whom they learned concepts and skills in childhood, by whom they were influenced to develop certain traits, and to whom they would go for counsel in case of specified problems at the time of responding. Our basic design rested on the analysis of variance in which there were five main effects as follows:[4]

1. structure of the nuclear family: presence or lack of an older brother
2. function of family: high or low familial socioeconomic status
3. exposure to fraternity: long or short duration of S's membership
4. ethnicity: WASP, Catholic, Jewish, black
5. contextual variable: ethnic homogeneity or heterogeneity of the campus

The results of this analysis are summarized in Table 3-1.

Our Findings

We had hypothesized that Ss with older brothers would report more influence from the nuclear family and less from peers. We made no specific predictions about either parent or the extended or total family. (We use "total family" as a category to register the influence of nuclear family plus that of extended kin.) We found that where Ss had older brothers, they reported, as hypothesized, that they were more influenced by their nuclear families than did Ss without older brothers. Those with older brothers also reported being more influenced than did Ss without older brothers by mothers, extended families, and total families, but less by fathers, fraternity brothers, and all peers.[5] (There was an exception to the last generalization: Those with older brothers tended to register greater influence from girl friends with respect to one of six categories of traits—the trait of nurturance-receptivity.) We have interpreted these results as consistent with our hypothesis that a structure with more appropriate models—in our study, Ss having older brothers as well as fathers—should prove more influential than a structure with fewer models—in our study, Ss having fathers but no older brothers.

Our functional hypothesis was supported both with respect to family and fraternity. Ss from families of high functionality (high relative socioeconomic status) tended to report greater influence of the nuclear, extended, and total family, as well as of the prime functionary—the father—than did Ss from families of low functionality. Generally, however, familial status did not correlate with maternal influence. The one exception showed maternal influence to be greater with low rather than with high familial status. Peer influence, especially of fraternity brothers, tended to be associated with low familial SES and thus, we conclude, with low familial functionality. Except for the slight indication that maternal influence might be correlated with low familial SES, these results are consistent with our theoretical expectations and lend confirmation to our schema.

Those who had longer exposure to the fraternity were older than those with brief exposure. We had expected to find among older Ss evidence of diminished influence of the family and increased influence of peers. The data generally confirmed this expectation. The one exception was that the age of S (and length of exposure to fraternity) seemed unrelated to the influence of the father; that is, although the influence of the mother, of nuclear, extended, and total family was lower among the older Ss, the influence of the father was uncorrelated with age.[6]

We had guessed that families of the ethnic category we had found to have the most extended familism and the most functional interaction with kinsmen—the Jews—would have great influence over their sons and that families of the category with the least extended familism—the WASPs—would have the least influence. We had not felt able to predict for the blacks. In accordance with these expectations we did find that there was a low level of influence among WASP mothers, nuclear families, and total families. WASP fathers, however, did not prove to be especially uninfluential. In accordance with our vacuum theory of influence (to be discussed below), WASP ethnicity was associated with high influence of fraternity brothers and total peers (although the only significant outcomes involving girl friends showed low influence with respect to two of six categories of traits—those pertaining to life style and to means of achieving goals). The evi-

TABLE 3-1. Conditions of Five Main Effects Associated with Familial vs. Nonfamilial Influence for Four Categories of Influence

Main Effect and Category of Influence	Familial Models					Nonfamilial Models		
	Father	Mother	Nuclear Family	Extended Family	Total Family	Fraternity	Girl Friend	All Peers
Familial structure: Does S have an older brother?								
Identification	No				Yes			
Socialization in childhood	No							
Influenceable traits	Yes	Yes	Yes	Yes	Yes	No	Yes	
Contemporaneous problems			Yes			No		No
Familial function: Socioeconomic status of S's family relative to families of other members of S's fraternity								
Identification	High	Low	High			Low		
Socialization in childhood	High							
Influenceable traits	High		High	High	High	Low		
Contemporaneous problems	High		High	High	High	Low		Low

Duration of exposure to fraternity							
Identification		Short		Short	Long		Long
Socialization in childhood	Short	Short		Short	Long	Long	Long
Influenceable traits		Short	Short	Short	Long		Long
Contemporaneous problems	Short	Short	Short	Short	Long		Long
Ethnicity of family (and of fraternity)							
Identification	B,C,W̄,J̄ / J	B̄,W̄ / J	B	B̄,W̄ / J	J̄,B̄		C,B̄
Socialization in childhood							C
Influenceable traits	B,W̄	J,W̄	B	J,W̄	C,B̄	C,J,W̄,B̄	C,B̄
Contemporaneous problems	J	J,W̄		J,W̄	C,W̄,J̄,B̄		W̄,J̄,B̄
Ethnic homogeneity or heterogeneity of campus							
Identification	Het	Het		Het	Hom		Hom
Socialization in childhood	Hom					Hom	
Influenceable traits							Hom
Contemporaneous problems							Hom

Legend:

Ethnicity: W = WASP; C = Catholic; J = Jewish; B = Black; W̄ = non-WASP, etc.

Ethnic homo- or heterogeneity of campus: Hom = homogeneous; Het = heterogeneous.

59

dence concerning Jewish ethnicity was very different from what we had expected: slight evidence that Jewish fathers were highly influential (only with respect to contemporaneous problems), mixed evidence about the nuclear and total family (high on contemporaneous problems, low on early socialization), and fairly consistent evidence of low influence on the part of Jewish mothers. Catholic ethnicity showed up as important with respect to peers, whereas blacks and Jews seemed especially uninfluenced by peers. (The low degree of influence of peers among blacks may have been affected by their being the only ethnic category lacking fraternity houses, and of course this lack of houses was no doubt related to their relative poverty.) With blacks the usually reciprocal relationship between familial and peer influence appears: among them the evidence is that the influence of mother, nuclear, extended, and total family is relatively high and that of peers relatively low. Perhaps it should be emphasized that whereas the greater influence of the black mother than of the black father is frequently interpreted as related to the female-headed family, such a familial arrangement does not prevail here. All the Ss whose responses were used in the quantitative analysis reported having intact parental marriages and both parents still in the home.

It may be recalled that, being uncertain whether to base our study on several ethnically homogeneous campuses or on a single heterogeneous campus, we decided to do both. Consequently, no hypothesis was associated with this main effect. Ethnic homogeneity of campus seems correlated with the influence of peers. Perhaps this is because the homogeneous campuses were smaller and more *gemeinschaftlich* than the single heterogeneous campus—a large state university. The relation of this variable to familial influence seems mixed and difficult to interpret. Of course it is important to keep in mind that the data of this study are not behavioral (observational) but, rather, are reports of college students as to who they believe have been most influential in their lives.

We have not worked out a satisfactory technique for measuring the totality of influences on each S from birth to the moment of testing that would enable us to calculate a distribution of proportion of total influence by type of source (father, fraternity brother, etc.). A very rough approximation to that kind of information may be derived, however, from averaging the distributions of influence over several areas of questioning. It is recognized that to do this involves us in assumptions we cannot possibly support, such as that (1) we have measured each set accurately, (2) that the several sets of measures are of equal importance in making the S what he is today, and (3) that no other kind of influence has existed. If we agree to tolerate these untenable assumptions for the purpose of obtaining a crude distribution of total influence, we find that the older brother accounts for something like 8 percent of the total influence, which for Ss not having an older brother tends to get distributed among father, fraternity brothers, and unrelated adults. Other results from this crude calculation are as follows: The father is reported to be the prime source of influence about a quarter of the time, the mother about a sixth, the nuclear family as a whole a little over half the time, the fraternity about a tenth, all peers (including the fraternity) around a quarter, other unrelated adults about a tenth, and the self around a fourteenth. The extended kinsmen account for only around 2 percent of total influence. Of course, by altering the weights assigned to early and contemporaneous spheres of influence, we could vary the proportion ascribable to family and to peers.

This study was designed in the hypothetico-deductive tradition with the theory stated, and, in fact, published (Winch, 1962) well in advance of the gathering of the data in 1965. If it had been possible to do our study in a truly experimental manner, most of the potential sources of invalidity would have been eliminated and there would have been relatively little need to seek alternative explanations of findings. On the other hand, if we had done an exploratory-inductive study[7]—where both the findings and their interpretation flow from the data—any interpretation we might offer could not be rated higher than a plausible hypothesis along the spectrum of tentative certainty from informal speculation to scientific law.

When Babe Ruth turned to a booing crowd, pointed to a spot in the bleachers where he would hit the next ball, and then proceeded to do just that, he did not conduct a scientific experiment, but the correspondence between the prediction and the result was convincing. Our situation is that we made some predictions on the basis of our structure-function-resource theory of influence and, in the main, our predictions have been confirmed.

The Structure-Function-Resource-Vacuum Theory of Influence

Our theory began with a sociological aspect pertaining to the structure and functioning of social systems and a social psychological aspect whereby the Janus-faced approach to function yielded the formulation: function $\rightarrow$ resource $\rightarrow$ influence. Having scrutinized the data gathered for the illumination of this theory, let us now set about to reformulate it.

We shall need ten propositions, the first six of which are findings of the present study of male college students:

1. The influence of the father is generally greater than that of anyone else.
2. The influence of the father correlates positively with the socioeconomic status of the family.
3. The influence of the mother is for the most part uncorrelated with the family's status. Such indication of correlation as exists suggests that the correlation may be negative.
4. More clear-cut associations with maternal influence arise from ethnicity— with black mothers tending to register much influence and Jewish mothers relatively little—and age (or duration of exposure to peers)—with

evidence that maternal influence decays although paternal influence does not.

5. The correlation between the influence of peers and the socioeconomic status of the family is negative.

6. The influence of peers tends to be low for blacks and Jews, high for Catholics and, to some extent, for WASPs.

From these findings we may offer the following inferences:

7. Since the influence of the father is positively correlated with SES and that of the mother is generally uncorrelated with SES, it follows that as SES decreases, the influence of the mother relative to that of the father increases.

8. Since the influence of the father is positively correlated with SES and that of the fraternity is negatively correlated with SES, it follows that as SES decreases, both the relative and absolute influence of the fraternity increases.

In addition, the following propositions are relevant:

9. The family has the first opportunity to influence the S; the opportunity of peers comes later, and especially is this true of fraternity brothers.

10. Although not all studies have come to the same conclusion, there is a general finding that the power of husbands relative to that of wives is positively correlated with familial SES. Rodman (1972) proposes that the exceptions to this generalization can be explained on cultural grounds; for example, the "modified patriarchy" of such relatively unindustrialized societies as those of Greece and Yugoslavia.

Let us consider the resources contributed by father and mother through their functional activities (i.e., their task-oriented behaviors). Virtually all of the fathers were employed—mostly in business and the professions. Most of the mothers were housewives and not in the labor force. Perhaps it should be recalled that the year of data gathering was 1965, and that as far as could be determined from the questionnaires each S was living with his original (biological) father and mother. Moreover, the fact that we are considering a sample of male college students who were members of fraternities, all of whose parents were still married to each other, biases our sample away from the general U.S. population in the direction of the traditional nuclear family. Taking note of this bias, let us assume that the prime familial function of the father was generally perceived to be that of status-conferring and that familial SES was a measure of the quality of the father's performance of this task. It is reasoned, then, that the father, by means of successful performance, was seen as providing the members of the family with material and psychic resources.

The influence of the mother (as well as that of the older brother) seems to have been about the same across the spectrum of statuses. Let us assume that the chief maternal functions were seen to be those related to child care (the parental function) and management of the household. The adequacy with which the mother carried out her assignment need not be related to the status the father conferred. It would seem likely that there were many women at all status levels who were regarded by their children as fine parents and/or housewives and that there were others—again without regard to social status—whose performance in one or both of these areas might be deplored by their children.

If, then, the influence of the father was less at the lower statuses (because he brought in fewer resources that could become rewards), this served to create a vacuum of influence so far as the son was concerned. One response was for the son to develop an increment of self-reliance, and this was suggested by data not shown in the present report (Winch and Gordon, 1974: 81). Another response was for him to become more reliant on extrafamilial figures—for example, fraternity brothers. Another way of phrasing the notion is that the family has the first opportunity to influence the boy. If the opportunity is missed because of the lack of resources, then the boy looks for the resource → reward → influence sequence from some other social system or relationship. We chose to study Ss who were members of a second social system—the fraternity. It turned out that although the relation between the influence of father and that of mother was not reciprocal, the relation between the family's influence—chiefly, of course, that of the father—and that of the fraternity did tend to be reciprocal.

This discussion of familial influence on the development of the son is related to the ongoing consideration in the literature on marital power. In particular we see our formulation to be consistent with Rodman's (1972) theory of marital power based on resources in a cultural context. As Rodman suggests, the American cultural context can be regarded as deriving from a society moving through a state of transition toward a norm of equality of the genders.

To the extent that we are moving not only toward equality of power of husband and wife but also toward a substantial reduction of the differentiation of gender roles, it would seem to follow that future studies should show an increase in the influence of mothers on sons and quite possibly a pattern of maternal correlates parallel to the paternal, including a positive correlation of maternal influence with familial SES.

Notes

1. The Janus-faced view of social function is that it both reinforces the social system and rewards the individual member.

2. Each S reported his family's income, his father's occupation, and the extent of his father's education. These three indicators were weighted equally and combined into a single measure of SES. The resulting distribution within each fraternity was dichotomized at the median. On this basis each S was assigned to the "high" or "low" category of relative SES.

3. The black and WASP schools were small private colleges. The Jewish and Catholic schools were larger, private, and more urban. The ethnically heterogeneous institution was a large state university.

4. The design called for 336 Ss, but it was not possible to get the desired number of Ss with each combination of attributes. The original design involved six main effects, but it developed during the research that one of the main effects was duplicating another. For an account of these problems as well as the questionnaire and sampling procedure, see Winch and Gordon (1974).

5. In this context, nuclear family refers to S's parents and siblings; extended family refers to other kin outside the nuclear family; and total family refers to the nuclear family plus extended family.

6. Interviews with a subsample of the Ss led to the impression that, as the son passed through his college years, he began to see his father as becoming increasingly influential in his life.

7. Corresponding to the Campbell-Stanley (1963) one-shot case study and to our (Winch-Spanier, 1974: Chap. 1) clinical method.

Chapter 4

The Curvilinear Relation Between Societal Complexity and Familial Complexity

Rae Lesser Blumberg
Robert F. Winch

Under what conditions does the family wax and wane in complexity? In this chapter, we combine insights from our own U.S.-based survey research with cross-societal macro-level data, and propose one sort of answer. First, we suggest economically linked factors—that may be investigated at both the macro and micro levels—establish the general parameters of the modal family organization for the group or society in question. Specifically, we propose the concept of "societal complexity" (and a series of basically economic indicators) as our major independent variable so that we may examine the full range of the evolutionary continuum of human societies, ranging from hunting-gathering bands to contemporary industrial nations. We then propose that societal com-

Based largely on Winch and Blumberg (1968), Blumberg (1970), and Blumberg and Winch (1972).

plexity is curvilinearly related to familial complexity, such that the most elaborate family organizations are encountered at intermediate levels of societal development. Using data from Murdock's Ethnographic Atlas (1967) and a sample of contemporary Third World nations (Adelman and Morris, 1967), we find empirical support for our proposition—never before tested quantitatively or cross-culturally—of a curvilinear link between societal and familial complexity. Moreover, the results help set the stage for further theoretical development concerning the "conditions under which" families both increase and decrease in organizational complexity. As our jumping off point, let us begin with a study which has been quite influential in presenting cross-cultural indications of a contemporary near-worldwide *decrease* in the organizational complexity of families. We then move to combine it with evidence concerning factors linked with an *increase* in complex familism.

Goode's Thesis

Goode (1963) has proposed that correlated with the trend of societies toward modernization, industrialization, and urbanization—his summary term is "world revolution"—there is a convergence of diverse familial forms onto the conjugal family system. The main characteristics of this system, he asserts (n.d.), are as follows:

1. The extended family pattern becomes rare, and corporate kin structures disappear.
2. A relatively free choice of spouse is possible, based on love, and an independent household is set up.
3. Dowry and brideprice disappear.
4. Marriages between kin become less common.
5. Authority of the parent over the child, and of the husband over the wife, diminishes.
6. Equality between the sexes is greater; the legal system moves toward equality of inheritance among all children.

Goode notes that the conjugal family is found in technologically simple societies, such as the Eskimo, as well as in urban, industrial, Western ones. But by defining the conjugal family in terms of the fading away of a series of preexisting familial prerogatives, Goode places the conjugal family of primitive societies beyond the reach of his conceptual framework. Accordingly, he cannot address the general question of the occurrence of the small family—whether it be called the nuclear or the conjugal family. As we shall see, the literature is indecisive as to the determinants or correlates of familial complexity and thus the question warrants investigation.

To explore this question, we suggest replacing Goode's term "world revolution" with the concept that we shall call "societal complexity." Goode's world revolution notion would embroil us in two major disadvantages avoided by our proposed alternative. First, it would largely confine our attention to contemporary changes among relatively complex nations, whereas we wish to explore societies both simple and complex, both ancient and contemporary. Second, the underlying notion of the world revolution—the headlong, essentially parallel transformation of nations around the globe toward greater "modernization," as well as industrialization and urbanization, has come under increasing criticism since Goode published his book in 1963. In fact, a new paradigm, the "world capitalist system" approach, now strongly challenges the assumptions of "modernization" theorists. Our notion of societal complexity would seem to substitute a concept that underlies *both* the modernization and world capitalist system approaches. Let us explicate each point in turn.

Societal Complexity: Toward a Clarification
of the Independent Variable

Basically, our concept of societal complexity substitutes the mainline trend of societal evolution for time-bound and now controversial notions of a contemporary world revolution into modernity and development. Evolutionary theory itself has had a rather checkered history in the social sciences, but few would dispute that over human history on this planet, the mainline trend has been for societies to become more complex in their totalities and more differentiated in their parts. Specifically, regardless of the theory of development or dynamic of social transformation they espouse, few social scientists would dispute that from the hunting-gathering bands of the Pleistocene (or their contemporary survivors) to today's industrialized societies, both capitalist and socialist, the following have increased greatly: technological development, organizational complexity, and structural differentiation. It is precisely this direction of change that is measured by the term "societal complexity." As will be further explicated below, it is the techno-economic component of societal complexity— in Marxian terms, the "forces of production"—that we see as the most frequent and important source of major social change, and hence the leading component of societal complexity. But the concept of societal complexity itself involves no theory or dynamic of social change. It is merely a description of the net state of the system at different points along the evolutionary continuum. Indeed, the idea that societies have developed from simple to complex states has been shared by theorists with totally divergent theories of the end states and dynamic involved. The notion is incorporated in the societal evolution theories of Spencer (1910) on the one hand and Marx (1968) on the other. It also is encompassed in such polar ideal types as Tonnies' *gemeinschaft-gesellschaft* (1940), Durkheim's *solidarité mécanique-solidarité organique* (1933), and Redfield's folk-urban continuum (1947). More recently, it informs the work of Lenski (1970). The immediate benefit to us of adopting a societal complexity perspective is that we are able to scrutinize the entire spectrum of societies from simple to complex and then to hypothesize that societal complexity is curvilinearly related to nuclear familism.

The second advantage of the societal complexity concept is its transcendence of the controversial and probably culture-bound formulation of a convergent world revolution in which essentially parallel national-level processes transform traditional-agrarian to modern-industrial countries. When Goode wrote, the bulk of the (non-radical) literature optimistically saw the nations of the world rushing toward a similar future in which they would become more "modernized," "developed," "Westernized," "decolonialized," "industrialized," and "urbanized." In short, "they" would become more like "us," the Western capitalist industrial nations. Of the above terms, urbanization *has* increased all around the globe. But the uniformity of the other alleged trends, and the thesis of parallel development itself have come under attack both theoretically and empirically. A darker side of this world revolution is now increasingly in the spotlight: the simultaneous fostering of *under*development in various Third World countries as the reverse side of the coin bringing development to a relatively small group of industrial, largely Western capitalist nations. This apparent paradox is explained by the world capitalist system paradigm. Under this formulation, the historical emergence of a worldwide capitalist economic system has conditioned and constrained the development of various countries in diverse ways. For some, their position in the world economy leads to dependence (e.g., as specialized and vulnerable suppliers of raw materials), not development (see Wallerstein, 1974 and Frank, 1969 for some of the basic arguments of this approach). But whether one views the transformation from traditional agrarian societies as occurring under the modernization or world capitalist system dynamic, one would expect that, in general, their levels of family organization would decrease in complexity as that transformation proceeded. In short, our concept of societal complexity remains a static model, not a dynamic theory, of social change, but it permits us to focus on how family organization changes in response to its mainly economic components.[1]

The Nimkoff-Middleton Study

Now let us consider the perspective of societal complexity and see how it contributes to the analysis of (1) the emergence of either the nuclear or the extended familial system and (2) sources of variation in familism within societies.

Using evidence overwhelmingly drawn from the "simpler" side of the continuum of societal complexity (which we may conceptualize as ranging from hunting-gathering bands on the left to advanced industrial societies on the right), Nimkoff and Middleton (1960) have tested the hypothesis of a correlation between type of subsistence pattern and type of familial system. The evidence is drawn from the 549 of the 565 cultures in Murdock's (1957) "World Ethnographic Sample" (WES) that could be coded on these two variables. Coding for type of subsistence was with respect to Murdock's categories as to the presence or absence, and the importance of, such subsistence activities as hunting and gathering, fishing, animal husbandry, and agriculture. Type of familial system was dichotomized into independent[2] and extended.

Hunting and gathering tended to have independent familial systems, whereas extended familism was the prevailing pattern among societies on a more complex level of subsistence—sedentary agriculture with part-time herding.

Continuing their secondary analysis, Nimkoff and Middleton isolated four factors that appear to influence type of familial system through their association with type of subsistence: (1) abundance and stability of the food supply; (2) degree of demand for the family as a unit of labor; (3) amount of geographic mobility involved in subsistence activities, and (4) amount and nature of property. The first of these factors can be considered to be the most important in the sense that the only deviant cases of extended familism among hunting and gathering peoples occurred among those whose food supplies were unusually plentiful and regular for that type of subsistence, and also in the sense that, statistically speaking, food supply "explained" the correlations between the other three factors and type of familism. In short, a relatively ample and regular food supply, high use of the family as a laboring unit, low necessity for geographic mobility with respect to subsistence, and strongly developed concepts of property (especially land) as owned collectively rather than individually were associated with the maximum probability of extended familism, and of course the reverse conditions were associated with familism of the independent-conjugal-nuclear type.

One other factor emerged as important: in societies complex enough to have stratification (which presupposes an assured food supply and the concept of property), this factor was positively correlated with extended familism even when type of subsistence was held constant.

Having concluded that type of subsistence, type of familial property, and degree of stratification are related to type of familial system among the simpler societies in the WES, Nimkoff and Middleton extrapolated beyond their data and proposed that some of the same relationships should hold among the modern industrial societies. In the latter type of society there are a low demand for the family as the unit of labor (since individuals are hired for cash on achievement criteria) and a high degree of geographic mobility in the pursuit of subsistence (the hunter pursues his game; the industrial worker or bureaucrat, his job). To be sure, the concept of property is more highly developed among the modern practitioners of nuclear familism, but Nimkoff and Middleton suggested that the shift from both or either group-owned land to land individually acquired or to disposable cash makes for the easier emergence of nuclear familism.

From these considerations it seems to follow that there is a curvilinear relationship between societal complexity (as measured by type of subsistence) and familial complexity, as follows: at the simplest level of subsistence (hunting and gathering) there is a tendency toward a nuclear family system; at the intermediate level of subsistence (sedentary agriculture and herding) the tendency is toward an extended family system; and with the industrial type of economy there is again a tendency toward a nuclear family system.[3]

As we have noted, the Nimkoff-Middleton study is based upon data drawn from ethnographies concerning 549 of the 565 societies in Murdock's WES. Most of the other studies of societal complexity cited here are based on the WES or an early version of the WES (both or either the Cross-Cultural Survey or the Human Relations Area Files) or on some modification of one of these data banks. Since this remark can be applied to the studies by Naroll, Freeman-Winch, Freeman, and Tatje-Naroll, it follows that these studies have a considerable number of societies and ethnographic sources in common. For this reason it is necessary to conclude that these different studies cannot be regarded as independent studies of the same or similar hypotheses. Rather, similarities of results between studies can be thought of as registering "alternate forms" reliability in the sense of measuring equivalence of various ways of coding information from a largely common set of societies.

Another important qualification to keep in mind in interpreting these results is that these studies of societal complexity have been secondary analyses: that is, the social scientists who have performed these studies have been using data that were not gathered for this purpose, nor indeed were the data coded with this purpose in mind. All data must be coded before quantitative analysis can be undertaken. The difficulty with secondary analysis is that the user of the data often does not know the rules that were followed in coding the data; hence he cannot know which information has been included and which excluded. With respect to the WES, however, the situation is unusually good since Murdock has specified in considerable detail a set of 15 variables that have been coded and since then Sawyer and LeVine (1966) have factor-analyzed intercorrelations among these variables. Of the nine factors extracted by Sawyer and LeVine, the first four were Murdock's "basic types of economy": agriculture, animal husbandry, fishing, and hunting and gathering. The next four factors related to variations in the familial system: nuclear family household, patrilineality, matrilineality, and cross-cousin marriage. The final factor was that of social stratification.[4]

The results of the Sawyer-LeVine study do not indicate that there is anything spurious about the correlations reported by Nimkoff and Middleton. What these results do indicate, however, is that since other information was not included, it was not possible to find any other type of correlation—for example, that the nature of the value system or of the religious organization might have any influence either on the level of subsistence or on familial complexity.

A final comment on the methodology of our problem is that the measures of societal complexity based on the WES or some derivative of it cover mainly the left side and not the full range of complexity. With such a measure, therefore, it is not possible to test a general hypothesis about societal complexity.

The Winch-Greer-Blumberg Studies

Results of the Winch-Greer-Blumberg studies have been presented in Chapter 2. We shall be recalling those studies here in addressing our second question, which concerns the factors involved in *intra*societal variation in nuclear families.

It will be recalled that there were two such studies. One (Winch, Greer, and Blumberg, 1967) was carried out in an upper-middle-class suburb of Chicago, and it was found that Jews were more familistic than Catholics or Protestants. In the second study (Winch and Greer, 1968), based on a probability sample in Wisconsin, Catholics and Lutherans were more familistic than "other Protestants," but the degree of correlation was considerably less than in the suburban study, and it disappeared when one or both spouses were migrants.

Some parallels can be drawn between the variables proving significant in the foregoing two studies and the four factors that emerged in the Nimkoff-Middleton analysis of the simpler societies of the WES:

1. *Migration* emerged in all of these studies: the degree of extended familism was lower among those who were geographically mobile. Nimkoff and Middleton report that, for the simpler societies, mobility was completely related to type of economy.

2. *Property in the form of land* was associated with extended familism among the societies of the WES. In Wisconsin the degree of extended familism was higher among rural than among urban nuclear families. Although we do not have data on this point, it seems plausible that land ownership might be more common among rural than urban residents.

3. *Family as a unit of labor* correlated with extended familism in the Nimkoff-Middleton study. In the suburban study it was discovered that those families wherein the father had never been associated in a family business were likely to be high in extended familism. It would seem that the rural families of Wisconsin— at least to the extent that they are farmers—would also make some use of their families as workers, and it will be recalled that (with the qualifications noted in the last chapter) rural families were more extended-familistic on the average than were urban families. It is consistent with this presentation that among farm families and among those where the head had been in a family business, the high scores on extended familism were especially high on functionality—their exchange of goods and services with kinfolk.

Evidentiary Standing of the Curvilinear Hypothesis

Having surmised that the data of Nimkoff and Middleton on primitive societies and the data of Goode on developing and complex societies could be reconciled through the hypothesis of a curvilinear function, we may recall that such an idea has been in the literature for at least half a century. This idea was expressed by Lowie, Forde, and Fortes. Using the terms "sib" and "family" to refer, respectively, to unilateral kin groups, which are large, and to bilateral kin groups, which are small, Lowie (1920: 148, 150) asserted that the family prevailed in the simplest societies and that the sib appeared "only when horticultural or pastoral activities have partly or wholly superseded the chase as the basis of economic maintenance." He added that the residence of the nuptial couple with kin and the transmission of property rights were important conditions favoring the establishment of unilineal descent (p. 157).

Forde (1947: 218) phrased the point somewhat differently in holding that "poverty of the habitat, the rudimentary character of productive techniques, or the combination of both . . . severely limit the scale and stability of both separate settlements and of the wider community" and thus inhibit the development of a large familial system. He went on to say that as societies develop centralized political authority, they create conditions unfavorable for the large unilineal kinship group (p. 223).

Fortes (1953: 24) concurred and indicated that conditions most favorable to the unilineal descent group seemed to exist "in the middle range of relatively homogeneous, precapitalistic economies in which there is some degree of technological sophistication and value is attached to rights in durable property." At the level of the simplest societies, Fortes saw the absence of durable property as hindering the development of large familial systems, whereas at a considerably higher level of complexity he believed the introduction of money and the development of occupational differentiation were factors that would contribute to the breakdown of large families and the fostering of small familial systems.

It is not clear from a reading of Lowie just how many societies he believed he had presented in support of the hypothesis; in any case the number would be small. He appears to have believed that there was no negative instance, a belief that seems no longer tenable. Both Forde and Fortes relied on a dozen or so societies to support their statements of the case.

In his review of the relevant literature, Marsh (1967: 73) asserts that "a number of anthropologists . . . have for some time been demonstrating that, in effect, the overall relationship between societal differentiation and kinship solidarity is more nearly curvilinear [than linear]." Thus, without providing any new evidence, Marsh seems to find that the curvilinear relationship has been asserted often enough to be regarded as empirically established.[5]

As stated above, the findings of Nimkoff and Middleton were based on Murdock's WES. It is relevant that two other studies using prior or subsequent versions of the WES and beginning with the same categories of familism (but combining them differently) asserted conclusions very different from those of Nimkoff and Middleton. The first of these studies is by Murdock (1949: 189), who concluded that types of descent groups are uncorrelated with societal complexity. The second, by Osmond (1969), used the Ethnographic Atlas (Murdock, 1967). She recoded the variable of familial organization into "limited" and "general" types and found a predicted relationship between increasing societal complexity and the limited form of familial organization. In short, Nimkoff and Middleton found a positive correlation between societal and familial complexity, Osmond found a negative relationship, and Murdock found no association.[6]

In conclusion, Lowie, Forde, and Fortes supported their thesis by adducing examples. Murdock, Nimkoff and Middleton, and Osmond examined the question with data from the Ethnographic Atlas (EA) or its predecessors, and they came to complete dissensus. (It was noted at the beginning of this chapter that Goode found the relationship between societal complexity and familial complexity to be negative over the range of developing and developed countries.)

Although our theoretical bent agrees with that of Marsh, we cannot see that he has presented convincing evidence in support of the curvilinear hypothesis. Accordingly, we believe it is in order to scrutinize the available data and to determine the conclusion to which they lead. To test the hypothesis of the curvilinear relationship, whose antecedents we have traced over the last half century, we shall begin by utilizing the EA.[7] For familial complexity, we shall propose a fourth coding of the basic Murdock familism variable, the other three codings being those of Murdock, Nimkoff-Middleton, and Osmond (see Blumberg, 1970).

Variables and Indicators

Societal complexity is the independent variable in our problem. It is conceived as a continuum ranging from the simplest hunting-gathering types of bands to the most complex urban-industrial type of society extant today. Our unit of analysis is the society, and all known societies are assumed to be arrayed along the continuum of societal complexity.

As operationalized with Murdock's (1967) EA, a variety of aspects of societal complexity are measured. We shall make use of several of these subsumed under two major dimensions of societal complexity—namely, technology and social organization.

Our index of technology is a composite of two measures of the mode of subsistence: (1) subsistence economy, and (2) type and intensity of agriculture. Both of these are variables in the EA.

Subsistence economy consists of the following categories: gathering, hunting, fishing, herding, incipient agriculture, horticulture or extensive (shifting) agriculture, and intensive agriculture. However, two of these categories—fishing and herding—failed to fit into any ordinal arrangement of categories with respect to level of technological complexity. Lenski (1970) encountered this problem in his analysis of 915 of the 1,170 societies comprising the EA, and he explained it by noting that fishing societies generally tend to be located in environmental niches that are unusually favorable with respect to food. This favorable situation permits them to grow larger and to be more sedentary than other societies at such a simple level of technological development. Considered by many to be an adaptation of agricultural societies to arid conditions, herding societies tend to be nomadic and to have small local community populations. They often expand politically and in other ways to levels commensurate with their relatively complex semiagricultural technology. Accordingly, we decided to reduce the 1,170-society EA sample by dropping the fishing and herding societies. This left us with 962 societies.

The second component of technology, type and intensity of agriculture, engaged our interest because it provides more refined classification among agricultural categories. In particular, it provides a coding scheme that divides intensive-agriculture societies into those with and those without irrigation. The supposition is that societies with irrigation represent a higher level of organization and hence of complexity than do their nonirrigating counterparts. This distinction permitted us to hope for better discrimination among the moderately and highly complex societies of the EA. This is desirable in the light of our plan to demonstrate a curvilinear relationship between familial complexity and societal complexity, and in view of the truncated range of societal complexity represented by the EA. With few exceptions, the most complex societies in the EA are moderately complex agrarian states with some urbanization (e.g., the Ashanti); industrial societies as such are ignored.

By combining these two indexes, we were able to distribute 933 of the 1,170 societies of the EA into the following technological categories: hunting-gathering, incipient agriculture, extensive agriculture or horticulture, intensive agriculture on permanent fields, and intensive agriculture with irrigation.

Our measures of the social organizational dimension of societal complexity stem from a discussion by Goldschmidt (1959) of the consequences of technology for social organization. We reject his argument implying that technology is the "prime mover" (although we tentatively agree with Lenski that it seems to have figured more often and more importantly as the source of autogenous change in the other dimensions of societal complexity than vice versa), but we accept his social variables as the basis for the additional aspects of societal complexity measured in this chapter. From the limited set of variables available in the EA, we have chosen the following four to approximate those of Goldschmidt: (1) mean size of local community; (2) permanence of settlement (the nomadic-sedentary dimension); (3) stratification (ranging from none to a system based on social classes); and (4) political complexity (number of levels of jurisdictional hierarchy beyond the local community).[8]

We conceive of familial complexity, our dependent variable, in terms of familial structure, functionality, and influence. With respect to the EA, we are able to operationalize familial complexity only with respect to familial structure.[9]

We have dichotomized the family-organization variable of the EA. A society is classified as having familism of low complexity if its system is the independent nuclear family[10] with either (1) monogamy or (2) only limited or occasional polygyny (less than 20% of all unions).[11] All other familial forms as coded in the EA are classified as showing familism of high complexity. This category includes independent families in which polygyny covers more than 20 percent of all unions. Also classified as high complexity are all types of extended familism (e.g., joint, stem, etc.), irrespective of form of marriage.

The Test
Ideally, we should be able to measure extended familism with an interval scale. Indeed, we feel that the nature of the data allows us to employ only the crudest kind of scale—the dichotomy. We regard our scale of societal complexity as ordinal. If we could measure both variables with an interval scale, it would be possible to fit a curvilinear line of regression and test the significance of the increment of explained variance beyond that accounted for by a linear function. Unfortunately, there seems to be no single statistic that can perform this func-

tion unless the data are in interval form.[12] Accordingly, we shall look for evidence of curvilinearity in the proportions of low and high extended familism as we look across the ordinal categories from low to high societal complexity.

Correlations in social science being what they are, we do not predict an invariant relationship, but only a tendency. Our hypothesis leads to the prediction that the proportions of societies with a high level of familial complexity will be at a maximum somewhere in the intermediate range of societal complexity, probably among those with settled agriculture. There should be a minimum of highly familistic societies among those with low societal complexity—that is, hunting-gathering societies. And the proportion with high familism should be falling off at the upper end of the range of societal complexity in the EA series, even though the range of this series falls considerably short of modern industrialized technological levels. Accordingly, within the range of the data of the EA, we believe the curvilinear relationship will emerge even though the right end of the curve will not be able to decline as far as it would with a complete distribution of societal complexity.

Findings

As stated above, two dimensions of societal complexity are presented: the technological (measured by the composite index of subsistence complexity) and the organizational (measured by four indexes). Then we turn to multivariate analysis to draw a clearer picture of the relationship of societal and familial complexity.

Table 4-1[13] shows familial complexity cross-tabulated with the technological dimension of societal complexity. This measure of subsistence complexity shows a substantial curvilinearity (or nonmonotonicity). High familism prevails in 54 percent of the hunting-gathering societies and rises to 80 percent in both the categories of extensive agriculture and intensive agriculture without irrigation. With irrigation, the percentage falls off to 65 percent. Thus, the point of inflection occurs among the large group (over three fifths of the sample) of societies practicing agriculture, but without the added refinement of irrigation.

The relationship between familial complexity and each of the four aspects of social organization is shown in Appendix F, Tables F-17 to F-20. Actually, because the permanence-of-settlement variable was not expected to discriminate at all between medium and more complex societies, we predicted only that we would find more low-complexity familism among the nomadic societies. But, for the remaining three variables, we proposed to find a curvilinear relationship with societal complexity. In brief, our expectations are supported by the data.

The inflected, rather than the monotonic, prediction is confirmed in Appendix Table F-17, the cross-tabulation of mean size of local community with familial complexity.

Cross-tabulating permanence of settlement with familial complexity (Appendix Table F-18), upholds our expectation that nomadic groups are much more likely (46% vs. 25%) to have low familial complexity than non-nomadic groups.

Turning now to stratification, whose cross-tabulation with familial complexity

TABLE 4-1. Relationship between the Technological Dimension of Societal Complexity and Familial Complexity: Ethnographic Atlas, excluding Fishing and Herding Societies

Familial Complexity	Subsistence Economy					
	Hunting and Gathering	Incipient Agriculture	Extensive Agriculture or Horticulture	Intensive Agriculture on Permanent Fields	Intensive Agriculture with Irrigation
High	53.9%	65.1%	79.5%	80.4%	65.2%
Low	46.1%	34.9%	20.5%	19.6%	34.8%
No. of cases* (N = 933)†	(180)	(86)	(415)	(163)	(89)

*C = .23, C̄ = .33, P < .001; G = .23, P < .001.

Note: Percentages are based on the frequencies excluding the no-information category. The C and C̄ are defined only in the positive range, but the range of G is from −1 to +1, and thus a positive value of G reflects a situation wherein one variable increases as the other does; a negative value indicates that one decreases as the other increases. Two-tailed values of P are shown. As explained in the text, the unit of observation in Appendix Tables F-17 to F-25 is a society as reported in the Ethnographic Atlas (Murdock, 1967). For the reason stated in the text, fishing and herding societies have been excluded from Table 4-1 and Appendix Tables F-17 through F-25.

†Excluded are 22 societies about which there is no information on subsistence economy, 7 societies about which there is no information on familial complexity, 120 fishing societies, and 88 pastoral societies, or a total of 237 societies. The number used for analysis is 933 (237 + 933 = 1,170). Any total less than 933 in Appendix Tables F-17 to F-22 indicates that information was not available on all cases.

is given in Appendix Table F-19, we find another confirmation of the curvilinear hypothesis. The percentages for high familial complexity rise from 66 percent to 79 percent and fall back to 67 percent. But, although the percentages indicate curvilinearity, they also indicate that the association between familial complexity and stratification is somewhat weaker than its observed relationship with other aspects of societal complexity.

The final indicator of social organization is that of political complexity. The percentages with high familial complexity are 59 percent, 83 percent, 83 percent, and 74 percent (see Appendix Table F-20). Once again we have demonstrated curvilinearity in the relationship between a measure of societal complexity and familial complexity.

In the multivariate analysis, we are interested in specifying the relationship between societal complexity and familial complexity. Because our model sees technology as more frequently setting general limits for social organizational components of societal complexity than vice versa, we use as the control variable subsistence economy, which is one of the indicators of the technological dimension of societal complexity. We shall examine the cross-tabulations of familial complexity with each of the four social organizational components of societal complexity when technology, as measured by subsistence economy, is held constant (see Appendix Tables F-21 to F-24). When size of community is the predictor, the gammas are significantly positive for low levels of technology—hunting-gathering and horticulture—and become nonsignificant for higher levels. A similar pattern appears when political complexity is the index of social organization. The other two indexes show nonsignificant correlations at all levels of technology. Although the statements must be regarded as quite tentative, the following two inferences are suggested by these findings:

1. The data on size of community and political complexity suggest that, at low levels of technology, the large family system is fairly highly correlated with urbanization and political complexity, but that this correlation disappears at the higher levels of organization.

2. The data on permanence of settlement and stratification suggest that the social organizational and the technological indicators have a good deal in common and that, when we control for technology, the correlation of familial complexity with societal complexity tends to disappear.

Although this evidence is certainly not conclusive, it is again consistent with our curvilinear hypothesis and its prediction that we should be encountering a point of inflection in the relationship between societal and familial complexity.[14]

Discussion

We have seen in Table 4-1 and Appendix Tables F-17 through F-20 a partial demonstration of the curvilinear hypothesis. Among societies of low societal complexity, relatively few have large familial systems. The point of intermediate societal complexity, where large familial systems are most frequent, is characterized by "extensive agriculture" and "intensive agriculture without irrigation"

(Table 4-1), largest towns in the range 200 to 5,000 (Appendix Table F-17), hereditary aristocracy (Appendix Table F-19), and one or two levels of political hierarchy beyond the local community (Appendix Table F-20).[15]

Thus, Table 4-1, and Appendix Tables F-17, F-19, and F-20 show (1) that the relationship is nonmonotonic, (2) that curvilinearity can be demonstrated even though the range of societal complexity represented by the EA is truncated, and (3) the maximum (point of inflection) occurs near the end of high complexity. The gammas of Table 4-1 and Appendix Tables F-17 through F-20 show that the prevailing linear (monotonic) trend within this range is for a positive correlation, that is, for societies and families both to increase in complexity. This is, of course, consistent with the finding of Nimkoff and Middleton.

What about Pastoral and Fishing Societies?

It will be recalled that, following the analysis of Lenski, we decided to omit fishing and pastoral societies on the basis of his conclusion that they did not fit into the same ordinal scale of complexity along which we were classifying other societies. We remained intrigued as to where the omitted categories would fall and, for this reason, ran a distribution with those categories inserted at such points as would maintain the smooth curvilinear function. The result appears in Appendix Table F-25. Since the function is nonmonotonic, the data do not uniquely determine the locations of the fishing and herding societies. If we have reason, however, to believe that these locations must fall either to the right or the left of the point of inflection, then we are dealing with a monotonic segment of the curve, and a unique solution can emerge. Here we note that Lenski (1970: 124-126, and fig. 6/2) classifies both fishing and herding societies as less technologically developed—at least in the technology they use—than advanced agrarian societies. Thus, Lenski's analysis encourages us to believe fishing and herding societies fall to the left of the point of inflection and that the sequence should be that shown in Appendix Table F-25.

What about Societies of Greater Complexity?

Formal proof of the curvilinear hypothesis would require (1) a set of societies covering the known spectrum of societal complexity, and (2) a set of observations yielding comparable data on societal complexity and familial complexity for all societies in that set. The analysis reported to this point is generally satisfactory,[16] except that the more complex societies are not represented. The consequence has been that we have been able to show the curve rising from its low values at the left end of the distribution (i.e., at the end representing low societal complexity), and we have been able to show that the curve attains a maximum before reaching the right end of the truncated distribution. Since the point of inflection has appeared within the range of the EA data, our hypothesis predicts that, over the range of the more developed societies, there should be a decrease in familial complexity as societal complexity becomes greater. Is there any way to bring data to bear on our hypothesis with respect to the remaining section of the distribution?

There is one study of economic development that contains some data relevant to our interest. Adelman and Morris (1967) have studied the pattern of interaction between specific economic and noneconomic forces in the process of development. They formulated 41 social, political, and economic indexes, determined their values for each of 74 countries, and then intercorrelated and factor-analyzed these variables. One of their indexes is called "character of basic social organization." For this index, they divide countries into those in which the predominant forms of basic social organization are "the immediate family group," "the extended family or clan," and those in which "strong tribal allegiances are widespread" (p. 29). (They trichotomize each of these categories to reflect the "moreness" or "lessness" of the variable.) The first two of the categories in the set of three are similar to those used in the early part of the present chapter. Unfortunately for our purpose, the third category (strong tribal allegiances) seems to be a different dimension of analysis.

Adelman and Morris provide data on a sizable sample of countries. They state that their sample excluded developed countries but, even so, the resulting set of 74 countries represented a considerable addition to the distribution represented by the societies of the EA. If we use gross national product per capita as an index of the degree of development, their set of societies covered the range from $40 per year in 1961 (represented by several African countries—Chad, Malawi, Niger, etc.) to $814 per year (for Israel).[17]

In constructing his index of societal differentiation (to be discussed in the next section) Marsh (1967) assumed that any present-day social organization sufficiently developed to be called a "country" would be developed to the point that it would lie above the most complex of the 565 societies included in the WES. Except for a few questionable cases (e.g., contemporary Laos being scored as more differentiated than the Rome of Trajan), his assumption seems generally plausible. We are making a more modest assumption—that present-day nations are more societally complex than those societies of the EA that fall below our point of inflection. Because we assume the countries of the Adelman-Morris study lie above our point of inflection, we predict for them a negative correlation between societal complexity and familial complexity.

Because of the inappropriateness of "tribal allegiance" as a measure of familial complexity, we eliminated from our consideration all societies that were scored by Adelman and Morris as showing this form of basic social organization. After this exclusion, 43 countries remained (most of the eliminations occurring among the sub-Saharan African countries).

Aside from "basic social organization," which we interpreted as akin to our degree of familial complexity—that is, our dependent variable—Adelman and Morris used 40 social, political, and economic indexes. Presumably they anticipated that all of these would be related to the process of development. For the

43 countries that were scored by Adelman and Morris as having familial systems of low ("immediate family") or high ("extended family or clan") complexity, we ran correlations between degree of familial complexity and 25 of the 40 indexes that seemed to exhibit face validity as measures of societal complexity. Of these, 16 proved significant at the one-sided .05 level. All of these showed the direction of correlation that would be expected by our hypothesis—the more complex the society, the simpler the familial organization. This is consistent with the conclusion of Goode.

Appendix Table F–26 shows the bivariate distribution of the 43 countries as classified by Adelman and Morris into three levels of "socioeconomic development" and two levels of familial complexity. The resulting gamma of .88 reflects a nearly perfect correlation of the type predicted by our curvilinear hypothesis. A similar finding comes from Stolte-Heiskanen (1975), who makes a fourfold distribution of European countries on the basis of economic development and familism, the latter being measured by an index composed of rates of birth and marriage and proportions of children in the population, of women married, and of households that are large. The gamma of her table is .70.

Splicing the Continua of Societal Complexity: The Marsh Index

It will have been noted that the technological scale of societal complexity we have derived from the EA is quite different from the scale of socioeconomic development based upon the factor scores of Adelman and Morris (1967: 168). Their index of socioeconomic development is based on scores derived from the first factor in a factor analysis involving per capita gross national product and 12 measures of social change. This factor accounts for slightly over half of the intercountry variations in income per capita and, according to the authors, "represents a configuration of country attributes that is consistent with our intuitive understanding of the broad meaning of development." The data from the EA have supported the curvilinear hypothesis by showing a point of inflection that reflects the maximum proportion of large family systems among agrarian societies practicing a technology less complex than irrigated plow agriculture. The Adelman-Morris data support our hypothesis by exhibiting a monotonic trend in the negative direction.

Ideally, in order to provide a strong test of our curvilinear hypothesis, we would need a single societal complexity measure, which we could apply to a single set of data covering the entire range of societal complexity, from hunting and gathering to modern urban-industrial. No such measure and no set of such data are known to us. However, the effort of Marsh (1967: 329–374) to construct a spliced index of societal differentiation offers an approximation. He attempted to construct a single continuum of societal differentiation by splicing two sets of scores from (1) the 565 preindustrial societies of the WES and (2) 114 contemporary nations. The scores for the WES societies are summed from two variables: degree of political integration and of social stratification.

The resulting range of scores is from 0 to 7. For contemporary nations, Marsh spliced to the foregoing an index (with a range from 8.6 to 109.4) consisting of percentage of males in nonagricultural occupations and gross energy consumption per capita (in megawatt hours).

Unfortunately, for those wishing to update Marsh's index by scoring the 1,170 EA societies rather than the 565 WES societies, one of his two ethnographic variables, political integration, was virtually dropped in the EA. Only the first 400 of its 1,170 societies were coded on this variable.

Despite the small size of the sample resulting from applying Marsh's WES-derived index to the EA, and despite the nonhomogeneous dimensions of the two halves of the spliced scale, we have proceeded to apply Marsh's index to those societies of the EA for which the relevant data are available. Furthermore, Marsh provides scale values for 42 out of the 43 Adelman-Morris countries we have used in our secondary analysis. Therefore, we are able to construct a single table involving our simplest hunting and gathering societies up through Israel and Japan.[18] The results appear in Table 4-2. Naturally, we hope ultimately to come up with a better solution.

Conclusion

Our findings agree with those of Nimkoff and Middleton in that the linear or monotonic trend over the simpler societies of the Ethnographic Atlas is for the more complex to have the larger familial systems. Our data also agree with Goode in that there is a tendency for the more developed countries to have smaller familial systems. Our data reconcile the two findings by showing that there is a point of inflection, with the maximum proportion of large familial systems occurring among societies with extensive or intensive agriculture without irrigation, in societies whose largest towns are in the range 200-5,000, that have a system of hereditary aristocracy, and one or two levels of political hierarchy beyond the local community.

Accordingly, we believe that we have been able to provide an evidential basis for the curvilinear hypothesis that has been stated more or less as an accepted fact by writers from Lowie to Marsh. In subsequent chapters, we consider variables that account for the rise and fall of the extended family as societies change their levels of complexity.

Notes

1. Attempts to operationalize a continuum of societal complexity can be traced back to Hobhouse, Wheeler and Ginsberg in 1915 and the more recent efforts of Naroll and of Freeman and Winch in 1956 and 1957 respectively. Naroll constructed his "social development index" from data on 30 preliterate societies, and Freeman and Winch used a sample of 48 societies to establish a scale of societal complexity up to the emergence of written language.

TABLE 4-2. Percentage of Categories of Societal Complexity Having Large and Small Family Systems, Applying Marsh's Index-of-Differentiation Score to Data from Ethnographic Atlas (Marsh Values, 0–7) and Adelman and Morris (Marsh Values, 8.0–49.9)[a]

| Familial Complexity | Marsh Index-of-Differentiation Score | | | | | | | | | | |
| | EA Societies | | | | | | | | A–M Countries | | |
	0	1	2	3	4	5	6	7	8.0–19.9	20.0–29.9	30.0–49.9
High	45%	69%	71%	85%	78%	90%	88%	72%	62%	32%	10%
Low	55%	31%	29%	15%	22%	10%	12%	28%	38%	68%	90%
No. of societies or countries†	20	87	69	26	32	20	17	25	13	19	10

[a]Only 296 of the 1,170 EA societies have information on all variables necessary to be included in this table. Forty-two of the 43 countries used in our secondary analysis of the Adelman-Morris data were given scores by Marsh. None of these 42 countries scored above 49.9, although the maximum for all countries (achieved by the United States) was 109.4.

†C = .34, $\bar{C}$ = .48, P < .001; G = −.05; N.S.

In their sample drawn from the Crosscultural Survey and the Human Relations Area Files, Freeman and Winch (1957) found that emergence of the occupations of priest and teacher seems generally to occur after the development of a money economy and a recognizable government but before the emergence of bureaucrats or of a written language. There is no need to conclude that a social system will always change in the direction of greater complexity. When the process becomes clearly understood, it seems likely that the explanation will assert that one necessary condition for societal differentiation to occur is an increase in resources. For example, a surplus must be available to support a priest or a teacher. On the other hand, when resources become scarce, as in a disaster, the complexity of the social system affected can be expected to diminish.

Subsequently Freeman improved on the technique of Freeman and Winch, and Tatje and Naroll then reported that their procedure and Freeman's ranked societies very similarly with respect to complexity; the Spearman correlation was +.87. See Freeman (1957); Tatje and Naroll (1970).

2. Nimkoff and Middleton define families as independent if they "do not normally include more than one nuclear or polygamous family . . . and . . . if the head of a family of procreation is neither subject to the authority of any of his relatives nor economically dependent upon them" (p. 125). Although the terms are not identical, it appears that for the discussion of their study, we may regard the independent family of Nimkoff and Middleton to be equivalent to our nuclear family (whether isolated or not) and to Goode's conjugal family, as well as to Litwak's modified extended family (1960).

3. The reader is reminded that although we have spoken of societal complexity as our independent variable and familial complexity as our dependent variable, we have disavowed any claim for an invariant or unidirectional relationship between the two. As Goode has shown, the family is not merely a passive entity acted upon by the forces of industrialization; feedbacks are numerous and complex.

4. Murdock's criteria for including societies in his sample were: for each of his 60 cultural subareas, the largest society; the ethnographically best described societies; the societies constituting examples of each basic type of economy (noted above—the most complex is plow agriculture), and of each major rule of descent (matrilineal, patrilineal, double, or bilateral) represented in the area; the societies representing each linguistic stock or major subfamily found in the area; and other area societies representing distinctive cultures (p. 667). It is evident that such selective criteria grossly underrepresent modern nations, and this is indeed what occurs in the WES.

5. Note also that Marsh (1967: 72) reformulates the concept found curvilinearly related to societal complexity as "kinship solidarity," which he says is characterized by "(1) the number of people encompassed in a person's web of kin obligations and rights, (2) the extent of interdependence among nuclear families related by blood or marriage, and (3) the extent to which kin ties and obligations take precedence over nonkinship roles and relationships."

6. Goode (1963: 4) states that "no specific family forms seem to be correlated with the specific 'states' of the economic and technological evolution." In support of this conclusion, Goode cites Freeman and Winch (1957), who found

that two familistic indexes did not fit into a scale of societal complexity. On this point, it should be noted that Freeman and Winch used the monotonic Guttman scale as a model, and thus a curvilinear (nonmonotonic function) would have been interpreted as a scaling error. Moreover, it should be noted that the features of familial organization examined by Freeman and Winch were exogamy and mate selection and that they did not study familial complexity. Accordingly, none of the evidence in the Freeman-Winch paper refutes the nonmonotontic hypothesis of the present chapter.

Another study that showed a nonconsistent relationship between societal complexity and familial organization—apparently because of a linear constraint used in the quantitative analysis—is Lomax and Berkowitz (1972: 228, 236).

7. We are aware that the EA has been criticized by a number of anthropologists (e.g., see Naroll, 1970b) on a variety of grounds, including the codes, bias in sampling, and the presence of diffusion within some subsets of societies, with the result that the number of independent cases is alleged to be less than the total number of societies. As sociologists, however, we note that diffusion among contemporary industrial and industrializing nations has reached worldwide proportions, and yet cross-national analyses continue to be done. At this point, we accept the assessment of Lenski (1970: 137) that "Murdock's Ethnographic Atlas is the single richest source of systematically coded data on preindustrial societies."

Murdock has responded to these criticisms with more selective and smaller samples, the latest of which (Murdock and White, 1969) is down to 186 societies. Although difficulties arise with such small samples when one undertakes multivariate analyses, we are planning further studies with carefully selected small samples of societies.

8. We were able to find in the Ethnographic Atlas reasonably good approximations to four of the five variables Goldschmidt listed as "consequences of technological advance." If we use the list merely to identify other important aspects of societal complexity (i.e., reject his causal view of them as consequences), we find ourselves in the happy situation of having a list of societal complexity dimensions, most of which can be directly operationalized with existing variables of the EA. The set of consequences Goldschmidt proposed and for which we found equivalents in the EA are: size of group, indexed as mean size of local community; permanence of settlement, one of the variables of the EA; division of labor and organizational complexity, for which our equivalent from the EA is political complexity, ranging from no political integration beyond the local community to four such levels; and production of goods and services and concomitant degree of political and economic inequality, for which we propose the EA variables of degree of social stratification, ranging from absence to social classes. The fifth consequence of Goldschmidt is leisure, which we deemed irrelevant to our purposes.

9. Another constraint imposed by our wish to use the EA as data is the necessity to use the household rather than the familial system as the unit of observation. Although familial systems frequently coincide with households, it is our view that household is an ecological rather than a social systemic term, and certainly examples can be found of familial systems that do not coincide with households. The gravity of this difficulty appears mitigated, however, by the

fact that what we are treating as small familial systems are characterized by Murdock as "independent." See note 10 below.

10. Murdock (1949: 32) distinguishes between dependent and independent families on the basis that the former is absorbed into a larger familial aggregate whereas the latter stands alone. See note 2 above for the way Nimkoff and Middleton define independent families.

11. Here we follow Murdock (1949: 28), who says he set the dividing line between monogamous and polygynous societies arbitrarily at that point where societies with less than 20 percent of its marriages polygynous, no matter how favored plural marriages might be, were "considered monogamous with respect to the family though polygynous with respect to marriage."

12. It is possible, of course, to test for the significance of differences between the adjacent proportions in Table 4-1 and to check for a reversal in the signs of these differences. At the two-sided .05 level of significance, two of the four differences between adjacent proportions are significant: those between columns 2 and 3 and columns 4 and 5. Since these two differences are opposite in sign, these results support the curvilinear hypothesis.

13. Gamma (herein denoted as G) is an appropriate statistic to measure the monotonic association between ordinally scaled variables. Where the relationship is nonmonotonic or where one or both variables are nominally scaled, the coefficient of contingency is an appropriate measure of association. Unfortunately, the two statistics do not have a common metric such that, say, a value of .5 on one can be assessed as .1 better than a value of .4 on the other. Indeed, the coefficient of contingency has the defect that its maximum varies with the number of rows and columns in the table of contingency. For a 2×2 table, the upper limit is not 1.0 but .707; for a 5×5 table the upper limit is .894.) It is possible, however, to norm the coefficient of contingency (C) in the sense of rendering its maximum 1.0 by applying a correction. The corrected coefficient of contingency is denoted as $\overline{C}$. For each bivariate distribution, we shall report G, C, and $\overline{C}$, as well as the level of statistical significance for G and C.

14. It would be possible to summarize the effect of control variables by means of the partial gamma (Davis, 1967). However, this statistic is a kind of mean of the gammas within the categories of the control variable weighted by the number of cases in each category. Such a statistic would mask any trend across levels of the control variable, such as has been noted above when size of community and political complexity are the predictors.

15. We omit reference to Appendix Table F-18 since it was not designed to show curvilinearity.

16. The phrase "generally satisfactory" implies something less than total satisfaction. This quantum of dissatisfaction derives from various limitations of the data of the EA for our purposes: the truncated sample, a nonunidimensional coding of some variables, and the fact that only the crudest form of measurement, the dichotomy, could be used with the dependent variable, level of familial complexity. Even in the face of these difficulties, however, the burden of the evidence seems impressively supportive of our hypothesis, and accordingly we find the results of the analysis to be generally satisfactory.

17. Adelman and Morris (1967: 11-14) state that their variables are of three

types: "(1) those for which classification could be based on published statistics; (2) those for which it was necessary to combine statistical and qualitative elements; and (3) those which were purely qualitative in nature." Most of the indicators entering into the factor scores of socioeconomic development appear to belong to the first of these categories, whereas the variable on which we have classified familial systems appears to belong to the third. With respect to the qualitative variables, they say that they examined published and unpublished studies, classified the countries, and then sought expert opinions on their classification, either by means of circulating their classifications to "about thirty country and regional experts" or by interviews with experts.

18. Marsh (1967: 339) notes that his data on "percentage of gainfully employed males in non-agricultural occupations . . . refers most often to 1950, next most often to individual years from 1951 to 1958," and for about one fifth of the nations, "the figures refer to the 1940's." His data on the consumption of energy are for 1952. The data of Adelman and Morris (1967: chap. 1) are largely on trends over the period 1950–1964. Their synchronic data are generally for 1960. There are 52 countries for which Adelman and Morris report scores on their factor of socioeconomic development and for which Marsh presents his scores of societal differentiation. The correlation between these sets of scores is .78.

Chapter 5

A Review of Some Relevant Literature: Materialism and Evolutionism; Sharing; Using Ethnographic Data

Robert F. Winch

In Chapter 2 we noted that a generation or two back sociologists saw the American family as nuclear. Indeed, throughout much of the Western world, where sociology was being written, "family" was seen as referring to a married couple and their minor offspring. Of course people had relatives, but relationships outside the nuclear family seemed to be of little importance. Hence it appeared reasonable to make little distinction between family and household and to ignore familial relationships transcending households.

Over the years our awareness of the existence of variety in forms of the family has come largely from anthropology. Such exotic ideas as unilineal descent groups and polyandrous marriages expanded the thoughtways of sociologists. In the present chapter I shall present some of the thinking of anthropologists as to the determinants of variation in familial organization. Furthermore, as we shall see, historians have begun to study the family and to produce evidence that offers promise of increasing our understanding. Accordingly, before undertaking to present our model of familial organization in Chapter 6, it seems useful to consult those who have preceded us in exploring this terrain.

In the following section I take up macrosociological propositions. That is, with the society as the unit of analysis, we shall be seeing what we can learn about the structure and functioning of the familial system from the mode of subsistence, say, or from the gender of the workers chiefly responsible for production. In doing so we shall be attending especially to the impact on the family of the way a people goes about the task of making a living, and to the way in which changes in this important set of tasks appear to affect the organization of the family.

In the next section of this chapter the perspective becomes microsociological. There I take up influence as an interpersonal process based on resources that flow from the functioning and structure of the familial system, as well as of other subsocietal systems. Although the comparative literature speaks more forcefully about the structure and the functions of the family than about its influence on the behavior of its individual members, we shall find that there is one aspect of familial influence on which we can bring some literature to bear.

The greatest source of data containing appreciable variation in familial systems is the literature of ethnography—the study of relatively simple societies. Characteristically, each ethnographer reports on "his/her tribe"; however, these monographs, while rich in description, contain little information that is readily comparable across societies and very little that is immediately quantifiable. In the final section of this chapter, therefore, I shall examine efforts to produce banks of ethnographic data that are amenable to quantitative analysis.

Some Macrosociological Literature on the Structure and Functioning of the Family

Most of the writers to whom I refer in this section, and indeed throughout this chapter, are (or were) anthropologists. We are indebted to anthropologists for several ideas. First is the notion that where societies are simply organized, that organization tends to be coterminous with kinship and only as societies become more complex do more specialized structures emerge. Second is the awareness anthropology has given us of a wide variety of familial types—not only with respect to size but, more important, also with respect to form and function. Third is a technology of investigation, one of the fruits of which we have already remarked in our own society in the case of the Leichter-Mitchell report on familism among New York Jews. In the light of these contributions, it is in order to examine the writings of anthropologists and to note their conclusions with respect to determinants of familial organization.

Empirically based efforts to generalize about the world's familial and kinship systems can be traced back for at least two centuries. In 1771 John Millar, a

Scottish professor of law, proposed a succession of evolutionary stages of economy from hunting and collecting through pastoral, agricultural, and commercial. In this he was not original (for the evolutionary orientation was a part of the Scottish thought of that time) but he sought to relate these stages to marital relations, the status of women, and the modes of tracing descent among tribal and historical peoples (including the natives of the Malabar Coast of India, who have attracted such ethnologic interest in recent decades). Although Millar's conclusions are not presently regarded as valid (Harris, 1968: 31-33), it is of interest to see as far back as the eighteenth century a study relating types of economy to familial variation.

Marsh (1967) begins his discussion of intersocietal studies of the family by citing Morgan (1871) and Tylor (1889). Fortes (1969) reinforces the point by speaking of Tylor as "the true founding ancestor of what has come to be called cultural anthropology" and of Morgan as the "founding father" of the study of kinship. This early stream of theorizing sprang from the so-called unilinear evolutionists,[1] who attempted to make use of Darwinian notions to develop schemes of the way societies develop. Morgan (1877) formulated stages of collective life—savagery, barbarism, civilization—that tended to reflect levels of subsistence technology and exchange—gathering, horticulture, production for market, respectively. The first two of the stages of collective life were subdivided into lower, middle, and upper periods. Roughly correlated with these stages, Morgan thought, was a variety of familial forms based on types of marriage—group marriage (between sets of brothers and of sisters, including classificatory siblings), polygyny (with a patriarchal familial system), and monogamy (with exclusive cohabitation). In the pairing marriage (his term was syndyasmian, referring to the pairing of one man and one woman, a relationship without exclusive cohabitation and thought to continue at the pleasure of the man and woman), which was thought to prevail during early barbarism, the couple was enmeshed in a unilineal descent system that was originally matrilineal and changed to patrilineal as surpluses developed and children began to inherit property from their parents.

Engels (1972 [1884]) embraced Morgan's analysis, and he restated it in the language of the conflict of social classes. According to Engels, as technology developed—use of metals for weapons and tools, domestication of animals for food and milk, weaving, plow agriculture—there was an increase in productivity. It became useful to bring in additional labor, and prisoners of war became slaves. Classes arose as there developed a distinction between rich and poor. With the stage of civilization several considerations seem to have been thought influential in bringing about the monogamous family, a phrase to which Engels usually added "as an economic unit," and which I should interpret as the nuclear family. First, property became owned individually rather than collectively by the descent group. Second, control over property became a masculine prerogative. Third, whereas the household duties of women in the large-family system had been public and honored, they became private and constituted domestic service. Fourth, with the advent of the small-family system there came testamentary freedom, and the individual husband-father then wanted to be sure that his heirs were indeed his own children. Under these circumstances sexual fidelity was enforced on women while men continued to enjoy sexual freedom through adultery and prostitution.

Although Engels accepted Morgan's analysis, the two men differed in their response to the evolutionary interpretation. Near the end of *Ancient Society,* Morgan asked rhetorically whether or not the nuclear (his term is monogamian) family is permanent. His answer to his own question was that the family must change as society does. The family, he said, was "the creature of the social system, and will reflect its culture." Then he continued: "It is at least supposable that it [the family] is capable of still further improvement until the equality of the sexes is attained" (1877: 499). Strongly advocating the equality of men and women, Engels said: "The overthrow of mother right [i.e., the shift from matrilineality to patrilineality] was the *world historical defeat of the female sex*" (1972: 120; emphasis in original). To him the "monogamous family as an economic system" was an abomination. He advocated creating conditions favorable to the equality of the sexes, and he saw the first steps in this direction to be bringing women into publicly productive labor and the development of collective responsibility for the rearing and training of children.

As applied to the family, then, evolutionary theory postulated an early stage of group marriage. Subsequent stages of development included unilineal descent systems—first matrilineal and then patrilineal—and finally the monogamous nuclear family, which was seen by some as the highest form (e.g., Westermarck, 1891). Social evolutionism of the latter nineteenth century came under attack by Boas and his followers of the historical tradition in anthropology, and by the early 1920s they had succeeded in discrediting social evolutionary theory.[2]

In the 1940s Steward brought a new impetus to evolutionary thought. He analyzed archeological evidence from Mesopotamia, Egypt, northern China, Peru, and Central America, and concluded that there had been a considerable degree of parallel development in those five regions. He distinguished the following five developmental stages: hunting and gathering; incipient agriculture; formative (meaning the introduction of grain and techniques of irrigation); regional florescence (the increase in population and number of villages, and the incorporation of villages into political systems); and cyclical conquests. Applying the rubric of cultural materialism to this type of formulation, Harris (1968: 680) remarks:

> The entire sequence is wholly intelligible as a product of endogenous forces; increasing productivity, increasing population density, multiplication of village sites, warfare, intervillage and later intervalley coordination of productive processes, increasing social stratification and bureaucratic control of production and distribution, centralization of power, feedback to greater productivity, and population density. . . . Given the combination Homo sapiens, a nutritive and hardy grain, semiarid valleys, ample sources of water, terrain adaptable to irrigation, it was highly probable that irrigation civilizations would evolve, not once, but again and again.

In 1936 Steward published a formulation relating familial organization to the mode of subsistence in hunting and gathering bands. Noting that in adverse environments the density of population was under one per five square miles and that the bands averaged 50 persons and seldom exceeded 100, Steward stated that the bands consisted of several nuclear families and that ownership of their land was invested in the group. Reasons for forming the bands, according to Steward, were economic—"subsistence insurance" provided by the larger group—and political—"security in warfare or feuds" (pp. 332-333). Because the important activities pertained to subsistence and defense, continued Steward, it was advantageous to organize such groups around a core of resident males with the result that the bands tended to be patrilineal and patrilocal.

Some of the sequences proposed by the Darwinians continued to intrigue scholars. Murdock (1937) investigated whether or not matriliny preceded patriliny, and he also undertook to test the relative merits of three schools of interpretation of cross-cultural data: the unilinear evolutionist, the historical, and the sociological functionalist. Murdock concluded (1) that although relatively advanced societies tended to have patrilineal descent, the matrilineal pattern was not universally prior to the patrilineal; and (2) that the patrilineal and matrilineal patterns were both functional adjustments to elaborations of the male and female realms of activity. It was his judgment that the functional interpretation was best supported by the data. In a later study Murdock (1949) found conditions that seemed to favor unilineal descent groups. Extended families and clans, he said, were dependent upon rules of residence and would disappear if the rules were changed.

Schneider (1961: 5-16) has written instructively about unilineal descent groups and the patrilineal and matrilineal varieties. He says that by his definition three conditions are constant features of such descent groups:

1. every child is the primary responsibility of one woman,
2. adult men have authority over women and children, and
3. descent groups are exogamous.

He then defines parents:

4. the mother of a child is the woman with prime responsibility for the care of the child during infancy and early childhood, and
5. the father is the person married to the child's mother during this early period in the child's life.

The basic difference between patrilineal and matrilineal descent groups, he says, is that in patrilineal groups authority and descent both run through the male line, whereas in matrilineal descent groups authority runs through the male line but descent runs through the female line. Another difference is that, whereas patrilineal descent groups require the familial position of wife-mother, matrilineal groups do not require the position of husband-father. In patrilineal descent groups, then, the content of the position of wife-mother varies much less than that of husband-father does in matrilineal groups. Finally, in the patrilineal descent group the in-marrying female may be thought of as little more than a receptacle for the penis and/or a medium for the development of the fetus, whereas in the matrilineal descent group the male contribution to conception may be ignored. Although the correlation between lineality and the prestigious gender suggests the theoretical possibility that the in-marrying male in a matrilineal society might be regarded as no more than a packet of seeds, Gough (1971) doubts that there is any society in which men have only the role of insemination.

Goody (1969) has found a correlation between region and inheritance among preindustrial societies. In Eurasian societies there is a tendency for parents to distribute their property to offspring of both genders, whereas in Africa the tendency is for a parent to transmit property to offspring of the same sex. Inheritance by offspring of both genders, moreover, tends to occur in larger, more stratified, politically more complex societies having intensive (plow) agriculture and practicing monogamous marriage.

In Chapter 4 we noted (1) that Lowie (1920) concluded that large familial systems developed when horticulture and/or herding succeeded hunting and/or gathering as the prime mode of subsistence, (2) that Forde (1947) saw both rudimentary technology (low societal complexity) and centralized political authority (high complexity) as unfavorable for large familial systems, and (3) that Fortes (1953) asserted the curvilinear relationship between societal and familial complexity. Our findings in Chapter 4 are consistent with these observations. Lowie also considered the conditions that would push a unilineal descent system in the direction of matriliny or of patriliny. He saw the nature of the work as a basic determinant. When the soil is tilled with a hoe, he said, it is usually women's work. If this is the principal form of subsistence, there is a tendency for the familial system to be matrilineal. Especially is this likely to be so if tools and land are handed down from mother to daughter. The animal-drawn plow tends to make cultivation of the land men's work, and when this is the basic form of subsistence, there is a tendency toward a patrilineal system.[3]

Some of the foregoing points are summarized in what Naroll (1970b: 1239) calls a "main sequence theory" of kinship that he says is familiar to all anthropologists. According to this theory, the predominance in subsistence-linked activities of one gender or the other leads to residence of the nuptial couple near the family of the spouse whose gender is dominant. Seemingly related is the observation that in developed societies, where sons follow in their fathers' occupations, solidarity is greater between the nuclear family and the husband's relatives, and where there is no such occupational succession, solidarity is greater with the wife's relatives. Sweetser (1966) provides evidence from Finland and Sweden, as does Koyama (1965) for Japan.

Sixteen years after his publication cited above, Fortes (1969) seems to retract the kind of theorizing in his earlier article and to deplore writers who interpret familial systems as greatly influenced by economic and other extrafamilial factors. He speaks of Worsley's reanalysis (1956) of Fortes' own Tallensi data toward this end as "naive determinism." Fortes' criticism of "Worsley's fallacies" is extended to Leach's study of a Ceylonese village (1961), wherein Leach interprets descent and affinity as expressions of property relations. A third writer whose line of interpretation is in this vein and hence to be condemned is Tambiah (1965), who has also reported on villages in the Dry Zone of Ceylon.

In my judgment, Fortes does not make clear exactly what his position is. By implication it would seem that Fortes would like to believe that family and kinship are things in themselves, autonomous, uninfluenced by the rest of the societies in which they appear. Such a bald statement does seem to Fortes, however, to be untenable, for after castigating those mentioned above and after maintaining that the structure of the kin system cannot be "deduced from a knowledge of the economy or of any strictly economic process, practice, or institution" (p. 229), he says that he does not deny "that technological changes such as a shift from a subsistence economy to a cash and market economy may influence the form and operation of kinship institutions." The form of statement that he finally seems to condemn is the claim of "an exclusive causal connection," which he says "has never as yet been established" (p. 230). But so far as I am aware, no serious writer has claimed categorical determinism of the kin system by the economy.

In Chapter 4 we saw that Nimkoff and Middleton (1960) used data from 549 primitive societies to trace the increase in extended familism over "independent" familism[4] as the societal subsistence base varied in technological complexity from hunting and gathering to settled plow agriculture. As we noted, Nimkoff and Middleton attributed the rise in extended familism to four variables associated with settled agriculture as the principal mode of subsistence: (1) geographic immobility, (2) reliability and stability of the food supply, (3) the family as the unit of labor, and (4) familial control of property (particularly land). They found hunting and gathering to be associated with the converse of these factors. Our findings in Chapter 4 were in harmony with those of Nimkoff and Middleton.

Using a similar set of data, Aberle (1961) found support for Ogburn's notion of cultural lag.[5] Aberle stated that although matrilocal residence was necessary for matrilineal descent to develop, matrilineal systems could continue after the rule of residence changed. On the other hand, conditions he believed to be unfavorable for the continuation of matrilineal systems included: occupational differentiation, with the small household being the primary work unit for each occupation; the development of wealth based on movable property (herds, slaves, money); the development of a money economy; and the development of a bureaucratic political structure.

After analyzing 15 matrilineal societies with subsistence based on cultivation, Gough (1961b: 577) reports that the factors appearing most related to strength of the descent group are as follows:

1. localization of the group on a relatively permanent site, especially with joint ownership of land;
2. scarcity of land and heritability of valuable immovable property (buildings, trees, etc.);
3. production based on division of labor within the group;
4. the group's leaders controlling distribution of the fruits of production; and
5. incorporation of the descent group into a centralized state with consequent imparting to the group's leaders of the sanction of the use of the state's organized force.

Disintegration of the descent group, she found (1961b: 596), occurred with the rise of a market system granting individuals access to jobs and the opportunity to acquire personal property. Barth (1973) agrees with point 1 above by remarking that the disintegration of descent groups follows on the breaking up of joint landed estates. Adelman and Dalton (1971) concur in 5 by noting that the nuclear system emerges when individuals are offered access to a job market. But Benedict (1968) argues that the family, especially as a patrilineage, can be highly functional as a family firm, and Hammel (1972) asserts that the earnings of sons have helped preserve the extended family in the Balkans.

A number of studies of the family in Europe and North America have concluded that the form of family life has varied with economic, legal, and political conditions. Grønseth (1970) says that from about 100 to 500 A.D. Norway had a joint family system, but that population pressure and the division of land resulted in a shift such that by the ninth century "joint families were mostly dissolved . . . [and] the *stem* family-patterns [were] taking over" (p. 228). The polity and the church then "undermined the old lineage system and its functions" (p. 232) and among the poorer classes the result was that a nuclear system prevailed by the middle of the fourteenth century.

In the Middle Ages familial systems of nobles tended to be extended, whereas the familial systems of commoners tended to be nuclear (Berkner, 1973). On the same point, Goody (1973: 13) notes that in traditional China and Japan and elsewhere the scarcity of land has affected the poor more than the rich and results in a "widespread tendency . . . for 'stem families' to be found among the poor, and 'extended families' among the rich."

Greven's (1970) account of Andover, Massachusetts, during the colonial period relates familial organization to the availability of land. A son's marriage generally depended on his father's consent and the father's ability to provide for the couple's subsistence, usually in the form of land. It appears that the first generation to settle in Andover was largely able to provide for the second. Because of a high birth rate and a growing scarcity of land, however, the second generation was unable to provide for the third in the manner the first had provided for the second. As a result, there was a marked increase in geographic mobility in the third generation, with nearly two fifths of the sons leaving Andover. Greven cites the following factors as fostering migration among the sons in the third generation: the inability of fathers of the second generation to provide land for all of their sons; the fact that sons could not expect to make a decent living by working as laborers; and the consequent dependence of the sons on either land or trades for livelihoods. Greven reports that by the end of the third decade of the eighteenth century Andover's third generation "had created an astonishing variety of family forms ranging from extreme extension to isolated nuclearity with households varying in composition as well" (p. 171). By the fourth generation the economic basis for paternal control existed only among the wealthy. Summarizing part of his account, Greven says that the first generation founds a town, settles down, acquires land, and raises children; the second generation remains on the land of its parents; but the third generation is forced by demographic and economic pressures "to move in appreciable numbers to search for land and opportunity" (p. 275).

In a study of 46 peasant communities, Goldschmidt and Kunkel (1971) found patterns of inheritance to be related to familial organization in the following way: (1) where inheritance was impartible and patrilineal, the family tended to be patrilocal and stem; (2) where inheritance was patrilineal but partible, the family was patrilocal and joint; and (3) where the inheritance was bilateral, the family tended to be nuclear.

Habakkuk (1955) is among the historians who believe that patterns of inheritance have an influence on the growth of population. After pointing out that the significance of partible versus impartible inheritance varies with the availability or scarcity of land, he concludes tentatively and with other considerations equal that in regions where the inheritance is distributed equally there tend to be fewer children than in single-heir regions. "The typical family in the single-heir region tended . . . to consist of the owner and his wife with a large number of children, surrounded by a penumbra of celibate uncles and aunts, younger brothers and sisters" (p. 6). For nineteenth-century France, Parish and Schwartz (1972) found that the stem family tended to reduce fertility.

A number of writers emphasize that the environment, the technology of subsistence, and the interaction between these two factors constitute the most important set of influences that shape a society and its component subsocietal structures.[6] Among the neo-evolutionary writers of recent decades, White (1949: 390) sees technology (energy and tools) as the "hero" in the evolution of cultures. Lenski and Lenski (1974: 110) deny that subsistence technology is the source of all change in societies, but they view it as very important:

1. Technological advance is the chief determinant of that constellation of global trends—in population, language, social structure, and ideology— which defines the basic outlines of human history.
2. Subsistence technology is the most powerful single variable influencing the social and cultural characteristics of societies, individually and collectively—not with respect to the determination of each and every characteristic, but rather with respect to the total set of characteristics.

Because of these considerations, they conclude, "the first step in analyzing any society must be to determine its basic mode of subsistence . . . the most crucial factor operating in societal evolution." At another point the Lenskis observe (1974: 105): "The level of structural development in a society is a function both of its level of technological development and of the abundance of resources in its environment." (See also Heise et al., 1976.) A somewhat similar view has been expressed by Duncan. Commenting on Goldschmidt's classification of evolutionary stages (1959), Duncan remarks that Goldschmidt's categories constitute a typology of "basic ecological forms." Then Duncan continues (1964: 51-52):

> Significantly, the ecological differentia are systems of exploitive technology rather than, say, types of environment. An ecological approach to social evolution does not, therefore, require the assumption of environmental determinism, but rather that of a reciprocal relationship between technology and environment.

Hueckel (1975: 927) adds that a corollary of the assertion that societies adopt technologies compatible with their resources is the proposition that when the level of resources changes through depletion, technology is adapted to meet the emerging situation.

Adams (1968-1969) interprets the literature as showing that in traditional societies migration results from scarcity of land, which in turn follows from the nature of the inheritance system, the condition of the land, and the level of the death rate. High migration, he asserts, results in a weakening of the traditional family. Goode (1963) has concluded that as the nations of the world undergo modernization, industrialization, and urbanization, there is a convergence of their previously diverse but relatively complex and extended familial systems onto a simpler one he has termed the conjugal family.[7]

In concluding this section on anthropological and historical studies, perhaps we should note that it is frequently difficult to tell from an ethnographic account whether the anthropologist is reporting the family as the people studied actually live it or as they understand it should be (Nutini, 1965; R. T. Smith, 1973:124). Levy believes that the large familial systems reported in the literature are descriptions of ideal kinship and that "actual families throughout world history have varied very much less than most of us have assumed" (1965: 60). This line of reasoning seems to have stimulated (or at least to have been followed by) a mode of inquiry we may designate as demographic history of the family. On the basis of records about households—in various countries and over a variety of periods—investigators have come generally, but not universally, to the conclusion that a pattern of large families is a myth. For example, Laslett (1972a: xi) writes: "It is simply untrue as far as we can yet tell, that there was ever a time or place when the complex family was the universal background to the ordinary lives of ordinary people." It must be emphasized that the phenomenon studied in these investigations is not a society's familial system but, rather, its domestic family—that is, the statistics about related persons who share dwelling units. When discussing their work precisely, these writers are candid about what they are studying;

their standard index is called "mean household size" (MHS). But their interpretations are frequently phrased to apply to familial systems. (See, e.g., the title of a paper by Burch, 1967.) Twinges of doubt appear to bother Laslett on this point for there is an occasional statement of justification. Thus he writes—without any supporting evidence:

> If relatives had in fact been so intimately bound up in the family circle in pre-industrial England, then they would surely be found more often to have actually lived within it, more often that is than we found them to have done in the lists of inhabitants we have surveyed (1972b: 71–72).

And again: "I believe that a convincing case can be made out in favour of the household as the fundamental unit in pre-industrial European society for social, economic, even educational and political purposes" (1972c: 156).

Writing in the same volume, Goody (1972) points to the difficulty of interpreting this kind of study. In many societies, he notes, the term "household" is ambiguous. For example, among the LoDagaa of northern Ghana, he says, the domestic group might average sixteen persons, and it might include three productive units and a larger number of consuming units (based on the mother-child dyad) (p. 107).

> While large compounds form a household in the residential sense, they break up into smaller units for the major socio-economic tasks of reproduction, production and consumption. . . . In many parts of Ghana it is a common sight to see a young girl taking an evening meal from the compound where her mother lives to her father's house; later that night the meal may be followed by the cook. Which is the household? (pp. 116–117)

I concur with Goody and with Fallers (1965: 81–82) that size of the household does not necessarily inform us about the functionality of the familial system or about the numbers and familial positions of those members of that system who are involved in important common undertakings (functions). I agree with Gough (1961a: 545) that it is less fruitful to compare units sharing a hearth or house than to concentrate on the group of kin whose members cooperate in some instrumental activity, especially productive and/or distributive. Hareven's (1974: 323) view that the "exclusive reliance" of students of nineteenth-century American family structures on census data leads to a confusion of the census "enumeration unit with the actual organization of family life" is congenial to me. In her study of a black ghetto in the midwestern United States, Stack (1974: 31) remarks that the household is not a meaningful unit because one may eat in one household, sleep in a second, contribute resources to a third, and feel that he/she belongs to all three. Shanas (1973) points out that in six countries for which the data are available (United States, Denmark, Britain, Yugoslavia, Poland, and Israel) the right of old people to live separately from their adult children is recognized, but they tend to live near their offspring, to see them frequently, and to rely on their aid when needed. This constitutes further evidence that household and family are not isomorphic.

It is my impression that running through much of the literature on size of households is a tacit assumption that everywhere and under all circumstances people prefer to live in small groups, especially the nuclear family group, rather than in larger ones, such as those including extended kin. Although I cannot be sure, I incline to the belief that this is a false and ethnocentric assumption. I believe it is ethnocentric because it seems to be based on the value of privacy, which appears to be a relatively recent value, probably confined to Western civilizations. It seems false on the evidence that traditional China appeared to value large extended households and to fulfill these preferences when resources permit; it was the poor whose households were small (Buck, 1937; Hsu, 1943).

It is my view that household is an ecological concept in the sense of dealing with spatial distribution. Our concerns are not basically ecological in this sense, but have to do with the structure and functions of the family as a social system. Since our subject is the family (or familial system), let us study the family rather than its dwelling unit(s). The relation between household and family is an empirical question and problematic. Accordingly, using the household as the defining criterion of the family appears unwarranted.

Is Influence Based on Altruism or Exchange?

What do we want to know about influence? Our basic questions are: How is it that some familial systems control a high proportion of the behavior (including thoughts, aspirations, and fantasies) of their members whereas others do not? What are the characteristics of more, as contrasted with less, influential familial systems? Which categories of members' behavior tend to be most amenable to familial control? What is the means by which familial systems influence their members?

For the most part the literature has not spoken cogently to these questions. In Chapter 3 we presented a study designed to shed some light on the first three of the questions. Concerning the means of influence the literature does contain some interesting dialogue, to which we turn at this point.

It appears that the simplest societies are those whose subsistence comes from hunting and/or gathering. For societies located in arctic or subarctic regions, subsistence is necessarily limited with respect to gathering and hence derives largely from fishing and hunting. Where the environment is less harsh, it frequently turns out that a bulk of the caloric intake comes from gathering, with the more interesting and succulent part of the diet from hunting. It would seem that this combination of obtaining subsistence lies at the base of a division of labor between men and women and of a sharing that constitutes the basis of the nuclear family. Washburn and Lancaster (1972: 301) have phrased the analysis as follows:

> When males hunt and females gather, the results are shared and given to the young, and the habitual sharing between a male, a female, and their offspring becomes the basis for the human family. According to this view, the human family is the result of the reciprocity of hunting, the addition of a male to the mother-plus-young social group of the monkeys and apes.

Exchange theory suffices to explain in the short run such behavior as that of the hunting man and the gathering woman. Our query, however, pushes beyond this consideration into the longer run, even lifetime, exchanges and attitudes of trust.

The influence of ego over a kinsman is legitimized through the institutionalization of ego's claim on that relative. The particular relatives on whom ego may make legitimate claims and the substance of such claims vary from one society and descent system to another. More generally, we may ask on what is such a claim based? Fortes (1969) distinguishes two kinds of familial relationship: prescriptive altruism and exchange. The first of these, he tells us, characterizes blood relationships; it involves sharing and trust. The second characterizes the affinal relationships, and is based on quid pro quo.

Is Fortes' distinction empirically useful? That is, do the data support the assertion? We do not know the answer and do not know where to turn for systematic data. Fortes cites instances that illustrate the distinction, but we have no way of knowing how general its applicability may be. It seems reasonable to assume, however, that it is generally more applicable in unilineal than in bi- or ambilineal societies. Among the middle classes of our own society a giving, sharing, trusting relationship is ideally the basis of mate selection. This subculture gives primacy to marital over lineal or collateral claims, and hence gives a false ring to the formulation of Fortes.

With a stranger one may proceed on a basis of quid pro quo. With someone close—whether related by marriage or by blood or even not related at all—we give, share, and trust. How do we come to such differences in response? Prior to the latter type of relationship, we develop a set of experiences that are gratifying and lead us to anticipate future gratification; they are not very frustrating or threatening and give us little reason to anticipate they will become so. Past gratification becomes the psychic precondition of trust. Those we trust, moreover, can teach us to trust others, usually such kin as siblings and cousins.

Bloch (1973) remarks that what makes possible the prescriptive altruism to which Fortes refers is that the exchange between kinsmen takes place over a long period since each party expects the relationship to endure over his or her lifetime. He suggests that we might operationalize the morality of kinship in Fortes' sense by observing the period over which individuals in relationships tolerate imbalance in exchange—the longer the tolerated imbalance, the more moral the relationship. He goes on to cite instances wherein such trust is institutionally created among unrelated people on the basis of their economic interdependence. Pitt-Rivers (1973: 101) adds that "reciprocity alternates down the chain of generations, assuring that the grandparental generation will be repaid in the persons of the grandchildren to whom they are linked by that principal that Radcliffe-Brown first made clear." The familiar notion that children represent a form of social security is of course widespread and constitutes reciprocity whereby the parents give while vigorous and receive when feeble.

Insight into such matters comes from Stack's (1974) study of a poor black community in the United States. She shows how intensity of need leads to the

effort to establish relationships of trust and to the willingness to test relationships for adequacy of reciprocity. But we should note that trust and reciprocity
do coexist in these relationships. Her study suggests, moreover, that what distinguishes Fortes' two kinds of relationship is degree of trust. Fortes implies
that trust is ascribed, but in the barren world of the urban poor described by
Stack, trust is tested each day and daily achieved. Perhaps it is worth noting,
furthermore, that what from Fortes' perspective is prescriptive altruism is seen
by Comhaire (1956) as family parasitism, and according to Marris (n.d.) leads
upwardly mobile individuals in Nigeria to migrate over such distances that they
hope to be beyond the reach of kinsmen. (See also Marris, 1962: 138–140;
1970: 400.) For another recent discussion of altruism see Wilson (1975), especially Chapters 5 and 27.

Development of Cross-Societal Research
Based on Ethnographic Data

Propositions of the type considered in the above section on macrosociological
literature require macrosociological data for their empirical testing. In Chapter 2
we saw that in the United States, official data do not really pertain to the family
system (but rather to the domestic family). Hence, as we noted, some of the
types of American family distinguished in that chapter could not be derived
from official data. This state of affairs seems to characterize generally available
data on the family in the nation-states. So far as nation-states are concerned,
therefore, there seem to be no relevant data on the familial system that we can
use for the empirical probing of our ideas. These thoughts lead us to consider
the data that anthropologists have been publishing about relatively simple societies. Although such data are usually published as verbal descriptions, there has
been an extensive effort to render such data amenable to quantitative analysis.
We turn now to consider the history of this effort.

Quantitative analysis of ethnographic materials was initiated by Tylor (1889).
Harris (1968) reports that around the beginning of the present century Steinmetz (1930) undertook a catalog of tribes and that he had several students who
carried out statistical studies on evolutionary issues (e.g., Nieboer, 1900). In
1915 Hobhouse, Wheeler, and Ginsberg published *The Material Culture and
Social Institutions of the Simpler Peoples: An Essay in Correlation* (see note 3
of this chapter).

In the United States the effort to use ethnographic data comparatively for
drawing sociological generalizations began at Yale University with Sumner
(1906; Sumner and Keller, 1927). In the 1930s two Yale scholars, Murdock and
his graduate student Simmons, began the effort to improve on the anecdotal
method of Sumner and Keller and to make use of quantitative analysis of the
available ethnographic data. Simmons (1937) developed a roughly ordinal set of
scales of 109 "maintenance activities, political and social organization, and religious beliefs and practices" suggested by Sumner and Keller. In his statistical
analysis Simmons reduced the information utilized by collapsing his four-category

scales to dichotomies. He concluded that his data showed a "a rather remarkable agreement" with the generalizations advanced by Sumner and Keller. Subsequently, Gouldner and Peterson (1962) used Simmons' coding of 109 traits on 71 societies for a study of ethos.

Meanwhile, Murdock and his associates were building up their collection of data on the simpler societies with which to test intersocietal propositions. By 1937 their Cross-Cultural Survey was a going concern at Yale, and Murdock had begun to publish conclusions based on his intersocietal data. Murdock relates that during summers he used to lay out his notes on the seats of a vacant classroom, and thereby he began converting Sumnerian propositions into the bivariate distribution of contingency tables. In 1938 Murdock and his associates published the first edition of the *Outline of Cultural Materials* (cf. Murdock et al., 1950), which is a set of categories devised for the purpose of organizing ethnographic information. During World War II the defense establishment of the United States saw the relevance of the Cross-Cultural Survey and facilitated its development with federal resources. Gradually the Cross-Cultural Survey was built up to a repository of information on "150 human societies, historical and contemporary as well as primitive" (Murdock, 1949: vii). The culmination of this phase of the work may be seen in the publication in 1949 of Murdock's *Social Structure*, which used data from 250 societies to test a multitude of relationships about the family, the community, descent systems, and the terminology of kinship.

Presently it was realized that the fact that the Cross-Cultural Survey was located in only one place deterred potential users from doing comparative studies. In 1949 a new organization came into being to make available at selected institutions copies of the files of the survey. This organization was called the Human Relations Area Files (HRAF).

In 1953 Whiting and Child used data from the HRAF to examine some hypotheses about the relations among social structure, child-rearing practices, and modal personality structure. Whiting continued publishing studies in this area (1959, 1960, 1961). At about this time also Barry et al. (1957, 1959) were studying intersocietal correlates of socialization.

By 1957 the HRAF gave birth to the World Ethnographic Sample (WES)— 565 largely nonliterate societies for which data were available on punchcards about familial, economic, and other categories of variables (Murdock, 1957; see also Sawyer and LeVine, 1966).

The WES provided a rich lode of data for those interested in the classic anthropological variables concerning the family. See, for example, the collection of studies in Ford (1967) as well as in Nimkoff and Middleton (1960). Among others who made use of the WES were Udy (1959) and Swanson (1960).

In 1960 Murdock moved from Yale to the University of Pittsburgh, and there he established the journal *Ethnology*. In the first issue of this journal (Editors, 1962) he announced the establishment of the Ethnographic Atlas (EA), which he saw as a further development of the WES. It would offer improvements in coding and in geographic classification; it would present corrected data on societies already listed as well as data on additional societies. He saw this as an enterprise that would continue through succeeding issues of *Ethnology*. In 1967 Murdock published in *Ethnology* a summary article from the EA based on 862 societies. Subsequently, the data he has offered the scholarly public through the pages of *Ethnology* have also become available on a computer tape and have been extended to about 1,200 societies.

It should not be assumed that universal applause greeted Murdock's effort to make the rich data of ethnography available for cross-societal comparisons and ultimately for quantitative analysis. One major criticism took the view that the data about any society are properly interpretable only within the culture of that society. Ultimately this idiographic view—that each society is unique and that no generalization across societies is permissible—is social scientific nihilism. The answer to this view would seem to lie in the kinds and utility of the generalizations that are drawn from the data.

A second major criticism concerns the nature of the universe of human societies and whether any such data bank as those represented by the Cross-Cultural Survey, the World Ethnographic Sample, and the Ethnographic Atlas constitute such a universe (on this as well as on the previous point see Köbben, 1952). If not, how may that universe be specified, and what kinds of samples do such data banks constitute? And, indeed, what kinds of units comprise such a data bank? (Tatje, 1970; Naroll, 1970a; Naroll, 1970b).

A third line of criticism is that whereas scholars are usually interested in bringing these data to bear on processual (including evolutionary) propositions, the data are synchronic and thus preclude any conclusions as to direction of causative relationships (Jorgensen, 1966; Harris, 1968).

A fourth line of criticism is directed less at the data themselves than at the uses to which they are put. Vermeulen and de Ruijter (1975) complain that research based on cross-cultural surveys tends to be inductivist and empiricist rather than involving the testing of hypotheses. I believe the studies tend to reflect the stage of theorizing in the discipline as much as they do the constraining nature of the data and offer a study by Swanson (1960) as well as our own work (Chaps. 4 and 7) as examples of cross-societal studies designed to probe hypotheses.

Finally, among statistically oriented comparativists themselves there has been concern over what has come to be known as Galton's problem: that is, to what degree are phenomena the consequence of diffusion or, per contra, the consequence of independent development? If, for example, there are fifty known cases of a particular culture trait and all cases can be shown to have been diffused from a single source, then for statistical purposes the case should be counted only once. There seem to be three schools of thought about this matter: it is a fatal flaw in this kind of analysis (Loftin, 1972; Erickson, 1972); it is serious but remediable through judicious sampling of societies (Naroll, 1964; Murdock and White, 1969); it is trivial and should be overlooked (Ember, 1971; Greenbaum, 1972). (See also Driver and following comments, 1966; Driver and Chaney, 1970.) It is our judgment that there is some sense in all three views. However, the hazards that confront scientific discovery are many. Although it behooves us to be aware of diffusion as a possible interpretation and hence, where possible, to control for such a source of "error," there is no more reason to abandon our efforts because of Galton's problem than because of a host of other threats to the interpretability of empirical relationships (Campbell and Stanley, 1963, Winch and Campbell, 1969).

In response to the second line of criticism, Murdock established at the University of Pittsburgh the Cross-Cultural Comparative Coding Center (the 5 C's Project), whose activity was to present an expanded set of data and codes on a carefully and rationally selected sample of societies—186 well-described cultures pinpointed to the smallest identifiable subgroup of each society at some specific time (Murdock and White, 1969).

Although the emphasis in this presentation has been on the work of Murdock, it should be noted that (especially during the 1960s) others were trying to deal with problems of coding and sampling ethnographic data in a form to make them usable in cross-societal analysis. (See, e.g., Human Relations Area Files, 1967; Naroll et al., 1970; Naroll and Sipes, 1973.) Without taking away any credit from others in the field, I believe Murdock has done a gargantuan job in fulfilling the empirical and methodological implications of a mentor he never met, W. G. Sumner.[8]

Summary and Conclusions

Our review has revealed a continuing emphasis ever since the eighteenth century on what Harris has called cultural materialism, that is, a principle of techno-environmental and techno-economic determinism, which

holds that similar technologies applied to similar environments tend to produce similar arrangements of labor in production and distribution, and that these in turn call forth similar kinds of social groupings, which justify and coordinate their activities by means of similar systems of values and beliefs (1968: 4).

An implied element in the literature has been what Sumner called the "strain of consistency" (1906: 5-6). This means that although the culture of a society may contain seemingly inconsistent cultural traits at some given time, there will be a tendency for the culture to change in such a fashion that the inconsistency will be removed. For example, if a society should shift its subsistence base from gathering (generally a feminine activity) to the herding of large animals (generally a masculine activity) and if at the beginning of the period it should have a matrilineal and matrilocal system, the shift to the economy based on the masculine activity of herding would presumably generate a disposition for the society to emphasize the solidarity of males and hence to shift to a patrilocal and patrilineal system.

Many of the writers cited have interpreted familial organization in the light of cultural materialism. Among their conclusions we find the following propositions. Advancing technology makes possible a surplus and creates a demand for additional labor; these conditions are favorable to the development of slavery, social classes and inheritance, and inheritance in turn creates an emphasis on paternity and a double standard of sexual morality (Morgan and Engels). The need for defense facilitated patrilineal and patrilocal systems (Steward). Favorable to unilineal (large) systems were localization of the group on a permanent site with collective ownership of land and a familial system that was a productive and distributive unit and exercised intragroup political authority (Gough). Occupational differentiation, the availability of jobs for individual compensation, and a money economy all facilitate bilateral (small) familial systems (Adelman and Dalton, 1971: 512). In the next chapter we shall begin our effort to weave these considerations into a theory.

The Janus-faced notion of function emphasizes that the output of social systems can include resources, which enable some people to influence others. We may interpret our data in Chapter 3 as indicating that when resources become available to a category of persons, such as upper-status husbands-fathers, those persons become more influential over other members of the family. Conversely, when a category of persons is unable to control resources, as in the case of lower-status husbands-fathers, they may have so little influence and derive so little gratification that they withdraw from their marital unions and their families of procreation.

At first blush, Fortes' notion of prescriptive altruism seems inconsistent with exchange theory. He seems to be saying that exchange theory applies in some relationships—between spouses—but not in others—between blood relatives. When we introduce the considerations of time and trust, however, we see that receiving and giving are phased into the life cycle—children and the aged receiving and able-bodied adults giving—and what is critical is trust—that the recipient will also give—because a lifetime is involved in the cycle of familial exchange. Viewed in this way, the culture prescribes that the mother behave altruistically toward her small child. Years later, when the child is an adult and the mother is feeble, the direction of the prescribed altruism is reversed. Thus, with time and trust, prescribed altruism becomes exchange.

The ideas I have noted in the literature are compatible with structural-functional sociology. For example, another phrasing of Gough's analysis is that the more of the economic function the familial system fulfills, the more important, stronger, and larger the familial system will be. Steward may be interpeted as saying that goes for the political function, too. To the degree that I have succeeded in integrating such observations with those relating changes in the familial system to changes in the mode of subsistence, I am justified in characterizing this mode of theorizing as structural-functional-materialist-evolutionary.

Notes

1. Linear evolution assumes some specified sequence of stages of development. It is to be distinguished from multilinear evolution and curvilinear evolution. Multilinear evolution "assumes that certain basic types of culture may develop in

similar ways under similar conditions but that few concrete aspects of culture will appear among all groups of mankind in a regular sequence" (Steward, 1963: 4). In curvilinear evolution it is assumed that some societal structures are simple at the simplest level of societal complexity, achieve their maximum development at an intermediate level of societal complexity, and then become simpler again as societies become even more complex. Rosenberg (n.d.) has written insightfully on curvilinear evolution. The reverberations of the arguments between anti- and pro-evolutionists may have waned but they have not disappeared. See, e.g., the anti-evolutionary thesis of Nisbet (1969) and the vigorous response of Lenski (1975; 1976). See also Bierstedt (1975) and Wilson's (1975) effort to develop "sociobiology"—"the systematic study of the biological basis of all behavior" (p. 4)—within the framework of neo-Darwinist evolutionary theory.

2. But according to Harris (1968: 553) both Malinowski and Radcliffe-Brown seemed to accept the main assumptions of social evolutionary theory even though neither contributed to it. And even among themselves the Boasians were convinced they were not really antievolutionists. Certainly it should not be concluded that the Boasians dealt a lethal blow to evolutionary theory. Campbell (1975) writes spiritedly in its defense and cites numerous publications on the topic over the past quarter century.

3. Hobhouse, Wheeler, and Ginsberg (1915) reported that hunting and gathering peoples tended to be matrilineal, pastoral peoples tended to be patrilineal, and that agricultural societies were about evenly divided between matrilineal and patrilineal systems. Evidence from our version of Murdock's Ethnographic Atlas (N = 1,170) indicates that the situation is more complex than the foregoing statements suggest. Hunting and gathering peoples tend *not* to be unilineal; those that *are* unilineal tend to be patrilineal. Pastoral peoples are inclined to be unilineal and patrilineal, but the proportion of patrilineal peoples is lowest in incipient agriculture (or horticulture) and highest in intensive agriculture without irrigation. See the following table:

Percentage Distribution of Societies in Ethnographic Atlas by Unilineal, Patrilineal, and Matrilineal Descent for Selected Categories of Subsistence Economy

Category of Subsistence Economy	All Forms of Descent				Unilineal Descent Only		
	Patri	Matri	Other	N	Patri	Matri	N
Gathering and hunting	19.6	5.6	74.9	179	77.8	22.2	45
Gathering	19.8	4.2	76.0	96	82.6	17.4	23
Hunting	19.3	7.2	73.5	83	72.7	27.2	22
Pastoral	82.6	8.1	9.3	86	91.0	9.0	78
Agricultural	58.0	16.7	25.3	754	77.6	22.4	563
Incipient	31.0	21.8	47.1	87	58.6	41.3	46
Extensive	59.7	21.3	19.1	414	73.7	26.3	335
Intensive	64.4	7.5	28.1	253	89.6	10.4	182
Without irrigation	68.9	3.0	28.0	164	95.8	4.2	118
With irrigation	56.2	15.7	28.1	89	78.1	21.9	64

4. See Chapter 4, n. 2 above for Nimkoff and Middleton's definition of an independent family. To Murdock, the nuclear family is dependent if "in the presence of general polygamy or of extended families, which subordinate it in a larger composite family" (1949: 32).

5. The term "cultural lag" was coined by Ogburn (1922: 200–313). According to his formulation, a change in what he called "material" culture (as, e.g., in technology of subsistence) is followed by changes in what he called "adaptive" culture (as, e.g., in religious belief or system of inheritance). The interval between the changes is what Ogburn referred to as cultural lag.

6. See Parsons (1966) for the view that "normative elements" are more important than "material interests" in producing social change.

7. As we have noted previously, by this term Goode means a nuclear family embedded in a network of kin.

8. Although it should be noted that, in acknowledging his intellectual indebtedness, Murdock devotes considerably more space to Keller, under whom he studied, than to Sumner, who died before Murdock arrived at Yale (1949: xi–xiii).

Chapter 6

First Steps Toward a Model of Familial Organization

Robert F. Winch
Rae Lesser Blumberg

In this chapter we build on the findings and insights available in the literature and in our own work for the purpose of creating our model of familial organization. Having considered some relevant literature in the last chapter, let us summarize briefly the findings of our own studies before proceeding with our model.

From the suburban study we learned that familism correlates with ethnicity, nonmigration, and entrepreneurial occupations. The statewide study corroborated our findings with respect to ethnicity and nonmigration; it also showed some correlation between ruralism and familism, and revealed some ways in which the associations between these three variables and familism were qualified by each other and by socioeconomic status. The study of male college students supported the prediction that familial influence would increase with the presence of additional suitable models (structural condition) and with the rewards of high status (functional condition) and that the absence of these conditions tended to create a vacuum in familial influence. From the analysis of preindustrial societies and the extension of the scale of societal complexity into nation-states, we have

Based in part on Winch and Blumberg (1972) and Blumberg and Winch (1973).

seen a curvilinear relation between societal and familial complexity with maximum familial complexity occurring in settled agriculture.

Our purpose is to specify as precisely and yet as generally as possible the conditions that favor one or another type of familial organization. We shall propose a set of predictors of familial systems and seek to weave those predictors into a model for the purpose of portraying sequences and feedbacks.

In the next chapter we shall probe this model with presently available data. Then, after considering related matters in intervening chapters, we shall undertake to revise the model and point out directions of needed research.

Familial System: The Explicandum

We have postulated three dimensions of the familial system: structure, function, and influence. In Chapter 1 it was noted that structure refers to differentiated positions in the family.

In our formulation the family is the subsocietal structure having the basic societal function of replacement (or reproduction). Because of its function of replacement, the family has the opportunity to carry out the related functions of position-conferring, parentifying, and socialization-education. The newborn must be given a place in the society; through being born into his/her particular family he/she acquires an ascribed position in the society. The significance of this function is especially apparent in highly stratified societies. Because of helplessness the human infant must be nurtured to survive and, as soon as he/she is mobile, must be controlled in order to be shielded from the hazards that the infant has not learned to recognize. We conceive of nurturance and control as the parental functions. Finally the newborn has much to learn before he/she can qualify as a full-fledged member of society; the family may carry a large part of the responsibility for socializing and educating the child.

As a primary group—intimate and face-to-face—the family is a structure within which one can obtain salve for emotional bruises and company for the sharing of triumphs. This function of emotional gratification is variously referred to in the literature as tension reduction, affection, love, emotional support, and expressiveness of roles. It would, of course, be subsumable under the heading of familial function to investigate the manner in which and degree to which the family fulfills this function of emotional gratification.

Other Subsocietal Structures: The Explicantia

Our materialist-evolutionary orientation leads us to anticipate that the engines of societal dynamics are fired more by subsistence technology, the environment, and their interaction than by forces in other sectors of societies. In Chapter 4 we discussed the study by Nimkoff and Middleton (1960) in which they reported that among preindustrial societies familial organization was related to four economic factors:

1. reliability and abundance of food supply
2. demand for family (rather than individual) labor in subsistence activities
3. geographic mobility involved in subsistence activities
4. family-controlled property, especially land

As we noted at that point, our own results provided parallels for the second, third, and fourth factors, and our review of the literature plus our own theorizing convinced us of the importance of the first.

It is useful to note, then, that we use a structural-functional orientation for the purpose of describing a society and for placing the familial system within that society, and also for comparing societies as well as familial systems across space and time. A well known example of such an analysis is Ogburn's (1929) representation of change in the American family as resulting from the loss of several functions. Useful as structural-functional analysis is in this respect, however, it does not inform us why the shift in functions took place.

To account for the changes in the family is to look for the determinants of familial organization and for that task we look to the environment, the technology of subsistence, and how those factors interact, and how they produce changes in the family, directly and through other aspects of societies. We conceive this part of our task to be best characterized as materialist-evolutionary. And our total approach—to paraphrase the Lenskis (1974)—is structural-functional-materialist-evolutionary.

The Concept of Subsistence Environment

We postulate that the familism-influencing factors named by Nimkoff and Middleton and paralleled in our work reflect the effect of what we term "subsistence environment" on the society or subsocietal category. We think of subsistence environment as encompassing technological, ecological, and economic variables and as being closely related to current evolutionary theories. Tentatively, we define subsistence environment as the subsistence technology and the arrangements for exploiting it in a given ecosystem. Although evolutionary theory tends to relate such concepts to relatively homogeneous preindustrial societies, we think of it as applicable also in more complex societies, where it may impinge on such subsocietal categories as social classes and ethnic groups. It appears, moreover, that the groups sharing a given subsistence environment may cross-cut the usual socioeconomic categories. For example, corporate executives in our suburban study may be grouped more meaningfully with military personnel, enlisted as well as commissioned, than with such of their neighbors as are involved in family businesses.

We conceptualize subsistence environment as consisting of four components that influence the society or subsocietal category largely through the Nimkoff-Middleton factors mentioned above. The four components are:

1. level of subsistence technology

2. environmental constraints and potentialities (including the pressure of population on resources)
3. nature of work and division of labor (both societally and familially, and including unit of labor and mode of compensation)
4. surplus, capital, and the fruits of production

It appears that these four elements comprising subsistence environment may vary in importance from one situation to another. Accordingly, the reliability and abundance of subsistence for any given group may be profoundly influenced by any one or combination of these components. Nevertheless, most recent evolutionary theorists, including Lenski (1966, 1970), would argue that, historically, technology seems most determinative. We tend to agree. From the long-term evolutionary perspective, however, environment would seem almost as important, particularly for societies at simple, preagricultural levels of subsistence technology. Thus, we agree with Duncan's (1964) phrasing of "a reciprocal relationship between technology and environment" (p. 52). Furthermore, we believe he brings an emphasis otherwise lacking in evolutionary theory in stressing the importance of demographic variables and treating them in the nexus of environment. Below, we shall treat population pressure on resources as an integral component of our concept of environmental constraints (or potentialities).

In general, once societies have become technologically advanced enough to have widespread division of labor and differential concentration of capital, then the arrangements for exploiting the subsistence technology appear to increase in importance. This seems true for familism no less than for, say, social stratification. Thus, Wolf (1966) argues that for peasant societies, an emphasis on societal, as opposed to familial, division of labor is associated with nuclear familism.

The consequences of economic concentration seem to be of even more general importance. In particular, the relationship to means of production becomes central for those in a marginal position. To take an example, for the masses of shacktown dwellers of the fringes of most Third World cities, the most important determinant of the reliability and abundance of subsistence is the marginality and low level of their access to means and fruits of production. Owning no capital or land, they fail to find a steady market for the only production factor they do possess—their own labor. This is due to a techno-economic and demographic structure in which the number of stable jobs falls increasingly behind increases in available labor force.

The question now arises as to whether we view the four component dimensions of "subsistence environment" as the sole determinants of variations in family organization. The answer is no, for two main reasons. First, we shy away from any deterministic interpretation—feedback processes between subsistence environment variables, social organizational variables, and the family system are numerous and complex. However, from the standpoint of probability and frequency, we would have to say that we expect the subsistence environment factors to influence social organization and familism more often and more importantly than vice versa. Second, our review of the literature and hypothesizing leads us to incorporate into our theory concerning influences on familial organization, other social organizational and family-linked variables that intervene between subsistence environment dimensions and the family system of the group under study. Thus, the influence of subsistence environment is both direct and indirect, and to summarize what our theorizing and literature review have led us to postulate as the main influences on family organization, we have developed Figure 6-1.

Please note that Figure 6-1 does not contain what we conceive to be the less important feedback arrows. Note also that it is phrased in terms of societies as units of analysis. This latter point does not follow from any lack of interest on our part in explaining familial systems intrasocietally as well, but stems from the paucity of data for that type of analysis. Although we are not sure, we believe the model will also apply to categories within complex societies—for example, Jewish entrepreneurs and their families within the United States.

The Model

The Boxes of Figure 6-1 subsume the variables involved in the parallels between our and Nimkoff and Middleton's findings plus others culled from the literature, including that discussed in Chapter 5. Boxes 1 through 3 represent the components of subsistence environment.

Box 1A. Nature and Level of Subsistence Technology. The importance that the Lenskis among others attach to technology is supported by empirical studies (e.g., Berry, 1960; Schnore, 1961; Gouldner and Peterson, 1962; Sawyer, 1967; Sheils, 1969; Heise et al., 1976). The level of subsistence technology, moreover, tends to determine the extent to which and the manner in which the environment acts as potentiality or constraint and sets fairly close limits on the arrangement for exploiting the environment in a given ecosystem. For example, we should surmise that a gathering society organized around large work groups with a specialized and hierarchical division of labor would be unlikely to survive or even to exist. We consider this dimension as *primus inter pares* in our model when viewed in historical and evolutionary perspective. It seems to be the main determinant of the four factors found by Nimkoff and Middleton as influencing familial organization.

Box 1B. Environmental Constraints and Potentialities, Including Population Pressure on Resources. In general, we believe that where environmental abundance or uncertainty is above or below the norm at a given level of subsistence technology, then the familial system will follow suit. That is, we should expect to find it structurally "stretched" in the instance of abundance and "shrunk" in the instance of uncertainty, as compared with the modal pattern for the given level of subsistence technology.

Although most population theory treats increases in population as a dependent variable of technological and other environmental factors, evidence is now accumulating that population growth may occur independently of advances in subsistence technology. That is, such factors as in-migration and increased seden-

Figure 6-1 Tentative Model of Determinants of Familial Organization

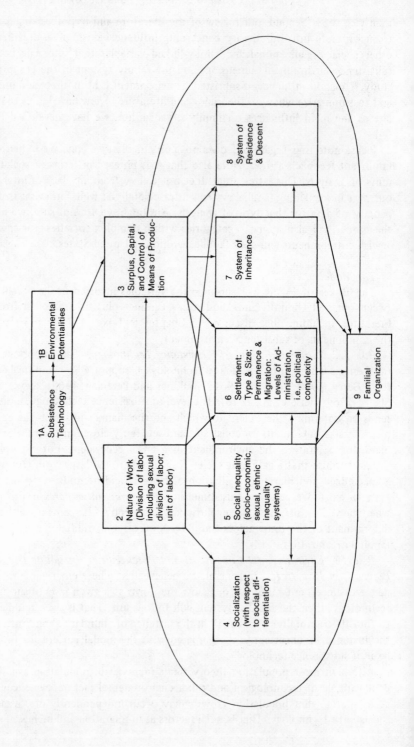

112

tarism, as well as abrupt changes in the ecosystem, can alter the balance between population and subsistence technology. Recent theories have emphasized the importance of demographic factors in the emergence of agriculture, which is regarded as one of the few important developments in the evolution of societal organization. Binford (1971), Flannery (1971), and Meyers (1971) all argue for population pressures as the "push" factor that made it adaptive for human groups to attempt to increase their food supply by turning to planting food rather than merely harvesting it (gathering). Boserup (1965) makes an analogous and better documented argument for the push factor behind the intensification of agriculture: the more mouths to feed per unit of land, the more intensively it is farmed.

It appears that population pressure translates its impact on familial organization in a variety of ways. One may view the Indian joint family as a method of avoiding distribution of the land under a system in which all sons inherit equally, but farming methods are not sufficiently intensive to avoid disaster if each son should attempt to operate his holding independently. Boserup believes that farming methods have not been intensified because colonial and present government policies of keeping food prices low, importing food, and levying taxes for land improvements have undermined the advantages of investing in agricultural intensification. Yet only the relatively better off Indian rural families have a sufficient existing resource base to support a joint family. For the remainder, the nuclear family is far more common.

Box 2. Nature of Work and Division of Labor.[1] Here we are interested in whether the subsistence activities performed by the group are done individually or cooperatively; whether the division of labor is predominantly in the family or in the society; whether compensation is in kind or in cash; and whether the unit of compensation is the individual or a larger, familial entity. Also we are interested in the sexual division of labor in subsistence activities.

As we have seen, some of the categories of subsistence technology of preindustrial peoples emphasize the work of women—gathering and horticulture (i.e., pre-plow agriculture)—whereas others emphasize the work of men—hunting, herding, and plow agriculture (Lowie, 1920; Murdock, 1949; D'Andrade, 1966; Murdock and Provost, 1973a). (See Table 6-1.) We have also noted observations to the effect that where there was an emphasis on the work of women, there would be a tendency toward matrilocal residence and matrilineal descent groups, but not necessarily toward high status of women. It should be recalled that even where matrilocality and matrilineality are the rule, authority is exercised by men. This point receives further treatment in Chapter 8.

Although subsistence technology and ecological considerations—including size of group—set limits, groups may still differ in their division of labor despite similar technological and environmental circumstances. Certain kinds of game may be hunted individually or cooperatively. In some Chinese communes it is reported that each brigade member receives his or her share directly whereas in others it goes to the male head of the household. These features appear to have implications for familial organization. Wolf (1966) sees the division of labor as

TABLE 6-1. Percentage Distribution of Societies by Gender Dominant in Basic Mode of Subsistence: Based on 1,170 Societies of the Ethnographic Atlas

Gender Dominant in Subsistence Activity	Gathering	Hunting	Fishing	Herding	Incipient and Extensive Agriculture	Intensive Agriculture with and without Irrigation
Percentages Based on All Societies in Subsistence Category						
Males	1	98	78	40	16	37
Females	76	0	1	0	34	11
Other (including equal, no information)	23	2	21	60	50	52
Percentages Based Only on Societies Wherein One Gender Is Dominant in Economic Activity						
Males	1	100	99	100	32	75
Females	99	0	1	0	68	25
No. of societies	96	84	120	88	505	277

central in accounting for extended versus nuclear familial patterns among peasant groups.[2] This is supported by both our and Nimkoff and Middleton's findings that demand for family labor is associated with more extended familism.

Box 3. Surplus and Social Relations of Production. Here we argue for the inclusion of what might be termed the "Marxian" component in the cultural core of recent evolutionary theory. Some economic anthropologists believe that the potentiality for surplus exists in virtually any economic system and that whether or not it is realized depends on other factors, such as a coercive governing elite. Be that as it may, we believe that the conversion of surplus into "advance" involves four contingencies: (1) the accumulation of surplus; (2) the conversion of surplus into durable capital; (3) the avoiding of concentration of capital in such fashion that production is restricted; and (4) the conversion of investment capital into growth. Historically, these have tended to form a sequence, although we agree that alternatives resulting in dead ends are possible. For example, the growth of population can prevent the accumulation of surplus; the distributive system (as in the case of the potlatch) can prevent the transformation of surplus to investment capital; ideology may override tendencies to concentrate capital (as in the kibbutz); and the economic behavior of those in control of capital can prevent its conversion into growth (as evidenced by the technostasis of most agrarian societies or by the nonproductive capital investment proclivities—vacant land, housing, consumption, Swiss banks—of economic elites in many Third World nations). Nevertheless, where concentration of capital and insufficient rates of growth combine to create groups with sporadic and/or inadequate access to subsistence opportunities, then the marginality of their relation to the means of production becomes the central determinant of their life chances and, we believe, a powerful influence on their familial organization.

Boxes 4 through 8 summarize the clusters of variables that our theory and our review of the literature have convinced us must be incorporated into a model of influences on familial organization. In general, we view them as consequences of subsistence environment, and hence as intervening variables. We do recognize the possibility, however, that each adds independent variance to the nature of the familial system.

Box 4. Socialization. We are interested in socialization with respect to two sets of variables affecting the organization of the family: attitudes and skills pertaining to subsistence activities and those pertaining to social inequality. Studies by Barry, Bacon, and Child (1957); Edgerton (1971); Pearlin and Kohn (1966); and Langman (1973) show relationships between mode of subsistence and socialization with respect to such attitudes as autonomy and independence versus obedience and conformity. It may be reasoned that the socialization for independence of children in hunting-gathering societies not only increases their probabilities of success in subsistence activities, but their proclivities for living in nuclear families in loosely organized bands. Similarly, socialization with respect to a society's inequality systems—socioeconomic, ethnic, sexual—will teach people, with greater or lesser success, to "know their place." These places in the social hierarchies tend to be associated with distinctive relationships both to subsistence environment factors and to familial organization.

Box 5. Social Inequality. There is considerable association between the components of a society's subsistence environment and its system of inequality (see Appendix E, Table E-1). Taking an evolutionary perspective, Lenski (1966: 437) posits a curvilinear relationship between the level of subsistence technology and that of the socioeconomic inequality system, stating that inequality achieves its maximum (and hence its point of inflection) among agrarian societies. Such a curve may also apply to the ethnic and sexual inequality systems, the other two dimensions of inequality that we have theorized are related to familism.

Nimkoff and Middleton have shown that even when level of subsistence technology is held constant, societies with more stratification are more likely to have extended family systems. In our opinion that conclusion must be qualified to take into account the work on intrasocietal variation in preindustrial societies by Sjoberg (1960), Goode (1963), Greenfield (1960), and Hsu (1943). Thus among highly stratified agrarian societies the elite tended to live in extended family systems and the culture tended to uphold them, but demography and poverty kept the households predominantly nuclear among the masses.

Our suburban study, reported in Chapter 2, illustrates that ethnic categories can vary with respect to characteristics of subsistence environment (the bureaucratic WASPs vs. the entepreneurial Jews) and that variation in such economic characteristics predicts familial organization. Thus to the extent that societies are internally heterogeneous ethnically and socioeconomically, we are sensitized to look for a plurality of types of family.

The same relationship seems also to be true with respect to inequality of sex roles. At the macrosocietal level, Barry, Bacon, and Child (1957) found correlations between type of economy (mode of subsistence) and the magnitude of sex-linked differences in socialization. They report that large sex differences in socialization are correlated with the growing of grain rather than root crops, nomadic rather than sedentary residence, keeping large or milking animals rather than small animals, and the hunting of large animals. This study does not indicate, however, in what way these differences in socialization relate to inequality of sex roles or have impact on the familial system. Another group of studies ignores socialization but explores how the subsistence contributions of the sexes are linked to their status and to their relative marital power (e.g., Blood and Wolfe, 1960; Rodman, 1972; Kaberry, 1953; Scanzoni, 1972). Also the structure of the family may be affected by the relation of each sex to subsistence: mother-headed households become possible when women have independent access to subsistence; polygamy is usually restricted to the wealthy; women's status tends to be low in societies where they have little part in subsistence activities.

Box 6. The Settlement. We consider several elements with respect to the nature of the settlement. First is the permanence or nonpermanence (nomadism) of the society. This is dependent on the mode of subsistence and—for preagricultural groups especially—on the lushness of the environment. As with

Nimkoff and Middleton, we are using the permanence of settlement as a macro-sociological indicator of the degree of geographic mobility required for subsistence. We realize, however, that whereas societies develop increasingly permanent settlements as they grow more complex, for individuals the relationship tends toward curvilinearity—individual mobility common among the preagricultural and postagrarian (i.e., industrial) societies.

Political complexity, as we have shown in Chapter 4, has a curvilinear relationship with familial complexity, only part of which was accounted for in multivariate analysis as due to the relationship between political complexity and level of subsistence technology. Thus, the political system can shape the organization of the family to its own ends (examples abound from Sparta to the kibbutzim). As we shall note in Chapters 8 and 9, the political system can affect the organization of the household (and probably also of the family) by establishing or eliminating a requirement that a family cannot qualify for welfare if there is an able-bodied resident male.

Box 7. Inheritance. This is the only box to come solely and directly from Box 3, surplus and social relations of production. It also leads directly to our dependent variable—familial organization, in Box 9. This is because the function of inheritance appears to be that it is the means whereby people who have accumulated some surplus try to assure its retention and concentration within a particular set of individuals. Some societies lack enough surplus or property to institutionalize means of passing these along to descendants. In some other societies the major resources, such as land, are communally owned, and although usufruct rights may be inheritable, the property itself is not. But where systems of inheritance do exist, they are overwhelmingly familial, that is, heirs tend to be consanguineally related. Thus, rules of inheritance may favor a man's sister's son, or the rules may specify the firstborn or last-born. As Appendix Table E-1 reveals, moreover, type of inheritance is highly associated with type of descent.

In the last chapter we noted studies relating familial organization to the availability of land, patterns of inheritance with special reference to inheriting land, systems of descent, and nuptial residence. See especially Greven (1970) and Goldschmidt and Kunkel (1971). It seems clear that inheritance has consequences for familial and household organization. For example, in the stem family, inheritance tends to be impartible, and the parents tend to live with the heir-designate rather than with any of their other children.

Box 8. Nuptial Residence and Descent. Nuptial residence refers to a society's rules or customs as to where a newly or recently married couple should live. Murdock and Aberle, as we saw in Chapter 5, have been interested in how rules of residence and of descent are intertwined. Exploring the degree of overlap between residence and descent should also be a useful way to illuminate familial organization. Patterns of change in residence during the life cycle (e.g., from wife's kin to husband's, or from extended kin to a separate household) may be ways of reconciling a pattern of descent that has become entrenched and a pattern of residence that is being challenged by new economic activities. Moreover, the rules of residence and descent suggest who the non-nuclear kin are likely to be in situations where the household includes extended kin. Finally, rules of residence that require periodic reconstitution of households may reflect a society's emphasis on life cycle and associated demographic and economic variables in organizing families.

Box 9. Familial Organization. We shall characterize the three fundamental dimensions we postulate for familial organization as follows:

1. Structure: the set of kin positions ego recognizes and with whose incumbents ego interacts.
2. Function: the giving and/or receiving of goods and/or services between kinsmen.
3. Influence: the degree to which and the categories of behavior with respect to which ego's behavior is controlled by kinsmen individually or collectively.

Some Concluding Remarks

One way of phrasing the type of question to which our functional orientation sensitizes us is that for each important function—production of food, for example—we ask: Is there some form of organization based on sets of kin? If so, we continue with the structural question: How are the co-actors in such sets related to each other? Finally, we may ask about the degree to which each co-actor's behavior is influenced by his/her participation in the functional kin group. And it is useful to know what are the rewards provided the co-actor by that group. We look to all of the extrafamilial variables in the other boxes as prospective determinants of what will be the structure and the functioning of a particular familial system under some particular combination of these other (materialist-evolutionary) variables.

It is customary to claim for a model that it exposes all assumptions and makes explicit all relationships among variables. The claim is justified where the model consists of a set of structural equations. The closer the model gets to the actual state of nature, however, the more dubious that claim seems. There are many hidden assumptions about every box in our model, and we cannot know when they are all exposed.

As the title indicates, this chapter represents our "first steps toward a model of familial organization." The arrows in our model represent the direction in which we believe the preponderance of influence flows; the absence of an arrow between any two boxes reflects our belief that there is no appreciable direct influence. The model summarizes a set of more or less educated hunches about a complex process stated in terms of a set of specified variables.

We have sought to relate the familial system to three of the other four postulated subsocietal systems. In the spirit of our predecessors, whose writing we have cited here and in Chapter 5, we have looked to the economy as the origin of causation: Boxes 1A, 1B, 2, and 3—subsistence technology, environment, work, and capital, respectively. Intermediate in the flow of causation have been education (Box 4) and the polity (Boxes 5 and 6, systems of inequality and settlement [including levels of administration], respectively). The remaining system—religion—has engaged our interest, and in due course we hope to integrate it more thoroughly into our thinking. It is our present opinion that probably the religious system has not tended to be a very frequent source of influence on the family, but that both the religious and the familial systems tend more frequently to receive influence from other systems—notably the economy and the polity— than to exert influence on those other systems.

Finally, it should be evident that we have been asserting a number of hypotheses, many of which have been reported as consistent with the data under more or less particular conditions—sometimes macrosociological, at others, microsociological. In their generality, these relationships are still largely problematic. They comprise a prospectus for our agenda of research.

Notes

1. Sociological theorists of social change tend to focus on social differentiation— the growth of a division of labor and the progressive differentiation of diverse institutions from a primordial, undifferentiated familial or community base— without ever considering the causes of that differentiation. This cause we link primarily to technological advance in interaction with environment, including population factors. Many of these theorists then go on to contrast ideal-typical traditional versus modern dichotomies with little consideration of the driving forces behind their view of social change. Such theorists include Durkheim, Redfield, and Marsh.

2. Wolf (1966) attributes the predominance of extended familism among peasant societies to the fact that conditions of production often made advantageous the permanent addition of other kin as laborers, and concomitantly encouraged division of labor within the family. However, his apparent attribution of nuclear familism among peasants to a stepped-up societal division of labor seems an oversimplification in terms of both his own discussion and our theory. All his examples share the emergence of a cash economy and wage labor in rural areas, which permit the individuation of land holdings. Moreover, one example—land fragmentation and nuclear families—shows the results of population pressure combined with partible inheritance patterns; another—nuclear families managing "farm factories"— shows the impact of technologically increasing intensity of cultivation. It would seem, then, that increased societal division of labor is insufficient in itself to lead to nuclear familism in peasant societies.

Chapter 7

Empirical Exploration of the Model

Robert F. Winch
Rae Lesser Blumberg

Having proposed a model to explain familial organization, we are confronted with the task of operationalizing it and asking the data to edit the model. We begin by considering the unit of observation. We have mentioned two. When talking about nonliterate peoples, our unit has been a society, with the implication that each such society is sufficiently homogeneous that the familial system of the ethnographer's account is an accurate enough representation for the society.[1] In complex societies like the United States we have indicated that several familial systems may coexist, each being more or less typical of some socioeconomic and/or ethnic category.

Early in this book we stated that our ideas implied a design of research that would span two or more societies and, *ceteris paribus,* the more societies, the more adequate will be the design. As we look about for data available for analysis, we are aware of none that would make possible a cross-societal study based on complex societies. On the other hand, the existence of a bank of relevant data on preindustrial societies—largely through the efforts of Murdock and his associates—makes it possible to explore these ideas with ethnographic data. We hasten to add that, as is usually the case in secondary analysis, the data will not

Based in part on Winch and Blumberg (1972) and Blumberg and Winch (1973).

prove entirely satisfactory for our purpose. Rather than await the arrival of the archangel with completely adequate data, however, it seems advisable to use the best data available, and for a first attempt at exploring our model we shall make use of Murdock's Ethnographic Atlas (EA), which was used in Chapter 4 in relation to our curvilinear hypothesis and was discussed further in Chapter 5.

Operationalizing the Model

From Chapters 4 and 5 the reader may recall that the Ethnographic Atlas makes available on a computer tape coded data for a considerable number of sociological variables with respect to a large number of mostly nonliterate societies. Our version of the tape lists 1,170 societies.

We have scrutinized the EA carefully in an effort to go as far as possible in using its codes as indicators of the variables in the boxes of Figure 6-1. Table 7-1 shows the results of this undertaking.

Most noteworthy and distressing from our point of view is the fact that of the four boxes we term "subsistence environment" (Boxes 1A, 1B, 2, and 3) we have an adequate measure of only one: subsistence technology. We shall use the categories: hunting, gathering, incipient agriculture, pastoral, fishing, extensive agriculture, intensive agriculture, and intensive agriculture with irrigation. The EA contains no usable code of environmental constraints or potentialities: from its data on climate, vegetation zones, and average community size it is impossible to assess accurately whether a given society lived in abundance or in privation. Nor are there indicators for surplus and the social relations of production. For the nature of work and division of labor we do find information on whether any of five modes of subsistence (gathering, hunting, fishing, animal husbandry, agriculture) or six economic activities (metal working, leather working, pottery, weaving, boat building, house construction) are organized as a craft or industrial specialty in a given society. As a gross summary of the presence versus absence of specialized occupations, our occupations index seems worth including in an operationalization of the model. Furthermore, the relative contribution of men versus women to economic activities is coded, and from this we have developed a trichotomy that we have called gender differentiation. What is in doubt is the value of either occupational complexity or gender differentiation as a measure of our core concepts. As noted above, then, we feel that we have an adequate measure of only one of the four core concepts: subsistence technology.

After Box 4 (socialization), which has no indicator, we are in better shape. Social inequality (Box 5) is represented by three indexes: caste, slavery, and social classes. Ethnicity is not coded for societies in the EA, and probably there is little ethnic variation within these relatively homogeneous societies.[2] The EA contains no code that measures sexual inequality.

The nature of the settlement (Box 6) is represented by three indicators: type, size, and political complexity. There are two indicators of the system of inheritance (Box 7)—one pertaining to land and buildings (real property) and the

TABLE 7-1. Categories of Analysis Proposed in Figure 6-1 and Relevant Indexes in Ethnographic Atlas

Box No. in Figure 6-1	Description	Index in Ethnographic Atlas
1A	Mode of subsistence (including technology)	Subsistence technology with following categories: hunting, gathering, herding, fishing, incipient agriculture, extensive agriculture, intensive agriculture, and intensive agriculture with irrigation.
1B	Environmental potentialities	None
2	Nature of work (including occupational differentiation and unit of labor)	For 11 economic activities (metal working, weaving, leather working, etc.) the EA indicates whether the occupational specialty exists. For each society we have constructed an index of *occupational complexity* by counting the number of "yeses." In addition, indexes of economic activities register gender specialization. From these measures of sexual division of labor we have constructed an index of *gender differentiation.*
3	Surplus and social relations of production	None
4	Socialization with respect to subsistence activities and social differentiation	None
5	Social inequality (socioeconomic, sexual, ethnic)	Three indexes register degree of stratification with respect to absence or presence and, if present, degree of development of (a) *caste,* (b) *slavery,* and (c) *social classes.* There is no index for sexual or ethnic *inequality.*

6	Settlement: type and size; permanence and migration; political complexity	One index (a) *type of settlement* reflects nomadism-sedentarism and also compactness of settlements. Another (b) *size of settlement* shows size and also presence of cities. A third (c) *political complexity* shows number of levels of jurisdictional hierarchy beyond the local community.
7	System of inheritance	One index (a) registers mode of *inheritance of real property*, and another (b) *inheritance of movable property*.
8	System of residence and descent	(a) *Index of residence of the nuptial couple.* Also we have combined indexes of patrilineal, matrilineal, and cognatic kin groups into (b) an index of *descent*.
9	Familial system (a) Structure	(a) The variables involving composition of dwelling units and type of marriage have been developed into a dichotomous index of *complexity of familial structure*. A society is classified as having low familial complexity if the household is typically based on the independent nuclear family, which includes a society having no more than 20 percent of its marriages polygynous.
	(b) Functionality	(b) None
	(c) Influence	(c) None

123

other to movable property. As might be expected with a bank of ethnographic data, nuptial residence and type of descent (Box 8) are coded.

It should be evident from the presentation to this point that we conceive of the familial system with its designated properties of structure, function, and influence to be the dependent variable of our analysis. However, data are available only with respect to structure. Data provided by the EA pertain to type of marriage (monogamous or polygamous) and composition of household (the particular combination of relatives said to live together). The mode of multivariate analysis we are contemplating requires the dependent variable to be scaled in either an interval or dichotomous fashion. Since Murdock's data are obviously not in the form of an interval scale, we elect to undertake this exploratory analysis with a dichotomy of familial structure (strictly speaking, of domestic families) into small and large. This is the same coding we used in Chapter 4, and it is also specified in Table 7-1. (Subsequently, we shall present and use an interval scale of familial structure.) Bivariate associations among these indicators are reported in Appendix E.

Scrutinizing the Model: AID Analysis and the Resulting Sample

At this point in our work the major purpose of our analysis is to get an estimate of how much of the variation in familial structure is explained—in a statistical sense—by the set of predictors we have selected and to see if there are any especially good or especially poor predictors. Also it may be of interest to note whether the results of a more systematically multivariate analysis than that performed in Chapter 4 confirm, refute, or elaborate the findings reported there. Finally, we shall be looking for any "deviant" societies that may increase our understanding of the problem.

Figure 6-1 might have led the reader to surmise that we should be planning a path analysis. Such is not the case—at least for the present. Path analysis requires interval scales, which we do not have, or their clumsy equivalent in dummy variables. (The 13 predictor variables we are using contain 71 categories.) Because of the nature of the data available we are treating the dependent variable as a dichotomy. Moreover, as suggested by our investigation of the curvilinear hypothesis (Chapter 4) and corroborated in Appendix E, some relationships among the variables are curvilinear (more correctly, nonmonotonic) whereas others are linear (monotonic).

A mode of multivariate analysis that does less violence to the variables and is suited to the linear-curvilinear problem just mentioned is the Automatic Interaction Detector (AID), a computer search program (Sonquist et al., 1973). We are using AID with a more definite purpose: to provide a first assessment of the strength of our model.

In its basic version, the AID procedure requires that every case have a value on every variable under analysis. If a case lacks an observation on any variable, that case is omitted. We began the analysis with a population of 1,170 societies (the entire set on our EA tape). Our problem involves one dependent and 13 independent variables. Data were missing on all variables. The missing data varied from 1 percent on familial structure and descent and 2 percent on residence and subsistence technology to 32 percent on the inheritance of real property and 54 percent on size of settlement. The cumulative result of the exclusions was that the number of societies dropped from 1,170 to 289, a reduction of 75 percent.

Any attrition raises the question as to the representativeness of the remainder. When the loss is as great as ours, the problem may become critical. Table 7-2 compares the regional distribution of our 289 societies with that of four other collections of societies presented by Murdock at different times. These are (1) the 1967 published version of the Ethnographic Atlas (862 societies); (2) the subsequent Ethnographic Atlas computer tape (our basic data source, with 1,170 societies); (3) the 412 clusters into which Murdock grouped the societies of the world (in 1967); and (4) his more recent (1968) set of 200 "world sampling provinces."

From Table 7-2 one can note that Murdock divides the world into six regions and that any over- or underrepresentation of our "289" in comparison with the regional distribution of another of the samples of the table tends to balance out when all the remaining samples of the table are taken into account.[3] While the reader is free to draw his or her own conclusion about the degree of our regional bias, we view our sample of 289 societies in a positive light. We required that every society have data on every one of 14 variables important for the analysis of the family. Thus the resulting sample *does* seem to be biased, but in the direction of the best reported societies in the ethnographic literature. On that basis we have the best data presently available.[4]

The AID is a program wherein the computer repeatedly dichotomizes a sample on the basis of the maximum squared correlation ratio (or ratio of the "between" sum of squares to the total sum of squares) between the dependent variable and combinations of categories of the predictor variables. In the process the original sample is fractionated into a set of mutually differentiated and internally somewhat homogeneous terminal groups, or subsamples. The process, including intermediate and terminal groups, can be portrayed visually as a "tree." (See Sonquist et al., 1973, and Appendixes D and E of this book.)

From the AID we can learn how much of the variance in the dependent variable the predictors can "explain" in a statistical sense, the combination of predictors that provides the "explanation," and some indication of which are the better predictors. Reasons for the qualifying adjective "some" are set forth in Appendix D, where the AID is discussed at some length.

Authors of the AID recommend a sample of two thousand or more and running the analysis on a random division of the original sample into two subsamples in order to establish the stability of the results. We have explained above how our sample size shrank to 289; we are simply using every case in the EA on which the relevant information is available. This state of affairs raises some question as to the stability of our results. To address this issue we shall show the outcome of an AID analysis based on two subsamples of our 289.

TABLE 7-2. Regional Percentage Distribution of the 289 Societies in the Present Analysis and of Murdock's Ethnographic Atlas (Two Sizes), His World Clusters, and His World Sampling Provinces

Region	Our Set of Societies (N = 289)	Ethnographic Atlas (N = 862)	Ethnographic Atlas (N = 1,170)	Clusters (N = 412)	World Sampling Provinces (N = 200)
Africa	27	28	35	21	16
Circum-Mediterranean	10	11	13	13	14
East Eurasia	16	11	9	16	19
Insular Pacific	11	15	12	17	16
North America	28	25	23	17	18
Central and South America	8	10	8	16	17
Total	100	100	100	100	100

Note: It is important to ascertain the nature of geographical distribution of societies in a sample because the six world regions represent varying modal levels of subsistence technology under indigenous conditions. Hence, different regionally distributed samples will show differences in the marginals for most variables related to level of societal development. However, we expect basic evolutionary generalizations to hold in any region: e.g., that gathering societies will tend to be small, politically acephalous, nonsedentary, occupationally unspecialized groups, whether in California or Ceylon.

For a reason to be explained later in this chapter, 7 societies were removed from the 289 and a second analysis was carried out on the remaining 282 societies. The effect of removing these 7 societies was to reduce Insular Pacific from 11 to 10 percent and to increase North America from 28 to 29 percent; the percentages of the other four regions were not changed.

Results

The outcome of the analysis by means of AID appears in Figure 7-1. Since we have scored the dependent variable 0 for small familial system and 1 for large, the means in the boxes of the figure register the proportion of large systems in each set or subset.

Table 7-3 responds to our quantitative question. Despite our having no indicators for four of our model's boxes, the indexes for the remaining boxes account for 40 percent of the variance. Nearly a half of the explained variance is based on Box 7, inheritance, and about a quarter is based on 1A, subsistence. The strong performance of the inheritance variables may be surprising to those who are acquainted with Murdock's view that "in actual application [these] codes . . . have proved inadequate" (1967: 167).

In Figure 7-1 the AID tree branches first on the variable of inheritance of movable property. Societies having either no inheritance or egalitarian inheritance (in which all children share equally) are split off from those having nonegalitarian systems of inheritance. (See Appendix Table D-10.) The nonegalitarian systems are overwhelmingly patrilineal. As we saw in note 3 of Chapter 5, patrilineal societies are uncommon at the lowest levels of societal complexity (gathering and hunting) and most prevalent among herding societies, where we find a tendency toward large familial systems.

Societies in which inheritance is absent tend to be of very low complexity (with the implication that there is little property to inherit), whereas those in which inheritance is equally apportioned among children of both sexes may be found either at the bottom or—more frequently—at the top of the range of societal complexity as that dimension is reflected in the EA. (Let us recall that contemporary developing and industrialized nations are not included in the EA.) Thus the first branching of the AID tree is consonant with the results of Chapter 4.

The curvilinear relationship is revealed in following the lower AID branch of absent or equal inheritance to its conclusion in Groups 32 and 33. The latter group represents the minimum in societal complexity. Not only do these societies lack inheritance, unilineal descent, and, with one exception, social stratification, but they consist almost exclusively of groups practicing the simplest mode of subsistence—19 out of the 22 societies in Group 33 are gatherers. Only 1 of the 22 has a familial system of high complexity. Group 32, on the other hand, seems predominantly composed of the most complex societies represented in the EA, with sons and daughters inheriting equally, bilineal descent, and—with the exception of four California gathering societies to be discussed below—predominantly based on a subsistence of advanced agriculture and having social classes. Only a third of the 13 societies in Group 32 have familial systems of high complexity as compared with 66 percent of the total sample of 289.

Turning to the upper branch of the AID tree, which emerges from nonegalitarian inheritance, we find two interesting end groups in which more than 90 percent of the societies have large familial systems. Both terminal groups are primarily on the agricultural level of subsistence (without irrigation). Below

TABLE 7-3. "Explained" Variance of Dichotomized Familial Structure by Concepts Shown in Figure 6–1 and Indicators from Table 7–1: Based on Sample of 289 Societies from Ethnographic Atlas Having Data on All Indicators

Box Concept and Indicator	Familial Structure		Explained Variance
	Large	Small	
1A Mode of subsistence			
Subsistence technology	Extensive agriculture; intensive agriculture without irrigation	Intensive agriculture with irrigation	.1003 (.1003)
2 Nature of work			
Number of occupations	No occupation reported craft or industrially organized	At least one occupation so organized	.0280 (.0280)
Gender differentiation			—
5 Social inequality			.0458
Caste		Absent	—
Slavery	Present		(.0331)
Social classes	Present	Absence of social stratification or complex social classes	(.0127)
6 Settlement			.0258
Type	Sedentary	Migratory	(.0103)
Size	Large	Small	(.0155)
Political complexity			—
7 Inheritance			.1675
Real property	Nonegalitarian	Egalitarian or no inheritance	(.0416)
Movable property			(.1259)
8 Residence and descent			.0345
Nuptial residence			—
Descent	Unilineal	Bilineal	(.0345)
Total			.4019

we shall discuss the apparent anomaly of gatherers coming out in both groups with highest and lowest proportions of large familial systems.

The branching process occurred most frequently as a result of the indicator of mode of subsistence, but this variable ranked second (behind inheritance) in percentage of variance explained. At this juncture, however, we cannot conclude that subsistence technology is really less important than inheritance in accounting for complexity of familial organization because, as Figure 6-1 shows, our model locates subsistence at an earlier stage than inheritance in the causal chain. We suspect that some of the explanatory power of inheritance comes from its acting as a surrogate for the surplus-and-social-relations-of-production box, for which we have no measure.

What about the interaction referred to in the name of the technique AID? With the construction of such auxiliary tables as those prepared for Appendix D it is possible to examine and to interpret interaction since the data can be laid out explicitly. For example, it can be seen by comparing Groups 3 and 4 of Appendix Table D-10 with Figure 7-1 that category 7 of subsistence economy appears in both the top and bottom branches. Category 7 is intensive agriculture. By checking earlier stages of the tree, one can see that intensive agriculture goes with large family systems ($\bar{Y} = .92$) when inheritance is unequal (tending toward impartibility) and with small families ($\bar{Y} = .33$) when inheritance is equal or there is no property to inherit.

The Anomaly of the Rich Gathering Societies

It will be recalled that as a result of the first branching process those societies on the upper branch in Figure 7-1 have unequal inheritance of movable property. Within the range of the EA these societies tend to be of intermediate technology, but there are eight societies that deviate by having a low level of subsistence—gathering. These are Shasta, Modoc, Atsugewi, and Eastern Pomo, all of north-central California; the Purari of the Bay of Papua; the Aranda of Australia's "red heart" desert; the Vedda of Ceylon; and the Chenchu of India.

In their analysis of deviant cases, Nimkoff and Middleton (1960) hypothesized that environmental abundance relative to a given mode of subsistence is likely to be involved in instances of large familism.

There is no doubt about the lushness of the ecological niche of the four California groups. Their subsistence is based primarily on gathering acorns from the many oak trees, plus salmon and other fishing and an approximately equal amount of hunting. All sources agree that the environment is one of general abundance although bad years are not unknown. All four of these north-central California groups have what Murdock terms the "small extended family" system as the predominant type, and all four have distinctions based on wealth. Two even use war captives as slaves.

The Vedda of Ceylon also mix fishing and hunting with their gathering, which is the dominant form of their subsistence. In contrast to California, however, honey rather than acorns forms up to half the diet. The prevailing type of

Figure 7-1 Proportion of Societies with Large Familial Systems in Subsets Generated by AID from a Set of 289 Societies in the Ethnographic Atlas

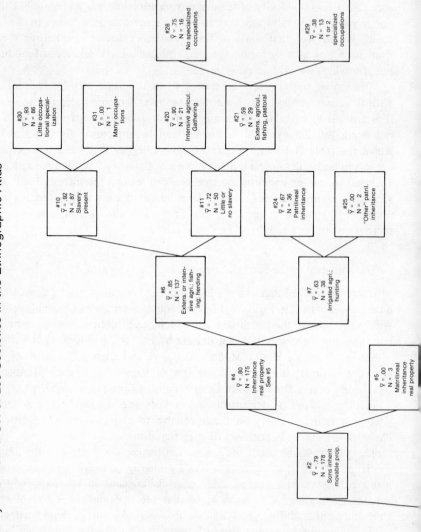

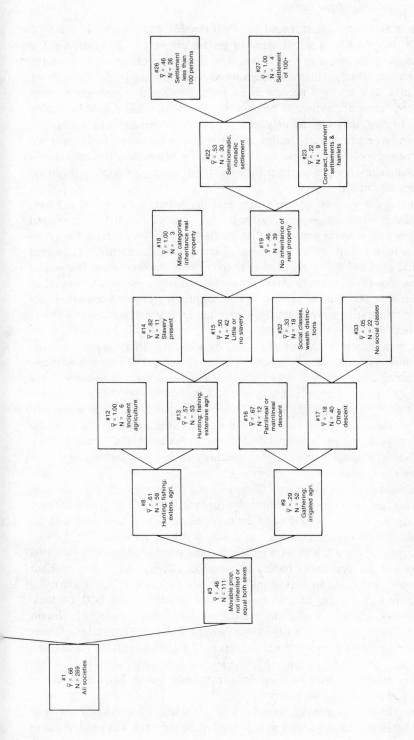

$\bar{Y} = .66$
N = 289
All societies

$\bar{Y} = .46$
N = 111
Movable prop. not inherited or equal both sexes
#3

$\bar{Y} = .61$
N = 59
Hunting, fishing, extens. agri.
#8

$\bar{Y} = .29$
N = 52
Gathering, irrigated agri.
#9

$\bar{Y} = 1.00$
N = 6
Incipient agriculture
#12

$\bar{Y} = .57$
N = 53
Hunting, fishing, extensive agri.
#13

$\bar{Y} = .67$
N = 12
Patrilineal or matrilineal descent
#16

$\bar{Y} = .18$
N = 40
Other descent
#17

$\bar{Y} = .82$
N = 11
Slavery present
#14

$\bar{Y} = .50$
N = 42
Little or no slavery
#15

$\bar{Y} = .33$
N = 18
Social classes, wealth distinctions
#32

$\bar{Y} = .05$
N = 22
No social classes
#33

$\bar{Y} = 1.00$
N = 3
Misc. categories inheritance real property
#18

$\bar{Y} = .46$
N = 39
No inheritance of real property
#19

$\bar{Y} = .53$
N = 30
Seminomadic, nomadic settlement
#22

$\bar{Y} = .22$
N = 9
Compact, permanent settlements & hamlets
#23

$\bar{Y} = .46$
N = 26
Settlement less than 100 persons
#26

$\bar{Y} = 1.00$
N = 4
Settlement of 100+
#27

family is also the small extended family (extended matrilineally, in fact). Although they do have a strong sense of private property of all kinds, which is rare among gatherers, they do not have crystallized distinctions based on wealth.

The other society with distinctions based on wealth, the Purari, probably belongs in a class by itself because of its fairly substantial dependence on more advanced forms of subsistence technology—horticulture and animal husbandry (pigs). In fact, they are the only group of the eight predominantly gathering societies to be permanently settled, and they live in the largest settlements and have the most complex political system. Their familial system is classified as of high complexity because of the prevalence of polygyny, not because they have an extended familial system.

General polygyny is also the reason that the Aranda are classified as having a familial system of high complexity. In their case we find that the "unequal inheritance of movable property" that resulted in their being regarded as a deviant case turns out to involve not capital goods but a religious artifact. The sacred Churinga is passed down from father to son. There is no statement that among the desert-dwelling, nomadic Aranda inheritance involves property that could be considered as the fruits of surplus. In fact, surplus is probably a rare experience for this frequently environmentally pressed group. Distinctions based on wealth are absent.

The final society in this set of eight is the Chenchu. Their economy is overwhelmingly gathering—Murdock classifies it as 80 percent of their subsistence—with sporadic hunting and some milking of bovines. It has been observed that the Chenchu are remarkable in their ability to endure hunger. This carries some intimation as to where on the scale of lushness-privation their habitat would fall. The Chenchu are the only society of the eight to have a familial system of low complexity; they live in independent monogamous units. Only patrilineal inheritance of movable property (predominantly their cows) causes them to be in this set of deviant cases.

The eight gathering societies of Groups 10 and 20 differ greatly from the non-inheriting (bar the Semang), small family (bar the Kung), 19 gathering societies of Group 33. The former eight and the latter nineteen were compared with respect to their distributions on each of the 13 predictor variables. They differed significantly at the .05 level with respect to nine variables, marginally (between the .05 and .10 levels) with respect to two more (slavery and division of labor by gender), and failed to differ significantly only with respect to the remaining two—caste and number of craft-specialized occupations—since both of these were totally absent from all 27 societies. The eight gathering societies of Groups 10 and 20 differed from the 19 gathering groups of Group 33 in that the former are more likely to have patrilocal residence, to be semisedentary, to live in a community of over 50 persons, to have a level of political jurisdiction above the local community, to have unilineal descent, to make wealth distinctions, and to inherit real and/or movable property.

What conclusions may we draw from the consideration of these 27 gathering societies? First, with the abundant ecological niche there tends to develop a large familial system—typically the small extended family consisting of a head and at least two married offspring—distinctions based on wealth, and the unequal inheritance of movable property.[5]

We may note that none of the gathering societies sharing the pattern of abundance—nor any of the gathering societies under consideration here—elaborated on the division of labor to the point of getting craft specialists in, say, gathering or boat building. Not only is occupational specialization absent but political centralization is rare among these societies, and these are both processes whereby certain individuals are alienated from general subsistence activities.

We know from the literature on the phenomenon of "macroband coalescence" that it is common for groups who live in small foraging bands during most of the year to coalesce into a macroband several times their normal number around the times of peak seasonal abundance. Among urban migrants in developing countries, taking in in-migrant kin as circumstances permit is a frequently mentioned phenomenon (Handwerker, 1973, on Monrovia, Liberia; Peattie, 1968, on Ciudad Guayana, Venezuela; Vatuk, 1973, on Meerut, India). Other studies have shown that among groups with an agricultural economy, such as the pre-Communist Chinese (Buck, 1937) and the (acculturating) Vedda (Brow, 1972), it appears that the head of the family tries to expand it so as to cultivate more land and consolidate wealth to be inherited. Conversely, another group of studies shows the family shedding members in times of adversity (see Chaps. 8 and 9 below). This literature includes treatises on the breaking up of the conjugal pair under the stress of male unemployment and marginality. Thus the family may react far more flexibly to economic conditions than has frequently been portrayed in a family literature that paints it as a largely traditional, change-resistant force.

However, for the family to be able to add or to shed members without reducing the prospects that those members will survive, it would seem that those members should be capable of forming or entering other subsistence units. This suggests that the "elastic" members are neither dependents nor specialists in nonsubsistence production.

Applying this reasoning to societies with simple technologies in economies of abundance, we infer that it would be adaptive to expand their families so as to consolidate their ability to accumulate and retain surplus. Correlates of surplus accumulation would be wealth distinctions to set off the more from the less successful families, and inheritance favoring those whose expansion of the family made the consolidation of surplus possible.

Conversely, building up the nonfamilial division of labor to exploit the economy could have disastrous consequences in a bad year. If a group needed five different classes of gatherers, and three of hunters and fishers, each specializing in a different area of subsistence activity, then the minimum foraging unit would be expanded considerably above that required by a group of what we may term "subsistence generalists." It seems unlikely that such a complex economic unit could be formed within the band size most characteristic of hunters and gatherers in nonexceptional environments, estimated by Lee and DeVore

(1968) to be about 25 persons, but it might be possible with the average of 50 reported by Steward (see Chap. 5 above). By the same process, political expansion, with its concomitant requirement of full-time administrators and military personnel, would also alienate certain members of the group from knowledge of basic subsistence activities. Instead, the elastic family and patterns of wealth and inheritance that would almost automatically be foregone in times of adversity result in no economic actors becoming alienated from normal subsistence activities.

It is our conclusion, then, that under favorable economic conditions gathering societies tend not to develop a division of labor or to expand their polity but, rather, to elaborate the family together with systems of inheritance status differentiation.

Exploring the Stability of Our AID Analysis

In multivariate analysis where tests of significance have not been derived or where they are based on dubious logic, it has been proposed that the original sample be randomly split into two mutually exclusive subsamples and that the multivariate analysis then be run on each subsample in addition to the parent sample. Then similarity of the results based on the two subsamples with those derived from the sample may be interpreted as evidence of stability of the results.

The sample of 289 societies that constitutes the base of the data for the present chapter was randomly split into two mutually exclusive subsamples of 139 and 150 societies. Details of the analysis appear in Appendix D. Here we report a summary of the findings.

The proportions of variance "explained" in the two subsamples were slightly larger (45 and 43 percent) than in the parent sample (40 percent). It may be recalled that our concepts varied in numbers of indicators from one to three. As might be expected, then, there is greater stability across the three analyses in the contributions of the concepts than of the indicators on which they are based. Inheritance has the maximum explanatory power for all three samples. Mode of subsistence, social inequality, and nature of settlement also appear as "explanatory" predictors in all three samples. On the other hand, the nature of work and residence and descent appear in only one subsample plus the parent sample.

In sum, the procedure of splitting our basic sample into two subsamples and then rerunning the AID shows concepts to be stabler than indicators, and in the context of "explaining" variation among nonliterate societies in size of familial organization the most stable of our concepts seem to be system of inheritance, mode of subsistence, social inequality, and nature of the settlement.

It is a familiar notion in statistical theory that the stability of an estimate is related to the size of the sample. For example, the variance of a sample mean is the variance of the population divided by sample size. In view of such considerations it is relevant to note that the AID makes use of very small clusters of cases. Indeed, it may dichotomize a set of k observations into one set of k - 1 cases and a second set consisting of only the k - th case. And the total explained variance receives an increment from this operation.

To get some feeling for the degree to which the variance being explained in our analysis resulted from small resulting subsets of observations, we decided arbitrarily that splits in which both resulting subsets contained at least 15 societies were of adequate size, but that those splits wherein one or both resulting subsets had less than 15 societies would be regarded as resulting in "small" groups. Again, the details of the analysis appear in Appendix D.

We summarize the results of this analysis as follows. First, of the 40 percent explained variance reported in Table 7-3, 17 percent was derived from splits wherein one or both of the resulting subsets had fewer than 15 cases. Conversely, 23 percent of the explained variance derived from splits that were satisfactory by the criterion that they resulted in subsets of 15 or more societies. Second, as would be expected, the splits resulting in small groups tend to occur late in the analysis. Third, it seems reasonable to infer that an indicator whose contribution to explained variance derives only from such unsatisfactory splits is one whose relevance to the explanatory system is probably not stable. Fourth, it appears that such splits do serve to make more homogeneous terminal groups. Finally, when we look at concepts rather than indicators, we see that again by this criterion system of inheritance and mode of subsistence appear in the "satisfactory" column ($N \geqslant 15$) of all three samples.

Refining the Analysis

After this analysis was completed, we decided to undertake some improvements and then redo the analysis.

One improvement has to do with the scale of the dependent variable. Up to this point we have used the simplest of all scales: the dichotomy. We have classified societies as having familial structures—or, more properly, domestic families (households)—that are either large or small. To refine our measurement of familial structure we have counted the number of positions in the domestic family.

Appendix C gives the details of this procedure. As can be seen in Appendix Table C-1, the range of positions runs from 2 to 13. The mean for all societies in the EA was 6.4, with a standard deviation of 3.5. Appendix Tables C-2 and C-3 show that not all integers in the range were used. No improvement in quantitative analysis resulted, however, from grouping values to eliminate hiatuses (see Appendix Table C-4), and thus the following analysis is based on the 2-13 scale.

A second improvement concerns the causal sequence of the concepts in our model. In our thinking, as well as in the comment by Professor Bernard Farber on our paper at the 1974 meeting of the American Sociological Association, there is a question as to whether we should view Boxes 7 and 8, system of inheritance and system of residence and descent, respectively, as part of the causal chain that results in one or another kind of familial system, or whether we should interpret those concepts as part of the familial system itself.[6] One way to resolve the dilemma is to declare that if Boxes 7 and 8 are part of the causal chain, they certainly seem to fall later in the sequence than Boxes 1A and 1B. If they are part of the familial system, on the other hand, one can still argue that they affect the familial structure. Accordingly, we have run an AID with the new scale of familial structure as the dependent variable, but this time the AID is being run in two stages. In stage 1 the predictors pertain to subsocietal systems other than the family, that is, to the economy and the polity. With residuals from this analysis we undertake a second AID in which the predictors are more related to the familial system, that is, the indicators of Boxes 7 and 8. In doing this, we have added an indicator—mode of marriage—to Box 8. This indicator specifies whether the practice in a given society is for goods and/or services to be transferred from the groom's side to the bride's (as in brideprice), from the bride's to the groom's (as in dowry), or in both directions, or whether there is no significant consideration at all.

One other change was made. It was discovered that among the 289 societies that had been analyzed, there were seven societies that practiced, or at least permitted, polyandry. Because we surmised that familial processes would be substantially different in polyandrous societies and because the number of those societies was too small for separate quantitative analysis, it was decided to drop them and to base our further quantitative analysis on the remaining 282 societies.

The outcome of the two-stage AID analysis appears in Figure 7-2 (stage 1), p. 138, and Figure 7-3 (stage 2), p. 140. In reporting the results we shall continue to attend the size of the groups resulting from the splits. Table 7-4 shows separately and then compositely the splits wherein no group had a frequency below 15 and, on the other hand, those steps wherein one or both of the resulting groups had an N in the range 1-14. See Appendix D for the details of the analysis.

Perhaps the first thing to be noted in Table 7-4 is that stage 1 accounted for nearly as much of the variance (37 percent) as did the entire single-stage AID (40 percent). It did this, moreover, with the big predictor—inheritance—excluded. Second, the two-stage procedure has increased the total explained variance from 40 percent to 49 percent. If we exclude the splits resulting in groups of less than 15, the explained variance rose from 23 percent to 35 percent. Another way of phrasing this point is that in the single-stage analysis the "unsatisfactory" splits contributed about one half of the explained variance; in the two-stage analysis their contribution is only about a quarter.

Perhaps the most interesting feature of Table 7-4 is the fact that every indicator except descent contributed to the grand total of explained variance. Thus we can see that the staging of the indicators prevented Box 7, inheritance, from overwhelming the boxes that occur earlier in the model. We had speculated that such an analysis might show the greater importance of Box 1A, mode of subsistence, but the outcome was in the opposite direction. In the original AID

TABLE 7-4. "Explained" Variance of Familial Structure, Scaled Intervally, by Concepts Shown in Figure 6-1 and Indicators from Table 7-1. Based on Two-Stage Analysis by Means of AID, by Size of Smaller Group Resulting from Split

Box Concept and Indicator	$N \geqslant 15$	$N < 15$	Total
	First Stage		
1A Mode of subsistence	.0347		.0347
Subsistence technology	(.0347)		(.0347)
2 Nature of work	.0427	.0172	.0599
Number of occupations	(.0135)	(.0172)	(.0307)
Gender differentiation	(.0292)		(.0292)
5 Social inequality	.1386	.0192	.1578
Caste		(.0192)	(.0192)
Slavery	(.1180)		(.1180)
Social classes	(.0206)		(.0206)
6 Settlement	.0680	.0512	.1192
Type	(.0560)		(.0560)
Size	(.0120)	(.0130)	(.0250)
Political complexity		(.0382)	(.0382)
Totals for first stage	.2840	.0876	.3716
	Second Stage		
7 Inheritance	.0372	.0374	.0746
Real property	(.0372)		(.0372)
Movable property		(.0374)	(.0374)
8 Residence and descent	.0322	.0070	.0392
Mode of marriage	(.0089)	(.0070)	(.0159)
Nuptial residence	(.0233)		(.0233)
Descent			
Totals for second stage	.0694	.0444	.1138
Totals for both stages	.3534	.1320	.4854

subsistence economy contributed 8 1/2 percent on satisfactory splits plus another 1 1/2 percent from small splits for a total of 10 percent. But in Table 7-4 its total is only about a third as great. On the other hand, the explanatory importance of social differentiation has risen more than four-fold—from around 4 1/2 and 2 1/2 percent to 16 and 12 percent, respectively.[7]

Summary and Conclusions

The model portrayed in Figure 6-1 lists 10 concepts. Of these we have found in the Ethnographic Atlas at least one indicator for each of six of the hypothesized predictors plus the dependent variable: familial organization. The three concepts omitted from our empirical exploration of the model are environmental potentialities, surplus, and the social relations of production. An investigation that leaves a third of the explanatory concepts unmeasured cannot be regarded as entirely satisfactory. But in this imperfect world a macrosociological study

Figure 7-2 Tree of First Stage of Two-Stage AID: Dependent Variable Is Interval Scale of Familial Structure

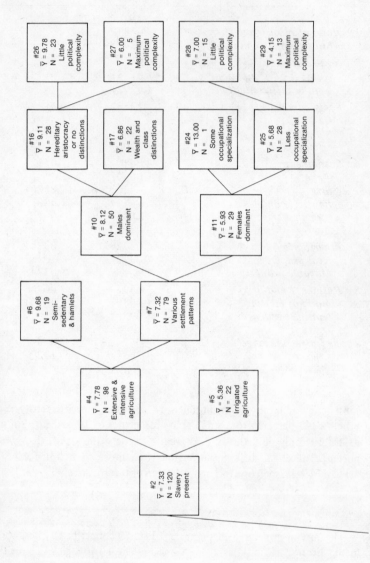

#26
Ȳ = 9.78
N = 23
Little political complexity

#27
Ȳ = 6.00
N = 5
Maximum political complexity

#28
Ȳ = 7.00
N = 15
Little political complexity

#29
Ȳ = 4.15
N = 13
Maximum political complexity

#16
Ȳ = 9.11
N = 28
Hereditary aristocracy or no distinctions

#17
Ȳ = 6.86
N = 22
Wealth and class distinctions

#24
Ȳ = 13.00
N = 1
Some occupational specialization

#25
Ȳ = 5.68
N = 28
Less occupational specialization

#10
Ȳ = 8.12
N = 50
Males dominant

#11
Ȳ = 5.93
N = 29
Females dominant

#6
Ȳ = 9.68
N = 19
Semi-sedentary & hamlets

#7
Ȳ = 7.32
N = 79
Various settlement patterns

#4
Ȳ = 7.78
N = 98
Extensive & intensive agriculture

#5
Ȳ = 5.36
N = 22
Irrigated agriculture

#2
Ȳ = 7.33
N = 120
Slavery present

138

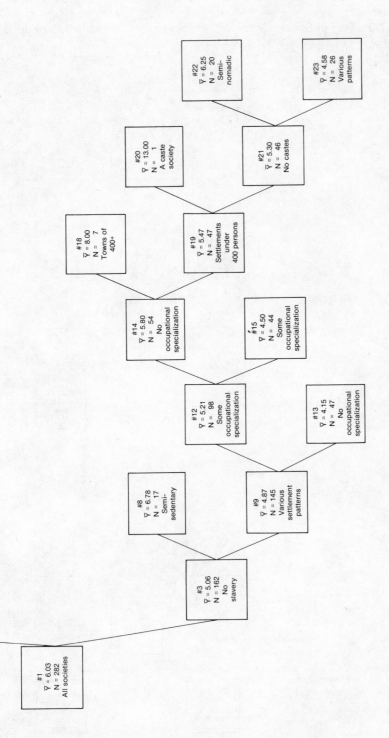

#22
V̄ = 6.25
N = 20
Semi-
nomadic

#23
V̄ = 4.58
N = 26
Various
patterns

#20
V̄ = 13.00
N = 1
A caste
society

#21
V̄ = 5.30
N = 46
No castes

#18
V̄ = 8.00
N = 7
Towns of
400+

#19
V̄ = 5.47
N = 47
Settlements
under
400 persons

#14
V̄ = 5.80
N = 54
No
occupational
specialization

#15
V̄ = 4.50
N = 44
Some
occupational
specialization

#12
V̄ = 5.21
N = 98
Some
occupational
specialization

#13
V̄ = 4.15
N = 47
No
occupational
specialization

#8
V̄ = 6.78
N = 17
Semi-
sedentary

#9
V̄ = 4.87
N = 145
Various
settlement
patterns

#3
V̄ = 5.06
N = 162
No
slavery

#1
V̄ = 6.03
N = 282
All societies

Figure 7-3 Tree of Second Stage of Two-Stage AID: Dependent Variable Is Interval Scale of Familial Structure

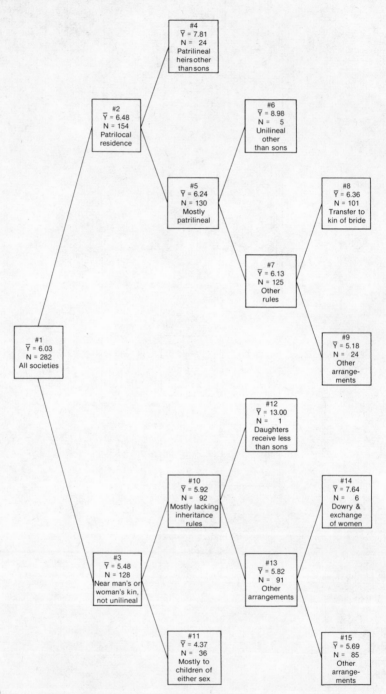

that involves measures of two thirds of all a phenomenon's hypothesized determinants is probably offering unusually adequate coverage.

The purposes of our investigation were to get some estimate of the explanatory power of the model, to see which of our concepts and/or indicators might prove especially strong or weak with respect to our problem, and to learn whatever deviant cases might be able to tell us. Given these objectives and the fact that most of the predictors were nominally scaled, we concluded that the Automatic Interaction Detector (AID) was the most appropriate technique of quantitative analysis.[8]

If our model should work perfectly, it would follow that the nature of a society's familial system could be predicted without error once we knew its mode of subsistence (Box 1A), its environmental potentialities (Box 1B), and so on through Box 8. Such a perfect model would explain all of the variation in familial systems, and the explanation would be complete both theoretically and statistically. Since AID is a search procedure, no test of significance exists for it, and thus we have no way of estimating the minimum proportion of explained variance that would assure that the model is better than chance. It is our impression, however, that studies in social science are regarded as having positive and plausible findings when the explained variance approaches 40 percent.

Since the AID requires that the dependent variable be scaled either intervally or dichotomously, we began by using the simplest possible indicator for a society's familial structure and classified it as large or small. The requirement of AID that every unit be scored on every variable, moreover, resulted in our losing three quarters of the societies in the EA and carrying out our analysis on the remaining 289. Our first run showed inheritance and mode of subsistence to be the strongest predictors and accounted for a total of 40 percent of the variance.

The tree resulting from the first analysis showed detailed confirmation of the curvilinear hypothesis set forth in Chapter 4: that small familial systems tend to fall toward the ends of the spectrum of societal complexity whereas large systems predominate at the intermediate level represented by intensive agriculture without irrigation. Since both the analyses of Chapter 4 and of the present chapter are based on the Ethnographic Atlas, there is no presumption that Figure 7-1 represents independent confirmation of the curvilinear hypothesis.

Having determined that our model would account for a reasonable proportion of the variation, we verified by the split-sample method (1) that the estimate of 40 percent was stable, (2) that the particular indicators doing the explaining were not stable, but (3) that the concepts of inheritance and subsistence seemed consistently good, and (4) that social inequality and settlement were also consistent predictors of familial organization. When we added the distinction between satisfactory and unsatisfactory splits on the basis of the sizes of the resulting subsets, however, the predictors in (4) showed up less well than those in (3).

At this point we offered two refinements in the analysis: (1) the dichotomy of size of familial structure was replaced by an interval scale reflecting the number of positions in the familial system; and (2) the AID was divided into two stages whereby clearly extrafamilial indicators were taken into account before indicators that are hypothesized to operate later in the causal chain and—depending on one's conceptualization—may be part of the familial system.

This AID accounted for about half of the variance, and a contribution was made by every indicator except one. We interpret these results as supporting the model.

Notes

1. As we saw in Chapter 5, however, the ethnographers are not in agreement in evaluating these descriptions. (The reader may recall the question as to whether such accounts represent what respondents say they do or what they say they believe should be done.) Other sources of confusion result from differing accounts by different ethnographers, resulting in part no doubt from their doing their field work at different times and also perhaps in different villages of the same tribe.

2. A scanning of seemingly relevant categories of the Human Relations Area Files revealed that there was not enough information on intrasocietal ethnic variation to warrant quantitative analysis.

3. A more detailed analysis of the deviations of our sample of 289 from the distributions of the four Murdockian samples in Table 7–2 is possible with respect to regional distribution. First, the sample of 862 societies derives from the summary article on the EA (Murdock, 1967). With respect to this distribution our sample of 289 seems overrepresented in East Eurasia, but shows a quite satisfactory fit in the other five regions. Second, we obtained our tape of the EA at a time when it consisted of 1,170 societies. With respect to this population of 1,170, of which our 289 constitute a subset, we find that the latter is overrepresented in East Eurasia (as before) and also underrepresented in sub-Saharan Africa. Third, in the above cited article (1967), Murdock grouped the societies of the world into 412 clusters. With respect to that distribution our 289 deviate in other regions from those previously noted—overrepresented in North America and underrepresented in Central and South America. Finally, in a more recent publication, Murdock (1968) has developed what he calls "world sampling provinces," the number of which is 200. With respect to this distribution, we are overrepresented in sub-Saharan Africa and North America and underrepresented in Central and South America. If, as Murdock seems to suggest, his 200 world sampling provinces represent his conclusion as to the regional distribution of the universe of primitive societies (although the "Standard Cross-Cultural Sample" described by Murdock and White is down to 186 societies), then it appears that our set of 289 represents an improvement over the parent set of 1,170 with respect to two regions (sub-Saharan Africa and East Eurasia), a deterioration with respect to two (Circum-Mediterranean and North America), and a standoff with respect to the remaining two (Insular Pacific and Central and South America).

4. See, for example, Naroll and Sipes (1973).

5. This pattern is most frequently encountered among a certain group of California gathering societies who lived by acorns, salmon, and other hunting, fishing, and gathering. A diffusionist could argue that the family, wealth, inheritance, and even modes of subsistence commonalities resulted from their close geo-

graphic connection, rather than their sharing a similar and abundant ecological niche, and, we should contend, a similar mode of exploiting it. After all, the unique combination of acorn and salmon economies dominated by gathering *are* found only in this delimited geographic region. But let us turn this diffusionist objection upside down. Granting the favorable ecology and assuming the disposition to imitate, we then ask why they did not copy the political organization that united two adjacent communities in only three of the thirty or more gathering, fishing, hunting groups from this area of California included by Murdock in the EA (Shasta, Tubatulabal, and Maidu)?

6. If one approaches such a question from the standpoint of test theory and multiple factor analysis, presumably the zero-order correlations and the configuration of those correlations with respect to the factors can give guidance. For example, if we had a single familial factor with high loadings of familial structure, marital residence, and both kinds of inheritance, and if those indicators had zero loadings on all other factors, the mutual affinity of this set of indexes would seem clear. In the present situation marital residence, descent, and the two inheritance indicators intercorrelate with respect to coefficients of contingency of .7 or higher ("corrected" C's of .77 or higher), but their correlation with the dichotomized scale of familial organization is at about the same level as with slavery—in the neighborhood of .3.

7. Despite the nature of our data there may be some who believe that a regression analysis is preferable to AID. We took a look at the possibility of performing a regression analysis with these data. Several difficulties arose. (1) Among our variables were some that correlated in a monotonic way with certain other variables but in a nonmonotonic way with still others; hence, whether left in their original form or transformed, they would violate any assumption of linearity. (2) If we had tried to solve the foregoing problem by means of the dummy variable technique, then we should have begun running thin with respect to degrees of freedom, since we should have had over 70 categories in our predictors and only 282 cases. Nevertheless, we arbitrarily omitted some of the least promising categories and ran a regression analysis with 35 categories to see what would happen. The biggest predictor (largest beta) was the "none" category of slavery (= -.36) and the next was very small settlement (less than 50 persons) with a beta of -.27. Class distinctions based on wealth and size of settlement between 50 and 100 persons were next with betas of .20 and -.19, respectively. For all 35 categories, the R^2 = .28 and was significant beyond the .001 level.

After dichotomizing the variables and analyzing the resulting fourfold tables, Gordon (1970) found no relation between familial structure (as dependent variable) and what we have called subsistence economy, type of settlement, or size of settlement, but he did find a relationship between each of these three predictors and nuptial residence. Where a relationship is curvilinear—as we have shown that between societal complexity and familial complexity to be—the relationship tends to be concealed if dichotomous categories are used.

8. We do not agree with the school of thought that maligns such techniques as alchemy (see, e.g., Einhorn, 1972). Rather, it is our view that any technique can be used stupidly.

Chapter 8

The Political Economy of the Mother-Child Household

Rae Lesser Blumberg,
with the assistance of
María-Pilar García

Over the past generation the mother-child dyad has become a focus of attention for both the research sociologist and the government policy maker. In the present chapter economic conditions—not race—are seen to be relevant to the occurrence of mother-child households. In the next chapter the question is raised as to whether a familial pattern based on mother and small child does indeed exist. — R.F.W.

In this chapter we shall consider two forms of the mother-child household that are characterized by the absence of a resident male head. First we shall treat the mother-headed household common among marginal lower classes in diverse wage labor societies, and then we shall consider the mother-child residential arrangement found among certain polygynous, largely horticultural tribes. Our reason for treating these two apparently so different forms is that we believe they share certain principles that account for their emergence under

Based on Blumberg with García (1974).

widely differing circumstances. For each we shall review extant conceptualizations, formulate our own structural hypotheses, and then present data to explore the propositions. The data concerning female-headed households come from the United States Census. The hypotheses concerning the mother-child dwelling unit are tested with data from the 1,170 preindustrial societies of Murdock's Ethnographic Atlas (1967). In both cases our hypotheses look to the relationship of the woman to her society's mode of production to account for the emergence of a male-absent household, and to her society's political economy to account for its persistence.

The Mother-Headed Household

Definitions and Review of Literature

Until recently the majority of studies of mother-headed households involved U.S. and Caribbean blacks, and mother-child residential arrangements are described almost exclusively among black African tribes (Murdock and Wilson, 1972). Murdock and Wilson emphasize that mother-child households are concentrated in Africa among groups that are ethnically Negro, and seem to have been imported as an "Africanism" into the New World with the slave trade. Nevertheless, they do assert that the "ultimate explanation must be sought in the social and economic conditions which gave rise to the mother-child household as the predominant indigenous form of family organization in Africa" (1972: 278). We shall go farther and argue that the relation with race is spurious, both on racial-historical and racial-biological grounds.

There are two other patterns usually described as mother-centered—the consanguineal and the matrifocal—on the ground that all three tend to occur among the economically marginal lower classes in a wide variety of wage labor societies. Neither of these other two forms, however, is defined as requiring the absence of a resident male head. Gonzalez, who prefers the term "consanguineal household," defines that term as a "coresidential kinship group which includes no regularly present male in the role of husband-father" (1959). The enduring relationships are those with blood kin, and of course these may include male relatives. The head of a consanguineal household is not necessarily a female: mother's brothers or other male uterine kin may run the show, as among the traditional Nayar (Gough, 1952).

R. T. Smith introduced the concept of the matrifocal family in his work on the black family of Guyana (1956). In a subsequent paper (1973) he says the term is intended to convey a state of affairs wherein it is women in their role as mothers who come to be the focus of relationships; the term was not intended to mean that women necessarily become heads of households. The working-class East Londoners described by Young and Willmott (1957) are matrifocal by this definition, even though marriages are stable and the males present. In short, some consanguineal households may be matrifocal and vice versa, and some of each type may be headed by the mother, but all three dimensions are analytically distinct.

Unfortunately, these three dimensions are generally jumbled together in the voluminous literature on mother-centered families. A more serious problem in this literature arises from the fact that early studies of this type of familism are confined to U.S. and Caribbean blacks, and until recently the dominant interpretation stresses either or both racial-historical and/or social pathological factors.

The racial-historical approach divides into two schools. In the first are those emphasizing African origins, such as the mother-child dwelling unit found in many polygynous African societies and the relative economic autonomy of the women (Herskovits, 1937, 1941, 1943; Herskovits and Herskovits, 1947; Bascom, 1941). The second harks back to the effects of plantation slavery on New World blacks (Frazier, 1939; Campbell, 1943; Henriques, 1953; King, 1945; Myrdal, 1944; Powdermaker, 1939; Simey, 1946; Woofter, 1930). Under slavery, it is held, strong structural bars to stable nuclear families emerged (e.g., absence of legal marriage among slaves). Later, continuing economic and other effects of racial discrimination militated against the lower-class black male's becoming the dominant figure in a stable family, the argument of this school asserts.

This slavery-based approach shades off into the interpretation based on social pathology. Frazier (1950: 277) viewed families deviating from the stable nuclear model as disorganized. It was his view that "the widespread family disorganization among Negroes has resulted from the failure of the father to play the role in family life required by American society." "Family disorganization," in turn, "has been partially responsible for a large amount of juvenile delinquency and adult crime among Negroes."

Probably the epitome of the approach linking social pathology and the black family was reached in the controversial "Moynihan Report" (1965). Moynihan considered the increasing incidence of female-headed households among poor urban blacks as a growing social cancer in the ghetto. In his words:

> At the center of the tangle of pathology is the weakness of the family structure. Once or twice removed, it will be found to be the principal source of most of the aberrant, inadequate, or anti-social behavior that did not establish, *but now serves to perpetuate* the cycle of poverty and deprivation (p. 30; emphasis added).

The orientations that link the female-headed households with blacks, social pathology, or, more subtly, a self-perpetuating "culture of poverty"[1] have been in decline in the literature of late. First, a long list of studies of both mother-headed and mother-centered households in nonblack populations has emerged, swamping an exclusively racial view. See Adams (1960) for statistics on female-headed households in a variety of Central and South American countries. In addition to Latin America, matrifocality has been observed in diverse Pacific groups (Calley, 1956—Australian aboriginal "mixed bloods"; Geertz, 1959—Java; Kay, 1963—Tahiti), native American tribes (Aginsky, 1947, 1949—Pomo of California; Boyer, 1964—Mescalero Apache), European populations (Lopreato, 1965—south Italian peasants; Wilson, 1953—Scottish mining community; Young and Willmott, 1957—East London), and other far-flung sites. Second, the focus of social pathology has also come under criticism from those stressing structural approaches. These structural views involve one or both of two main tenets: (1) the mother-headed household is not abnormal in and of itself; and (2) it is linked with structurally caused poverty in wage-labor societies, especially with the economic marginality of the male.

With respect to the first tenet, Adams (1960) has been influential in justifying the nondeviant nature of the mother-child household. It is not surprising that previous social scientists had considered the female-headed unit an aberration, for this was a group that tended to view the nuclear family as universal (Murdock, 1949; Parsons, 1955; Bell and Vogel, 1960) and the male as the rightful head of the house (Parsons and Bales, 1955). Adams rejects the view that the nuclear family is universal and universally fulfills a list of agreed-upon functions. Instead he proposes a structural conceptualization of the family, based on the dyad (of which the mother-child dyad is perhaps the basic biological unit) as the primary building block of family structure. This removes the mother-child household from the category of social disorganization while rendering irrelevant arguments as to just what universal functions the nuclear family is best filling, and/or whether it is indeed universal.

The second tenet, linking the mother-headed household to poverty and the larger class system of a wage-labor society, was first argued influentially by R. T. Smith (1956). In two of the three poor black villages he studied in Guyana (then British Guiana), he found that over a third of the households had female heads. Noting that the men of these villages were at the bottom of the color-class system, and that when they worked their jobs were "undifferentiated" with respect to status, he said that low status and lack of steady income resulted in the men's being unimportant in their households. It was because their occupational roles did not enable the men to make important contributions in status and income to their households, he concluded, that the households tended toward matrifocality. It should be noted, however, that his data show the economic opportunities in these villages to have been marginal for both sexes, and also that the males acted as a migratory reserve labor force in the larger capitalist economy (cutting cane on the sugar plantations for several months a year during "crop," migrating for long periods to work in the bauxite mines, etc.).

Smith has been criticized by Greenfield (1966), who argues that his explanation ignores the historical process whereby women-centered families arose, and by Gonzalez (1970), who feels he gives too much weight to the psychological effects of the male's inability to provide cash income for the household.

Greenfield's own study is of Barbados, and he agrees with Smith on the immediate causes of female-headed households among the poor (i.e., that low occupational prestige and low, unreliable income of the male create a psychological situation conducive to his departure). Furthermore, Greenfield's well presented data show a similar picture of the family, even though he regards the village he studied as somewhat more middle class occupationally than Smith's villages. (In his village Greenfield found that 44% of the families were "incomplete and based primarily on the mother-child relationship"–p. 143.) Other findings of

Greenfield that paralleled those of Smith were: female heads are older than their male counterparts; average age of household head is high for both sexes; and without property marriage is rare. Economically, the Barbados revealed in Greenfield's data seems even more distorted than Guyana; the island is a classic example of a one-crop (sugar) capitalist economy. There is not even any important subsistence agriculture. Furthermore, Barbados is overpopulated (despite emigration), and its people act primarily as a reserve labor force for the capitalist, technologically saturated, sugar plantations.[2] Only a quarter of the labor force is directly employed by the sugar plantations, and many of these for only the 20 weeks per year of labor-intensive crop activities. During the remaining 32 weeks, "hard times," people are pushed to alternate, even more marginal, economic pursuits. In sum, Greenfield provides a detailed portrait of mother-centered households on Barbados and excellent documentation of the structural factors that would seem to cause both the economic marginality and the low incidence of stable male-headed households among these people.

Amazingly, the explanation proposed by Greenfield for the origin of both the island's nuclear and mother-headed family forms involves not the structural conditions long characterizing Barbados' plantation economy but, rather, historical diffusion from seventeenth-century England. Capitalism, wage labor, and the small nuclear or mother-headed household arrived together as part of a larger Anglo-Saxon culture stream "into which the emancipated slaves were drawn two centuries later," he asserts. He documents that in medieval English villages legal marriage was contracted only if property was involved. ("Husband" meant a propertied villager; "wed" is the gift the groom gave the bride to signify her being vested in inheritance rights to his property.) In addition, records imply not only that the propertyless in rural villages lived in common-law unions, but also that many poor households had no resident males (p. 165). Yet, rather than considering the structural parallels as causal (i.e., the common position of the English and Barbadian poor villagers vis-à-vis the means of production), Greenfield implies that cultural diffusion is reason enough. On page 172 he quotes Cruickshank (1916): "The Barbadian Negro is an English rustic in black skin." This further means that Greenfield is deliberately silent on how matrifocality emerged in neighboring Caribbean islands lacking an Anglo-Saxon heritage. Contrariwise, he asserts that the essentially similar market-exchange capitalism and familial forms of Barbados and the United States may be due to common origin. Thus the correlation between economy and household might be the result of diffusion[3] rather than a functional relationship (p. 168). Greenfield's explanation might be more convincing if we did not have such a wide variety of studies showing functional relationships between economic factors and household form. These studies extend beyond the mother-centered household literature (where all the studies mentioned to this point show the covariation of economic marginality in a wage-labor economy and matrifocality). Handwerker (1973) has shown how economic factors affect familial structure among Bassa migrants to Monrovia, Liberia; and Opler (1943) has given an overview of the economic concomitants of polyandry. Our study of familial organization in 289 preindustrial societies showed that two economic indicators—subsistence economy and number of occupations—accounted for a quarter of the explained variance, and with the familial-economic variable of inheritance added, they accounted for nearly three quarters of the explained variance. When we allowed the structural variables (including the economic indicators) to operate first, they accounted for about 70 percent of the explained variance, but there was shrinkage in the proportion explained by directly economic indicators. (See Tables 7-3 and 7-4 above.)

That mother-headed households would be more frequent where women have economic options comparable or superior to those of the males of their class is proposed in Winch and Blumberg (1968: 90-91) and Blumberg (1970: 207-211). The greater participation of lower-class women in the labor force is also cited, and its correlation with domestic power discussed. Poverty and wage labor, the two old standbys of the matrifocal literature, are also invoked in these two writings. A further factor is posited in the 1968 article and explicated in the 1970 work: the absence of the family as the unit of labor, and the relationship of this factor to the mode of production. Thus, Blumberg contrasts the different sorts of occupations in which blacks and East Indians are found in Guyana. The blacks, about whose matrifocality Smith has written, tend to work as individuals for wages in settings such as factories or public bureaucracies (where members of a family would not normally be employed together). The East Indians are never discussed as having matrifocal familism. And, as both Blumberg and Despres (1970) note, they tend to be found in economic pursuits that are family based: for example, family farms and family-run shops. More generally, Blumberg observes, cross-societal evidence suggests that familial organization contracts and becomes more flexible under circumstances of unreliable or inadequate subsistence (Nimkoff and Middleton, 1960). The specific nature of the mode of production of the society will affect the sexual division of labor (see also Brown, 1970; Murdock and Provost, 1973a; Blumberg, 1974, 1976). Jointly, Blumberg (1970) implies, these factors tell us whether the "minimum household structure" expected to emerge under conditions of unreliable or marginal subsistence would be dyadic or require a male. Despite these suggestions concerning the unit of labor and the economic role of women, the Winch-Blumberg and Blumberg (1970) studies did not present an integrated theory accounting for the emergence, prevalence, and persistence of female-headed households.

In order to do so, we believe we shall have to go beyond the extant structural interpretations of mother-headed units in two ways. First, we should treat systematically the relation of the mother to the economic sector and the impact of this relation on her child-care responsibilities at different stages of the family cycle. This may give us some of the "missing links" to account for the origin of mother-headed families in certain groups. But, in order to account for their persistence, a second new element is necessary: a thorough analysis of the role of the larger political economy in maintaining the structural concomitants of mother-headed households in a given societal category, regardless of state rhetoric that may condemn such families as "disorganized" or as a threat to the polity. At this point let us outline in preliminary form the conditions under which we believe the mother-headed family emerges and persists.

Some Conditions for the Emergence, Prevalence, and Persistence of Mother-Headed Households

In general, although such units are most prevalent among the economically marginal lower classes in a variety of wage-labor societies, not all economically marginal lower-class groups in such societies have mother-centered households. Conversely, female-headed units may be found in wage-labor societies among groups that are not economically marginal (although, we suggest, not in very high proportion).

Accordingly, we distinguish four conditions for the emergence and prevalence of female-headed households, in general, and an additional one for its persistence when encountered among the economically marginal lower classes in wage-labor societies. Actually, conditions I, II, and III tell us among which groups, and when in their family cycle, mother-headed households can emerge. Condition IV adds a specification affecting how prevalent mother-headed households might become in a societal category. The word "poverty" is never mentioned in these four conditions. Yet it appears that they are fulfilled most frequently among groups that are not only poor, but also constitute a surplus labor population in the context of a larger political economy. Condition V ties together surplus labor and political economy to predict the circumstances under which female-headed households persist. All five conditions, we believe, are ultimately related to the mode of production.[4]

Condition I. The unit of labor, the unit of compensation, and the unit of property accumulation is the individual, independent of gender. (In societies where families are the unit of labor, and/or compensation is paid to the male head, and/or family property is corporately held, females rarely emerge as heads of households.)[5]

Condition II. Females have independent access to subsistence opportunities. This condition is a function of (1) there being viable economic opportunities open to females via: (a) their own work; (b) those of economically productive children whose labor or compensation they have access to; (c) inheritance; and/or (d) state-provided welfare; and (2) females being permitted, and in fact, able to head a separate residence and to control property.

Condition III. Subsistence opportunities open to females can be reconciled with child-care responsibilities. We must determine whether the female's own subsistence pursuits can be carried on simultaneously with child-care responsibilities (e.g., cottage industry, gathering).[6] If so, condition III is satisfied. If not, satisfaction of condition II might involve postponing formation of a mother-headed unit until young children can be cared for by a sibling old enough to do so, and/or some other child-care agent is available, and/or the children are not so young as to require "babysitting," and/or until the woman can arrange sufficient remuneration from a working child, property, inheritance, and/or state welfare to permit her to stay home.

Condition IV. The woman's subsistence opportunities from all sources in the absence of a male head are not drastically less than those of the men of her class.

As noted, all these conditions most frequently obtain among the economically marginal in wage-labor societies, accounting for the concentration of female-centered and female-headed households among such groups. In other words, mother-headed households are most prevalent among groups characterized as surplus labor. For mother-headed families to persist in a society over time, we argue, so too must the class of surplus labor. Accordingly, to account for the persistence of mother-headed households, we invoke:

Condition V. The political economy of the society produces and profits from a surplus labor population, and the female-headed household unit reproduces the surplus labor population. (This benefits those who control the political economy. To the extent that the political economy is controlled by extranational factors, the size of any surplus population and the extent to which it is internally beneficial to the society's elite become independent of their wishes). Where condition V is fulfilled, we predict that, state rhetoric to the contrary, programs that successfully reduce poor female-headed households will not be undertaken in the absence of a change in the structural conditions.

Discussion of the Conditions

Before deriving specific hypotheses from these conditions, we shall discuss some questions that they suggest.

Is bilateral kinship a necessary condition for mother-headed households, or is it just a correlate?

We believe that condition II—that females have viable independent subsistence opportunities—is almost never fulfilled in the absence of condition I—that rights to the means of subsistence be individuated—and that condition I is what most often breaks down existing unilineal systems. Therefore, we do not consider it necessary for a fully bilateral descent system to be present before mother-headed units can begin to emerge. Writings on contemporary Africa almost invariably show a link between the individuation of subsistence opportunities or property and the modification of traditional unilineal familial patterns. Handwerker (1973) shows a wide variety of flexible household structures among the patrilineal Bassa migrants in Monrovia, Liberia, including 13.6 percent female-headed households containing only maternal kin. The strongest immediate determinants of household composition in his sample seem to be economic marginality and ownership of property.

When might a patrilineal system not move in the direction of matrifocality if brought into a commodity-production economy under conditions of poverty?

One such set of conditions preventing the emergence of matrifocality involves groups whose women are economically totally dependent—that is, they are neither major subsistence producers under the traditional (usually dry agrarian or herding) subsistence base, nor are they able to find a place in the overcrowded wage-labor market, where traditional restrictions on female economic activity are buttressed by male unemployment. This situation is frequent in the (often Moslem) countries of the Middle East.

Despres' (1970) description of the East Indians who came to the Guyana sugar estates as indentured workers is suggestive. Both the East Indians and the African slaves who preceded them had patrilineal systems, but slavery had destroyed the African system. In contrast, the conditions of the East Indians' contracts guaranteed job security (minimal but steady) subsistence, and permitted a strategy of family employment. Men, women, and young boys worked in separate labor gangs (and presumably the young girls were engaged in child care). By contract, a certain proportion of their labor time was for pay rather than for the estate. With the pooled income they could rent more land to add to the family wet rice plot the owner assigned them and work that collectively in their free time as well. They could grow rice as a cash crop because their own food was guaranteed. Thus the family was able to act as the capital formation unit, and many families had accumulated enough at the end of the contract to trade their return passage rights for the right to buy government-subsidized irrigated land suitable for wet rice cultivation on a family basis. With family property they could retain patrilineal inheritance and engage in further family business ventures. Thus, in answer to our question about a patrilineally oriented family system persisting when brought into a commodity-production economy at poverty level, it seems that:

1. The early opportunities for familial employment and capital accumulation strategy permitted continuation of the patrilineal pattern.
2. The "minimum guaranteed subsistence" of the contract obviated the patterns of ad hoc reshuffling of household arrangements and resources that we believe accompany "feast or famine" economic uncertainty among other subsistence level groups.

Then we asked:

In general, what effect does a feast or famine pattern of unreliable subsistence have on the adaptation strategy of a group, especially its familial patterns?

Our response consists of several propositions.

1. *Proposition A.* Environmental uncertainty leads to flexibility. Whether among certain U.S. corporations (see, e.g., Perrow, 1967; Harvey, 1968), hunting and gathering bands (e.g., Lee, 1968, 1969, on the Kung Bushmen), or economic marginals in wage-labor societies (e.g., Stack, 1970; Calley, 1956), groups that have to cope with environmental uncertainty are characterized by flexibility of organization. Their adaptive strategies are dynamic and loosely structured in response to fluctuating conditions.

2. *Proposition B.* Unpredictable fluctuations of scarce resources lead to sharing and exchange. This kind of redistribution has been documented for both

hunting and gathering groups (Lombardi, 1973, and Sahlins, 1965, give numerous references), and wage-labor society marginals (see Valentine, 1970; Stack, 1970, 1974, for exchange networks among certain U.S. urban blacks; and Calley, 1956, for same among Australian aboriginal "mixed bloods"). Conversely, adding the criterion of scarce resources excludes Perrow's and Harvey's formal organizations. In general, it appears that groups facing inconsistent surplus tend to adopt a strategy of sharing and exchange of resources. Lombardi argues mathematically how such redistribution serves to smooth out fluctuations in net available resources (1973). Calley's study bridges hunting-gathering and wage-labor society marginal groups. The Australian aboriginal "mixed bloods" had practiced generalized redistribution in their traditional economy and more recently were practicing various kinds of "borrowing and counter-borrowing" on their reserves in northern New South Wales, where they eked out a precarious existence, functioning as the sporadically employed and underpaid local reserve labor force. (Government relief prevented outright starvation.) To generalize, it appears that in the hunting-gathering situation, the fluctuating and generally low levels of resources are caused by a combination of technology and habitat, whereas, in the wage-labor marginality situation, they are caused by the relation of the group to the larger political economy.

3. *Proposition C.* The flexibility and sharing and exchange characterizing groups facing inconsistent surplus extend even to household members, with the composition of co-residential groups changing flexibly and dynamically with changing circumstances. This is illustrated by Stack (1970) in her study of the "kindred of Viola Jackson," a U.S. black woman. Lee (1968, 1969) also describes shifting band composition among the Kung Bushmen. Indeed, many of the studies we have cited concerning the matrifocal family in wage-labor societies show instances of flexible family composition as adaptive strategy. Under the impact of economic and interpersonal changes in the situations of their members, household units form and reform, and often children are shifted around or informally adopted. Yet what is striking in this literature is that, despite adversity, these children do get cared for. Redistributing family members seems as adaptive a strategy for these people facing inconsistent surplus as redistributing food, money, and other resources. Two further points should be noted concerning this flexible household composition.

First, Stack shows that the pool of eligibles for this sort of exchange includes a loose bilateral group rather than just maternal consanguineals, as indicated by Gonzalez (1969, 1970).

The answer, then, to our question as to how a pattern of subsistence involving fluctuation of scarce resources affects households seems to involve: (1) organizational flexibility; (2) sharing and exchange; and (3) adaptive recomposition of households. These three properties, we believe, characterize the households of wage-labor society marginals through conditions I through V.

Second, Calley also found family composition frequently in flux, but throughout it all he found that the proportion of mother-headed households (about one third) in one group he studied remained "fairly constant."

Under what conditions will the proportion of female-headed units increase in wage-labor societies among groups which are not economically marginal?

Here we look to condition IV concerning the sex gap in resources. Does this mean that mother-headed households should multiply among middle-class women in industrial societies around the world as they enter the labor force in increasing numbers? Not necessarily. Presently, in a number of Western industrial societies, the higher the social class, the lower the rate of marital instability (Goode, 1962). This appears to be related to the fact that the size of the sex gap in resources also increases with higher social class. The income, education, and prospects of a lawyer's wife working as a secretary (or even as a teacher) are much worse compared to her husband's than is the case with the woman at the next typewriter married to a bus driver. Thus it makes sense for the lawyer's wife to protect her own and her children's upper-middle-class life style and status by staying married. Numerous studies have revealed how infrequent is court-awarded alimony and how very prevalent is male non- or undercompliance with court-ordered child support. In one example, Bart (1974) studied all whites receiving divorces in Chicago's Cook County three years previously and found that only half of the women reported receiving what child support the court had decreed (based on a 50 percent rate of questionnaire return).[7]

Nor does the evidence show that the increasing participation of middle-class women in the labor force is accompanied by a shrinking in the male-female gap in earnings or even education. Quite to the contrary, Knudsen (1969) demonstrates the gap in these areas has increased during the recent years of economic expansion that pulled so many U.S. married women into the labor force (see Oppenheimer, 1973). Nonetheless, as more women achieve the possibility—via work or welfare—of a viable (if lower) income by their own efforts, they may increasingly choose to set up a "home of one's own," to paraphrase Woolf. Recent statistics seem to bear this out.

In the United States the last decades may not have seen a general shrinking of the earnings gap between males and females, but one category—black females—did increase its real income faster than whites of either gender, or black males. The income of nonwhite women rose 260 percent from 1950 to 1968, as compared with, say, only 160 percent among nonwhite males (Farley, 1970). Also, especially since the mid-1960s, transfer payments (social security, welfare, etc.) have risen. Consequently, it is not surprising that the U.S. Department of Labor (1973) shows a concomitant rise in the proportion of households headed by females of all races, especially black ones. The explanation of the general rise in female-headed units since roughly 1960 seems to lie in the greater ability of certain groups of women to maintain an independent household rather than living with relatives. Among white women, the largest percentage gains were registered among those over 65, who tended to live alone (U.S. Department of Labor, 1973). Among black women, however, Farley (1970) shows that it was among younger females 15–34 and especially 35–44 that rates of household headship increased, and here the increase involved woman-headed households, not women living alone. Contrary to Moynihan's misleading pronouncements of a breakdown in the black ghetto family, this was not achieved by a reduction in the proportion of nonwhite married males heading households (for, in fact, this figure increased somewhat). Rather, Farley suggests, these additional female-headed units involved women who had previously been living with relatives and were now able to make it on their own.

In conclusion, even within rising general levels of absolute affluence and female-headed households, we would predict a higher proportion of mother-headed units among categories where the relative sex gap in resources is narrow, a situation still most frequent among the lower classes.

Now let us consider certain implications of condition V: (1) Under what conditions does a society's political economy produce and profit from a surplus labor population? (2) How does the female-headed household articulate with the surplus labor population?

With respect to the first question, critics of capitalism argue that the existence of a marginal lower class is a *"necessary and inevitable consequence* of a mature industrial capitalist system" (Sackrey, 1973, discussing the assumptions of Baran and Sweezy's *Monopoly Capital,* 1966; emphasis in original). However, a strong case can be made for the "necessity and inevitability" of such a class in two other types of society as well: (1) traditional agrarian ones, and (2) contemporary Third World nations. In all three types of society, it seems, the mechanism that makes inevitable such a class consists of the conjunction of two factors. Factor 1: On the one hand, those who control the political economy seem to benefit in two ways from the existence of adults who are normally marginal to the labor force: these adults reduce the bargaining power of the mainstream labor force (e.g., peasants in agrarian societies) by serving as potential replacements; and, moreover, they are conveniently available to be pulled into the mainstream labor force only when and if the need arises. Factor 2: On the other hand, many of the poor in those societies may find children to represent a benefit, not a cost—a possible solution to the problem of their poverty rather than its cause (Mamdani, 1972).

Let us now consider the three types of societies where a surplus labor force tends to emerge.

1. *Traditional agrarian societies.* Here, Lenski (1966) argues that 5 to 15 percent of the urban population in such societies consisted of a class he calls the "expendables"—coolies, beggars, prostitutes, street vendors, thieves, and so on—whose life conditions were so miserable that they did not reproduce themselves. Lenski believes, however, that they were replaced each generation because they represented the peasant population in excess of what the governing elite was willing to let survive, even at minimum subsistence level. Just because these sons and daughters of the peasantry were barely even a surplus labor force as adults does not mean they were not useful to their parents as children. Often the only one of the three factors of production (land, labor, capital) the peasant producer can control is labor costs—by growing his own labor force (Polgar, 1972). For peasants, children typically represent a net benefit in labor over the small cost

of maintaining them. Thus a large family is a rational investment under a mode of production where surplus is usually skimmed off the top by the governing elite before peasants can attempt to look after their own needs (Wolf, 1966).

2. *Third World nations.* Similarly, it has been argued that for large segments of the marginal urban poor in capitalist wage-labor societies— especially underdeveloped ones—children represent to their parents a potential net benefit rather than a cost (Schnaiberg and Reed, 1974; Blumberg, 1973), even if they ultimately swell the size of the surplus labor population. And it is precisely in the size of this reserve labor force that Third World societies are distinguished from both historical agrarian ones and advanced industrial-capitalist nations: these countries have tended to lose control of the size of their surplus populations.

Many of these Third World countries were previously traditional agrarian systems (and producers of a surplus population) before they were drawn into the world commodity-exchange system. Today they tend to be experiencing capitalist development in cities and key resource sectors while in the countryside cash crops are replacing subsistence agriculture without major reforms in the land tenure arrangements that had led to surplus population under the traditional system.[8] Add malaria control, smallpox vaccination campaigns, and other infant mortality–reducing measures, and the level of population pressure in the countryside should encourage either fragmentation of holdings and/or migration to the cities. Given the vagaries of the commodity cycle in the world market and the small size of these countries' "modern industrial" (and frequently capitalist, export-oriented) sector, it follows that the growth of urban jobs falls increasingly short of the supply of hopeful job-seekers. (This phenomenon is often known as "overurbanization"—Hauser, 1963; Browning, 1967.) Moreover, most of these countries are too poor to have adequate welfare programs.

In general, where viable subsistence opportunities exist for *females* in such societies, the probabilities are high for flexible bilateral kinship, and various manifestations of matrifocal families, including female-headed units. But the absence of welfare and the fact that the size of the surplus population may easily get out of hand may have especially disastrous consequences for such family units in this type of society.[9]

3. *Western industrial nations.* The situation in many of these countries is complicated by their exchange of marginal populations (when the economy is expanding, some northwestern European countries import as temporary workers some of the reserve labor force of countries to the south; the influx of illegal Latin and Caribbean immigrants is the U.S. analogue); we shall confine our attention to the United States. Here we find both a comprehensive welfare system and relatively high proportions of female-headed families among the urban poor. Moreover, scholars have argued that the welfare system, especially the program known as Aid to Families with Dependent Children (AFDC), actually promotes female-headed households by making it difficult for a family to get assistance while an able-bodied male head lives in the house (Safa, 1964).

A stronger criticism of U.S. public assistance charges that in this affluent country the primary effect—and perhaps purpose—of welfare "has been *to guarantee a marginal work force at the bottom of the economic order"* (Sackrey, 1973: 111, emphasis in original). Piven and Cloward (1971) make a forceful and detailed argument that the chief function of relief is to regulate labor by (1) expanding relief to restore order when social conditions such as "mass unemployment" threaten turbulence (post-Watts-riot welfare expenditures tend to support this view);[10] and (2) treating welfare recipients in times of full employment in such a degrading and punitive manner as to convince the laboring masses that this is a fate to be avoided if even the "meanest labor at the meanest rates" can be obtained (p. 4). In other words, welfare and unemployment compensation are pitched sufficiently below the prevailing wage rates as to make them a subsistence maintenance program into which surplus labor (especially male surplus) can be safely pushed in and easily pulled out as political-economic conditions warrant.[11] To Piven and Cloward, "relief arrangements are ancillary to economic arrangements" (p. 3).

But why should relief arrangements favor the formation of female-headed units when government rhetoric (e.g., the "Moynihan report") condemns that type of family as disorganized, crime producing, and poverty perpetuating? Faced with this paradox, should we give greater credence to the "relief arrangements" or to the rhetoric? Levin (1973), writing about why U.S. schools are financed to invest so much more money in wealthy than in poor pupils, invokes what he terms the "principle of correspondence" to argue that we should give greater weight to the activities and outcomes of a long established institutional sector than to its official liturgy.[12]

By this criterion, then, we find that despite conflicting and often crosscutting interests among different sectors of industry, southern versus northern states, and a patchwork of welfare and unemployment compensation laws, one outcome is clear:[13] policies that consistently favor the long-term sustenance of only women and children (among the able-bodied) have been with us for a long time. Not only are the existing number of marginal women and their households sustained, but we have never heard of a woman's welfare check being cut for an extra child. So it seems reasonable to take the long established built-in mechanisms that encourage and maintain female-headed households (albeit below the poverty line)[14] as an indication that this type of arrangement is successfully reproducing the next generation of the "marginal work force at the bottom of the economic order."

In answer to our second question, concerning the articulation of female-headed families and the surplus labor population in these different types of societies, we may conclude: in agrarian and Third World societies, the absence of welfare seems to mean that the crucial determinant will be the extent to which the woman can achieve a viable subsistence by her own and/or her children's efforts. Since the jobs open to such women might safely be characterized as marginal, and since welfare is not generally available, a woman might need both independent access to employment and the contribution of some of her children before making a go of a female-headed unit. This points to using children as possible solutions to the problem of her poverty (although it may not mean that women without resident husbands have more children than women of the same class with resident husbands). The individuation of property and the unit of labor make the mother-headed household much more likely in the Third World than in the agrarian situation. In the United States, by contrast, the economically marginal woman heading her own family has access to a welfare system that guarantees against starvation. If she stays on it, she may not be penalized for having additional children, and if she goes off welfare, she is unlikely to get beyond the status of "working poor," that is, become a member of a volatile, ill-paid secondary labor force[15] where once again a larger number of children may ultimately turn out to be a bonus if she can smooth out fluctuations in resources by her access to a flexible kin-based exchange network. Because of the nature of the welfare system, we must conclude that the articulation of the female-headed household with the larger political economy seems most direct in the case of the United States, where such a unit is encouraged to form and grow by long-standing laws.

Information about Female-Headed
Households in the U.S. Census

Despite the rather broad discussion of the implications of our five structural conditions presented in the preceding pages, what we are actually able to test at this point is limited by the available data. We shall propose that in the United States structure and not race is involved in producing high proportions of mother-headed units among certain sectors of the population—specifically, poor, urban residents. This we shall test with published data from the U.S. Census.

As we have pointed out above, much of the discussion of female-headed families in the United States is framed in terms of the phenomenon being one of social pathology among poor urban *blacks*. And a first glance at the figures tend to confirm that impression. According to the 1970 census of the United States, 23.1 percent of all urban households are female-headed (U.S. Bureau of the Census, 1973a: 957-959). By race, however, this breaks down as follows: blacks, 35.0 percent female-headed units; Spanish heritage, 18.4 percent; and others (mostly whites), 21.8 percent. Since both blacks and the Spanish-surnamed tend to be poorer than whites and the black rate is nearly double the Spanish rate, the notion that this is a specifically racial problem seems initially plausible.

To test the structural hypothesis, however, we shall break down the total urban population to examine categories of low income. Income data in the 1970 census pertain to the preceding year, 1969. For a family of four the poverty line in 1969 was said to be at $3,700 (Stein, 1970: 3). At low-income levels, the census graduates income in intervals of $1,000. As a rough approximation of the really poor—those well below the poverty line—we examine data for urban households with income under $2,000 in 1969. Even remembering that the data refer to households, not families, and thus can include people living alone such as elderly widows, we find it sobering that 64.5 percent of the urban households with income under $2,000 are female-headed. Broken down by race, the figures are even more interesting: blacks, 65.2 percent female-headed households; Spanish heritage, 52.2 percent; and others (including Orientals and native Americans, but overwhelmingly whites), 65.1 percent. Thus the figures for black and white American households at the lowest level of income are nearly *identical* with respect to the proportion that is female-headed.

Although we do not have data, the lower figure among Spanish-surnamed people may in part be explained by the problem of illegal immigration. People who are in the United States illegally are less likely to risk the female-headed-family-facilitating welfare rolls. If an accurate count of people of Spanish heritage were possible, moreover, it might show a male-skewed sex ratio of the sort found among other immigrant streams that would give the females of the category more opportunity to remain in male-headed households.

Now let us examine the data on urban households earning under $4,000 in 1969, which, given average household size, should still overwhelmingly pertain to people at or below the poverty line. Female-headed households are still in the majority—55.3 percent. By race the figures show: black, 59.2 percent female-headed; Spanish heritage, 43.9 percent; and other (again overwhelmingly white), 55.1 percent. With level of income controlled, then, the difference between blacks and whites in proportion of female-headed households seems much too slight to provide the basis for a theory of racial pathology. These data appear in Table 8–1.

As the foregoing data intimate and as Table 8–1 corroborates, the reason the total figures are so misleading is that median incomes are sharply different for the three racial categories. (The table also gives data to calculate the extent of the sex gap in income. The median income of a household headed by a white female was 37.3 percent that of a household headed by a white male and 52.9 percent that of a household headed by a black male. Meanwhile, incomes of households headed by black males averaged 70.6 percent of those headed by white males.)

Reflecting once again on the five conditions discussed above, we should not find it surprising that in the United States a majority of the poorest households of even urban whites should be female-headed. Two factors in particular seem important: (1) the high rate of female participation in the U.S. labor force (as of March 1970, 43 out of every 100 women over 16 were in the labor force [Stein, 1970: 6], and the figure has risen since); and (2) its fail-safe welfare system, Aid to Families with Dependent Children, which underwrites their survival.

The Mother-Child Residential Unit

Early in this chapter we noted that Murdock and Wilson had stated that the ultimate explanation of the link between ethnicity and the mother-child residential unit should be sought in social and economic conditions in Africa. Now we shall explore those conditions, but in a context not confined to Africa. Our data will be derived from Murdock's Ethnographic Atlas (1967), and hence we shall be limited in our study by the variables he has coded.

TABLE 8-1. Numbers of U.S. Urban Households by Selected Levels of Income in 1969 and by Sex and Race of Head, 1970

Race and Sex of Head of Household	N	%	Median Income	Households with Income under $2,000		Households with Income under $4,000	
				N	%	N	%
Total	47,672,276	100.0	$ 8,920	4,998,230	100.0	10,152,905	100.0
Male	36,670,772	76.9	10,431	1,773,922	35.5	4,534,666	44.7
Female	11,001,504	23.1	3,892	3,224,308	64.5	5,618,239	55.3
Black	5,259,391	100.0	5,740	1,004,485	100.0	1,909,805	100.0
Male	3,417,324	65.0	7,363	349,111	34.8	779,653	40.8
Female	1,842,067	35.0	3,038	655,374	65.2	1,130,152	59.2
Spanish Heritage	2,057,818	100.0	7,282	227,802	100.0	507,066	100.0
Male	1,679,156	81.6	8,144	108,794	47.8	284,213	56.1
Female	378,662	18.4	3,317	119,008	52.2	222,853	43.9
Other[a]	40,355,067	100.0	b	3,765,943	100.0	7,736,034	100.0
Male	31,574,292	78.2	b	1,316,017	34.9	3,470,800	44.9
Female	8,780,775	21.8	b	2,449,926	65.1	4,265,234	55.1

Source: U.S. Bureau of the Census. Census of Population: 1970. Vol. 1. Characteristics of Population. Part 1, U.S. Summary–Section 2, Table 258, pp. 960–961.

[a]The "other" category is derived by subtraction of black and Spanish heritage from the total. Since the proportion of Orientals and native Americans is very small, it is virtually equivalent to white

[b]Since values for the "other" category were derived by subtraction, no values for median income were available for this category.

We have been considering two mother-child forms of household: the mother-headed family and the mother-child dwelling unit. These two forms of household arise among quite different types of societies, but they do share two common elements. These are: (1) that the woman have the chance for a relatively autonomous subsistence contribution—in other words, that she be able to participate in production and control the allocation of at least a part of the fruits of her labors, or that she derive an equivalent amount of power from her embodiment of autonomous resources other than her own labor power (e.g., she may retain control of part of the bridewealth she costs her husband's kin group, or represent a needed politico-military alliance, or inherit from her own kin group); and (2) that those in control of the larger political economy find it in their interests that she be maintained in a specifically mother-child household unit. The two forms immediately part company in that the mother-headed family is just that, whereas even though the woman in the mother-child dwelling may have a home of her own, she is part of a larger polygynous family, of which she is not the head.

Murdock and Wilson (1972: 278) say that among the social and economic conditions that seem correlated with the mother-child dwelling unit are "the widespread occurrence of polygyny and slavery, both of which are appreciably more prevalent in Negro Africa than in any other major region of the world." We have found that the mother-child dwelling sometimes occurs—even in Africa—in societies without slavery, but never to our knowledge in the absence of polygyny.

Specifically, we expect the mother-child residence to be most common: (1) where women are concentrated, especially as producers, by general polygyny; (2) in the home territory of the husband's kin (i.e., marital residence with husband's kin and/or patrilineal descent); and (3) where women make a substantial contribution to the husband's kin's subsistence resources (either by their own labor, or through resources they embody or control).

These conditions are expected to be more common among societies practicing extensive hoe agriculture than among societies involved in other modes of subsistence. The data of the Ethnographic Atlas reveal that women are important contributors to hoe agriculture, men being the dominant labor force in only 16 percent of the world's extensive hoe cultivation societies. Perhaps this is because the demands of hoe agriculture do not seem to conflict with simultaneous child-care responsibilities (Brown, 1970; Blumberg, 1974). Moreover, most extensive agricultural societies are at intermediate levels of societal development. They seem already to have begun the route to stratification and societal complexity by attempting to increase production beyond the food and replacement stock needs of the group. In other words, they are attempting to realize the superior productive potential of extensive hoe agriculture, as compared with incipiently agricultural modes of production, by deliberate efforts to produce and accumulate surplus.

Elsewhere we have argued that the concentration of producers in a familial system of high complexity and the elaboration of the unilineal descent group are social organizational forms that flourish at intermediate levels of societal complexity—that is, after the beginning of deliberate surplus accumulation, but before the individuation of property and the growing power of the state combine to give youth subsistence opportunities not tied to family-controlled resources while undermining the economic basis of the corporate descent group (Blumberg and Winch, 1972, 1973; Blumberg, Winch, and Reinhardt, 1974). So too, we suggest, with mother-child residence.

All of the elements of the package we have been discussing—residence with husband's kin (and an associated phenomenon, payment of bridewealth to the wife's kin group for the loss of her services); unilineal corporate descent groups predominantly on the patri-side; the importance of extensive hoe agriculture; a high contribution of women to subsistence production; and their concentration as producers in general polygyny—tend to go together, at the predicted intermediate levels of societal complexity, in Africa. And Africa, of course, is where most instances of mother-child residence are found. We believe that it is this "package" rather than the "ethnic location" that influences mother-child residence.

To rephrase, if a woman who has a certain amount of strategic power—by virtue of her autonomous contribution to production, bridewealth vested in her, a political or military alliance she cements, or inheritance potential in her kin group—is brought to her husband's kin residence and/or descent group in a situation of general polygyny, there might well be a convergence of interest on the part of the woman and the husband's kin group in giving her the measure of independence represented by her own home. For the husband's kin group there is the desirability of insuring that her strategic resources (e.g., labor) remain within the group while keeping her from allying with others in a similar structural situation (e.g., the other co-wives in the household or village) and upsetting the household or kin group control structure. For the women, it represents a gain in autonomy and facilitates individual accumulation of property. Missionaries' sermons to the contrary, the status of women under polygyny is not necessarily low, even though they tend to reside with the husband's kin group and have mere usufruct rights to the lands they cultivate. Often, however, they may dispose of surplus production and are in a position to amass wealth by production and/or trade. Sometimes, in addition, co-wives are able to unite and win important powers (as among the Lovedu, where the co-wives are cousins; see Murdock, 1949). Preventing such an occurrence may be behind not only the kin group's approval of separate residences for co-wives, but also the two most common organizations of production under African hoe horticulture: the farming of scattered individual plots by individual women (Kaberry, 1953) or more centralized activity under direct male supervision.

Indeed, the absence of a separate residence under conditions of general polygyny may mean that the women are not important producers and/or holders of other strategic resources. Then separate units will be unnecessary, and the husband's discipline, backed by community sanction, should keep co-wives in line.

One other possible reason for the absence of a separate residence for co-wives is sororal polygyny. Women raised as sisters are presumably able to cooperate under the same roof, the argument goes (Whiting and Child, 1953; Stephens,

1963). Also, we might add, they are biologically unlikely to be numerous enough to constitute the threat of a producer alliance. It would seem, then, that there are two basic solutions to the problem of general polygyny: separate residence in the case of nonsisters, and the same dwelling for sister co-wives. Looking at sororal polygyny worldwide on the basis of EA data not shown here, we find 65 instances of sisters sharing a residence (none of which are in Africa or the adjacent Circum-Mediterranean region) versus 17 cases of sisters with separate dwellings (all but 3 of which are in Africa). Interestingly enough, our contention that female producers should be more likely to be separately housed is borne out: the subsistence contribution of women in societies where the sisters are housed separately is much higher, on the average, than in the societies where sister co-wives share their husband's roof. The situation is parallel for nonsororal polygyny: separate residence goes with a greater probability that the society in question will have a female-dominated sexual division of labor. Although the figures for sororal versus nonsororal polygyny illustrate that Africa and the Circum-Mediterranean seem to have hit upon the nonsister-separate-residence solution to general polygyny while peoples in the other regions with general polygyny have opted for common housing of sisters, the correlation of separate residence with female subsistence production seems more revealing than that with region. In fact, we predict a positive correlation between the importance of females in subsistence and mother-child residence, worldwide, and we find it. Part A of Table 8-2 shows a significant gamma of .45. While this is only moderate compared to the .8 or better gammas (not shown) between mother-child residence and (1) marital residence with husband's kin, (2) high bridewealth, and (3) patrilineal descent, we predict that it is not spurious.

To summarize to this point, we have predicted general polygyny and residence with husband's unilineal kin as the common elements in situations of mother-child residence. We have found that general polygyny, due to a coding artifact in the EA, is a prerequisite for mother-child residence, while residence with husband's (unilineal) kin group occurs in 94 percent of the cases of mother-child dwellings. Moreover, 87 percent of the mother-child residence societies fall into the highest category of brideprice, and 61 percent of them are dependent on extensive hoe cultivation as their dominant subsistence activity. Strong as these relationships are, we feel that when they are applied as controls, they will *not* wash out the basic relationship between a sexual division of labor in which women are important and the provision of separate mother-child dwellings. Nor, we argue, will holding region constant by examining only African cases eliminate the relationship, even though 71 percent of all African societies have mother-child residence.

As our first test of conditions conducive to mother-child residence, we predict that the relationship between sexual division of labor and mother-child residence will hold up when we apply successive controls from the rest of the "package," including limiting the test to Africa, where the package characterizes the overwhelming majority of societies. First, we control by eliminating societies lacking general polygyny, since EA coding categories make it impossible for them

TABLE 8-2. Testing the Relationship of Sexual Division of Labor with Mother-Child Residence for Spuriousness

PART A. The Basic Relationship Worldwide
Sexual Division of Labor in the Dominant Subsistence Activity

Household	Labor Force				Female Contribution to Subsistence Average Score[a]
	Male Dominant	Intermediate	Female Dominant	Total	
Mother-Child	14.3%	28.5%	39.9%	25.9%	40.9%
	(56)	(65)	(112)	(233)	
Other	85.6	71.5	60.1	74.1	32.4
	(335)	(163)	(169)	(667) Σ = 900	

$\gamma = .45$
$(\chi^2 = 51.2, 2df, p < .00001)$

PART B. Sex Division of Labor–Mother-Child Residence among Societies with (a) General Polygyny in (b) Africa

Household	Male Dominant	Intermediate	Female Dominant	Total	Average Score
Mother-Child	75.0%	88.7%	92.7%	87.7%	45.1%
	(36)	(47)	(102)	(185)	
Other	25.0	11.3	7.3	12.3	38.5
	(12)	(6)	(8)	(26) Σ = 211	

$\gamma = .46$
$(\chi^2 = 9.8, 2df, p = .0075)$

PART C. The Relationship among Societies with (a) General Polygyny in (b) Africa practicing (c) Extensive Agriculture having (d) Marital Residence among Husbands' Kin; and (e) Highest Brideprice

Household	Male Dominant	Intermediate	Female Dominant	Total	Average Score
Mother-Child	62.5%	84.0%	92.5%	86.8%	48.3%
	(10)	(21)	(74)	(105)	
Other	37.5	16.0	7.5	13.2	41.9
	(6)	(4)	(6)	(16) Σ = 121	

$\gamma = .59$
$(\chi^2 = 8.1, 2df, p = .0177)$

PART D. The Relationship among Societies with (a) General Polygyny in (b) Africa practicing (c) Extensive Agriculture having (d) Descent = Patrilineal, and (e) Highest Brideprice

Household	Male Dominant	Intermediate	Female Dominant	Total	Average Score
Mother-Child	61.5%	85.7%	92.3%	86.9%	48.1%
	(8)	(18)	(60)	(86)	
Other	38.5	14.3	7.7	13.1	40.7
	(5)	(3)	(5)	(13)	
				99	

$\gamma = .57$
$(\chi^2 = 0.5, 2df, p = .0387)$

[a]This is an index composed of female contributions to five subsistence activities: gathering, hunting, fishing, herding, and agriculture. A score of 40.0 would indicate that women did a total of 40% of the work in their society's subsistence base (and that the males' score would be 60%). Worldwide, for the societies of the EA, the median female contribution to subsistence is around 37%.

to be coded as having the mother-child dwelling form. At this point, we also drop non-African societies, predicting that even within African societies with general polygyny, mother-child residence is more likely where women are important producers of subsistence. Part B of Table 8-2 shows that the gamma remains the same (.46), and even though we have dropped from 900 to 211 cases, the relationship remains significant.

To summarize the presentation of a whole series of control tables, in Part C of Table 8-2 we shall add three more controls: residence with husband's kin; highest level of bridewealth (either substantial brideprice or exchange of women); and extensive hoe agriculture as the dominant base of subsistence. This brings us down to 121 cases but produces a gamma of .59, which remains significant.

Finally, we present Part D of Table 8-2 to show what happens when patrilineal descent is substituted for marital residence with husband's kin in the series of controls used in Part C. Since marital residence is with husband's kin even in the situation of matrilineal descent with avunculocal residence (i.e., where the groom goes to live with his mother's brother), we end up with fewer cases than in Part C—only 99. But the gamma is still .56 and still significant.

In sum, restricting our attention to societies within Africa characterized by the variables we have identified as strongly associated with mother-child residence, we have confirmed our prediction. The relationship between the importance of women's contribution to subsistence and mother-child dwelling has not washed out.

A second exploration of our notion of the determinants of a "home of one's own" for co-wives involves the Automatic Interaction Detector (AID). We begin by restricting the AID run to societies with general polygyny. Of the 1,170 societies of the Ethnographic Atlas, 564 have general polygyny. Since AID requires every case to have a value on every variable under analysis and not every society did, we emerged with 273 societies on which to examine our ideas as to the major variables found in the EA that influence the mother-child household.

First, to measure the potential resources that might win a separate house for a co-wife, we include three variables: sexual division of labor in the dominant subsistence activity; bridewealth; and inheritance of movable property. The EA contains codes on the inheritance of both real property and movable property. We chose movable property because of the large (and expected) association of mother-child residence with residence with husband's kin. So if the woman is to inherit something that can be easily convertible to a resource relevant for the husband's kin group, it would seem necessary to be portable (e.g., money, tools, herds, slaves) rather than fixed (e.g., land, coconut palms). Our reasoning was that if co-wives were important in the production of subsistence, commanded a high brideprice (especially if some of it remained in the women's rather than their parents' control, which unfortuantely is not specified in the EA codes), and were persons to or through whom movable property was inherited, they would be more likely to have separate housing.

Second, to measure the fact that mother-child residence is much more likely where the co-wife joins the husband's kin group, we chose two variables: prevalent marital residence and system of descent.

Third, to tap a variable that is important in determining the sexual division of labor, the level of societal complexity, and in fact many of the other variables in this analysis, we include subsistence economy as our basic measure of the techno-economic base.

Fourth, we measure various additional indicators of societal complexity, in keeping with our prediction that the mother-child residence phenomenon is most prevalent at intermediate levels of societal complexity—in other words, is curvilinearly related with what we may term "evolutionary" variables. Those we include are stratification, political complexity, number of craft-specialized occupations, and permanence of settlement. These four indexes of societal complexity complete our basic list of 10 predictors.

In addition, however, there is the potentially confounding variable of region (i.e., is it really an ethnically black African phenomenon?). We have argued that "Africa" seems to stand for a summary or surrogate measure of a whole package of traits (of which the residence, descent, brideprice, and subsistence economy predictors, the general polygyny filter, and the mother-child dependent variable are components) that go together for functional rather than racial or even geographic diffusion reasons. To test this idea we shall run AID twice—once without region included among the predictors, and again with it. If we are right, the total percentage of variance explained should not be significantly less when region is eliminated from the analysis.

The results confirm our expectation. In both analyses the predictor variables accounted for 58 percent of the variance. As a comparison of Figures 8-1 and 8-2 will reveal, however, the decision to incorporate or to exclude region changes the appearance of the branching "tree" that is AID's hallmark. Let us follow the two trees as the program attempts to isolate the highest versus the lowest branches, that is, those leading to the group of societies maximally and minimally likely to have separate mother-child dwellings.

First we shall consider the AID run from which region was excluded. The first branch is formed by splitting the 273 societies (64 percent of which have separate mother-child residences for co-wives) into two groups on the basis of subsistence economy. Those with extensive hoe agriculture, herding, or intensive agriculture with or without irrigation are put into the upper branch (N = 206, 80 percent with mother-child units) that will eventually isolate the societies most likely to have separate mother-child dwellings for co-wives. Let us follow this upper branch to its apex—the set of societies having the highest incidence of mother-child residence. The next split is on the variable of brideprice, with eight societies having the two lowest brideprice categories (token exchange of gifts, or total absence of brideprice) being split away. (As we had expected, these have a lower incidence of mother-child residence.) The main upper branch next divides on sexual division of labor, separating societies where females predominate in the main activity of subsistence. The 88 female-labor societies form an "end group" in that no other meaningful sub-branches are split off from them. And we find that 91 percent of this end group have the mother-child household.[16]

To summarize the results of this first AID tree, from which region was ex-

Figure 8-1 AID Tree for Mother-Child Residence Among Societies with General Polygyny, Region Excluded**

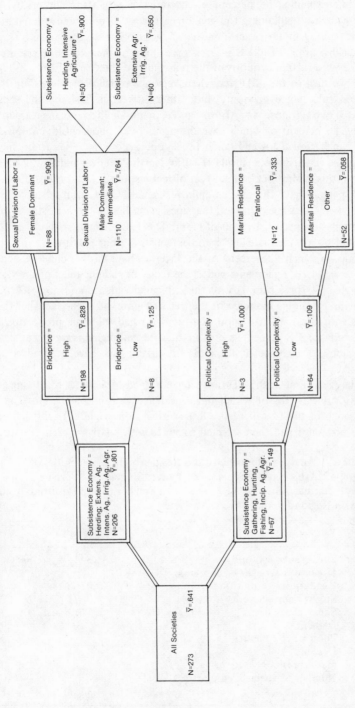

*Note that the proportion of societies with mother-child residence is almost as high for this end-group as in that indicated as our maximum.

**Double lines signify theoretically predicted main branches leading to maximum and minimum values of dependent variable.

167

cluded, we explained 58 percent of the variance with 10 predictors, with sub-sistence economy explaining the greater part, and—as predicted—sexual division of labor figuring in the determination of the maximum occurrence of mother-child dwelling units. (Table 8-3 gives a summary of the explained variance and note 16 gives a further synopsis of the remainder of the tree in Figure 8-1.)

Now we turn to the AID tree where region was included. Here the first split is not on subsistence economy, but rather on region. Thereby the sample is split into two groups: an African and Circum-Mediterranean group of 184 societies, 86 percent of which have the mother-child household, comprising an upper branch, and a lower branch of 89 polygynous societies from the other four regions (East Eurasia, Insular Pacific, North America, and South America). Of course this is Murdock's (1967) set of regions. In the latter set of 89 societies only 15 percent have the mother-child residences. Once again let us follow the upper branch to its apex. In fact, that apex is reached in the next step, when the tree branches on sexual division of labor. The 132 societies with either female-dominated or intermediate labor forces constitute our maximum mother-child end group, in which 92 percent of the societies have mother-child residences.[17] Thus, for this tree, region emerged as the factor explaining most of the variance. (See Table 8-4 for a summary of the explained variance and note 17 for a re-view of the remaining branches of the tree of Figure 8-2.) The fact that the AID analysis with and without region as a predictor had the same proportion of ex-plained variance, 58 percent, seems to indicate that region is serving as a symbol for the joint occurrence of the sorts of variables we have referred to as our package.

Let us recall that both AID runs were confined to societies practicing general polygyny, nine tenths of which have residence with husband's kin. The maxi-mum branch of the tree in Figure 8-1 (with region excluded) split first on sub-sistence economy and then selected societies with relatively high brideprice, in

TABLE 8-3. Analysis of Mother-Child Residence in 273 Societies of Ethnographic Atlas Having General Polygyny: "Explained" Variance Contributed at Each Step of AID, by Size of Smaller Group Resulting from Split—with Region Excluded from Analysis

Step	Indicator	$N \geqslant 15$	$N < 15$
1	Subsistence economy	.3418	
2	Mode of marriage (brideprice)		.0605
3	Gender differentiation	.0165	
4	Subsistence economy	.0271	
5	Social classes		.0167
6	Descent		.0161
7	Political complexity		.0362
8	Descent		.0133
9	Marital residence		.0118
10	Number of specialized occupations		.0412
	Total .5812 =	.3854 +	.1958

Figure 8-2 AID Tree for Mother-Child Residence Among Societies with General Polygyny, Region Included**

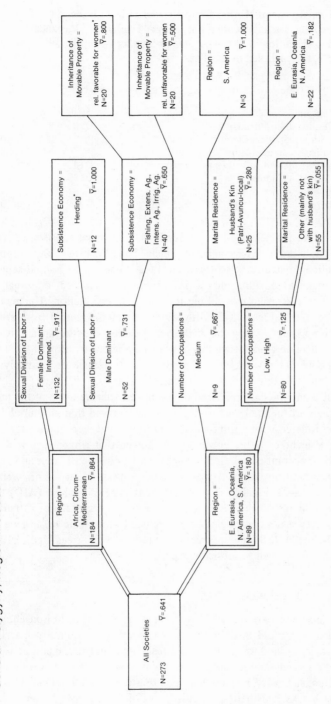

*Because the N is so small, we do not treat this as the maximum end-group.

**Double lines signify theoretically predicted main branches leading to maximum and minimum values of dependent variable.

169

TABLE 8–4. Analysis of Mother-Child Residence in 273 Societies of Ethnographic Atlas Having General Polygyny: "Explained" Variance Contributed at Each Step of AID, by Size of Smaller Group Resulting from Split–with Region Included in Analysis

Step	Indicator	$N \geqslant 15$	$N < 15$
1	Region	.4472	
2	Gender differentiation	.0205	
3	Number of specialized occupations		.0378
4	Subsistence economy		.0180
5	Inheritance of movable property	.0143	
6	Marital residence	.0139	
7	Region		.0281
	Total .5798 = .4959 + .0839		

which women are the primary labor force in the dominant subsistence activity. Principally, these are extensive agriculturalists. Thus the results seem supportive of our paradigm that asserts co-wives are most likely to be housed separately when they make a contribution too important to be ignored—or foregone—to the resources of the group controlling the means of production. The maximum branch of the tree in Figure 8–2 (with region included) resulted from an initial split on region. Then, among the African and Circum-Mediterranean groups, it reached its top value among societies in which the sexual division of labor in the main subsistence activity was either predominantly female or relatively equal by gender. Here, too, our predicted sex variable emerges.

Finally, it seems we have rendered untenable an interpretation of the mother-child dwelling unit on the basis of race. First, we showed that mother-child residence was correlated with a number of conditions that were more prevalent in Africa than elsewhere. Next, however, we showed that what we viewed as the substantively important correlation between sexual division of labor and mother-child residence held up within Africa—even when these other factors were held constant (Table 8–2). Finally, using a different type of analysis (AID) to predict mother-child residence, we explained the same percentage of variance (58 percent) whether region was included or excluded as a predictor, and we found that both the region-included and region-excluded AID "trees" led directly to the importance of women as subsistence producers.

Summary and Conclusions

We have analyzed two very different types of mother-child household: the female-headed household most prevalent among the economically marginal in wage-labor societies, and the mother-child residential unit found among societies with general polygyny and residence with the husband's kin or descent group. In the case of female-headed households, the literature for a long time had focused primarily on blacks and their specific history. In the case of mother-child residential units in polygynous societies, Murdock and Wilson (1972) did speak of the phenomenon as concentrated in the Negro societies of Africa, but they counseled a search for an "ultimate explanation" among social and economic conditions.

For both of these types of mother-child family, we have managed to eliminate any effect of race while highlighting the importance of the relationship of the woman to her society's mode of production as crucial for the genesis of the mother-child familial form in question. For its persistence, we have speculated, we must look to the degree to which the mother-child household serves the interests of those who control the society's political economy.

Notes

1. In a less blatant form, the writings about the "culture of poverty" also blame the victim. And to Oscar Lewis, who originated the "culture of poverty" approach, one of its characteristics is matrifocality. Since Lewis was not studying blacks and claims cross-cultural validity for his approach, this represents an extension of the racial social pathology focus to a worldwide nonracial perspective. Adherents of this approach from the liberal Lewis (see especially 1966) to the ultraconservative Banfield (1970) may point to structural conditions (e.g., high unemployment rates, low wages) as influences in creating the poor. But what keeps them poor, these authors argue, is their self-perpetuating culture of poverty. Nonetheless, matrifocal families play a less central role in the transmission of poverty in this approach than in that of Moynihan.

2. According to Greenfield, "The sugar industry has developed to the limits of the present level of technology and cannot be expanded by capital investment" (pp. 69–70).

3. Although he does not name it, Greenfield has invoked the specter of Galton's problem, which was discussed in Chapter 5.

4. Elsewhere (Blumberg and Winch, 1973; Blumberg, Winch, and Reinhardt, 1974) we have discussed three major components of the mode of production: the subsistence technology, the division of labor, and the social relations of production. The first two are jointly considered the "forces of production," in distinction to the "social relations of production" in many Marxian definitions (see, e.g., Edwards et al., 1972: 50).

5. Females might occasionally emerge as heads of three-generation families under some unusual corporate family circumstances (e.g., in mother-daughter matrilineal inheritance systems, which are extremely rare; or in the instances where the widow in a patrilineal inheritance system retains control of her husband's assets, these more frequently pass to the sons or husband's brother without the widow becoming family head).

6. Ester Boserup (1974: 18) notes: "In most developing countries . . . nearly all of the women employed in urban areas do part time domestic work or are engaged in such activities as crafts, home industries or trade. In these home-based occupations, it is possible to continue child-bearing and earning wages. In fact, children, from an early age, can contribute to such enterprises."

7. Folklore has it that rich heiresses and successful Hollywood actresses are the most multiply divorced categories of females in the United States. If true,

it may in part reflect the low resource gap between these women and their mates. For a more general discussion of relative resources of each spouse and domestic power, see Scanzoni (1972).

8. These comments concerning surplus labor are more applicable to Asia (and, to a certain extent, parts of Latin America), with their plow-agriculture agrarian base, than to sub-Saharan Africa, where the traditional subsistence base was (and still is for the most part) hoe horticulture. Surplus labor populations under traditional conditions seem generally confined to the more complex, stratified, and urbanized agrarian systems.

9. It may be that the sorts of exchange networks described for lower income marginal categories, and especially those of mother-headed households (e.g., Stack, 1970, 1974, for the U.S.; Peattie, 1963, for Ciudad Guayana, Venezuela), require the input of at least some surplus in order to be viable. Otherwise, with no surplus in the system and some members falling below zero net available resources, the network might increase the level of general hardship without necessarily saving the worst-off members—and collapse. The visible numbers of little shoeshine/errand boys on the streets of certain Third World cities are sometimes popularly attributed to a two-step process of poverty and abandonment: the father leaving the mother, and she leaving the eldest male child to shift for himself, more or less. The family origins and reasons for homelessness of such children constitute empirical questions, but in the absence of general welfare it can be speculated that the failure or absence of the exchange network might be associated with such outcomes.

10. According to Sackrey (1973: 92–93), "The number of families receiving AFDC funds more than doubled during the 1960's, though it had increased by only 17 percent during the 1950's; and in New York and California, the rise during the 1960's was even greater than the national average, with most of the increase occurring after 1965." A summary of Sackrey's figures taken from the *Statistical Abstract of the United States: 1971*, p. 271, shows total government expenditures on public aid to the poor at $4.1 billion in 1960; $6.3 billion in 1965; $8.8 billion in 1967; and $13.2 billion in 1969. Urban riots began in 1964, but clearly other factors also influenced the dramatic post-1965 increase in welfare expenditures.

11. Sackrey notes of the Piven and Cloward argument that it "also explains the relatively low welfare payments in southern states. Since wages in the South are relatively low, it is necessary, in order to regulate the labor force, to keep welfare payments below local wages so that when jobs do appear, welfare recipients can be forced into them at wages higher than their welfare payments" (p. 112). On the other hand, one can argue that low and stringent southern welfare and unemployment benefits encouraged migration at a time of massive agricultural mechanization and displacement of the rural agricultural population. Piven and Cloward cite a Presidential Commission on Rural Poverty finding that in only 15 years, between 1950 and 1965, U.S. farm output rose by 45 percent while farm employment fell 45 percent. Accompanying this has been a great wave of rural-urban migration. With both wage and welfare rates more attractive in the North, many black farm families (4 million since 1940) joined the tide. Especially in the 1960s, when black voting first became a realistic possibility in the South, a welfare policy that encouraged migration must have seemed attractive to local officials (see note 13 below).

12. Despite official rhetoric of equal opportunity, "schools are financed in such a way that they invest far more in the children of the rich than in the children of the poor . . . tracking and curriculum serve to sort and select children in such a way that the children of blue-collar occupations . . . and the children of the elite will be socialized for positions consonant with their class of origin," Levin writes (1973: 9). To some critics, nonetheless, these inequalities are the result of "institutional mindlessness." Instead, Levin suggests, in a stable social setting the schools' activities "will correspond to and serve the social, economic, and political relations" of the larger society. We apply Levin's principle of correspondence" to the long-established policies of the welfare sector.

13. Welfare is largely funded by Washington, but the states are primarily responsible for the programs and rates paid; administration is state or local (see Handler, 1972, for a good general discussion). States run the unemployment compensation programs pretty much as they see fit. With AFDC, "local government exercised most of the control and paid only about 10 percent of the cost; the states virtually exercised the rest of the control and paid only about one-third of the cost" (Handler, p. 116). Examples of conflicting interests are many. For instance, the interests of some politicians in a southern state in keeping welfare rates so low as to encourage out-migration of displaced black agricultural laborers who now have become actual or potential voters may conflict with those of a manufacturing city in the state which may favor a somewhat less penurious standard so as to insure that enough of a surplus labor force remains to take care of fluctuations in local labor needs at low costs to local industry. Conversely, northern cities and states may want a shrinking gap between northern and southern benefit levels so as to stem the tide of migration, and they may want more federal money to help keep welfare and unemployment payments high enough to stave off urban unrest without bankrupting them.

14. U.S. Department of Labor (1973: 8) figures show:

> Of the 6,191,000 families headed by women in March 1972, 2,100,000 or 34 percent, had incomes below the poverty line in 1971. The comparable proportion for families with a male head was 7 percent. Among those female-headed families where there were related children under age 18, 45 percent were poor. Of those families where the related children numbered five or more, 76 percent were poor. About one-fourth (27 percent) of all white female-headed families had incomes below the low-income level in 1971, but more than half (54 percent) of all black female-headed families had this little income. Thirty-seven percent of the white female-headed families with related children under age 18 were poor in 1971; the comparable proportion for black female-headed families was 60 percent.

In this context, it is interesting to note Stein's statistic that three fifths of female-headed households with children were receiving some welfare assistance. In fact, as Stein's (1970: 5) data show, female-headed households are becoming a larger proportion of the below-the-poverty-line population: "In 1969, 47 of every 100 poor families with children were headed by women. In 1959, the proportion was 28 out of 100."

15. The notion of a dual job market has been an important new development in economic theory (see Gordon, 1972, for an excellent discussion and numerous references). Here we find the ill-paid, often unstable jobs of the secondary labor force, jobs that lead nowhere: "they are not connected to job ladders of any sort" (Gordon, 1972: 45). They are often in small, nonconcentrated industries with low and volatile profit margins, high labor intensity, elastic demand, and intense competition; and even when they are not, women, minority groups, and

those with low education are disproportionately found holding them. These findings are supported by the results of the University of Michigan five-year longitudinal study (Morgan et al., 1974) of the factors influencing economic well-being among 5,000 U.S. families. They found that most of the major determinants of well-being were beyond individual control—for example, sex, race, education, and age. However, it turned out that "family composition change is the most important of all the variables we included in our analysis of changed well-being." Partly for this reason, there proved to be a considerable and surprising amount of movement in and out of poverty: "Only 9 percent of the 5,000 families were in the bottom fifth of the income distribution in each of the five years. On the other hand, 35 percent of the families were in the bottom fifth during at least one of the five years" (Chapman, 1974, reporting on the study). Concerning the relationship between sex of the household head and being consistently in poverty, the study found: "A family's chance of being persistently poor is about twice as great if the head is a woman" (Morgan et al., 1974: 336).

16. There is one other sub-branch that is almost as high on this upper section of the tree. It is formed from the group of societies with male-dominated or intermediate sexual division of labor by another split on the subsistence economy variable. Societies with herding or intensive agriculture as their dominant subsistence base (N = 50) prove to have mother-child residence in 90 percent of these cases. The other end group on the upper tree is composed of 60 irrigation or extensive agriculture societies in which 65 percent have mother-child dwellings.

The lower branch of the tree contains 67 gathering, hunting, fishing, or incipient agricultural societies of which only 15 percent have the mother-child unit. After dropping two high-political-complexity societies with mother-child residence, the computer splits the remainder (with low political complexity) on the variable of marital residence. Twelve societies with patrilocal residence are split away from the emergent minimum mother-child sub-branch; three have mother-child dwellings. The remaining 52 societies constitute our "minimum mother-child residence" end group—only 3 of the 52 cases (6 percent) have this household form.

17. Following out the remainder of the upper branch of Figure 7-2, we start with the sub-branch involving the male-dominated division of labor. It next splits on subsistence economy, where 12 herding societies, all with mother-child residence, are distinguished from the remaining 40 (fishing, extensive agricultural, intensive, or irrigated agricultural groups). These 40 split into two end groups of 20 each on the variable of inheritance of movable property. Where inheritance is matrilineal, or "other patrilineal heirs" are rewarded (Murdock, 1967, does not further specify, unfortunately), 80 percent of the 20 societies have mother-child residence; in the 20 where inheritance is either classically patrilineal or involves "daughters receiving less than sons," the proportion with mother-child residence is only 50 percent. The inheritance categories in the former instance might favor women relatively more, thus giving them enough of a resource to justify separate residence, but the coding is not sufficiently explanatory to judge.

Last, we follow the lower branch to the end group of societies with the minimum proportion of mother-child residence. The 89 societies from the remaining four world regions are first split on political complexity to spin off nine medium complex societies, which, furthermore, have one, two, or three occupations organized as crafts (an intermediate level), and a somewhat higher proportion of mother-child residence. Next, the main lower branch continues with the lowest (no specialized occupations) and highest (four such crafts) complexity societies— in accordance with our suggestion that the mother-child residence is maximal at intermediate levels of societal complexity. These high- and low-complexity societies are next split on marital residence, where those 25 societies with patrilocal or avunculocal (both husband's kin) patterns—and more mother-child residence—are split off. The remainder constitute our minimum mother-child household group, where only 5.5 percent of the remaining 55 societies have this form. (The last split separates three South American societies, all of which have mother-child residence, from the remaining three world regions, a residual pool of 22 societies of which 18 percent have mother-child domiciles.)

Chapter 9

Inferring Minimum Structure from Function: Or Did the Bureaucracy Create the Mother-Child Family?

Robert F. Winch

Dyads of the Nuclear Family

Most women marry, and since the sex ratio of the nubile is usually near unity, so do most men. Most women bear children, and it appears that they usually marry before they deliver if not before they conceive their first children. Out of this triad of human beings comes what Murdock (1949) has called the nuclear family.[1]

It has been a convention to regard this triadic family—husband, wife, offspring—as the basic unit or building block in the sociology of the family. In re-

Based on Winch (1975).

cent years, however, the unity of this formulation has been called into question. Richard Adams (1960) has pointed out that in numerous contexts, and he cites Central America in particular, the dyadic mother-child family seems both functional and stable. He and writers who are racially sensitive point out that the analyst who begins with the triadic nuclear family as a base is driven by inference to the regrettable conclusion that the mother-child family is a deviant and degenerate familial form. To overcome this state of affairs, Adams has proposed that the basic unit or building block for theorizing about the family should be the dyad rather than the nuclear triad. In my judgment Adams' formulation does provide a desirable flexibility in thinking about the family, and accordingly I accept his recommendation to regard the familial dyad as the basic familial unit.

The acceptance of Adams' recommendation raises the question as to whether or not there is some particular familial dyad that should be regarded as "basic," that is, of greater importance than other dyads. If we ignore the distinctions of age and gender among offspring, the nuclear family consists of three dyads: husband-wife, father-child, and mother-child.[2]

As I have argued in this book and elsewhere (Winch, 1963, 1971, 1972) analytically a society has five basic structures (economy, polity, church, school, family), each with a basic societal function, and that the basic societal function of the family is replacement (or reproduction). Obviously the sexual dyad is required to carry out the function of replacement, and it results in parent-child dyads. Of the three dyads noted above it can be argued that, although the sexual is necessary for reproduction, the copulative process is brief. On the other hand, the survival of the infant resulting from the reproductive function requires prolonged care by an adult, and that adult is the mother almost everywhere, under almost every level of societal complexity and variety of culture.

As Gough (1971) and van den Berghe (1973) point out, humans share with anthropoid apes a physiologic state of affairs that is conducive to the establishing of this dyad. This state of affairs centers on the relative immaturity of the newborn, their prolonged helplessness, their need for nurturance and protection if they are to survive, and the indisputable fact that they enter the world from their mothers' bodies whereas their paternity may be unknown. Scholars are not the only ones to take note of these considerations, as Radcliffe-Brown (1950: 77) remarks:

> In primitive societies, whether they have matrilineal or patrilineal institutions, it is normally recognized that the closest of all kinship bonds is that between mother and child.

In the same vein, Margaret Mead has written of the family as a mother with her child and a man to look after her. Barnes (1973) writes that there seems to be scientific consensus that a mother's response to her infant is to some degree innate or genetically determined, whereas there is no evidence that a father is programmed genetically to behave differentially to a child merely because he sired it. (See also Ainsworth, 1973.)

Do All Preindustrial Children Have Fathers?

Given the fact that a sexual relationship may be quite brief whereas a mother-child relationship should last at least long enough for the child to be able to fend for itself,[3] one might reasonably expect to find mother-child families rather than nuclear families predominating among simpler peoples. Such is not the case. Murdock reports that among gathering bands—and indeed among societies at a variety of levels of complexity—the nuclear family is universal, although in many cases it is embedded in larger familial systems (1949). Subsequent writers have challenged Murdock's claim. The Nayar on the Malabar Coast of India in the eighteenth century (Gough, 1960) and certain kibbutzim in Israel (Spiro, 1956) have been noted as negative cases, and other writers have been asserting that a frequently appearing form in some segments of complex societies is a mother-child family, sometimes with matrilineal extension (e.g., Adams, 1960; Blake, 1961; Clarke, 1957; Frazier, 1939; Gonzalez, 1969; Greenfield, 1966; Henriques, 1953; Otterbein, 1965; Rainwater, 1966; M. G. Smith, 1962; R. T. Smith, 1956; Stack, 1974).

What should we conclude about this dispute? Let us divide our conclusion into two parts in order to consider separately the relevant bodies of literature: ethnographic accounts of relatively simple societies written typically by anthropologists and studies of more complex societies using ethnographic techniques or sometimes the technique of the survey.

From the studies of simpler peoples we get the definite impression that normally a mother has a husband and a child has a father, although the genetrix and the pater may be different men and that difference may even be normatively recognized. The number of simple societies extant today and through history is of course unknown. In his Ethnographic Atlas, Murdock lists data on around 1,200 societies. There are a few societies on which the data are not complete with respect to the family—around a dozen—but in all of the rest the husband-father is reported to be a normal member of the familial system. On the basis of this very substantial summary of the ethnographic literature, it appears that there is at least 99 percent unanimity that the nuclear triad is present in the familial system.

The observation that the nuclear family is nearly universally present leads to the question: Do the reports we are considering pertain to behavior or to norms? The existence of mother-child familial patterns in more complex societies leads us to ask: What does this imply for Malinowski's "principle of legitimacy"?

A few pages back we noted the difficulty of determining whether an anthropologist is reporting actual or ideal patterns of the family. Barnes (1971: 32–35) cites the confusion between behavioral and normative data in the Ethnographic Atlas as one of his objections to the attempt to quantify such information. With this reservation in mind, what can we conclude about the husband-father in primitive societies? Although it may sound weak, the strongest conclusion we are justified in drawing without further investigation is that almost all accounts of life in the simpler societies report that the child belongs to a family that includes the father as well as the mother and that virtually nowhere is the contrary reported as either a cultural norm or a statistical fact.

Fathers in Developing and Developed Societies

With respect to complex societies, especially those developed enough to have good household statistics, we are able to see that the marital couple is a household norm and that a very high proportion of children live with both parents, but that there are segments of some of those societies where a resident husband-father is in the minority. U.S. data on this point were presented in Chapter 2 (see Table 2-3).

Although Malinowski lacked statistical support for his belief, he asserted that in all societies the father has been regarded as indispensable to the child (1929). He spoke of this as the "principle of legitimacy." In sociological terms what this means is that the family has the responsibility both to the society and to its offspring to give the child a familial identity by means of which members of the society are able to place the child. This is what was referred to in Chapter 1 as the position-conferring function. Malinowski was declaring that if the child had no pater, the child could not be accorded a position in the society. The phenomenon of mother-headed families in segments of developed societies has thrown this view into serious question. Some writers (e.g., Blake, 1961) seem to believe in the Malinowskian position whereas others (e.g., Henriques, 1953) demur. The facts seem to be that children from mother-child families do get identities from their mothers. In some settings the prestige accorded the identity is diminished if it comes from the mother rather than from the father. The dispute referred to above seems to have revolved around the question as to whether this was so, and if so, by how much. Fortes (1969: 258) has used the terms "half-legitimate" and "quasi-legitimate" to refer to this state of affairs.

As nearly as we can tell, then, among the simpler peoples marriage is nearly universal[4] —both with respect to all eligible adults in any given society and with respect to virtually all societies at a level of complexity below that of nation-state. With respect to the latter category of society, there tends to be a greater degree of cultural heterogeneity involving a variety of ethnicities and socioeconomic levels. While it would appear that marriage is the approved and usual state for eligible adults, there are within a number of societies subsocietal categories in which it is a recognized and perhaps majority practice for households to be female-headed, that is, to have no resident husband-father.

Some Questions about Husbands-Fathers

Granting the foregoing observations to be true, we are confronted with the following questions:

1. Why is there a husband-father in the familial system of nearly all simple societies?

2. Why does the statistical majority in the more complex societies show a pattern whereby there is a husband-father in the familial system?
3. Why is there a pattern of absence of husband-father in segments of the more complex societies, and what are the characteristics of those segments?
4. Does the absence of the husband-father result in a mother-child familial pattern?

The Husband-Father in Preindustrial Societies

Sumner and Keller saw marriage as a cooperative arrangement in the interest of self-maintenance (1927: vol. 3, pp. 1505, 1508). Murdock (1949: 8) has spoken of marriage as existing "only when the economic and the sexual are united into one relationship." In part, his explanation runs as follows:

> The man, perhaps, returns from a day of hunting, chilled, unsuccessful, and with his clothing soiled and torn, to find warmth before a fire which he could not have maintained, to eat food gathered and cooked by the woman instead of going hungry, and to receive fresh garments for the morrow, prepared, mended, or laundered by her hands. Or perhaps the woman has found no vegetable food, or lacks clay for pottery or skins for making clothes, obtainable only at a distance from the dwelling, which she cannot leave because her children require care; the man in his ramblings after game can readily supply her wants. Moreover, if either is injured or ill, the other can nurse him back to health. These and similar rewarding experiences, repeated daily, would suffice of themselves to cement the union. When the powerful reinforcement of sex is added, the partnership of man and woman becomes inevitable.

It appears that both among the higher apes and among humans at the simplest technological level (gathering and hunting), the probability of survival of the young is increased if the mother-child dyad is expanded into the triad of the nuclear family with a consequent gender-linked division of labor whereby the adult female specializes in child care while the adult male specializes in defense. As Gough (1971) remarks, moreover, the inclusion of the male into this familial group for both apes and humans seems abetted by the fact that—unlike the situation in many other species—female apes and humans are sexually active around the calendar.

In the previous paragraph I referred to a very crude division of labor as being the probable basis for an increased probability of survival of the mother-child dyad. Is there more that can be said about the gender-linked division of labor? After noting that the fact of some division of labor between the sexes is practically universal, Lévi-Strauss says that the actual tasks given to one sex or the other vary from one society to another: "The Boróro women till the soil while among the Zuñi this is man's work; according to tribe, hut building, pot making, weaving, may be incumbent upon either sex" (1960: 275).

It would be wrong, however, to regard hunting and child care as the only consistently gender-linked activities. Murdock and Provost (1973a) have analyzed the gender distribution of 50 technological activities or tasks in a sample of 185 preindustrial societies, deriving four categories of tasks: strictly masculine, largely masculine, "swing" activities (predominantly masculine in some regions but predominantly feminine in others), and largely feminine. They found no task that was universally feminine. "One can," they continue (p. 210), "name activities that are strictly feminine, e.g., nursing and infant care, but they fall outside the range of technological pursuits."

Among their strictly masculine tasks were hunting large land and aquatic fauna, smelting of ores and metalworking, and lumbering and working in wood. Their largely feminine activities included cooking, laundering, gathering fuel, and fetching water. Among the swing activities were generation of fire, preparation of skins, and the planting, tending, and harvesting of crops. With respect to feminine participation, Murdock and Provost quote with approval from an article by Judith Brown (1970: 1074) as follows:

> The degree to which women participate in subsistence activities depends upon the compatibility of the latter with simultaneous child-care responsibilities. Women are most likely to make a substantial contribution when subsistence activities have the following characteristics: the participant is not obliged to be far from home; the tasks are relatively monotonous and do not require rapt concentration; and the work is not dangerous, can be performed in spite of interruptions, and is easily resumed once interrupted.

Murdock and Provost add that such feminine tasks require nearly daily attention and for this reason are not compatible with many tasks that require protracted absence from the household—for example, warfare, hunting, fishing, and herding.

We may summarize the findings of Murdock and Provost and of Brown as follows:

1. Male activities tend to require strenuous physical exertion and strength; although female activities may demand a considerable output of energy, they are usually less demanding of great strength.
2. Male activities tend to require spatial mobility and absence from the hearth; female activities tend to be local.
3. Male activities may involve continuous effort for considerable blocks of time; female activities involve only a few hours at a time when they are done away from home.

Underlying points 2 and 3 is the implication that women (and not men) are responsible for rearing small children. As life is lived among the simpler peoples, this set of considerations, which Sumner, Keller, and Murdock think of as economic, provides the basis for interdependence between a man and a woman. To us this appears to be a plausible causal statement although we cannot be quite as convinced of its truth as was a Boróro informant who explained to Lévi-Strauss that the reason a 30-year-old fellow tribesman appeared unclean, ill fed, sad, and lonesome was that he was a bachelor (1960: 269).

In any case it seems reasonable to believe that in these relatively simple societies with their quite clearly defined gender roles, husband and wife are interdependent, and this is conducive to the survival of their children.

The Husband-Father in More Complex Societies

The second question posed on page 180 asks why the familial pattern of more complex societies tends to include the husband-father. Of course, the conventional answer to this question involves mate selection based on mutual love and procreation as an expression of that love. Another way of responding to the question—one that is more consistent with the functional views of Sumner and Murdock—comes from a study by Gonzalez (1969) about the Black Caribs of Guatemala. It is difficult, if not impossible, says Gonzalez, for one woman "to function effectively as a mother, housekeeper, wage earner, and cultivator all in one." With the coming of children, she continues, a woman finds it necessary to form a cooperative relationship with some other adult, whether or not she lives with that person. "It is only in societies that provide institutions such as nursery schools, supervised playgrounds, and the like, that a woman with children can successfully carry on alone" (1969: 99).

The passage from Gonzalez poses the following question: Since (or if) a mother with one or more small children cannot function effectively in all of the numerous roles mentioned, to whom does she turn for assistance in getting these responsibilities under control? Which of the various roles listed by Gonzalez can or must the woman carry out for herself, and which can or will she arrange to have fulfilled by someone else? Most women in complex societies apparently enter into nuclear families. Either they become full-time housewives and mothers during the greatest dependency of their children or, if employed, they turn to relatives, hire another woman, or pay an agency to fulfill many of the responsibilities of housewife and mother. This solution is in the spirit of the division of labor discussed on pages 180-181 above, which in one version or another has been around for several thousand years.

Conditions of the Absent Husband-Father

Under what conditions does a woman not take a husband to divide up the role set Gonzalez had characterized as onerous? Here we take up the third question from page 180. Steward and Gough have reminded us that under some conditions protection is a familial activity and, where this is so, males are highly useful. But here we are considering developing and developed societies in which the polity is at least nominally responsible for maintaining order, and hence for protecting persons. When the utility of the male as protector diminishes in importance, what considerations become salient in determining whether or not a woman takes a husband? Under these conditions the woman may believe that she is too young to "settle down yet" (Rainwater, 1966). Or she (or whoever else may be responsible for selecting her mate) may be unable to find a man whose present and potential characteristics appear to qualify him for fulfilling the desired roles, usually those of providing income and social status.[5] Assuming the young woman to be not unduly unattractive and her mate-selective criteria to be reasonable, these circumstances are most likely to occur at the bottom of the spectrum of socioeconomic statuses. In her investigation of the Black Caribs of Guatemala, Gonzalez concluded that the men's being involved in migrant wage labor was a necessary condition and that the migratory nature of the men's work (from villages to towns and cities) resulted in a low sex ratio (relatively few males per 100 females) and made it difficult for husband-wife couples to form and remain together.

Stack (1974) adds unemployment, underemployment, the insecurity and instability of employment of men, and welfare laws as conditions that discourage women from forming nuclear triads in the United States. She reports that the culture of the black ghetto she studied in the midwestern United States defined marriage as a risk to the woman and her children and a threat to the durability of her kin group. (Making a similar point about the Black Caribs, Gonzalez says that since a woman is never sure a man will return, it is a rare woman who can afford to detach herself from her consanguine group.) When a young woman in that ghetto first becomes pregnant, according to Stack, she and the prospective father do not usually set up housekeeping together but, rather, each remains in the home where she and he were raised. She does, however, look to him and especially to his female kin (mother and sisters) for some financial help. Clarke (1957) reports a similar pattern for Jamaica.

Pointing out that among the lower-class blacks of Guyana the household is primarily a child-rearing unit wherein the man provides economic support for the woman, R. T. Smith (1956, 1973) says a woman is likely to accept a man's authority during her child-bearing period and gradually thereafter to assert her autonomy.[6] The children derive nothing of importance from their father—neither property nor group membership. These men are wage laborers and are at the bottom of the economy. They have little prospect of steady employment, and there is little status differentiation among them. The mother early becomes the focus of her children's affections and with her children gradually becomes also the center of an economic and decision-making coalition. It is this centrality of the maternal role—whether the husband-father is present or absent—that Smith says characterizes the matrifocal family. In this study most female heads of households had passed through menopause, and the structure of the family tended to consist of the woman, her daughters, and their young children. A quite different state of affairs prevails in the upper fringe of this stratum. Where factors of prestige operate, the occupation of the husband-father becomes significant, and he becomes a reference point for others of the household group. Smith goes on to indicate that in a strongly patrilineal society such as the Tallensi (as contrasted with bilateral Guyana), the man who is head of the compound also heads a property-owning group and the children belong to a patrilineage of which he is head. Thus he directs economic, political, and position-conferring functions.

Schneider and Smith (1973) analyze the familial pattern of the American lower class in terms that seem completely applicable to the Guyanese pattern described just above and to the mother-child pattern seen elsewhere:

> The one thing that is abundantly clear is that the marital relationship is not the basis of family structure in the way it is for the middle class, and that marital disruption does not give rise to a broken home. A broken home in the

lower class would be one in which a mother abandoned her children, leaving them to be taken care of by the father (p. 95).

Among the lower class, also, they note an emphasis on "help, cooperation, and solidarity with a wide range of kin . . . upon keeping open the options—upon maximizing the number of relationships which involve diffuse solidarity . . . a tendency to *create* kinship ties out of relationships which are originally ties of friendship" (p. 42).

In conclusion, it appears that with rare exceptions (notably the Nayar and the kibbutzim) where conditions permit, the nuclear triad is in the familial system. Conditions that deter or prevent its developing include low and irregular income on the part of men plus perhaps their frequent and prolonged absence to work elsewhere, as well as the opportunity for women to obtain income through their own employment, the employment of their children, and/or welfare. It appears that where conditions are unfavorable for the establishment of the nuclear triad, the standby arrangement is a maternal-consanguine family, which is able to function stably and rather efficiently under such adverse conditions.

Is There a Pattern of the Mother-Child Family?

Although the heroic mother is a figure that appears to have been more or less in the consciousness of man since the dawn of history, it seems that it is really since the days of Brecht (1941) and Frazier (1939) that we have been aware of a phenomenon that has come to be known as the mother-child family. I think we are entitled to ask why it is that we sociologists became aware of the pattern of the mother-child family only over the last third of a century. To the skeptic this raises the further question: Does the mother-child family exist as a familial pattern?

In some ways this is a question parallel to: Is the family universal? The answer to the latter question is of course yes or no, depending on one's definition. If we define the family as whatever structure carries out the familial function, define the familial function as reproduction, and build the notion of reproduction into our definition of society, then it becomes a logical necessity for every society to have a family, just as it has an economy, a polity, and so on. On the other hand, if we define the family as a particular configuration of familial positions interacting with each other in particular ways and locations, it always seems possible to find some situation in which the specified pattern is absent.

As we have seen, the literature on the mother-child family has not involved primitive societies. Rather, it began with Frazier's account of the black family in the United States (1939). Since then a dozen or more studies have described the mother-headed family in the islands of the Caribbean and the lands of Central America, as well as in areas of cities in the United States inhabited by impoverished blacks. There is much similarity in these accounts, and the consensus among these writers lends plausibility to the surmise that there may be some underlying sociological generalizations awaiting our analysis.

Rather than consider each monograph in turn with the evidence it provides, I propose to construct a composite picture of what happens in these various settings as the girl becomes pregnant for the first time and moves through the childbearing years.

It appears that as a girl enters puberty she is typically not well informed about sex. Blake (1961: 77) reports that "mothers appear to withhold [sex] information [from their daughters] intentionally as part of what they feel to be the only feasible methods of parental control." Of course, such parental controls prove ineffective, and the girls become pregnant. (Blake, p. 46, reports that among her Jamaican respondents the median age at first intercourse was 17. For the black ghetto he studied in St. Louis, Rainwater, 1970: 309, gives a similar figure.) In Jamaica (Henriques, 1968) and Barbados (Greenfield, 1966) it is reported that news of a girl's pregnancy is received by her mother (and, if he is present, her father) with outrage. Clarke (1957: 99) states that there appear to be four "almost ritualized stages" in the mother's behavior on discovering her daughter's first pregnancy: (1) The girl is noisily upbraided, beaten, and frequently expelled from the house. (2) The girl takes refuge with a neighbor or kinswoman. (3) Kinfolk or neighbors intercede with the mother on the daughter's behalf. (4) The girl returns to the mother's house to await the birth of her child.

Typically, then, it appears that the girl bears her first child while she is still a member of her mother's household, and of course in some cases her mother's husband is present in the household. Seldom, however, does it appear that the girl's lover—that is, the father of her firstborn—enters significantly into the post-conception interaction. It seems generally to be reported that his identity is known, and thus paternity is socially conferred upon the newborn. On the other hand, his economic position is such that he is in no position to contribute meaningfully to the support of the young mother and infant. After the child is born, responsibility for its rearing frequently falls to the girl's mother, while the girl resumes her social career in her adolescent peer group and/or enters the labor force and contributes earnings to her mother's household.

On the basis of his study in Guyana, Raymond T. Smith has proposed a three-stage development of the relations between men and women; the first stage, which we have just noted, is that they are lovers without common residence. The girl may have more casual affairs and resulting children, whose rearing she may entrust to her mother, but presently she is likely to enter the second stage: a more enduring liaison with common residence and with or without legal marriage. Once men pass the age of 40, Smith writes, they have usually become heads of households, and most male heads of households are living with their legal or common-law wives. The third stage arrives with the departure of the men, because of death or other reasons, and women become heads of households—usually after they have passed through menopause (Smith, 1956: 61-65).

There comes a time, apparently, when it is either impossible or counternormative for the young woman to continue delegating responsibility to her mother for child rearing. This is a critical time in her life for, as Rodman (1971: 183) remarks, a woman left alone cannot both care for and support her small children. At this point there are three possibilities: she may find some other woman (usually a relative) to rear her children, she may work out an arrangement of mutual assistance with other women in a similar situation, or she may form a liaison with a man, whereby he assumes financial responsibility for her children (plus perhaps his own, who join the household), while she becomes a housewife and child-tender. Because of the difficulty of her situation, the woman, in exchange for the man's support, is usually willing to remain sexually faithful to him and accept domination from him that she would find intolerable later in her life after one or more of her children are old enough to begin contributing to the household.

Once the children are old enough that some can care for others and the mother is no longer needed to care for them, she is likely to reenter the labor force. It appears, moreover, that later as the children begin to find jobs and contribute to the household, the mother may be well on the road to starting another cycle whereby she will look to her children for support of the household and withdraw from employment to care for the first of her grandchildren—the offspring of her oldest daughter's first pregnancy. While this is going on, a considerable proportion of the men disappear. Partly this results from differential mortality. On the average, men marry women younger than themselves, and men generally have shorter life expectancies than do women. But some who disappear have just gone elsewhere. As the children become economically productive, their mothers' husbands are less needed, their domination becomes less tolerable, and their economic marginality renders their usefulness unreliable. Gonzalez (1969: 117) reports that during hard times men are likely to return to their consanguineal kin for food and shelter. R. T. Smith (1956: 65, 152) says that the resulting structure of the familial system he studied consists of a woman, her daughters, and the daughters' children.

M. G. Smith (1962: 255) believes there is not a single sequence of stages such as that noted above, but that what he calls "mating organization" varies, and that the particular mating system determines the nature of the familial structure. Other writers, he says, have exaggerated the importance of the maternal grandmother and have underestimated the significance of collateral kin in helping mothers and their children.

Several paragraphs above I noted that a lone woman with small children faced three possibilities. Stack's (1974) study of impoverished urban blacks in the United States emphasizes the solution of mutual assistance with other women. In her study there are mother-child households, but there is no mother-child family. The family is larger. Every mother is involved in a network of mutually supportive relationships. It appears that these relationships are with kin (usually female kin) where the woman has kin in the community which she generally does. But where she does not have local kin, it appears that she establishes a relationship of mutual aid with friends, who come thereby to serve as kin-surrogates.

Thus the situation that Stack describes might be characterized in Gonzalez's phrase of the "consanguineal family," with the addendum that it is sometimes based on fictive consanguineality. (See also Aschenbrenner, 1975.)

It turns out that when we examine the literature on the mother-child family, there may be mother-child households, although these frequently turn into three-generational uterine descent systems. Moreover, since the mother-child dyad can hardly be self-sufficient when the child(ren) is (are) small and dependent, we find that the mother normally finds some source of support. If that source is a husband or a lover, the resulting familial system is a nuclear family—whether the man-woman relationship is a legal marriage or not. If the source is a mother, brother, sister, or other blood relative, the resulting familial system is consanguineal. The arrangement may be assisted by the state through its welfare system, which is usually inadequate to the mother's needs. I am disposed to conclude, therefore, that the image of the mother-child family struggling along by itself with the children all dependent probably seldom exists—Brecht and Frazier notwithstanding—and then probably only as a temporary state of affairs while the mother tries to complete arrangements for one of the three possibilities I have referred to above.

Related to the foregoing is the fact that in many of these reports parents of both young boys and girls oppose their entering marriage. While offspring are capable of earning income and are still unmarried and without commitments to others, the parents can generally influence their offspring to direct a substantial portion of their earnings into the household of the parent. To the parent(s), then, the offspring's marriage signifies a reduction or termination of a source of income. To the boy, parents tend to communicate (1) that the girl is not good enough, and (2) that she will consume all his earnings and perhaps even run him into debt. To the girl, the message tends more toward the vein that men are not dependable, and that the only trustworthy support is from her blood relatives, especially her parents and siblings. The economic marginality of males in these settings both lends plausibility to the point and implies that they too will be responsive to the suggestion that affinal ties are less reliable sources of support than are consanguineal.

According to these views, marriage tends to favor the nuclear family over the consanguineal family. It is favorable to the nuclear family in the sense that it provides legal safeguards for the transmission of property from a deceased spouse to a surviving spouse and their children. Conditions conducive to the avoidance of marriage, therefore, are a lack of property to transmit, and a preference to transmit property through the uterine line. (Here Oppong, 1974, is relevant.)

In pulling together these ideas, I begin by noting Greenfield's (1966: 110) definition of the family as an institutionalized pattern of child care and Stack's (1974: 33) elaboration that the family is an organized, durable network of kin and non-kin providing for the domestic needs of children and assuring their survival. But as Gonzalez (1969: 99) has pointed out in the passage cited above, it is difficult, if not impossible, for a single woman to fulfill all the roles involved in maintaining a household and caring for small children, and it becomes possible only in societies providing such systems of support as nursery schools and supervised playgrounds. To this, Stack (1974: 83) adds: "Close female kinsmen in The Flats do not expect a single person, the natural mother, to carry out by herself all of the patterns which 'motherhood' entails." And she concludes that these roles involve being provider, discipliner, trainer, curer, and groomer (p. 84).

These considerations lead me to conclude that in none of these situations does the familial system consist of a mother and her small, dependent children only. Rather, there tend to be at least two adults, one of whom assumes an economic and the other a parental role. Thus the functional system to which we apply the term "family" seems always to include these two distinct familial positions with distinct incumbents. This is the line of reasoning that leads me to conclude that if a true mother-child family can be found in the sense that it is functionally independent, then it is probably a temporary arrangement resulting from a fairly recent departure of some adult and lasting only as long as it will take the wife-mother to establish a familial or quasi-familial relationship with another adult. For the United States this inference has received strong empirical support from a study by Ross and Sawhill (1975). After an analysis of data from the U.S. Bureau of the Census and from the University of Michigan's Panel Study of Income Dynamics, they conclude that "for most women, single parenthood is a 'time of transition' between living in one nuclear family and another" (p. 159). Indeed, they regard this finding as so salient that they entitle their book *Time of Transition.*

It should be noted that the literature on the mother-child family, which we have been considering, pertains to subsocietal categories at the bottom of the socioeconomic hierarchy. The disadvantaged situation of these people frequently enters into the explanation of the absence of husbands and fathers from their households, and it is among the economically depressed that the mother-child households are most frequent. This observation does suggest a question, however, as to whether the inability of the mother to take care of dependent children by herself would be mitigated in other economic strata of developing and developed societies.

Wealth, of course, does make possible the purchase of domestic service. Nineteenth-century novels acquainted us with numerous domestic occupations: governesses, chambermaids, parlormaids, cooks, butlers, gardeners, and so on. It seems that where there is adequate wealth and where the labor force provides the human resources, there is a disposition to transfer domestic and parental activities from family members to servants. And since the activities involved are those traditionally assigned to the wife-mother, the effect of such a transfer is to render the wife-mother relatively functionless. In other words, among the wealthy the opportunity exists to substitute the ability to buy domestic service for the carrying out of a number of activities usually regarded as wifely-maternal responsibilities—maintaining and cleaning quarters, providing meals, and caring for children. (On the other hand, in many situations of wealth and privilege, the woman does retain the roles of sexual partner, genetrix, and hostess.) In this light, given means and a labor force of willing, skilled, and reliable domestic personnel, a single parent of either gender can cope.

In the middle classes, however, a single parent may have more limited means and may encounter difficulty in finding and retaining the service of skilled and reliable domestic help. Hence, it would appear that the middle-class single mother can probably cope better than her lower-class counterpart, but her problems are still likely to be substantial.

Essentially, this analysis has concerned child care as a problem confronting the manless mother of small children. Another way of looking at the problem is from the viewpoint of fostering or child-lending. (*Fostering* refers to a state of affairs wherein a child lives away from his/her natural parents and is cared for by some other adult or adults.) Such "dispersed" youth are estimated to represent at least a quarter of all children in Belize (formerly British Honduras), according to Sanford (1974), who says the rearing of children is seen as a responsibility of kin rather than of the genetrix alone. Fostering or child-lending is reported to be widespread in the West Indies (e.g., Horowitz, 1967; Otterbein, 1966; Philpott, 1973), as well as among Polynesian peoples (Carroll, 1970); and even among low income blacks in a midwestern community (Stack, 1974).

And What about the Bureaucracy?

Having concluded that the mother-child family is myth rather than reality, what have I to say about the bureaucracy, and about which bureaucracy? First, I believe that the myth was perpetrated by our system of social bookkeeping known as the U.S. Bureau of the Census, which reports a sizable and increasing proportion of mother-child households. For some time social scientists have been pointing out that the familial system is not identical with the household. Unperturbed by these suggestions, our Bureau of the Census continues to define the family as those related persons occupying a common dwelling unit. On this point I quote again from Stack (1974: 31):

> It became clear that the "household" and its group composition was not a meaningful unit to isolate for analysis of family life in The Flats. A resident in The Flats who eats in one household may sleep in another, and contribute resources to yet another. He may consider himself a member of all three households.

In the United States we have a second bureaucracy that serves to create and maintain the myth of the mother-child family. This is the welfare system, which continues to penalize families with a visible husband-father. Ross and Sawhill (1975: 97) point out that under the Social Security Act and related rulings: "If children in families are in economic need they will be eligible for assistance in virtually every case except where they are living with both natural parents. . . . Once a family with few or no earnings or other resources becomes female-headed, acceptance [on welfare] is quite likely."

Summary and Conclusions

Mother, father, child—these are the elements of what we think of as a family. But are they all necessary? Postulating that reproduction is the family's basic societal function and noting the brevity of the copulative act, we have proposed that the minimum familial structure should be a mother-child family. Then we consulted the evidence.

What do we find to be the conditions under which the familial system does not include a husband-father?

1. The husband-father is consistently reported in preindustrial societies. The only known exception is the Nayar. In this society the pattern was not a mother-child family but an extended matrilineal descent system.
2. There are some developed and developing societies wherein the mother-child family has been reported. In these, however, the ethnographic evidence seems to indicate that in the absence of the husband-father the mother makes arrangements with other (usually female kin) adults to help with the multifarious roles associated with motherhood.
3. Hence the familial pattern should be known *not* as mother-child but as mother-centered, or matrifocal, with matrilineal extension, which is sometimes fictive.
4. Where it occurs, the absence of the husband-father seems usually to be associated with the following conditions and situations:
    (a) economically depressed classes
    (b) the individual as the unit of labor
    (c) the man, if employed, tends to be a migrant worker
    (d) the man is not able to make a contribution to the family with respect to the position-conferring function

The data from primitive societies instruct us that our hypothesis about the prevalence of mother-child families is wrong. The remarks of Murdock, Gough, and Steward suggest why: in simple societies the family is always more than a replacement institution. It seems likely that what Gonzalez said about mothers—that they need another adult to help with the numerous roles associated with motherhood—is true of preindustrial as well as developing and developed societies. It seems more than likely, furthermore, that her remark might be generalized to include a single parent of either gender—that is, that in any society, the rearing of one or more dependent children involves a set of tasks requiring either two or more adults or considerable institutional support for the single parent.

Then what about our functional analysis? It appears that we have learned that there are additional corollary functions to the function of replacement. One surely is the economic function. The quotation from Murdock has suggested something of the gender-linked division of labor among hunting and gathering peoples. One conceivable inference from the absence of any (or at least any appreciable number of) societies without normative marriage is that societies have concluded that gender-linked division of labor is good, and probably those (and some may have tried it) without such a division of labor may have died out before any enterprising ethnographer could write their story. We may note that Gough and Steward also refer to the protective function of the family. Thus we may come to the hypothesis that among preindustrial peoples there is a set of functions that the family fulfills: replacement, economic, and political (with emphasis on its protective aspect).

When we look to developing and developed societies, we see a picture in some ways different, in some ways similar. Most obvious is the difference that in these societies the mother-child family has been reported. Does this mean, per Gonzalez, that these societies are providing institutional support? Since the prevalence of such families is reported to be greatest in the least affluent strata of these societies, it seems unlikely that such mothers can afford servants, day-care nurseries, frozen foods, and so on. Rather, according to the writers cited, mothers of small, dependent children are usually involved in familial networks beyond the mother-child dyad. The patterns noted include a man and/or the mother's mother, and/or the mother's other matrilineal kin, usually a sister, but possibly fictive kin. And thus we are justified in speaking of the mother-centered, or matrifocal, family with (sometimes fictive) matrilineal extension. It seems that as an actuality, where there are small children, the mother-child family is not a pattern but a temporary phenomenon (enduring only until the departed adult can be replaced), and that it is a creation of the modes of social bookkeeping and of the administration of welfare. For all types of society, therefore, the thrust of this argument is that where there are small, dependent children, it has been the pattern to have at least two adults to fulfill the provider and child-tender roles.

Finally, it is likely that some critics of traditional forms of the family will interpret this analysis as conservative and pro–nuclear family or perhaps pro–extended family. Not so. Like science generally, it merely reports the extant data. This analysis does not deny the possibility that other solutions to the problem of child care may become widespread.

Notes

1. Also called "elementary family" by Radcliffe-Brown (1950: 4) and, with the condition of being embedded in a network of kin, "conjugal family" by Goode (1963).

2. Distinguishing gender of offspring as well as of parents, Hsu (1971) postulates four positions in the nuclear family and eight resulting dyads. He believes that some one of these eight dyads tends to be dominant in any kinship system. Characteristic of whatever dyad is dominant, he says, is a set of attributes that are dominant also in that they "determine the attitudes and action patterns that the individual . . . develops toward other dyads" (p. 10). In the work cited, Hsu discusses the following dyads: husband-wife, father-son, mother-son, and brother-brother. Hsu is interested in the psychological consequences of such arrangements but does not speculate on conditions that bring about the dominance of one or

another dyad. Hsu appears to be less interested in the structure of a social system than in what he calls its "content," which he says refers to characteristics of the social system that "govern the tenacity, intensity, and variety of interaction among individuals" participating in the system (p. 6).

3. At the hunting-gathering level of subsistence it has been estimated that breast feeding is continued until the child is 2 1/2 to 3 years old because of the unavailability of foods soft enough to permit weaning (Dumond, 1975: 715).

4. Although it is not always easy to tell who is married to whom.

5. In view of an apparently widespread tendency toward hypergamy, moreover, the women at the top of the spectrum of socioeconomic statuses also have some difficulty finding husbands, but their situation is not relevant to the present discussion because they are relatively unlikely to bear children premaritally.

6. Greenfield (1966: 108) makes a somewhat similar observation about the black family in the Barbadian village he studied: that the authority of the father weakens as soon as the working sons begin to contribute money to their mother.

Chapter 10

Summary and Conclusions: Review; Second Steps Toward a Model of Familial Organization; Suggestions for Needed Research

Robert F. Winch

Review of Findings

The family in some form is found in all societies, and everywhere it has been the subsocietal system through which the society has replaced members lost through death or migration.[1] Almost everywhere the family also performs other functions: socializing the young, giving them positions in the society, and providing emotional support to the adults as well as to the children. More varied is the degree to which the family performs as a unit in the realms of the economy, the polity, and the church. It was my view, stated in Chapter 1, that the organi-

193

zation of the family—its structure and its influence—would vary with the functions it performed.

In our suburban study, reported in Chapter 2, we found that Jews reported more kin than did Christians and reported more interaction with those kin, and that the interaction was more functional. In that sample Catholics were intermediate in isolation extended-familism between the Jews and the Protestants. In our statewide sample, which lacked an analyzable number of Jews, Lutherans appeared to be as familistic as Catholics, and both were more so than other Protestants but considerably less so than the Jews of the suburban sample. To some extent the familism of the Jews was associated with their being more entrepreneurial and less migratory than the Christians, but this did not account for much of the difference (see Table 2-6). We surmised that the migration of the Jews differed from that of the Christians in that it tended to be more linked to the location of kin whereas among Christians it was more linked to jobs, especially in large-scale organizations. Furthermore, we found in Chapter 2 that there was reason to avoid thinking about *the* American family because there appear to be a variety of patterns—each associated with different conditions of disadvantage or advantage.

Familial influence as the consequence of structure and function was the topic of Chapter 3. Based upon a study of male college students, the conclusion was that the data seemed to justify a structure-function-resource-vacuum theory of influence—that familial structure had implications as to the presence or absence of suitable models (for imitation), that function implied resources that might become rewards, and that if suitable models and/or resources were lacking in the family, they would be sought elsewhere with the consequence that the family would be relatively noninfluential.

Our quest for correlates of familial organization continued into Chapter 4, where we showed that the complexity of the family is related in a curvilinear manner with the complexity of the society—that is, that large systems occur most frequently among societies engaging in settled agriculture, but before they come to the organizational complexity involved in irrigation.

In Chapter 5 I took note of variables thought by various scholars to affect the way in which the family is organized. In particular, it was widely thought that the way in which people make their living would be reflected in familial organization and that changes in the mode of subsistence would provide the principal dynamic of familial change. Consideration was also given to the social cement that binds the members of the family to each other, and the chapter concluded with a discussion of ethnographic data banks.

In Chapter 6 we sought systematically to evolve a set of determinants of the familial system. Our orientation involved looking to the mode of subsistence and changes therein—especially technical changes—as the most powerful determinant and one that we anticipated would influence familial organization both directly and through other sorts of variables, such as the way in which work is organized, the control of means and fruits of production, socialization and social inequality, and properties of communities. Furthermore, we thought that forms of descent, nuptial residence, and inheritance would be influenced by the predictors mentioned in the last sentence. In these terms we traced a hypothesized model from the techno-environmental conditions of making a living through conditions of social and political organization to the familial system itself. This we labeled a materialist-evolutionary approach to the explanation of the structure and functioning of the family.

Chapter 7 saw our effort to bring Murdock's Ethnographic Atlas to bear on our model. Although we lacked indicators for important variables and suffered severe attrition so that we were able to analyze only about a quarter of the 1,170 societies, we concluded that with a purely synchronic model we could account for 23 percent of the variance in our dependent variable (size of familial system), or 40 percent if we included splits in the AID analysis that involved small resulting sets (of less than 15 societies). The technique of dividing the sample into mutually exclusive subsamples showed that predictors other than subsistence economy and rules of inheritance made unstable contributions to "explained" variance. Further analysis with a two-stage pseudodiachronic model suppressed the "explanatory" importance of inheritance and allowed more variables hypothesized to operate earlier in the causal chain to register their influence. Moreover, in the two-stage analysis the explained variance rose to 35 percent, or 49 percent including small splits.

In Chapter 8 economic conditions conducive to the existence of the mother-child household were proposed and it was suggested that the occurrence of this form was related to the woman's opportunity to acquire subsistence and to do so in a manner compatible with child care. Although Blumberg with García were unable to subject these conditions to systematic empirical test, they did show the error in attributing this form to race, and they established correlations, again with economic variables, of the separate mother-child household among polygynous societies.

In Chapter 9 I challenged the notion that the mother-child dyad had developed anywhere into a familial pattern. The evidence seems to indicate that one woman cannot serve simultaneously as tender of small children, household maintainer, and provider. It appears that women who are thrust into a situation demanding that they simultaneously fulfill all three roles generally extricate themselves from it through forming a new liaison and/or seeking help from relatives, friends, or agencies. Thus the functioning familial unit comes to involve one or more adults in addition to the mother.

Second Steps Toward a Model of Familial Organization

The situation resulting from our AID analysis (Chap. 7) is that (1) we hypothesized a set of variables to predict familial organization, (2) we developed a model of that set of variables, (3) we located indicators for most of the variables, and (4) all of the indicators made contributions to the explained variance in one or both cases (see Tables 7-3 and 7-4, and also Appendix Table D-3). Thus, although these analyses cannot be construed as constituting a rigorous test of the model, the data are consistent with the hypothesized model asserting that familial organization is the consequence of subsistence environment and related subsocietal patterns.

Having presented our model and having subjected it to the best available empirical test, we come now to read the cues that the data offer for the improvement of the model. Improvements in our model would presumably involve one or more of the following: detecting omissions in the set of explanatory concepts, detecting irrelevant or tautological concepts, and discovering incorrectly drawn arrows. In other words, potential improvements consist of concepts to be added and/or to be discarded and/or relationships to be altered.

With respect to the detection of omissions, I feel our situation is not so much a problem with Figure 6-1, the model, as with Table 7-1, the set of indicators we were able to derive from the Ethnographic Atlas. As noted in Chapter 7, we had no index at all for Boxes 1B, 3, and 4, environmental potentialities; surplus and the social relations of production; and socialization with respect to subsistence activities and social inequality. Moreover, we regarded as inadequate our two indicators for Box 2, the nature of work. It is our judgment that it would be important to undertake the creation of codes for Boxes 1B, 3, and 4 as well as additional codes for Box 2, and to do this for as many as possible of the societies of some rational sample (e.g., Murdock's 186).

Operationally, redundancies or irrelevancies are indexes that fail to "explain" any variance, and our evidence appears in Tables 7-3 and 7-4 as well as in the tables from Appendix D. In our original AID, 4 of the 13 indicators were candidates to be dropped by this criterion. If we were to adopt a strict criterion and eliminate indicators that accounted for variance only while making splits resulting in small groups, we would be left with just four.

If we were to accept only indicators that explained variance on both of the randomly drawn subsamples, we would also be left with four, and if we then added the strict criterion about size of split group, we should then have disposed of all our indicators but one—subsistence economy.

It may be recalled, however, that we decided that it would be consistent with our theory to break up the AID analysis into two stages. By doing this, we increased our total explained variance from 23 to 35 percent, and with the small resulting splits included, from 40 to 49 percent. In this operation 10 out of 14 indicators made some contribution to the 35 percent, and every indicator except descent made some contribution to the grand total of 49 percent.

Our experience here leads to the surmise that instead of dropping *any* of the indicators in our present set (all of which were selected for their theoretical relevance), it would be more rational to scrutinize the model (Figure 6-1) to see whether it might be advisable to go from a two- to a three- or higher-stage analysis.

The basic AID procedure gives simultaneous access to all predictors in the explanatory process. We may recall, however, that the predictors in Figure 6-1 are arranged in three levels of antecedence to the dependent variable of familial organization. Theoretical misgivings about the relation of Boxes 7 and 8 to Box 9 led us to detach Boxes 7 and 8 from the rest of the predictors to set up the two-stage analysis. Since the results seem to indicate this to have been an advisable tactic, we should now consider pursuing the logic and move to a four-stage analysis as follows:

Stage	*Content*	*Boxes*
1	Economic: techno-environmental	1A (and 1B if indicators become available)
2	Economic: social relations of production	2 (and 3 if indicators become available)
3	Sociopolitical	5 and 6 (and 4 if indicators become available)
4	Familial: inheritance, residential, lineal	7 and 8

This formulation leads us to rearrange Figure 6-1 as shown in Figure 10-1.

Figure 10-1 represents a second version of our model of familial organization that, as the figure implies, is necessarily still crude. The continuing crudeness is multiply determined. One reason has to do with the fact that some boxes in both figures have no indicators. The crudeness of some of the available indicators is another reason, and low coefficients of association may reflect error of measurement rather than lack of covariation at the conceptual level. Some of the crudeness reflects the lack of a more powerful technique of quantitative analysis. Some has to do with the lack of longitudinal data, which might enable us to determine direction of causation[2] and presence of feedback loops.

Appendix Tables E-1 and E-2 show that the lowest median measures of association—both $\bar{C}$ and G—come from gender differentiation. This is an indicator for Box 2, the nature of work. Second lowest median with respect to $\bar{C}$ is the dichotomized measure of familial structure, while the interval scale measure of familial structure is second lowest with respect to G. These are the two indicators of Box 9, familial organization.

In the case of the nature of work, we see that the other indicator, number of occupations, has a median $\bar{C}$ and a median G of .51, both considerably better than average, and suggesting that this indicator is measuring something. Neither indicator of Box 2, however, has a sizable degree of association with Box 9, which leads to the thought that the arrow between Boxes 2 and 9 might be scratched.

Appendix Table E-2 shows that the indicators of familial organization do not have high gammas generally. Appendix Table E-1 shows that the coefficients of contingency of familial organization are highest with the indicators of Boxes 7 and 8. For the boxes having indicators, it appears that the other arrows of Figure 6-1 receive support.

For these reasons I propose that Figure 6-1 be redrawn with four layers of predictors, as shown in Figure 10-1 above, and that Box 9 be connected only with the fourth layer, Boxes 7 and 8.

Functions as Sources of Reward

As I indicated in Chapter 1, I believe that there is one type of analysis that is especially conducive to the integrating of sociological and psychological con-

Figure 10-1 Revised Model of Determinants of Familial Organization

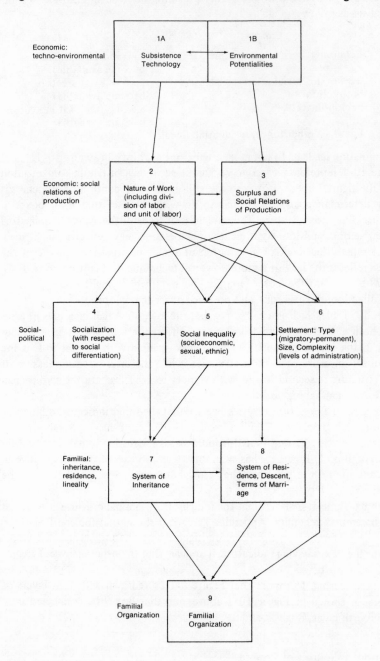

siderations. This is the Thibaut-Kelley social psychology of groups. This variant of exchange theory postulates that the individual member of a social system— and their interest is in small groups—is induced to join or to remain in the organization on the basis of experienced and anticipated benefits or rewards and is induced to leave on the basis of an experienced or perceived alternative that seems more rewarding or beneficial.

Thibaut and Kelley did not go into a systematic formulation of rewards. That is the point at which the individual-oriented aspect of our Janus-faced notion of function is helpful. Table 10-1 is organized to show how the various functions *can* reward members of families and thereby induce them to remain in and work for the familial system. It should be noted that the absence of a reward is represented in Table 10-1 as a neutral condition—neither inducing the individual to remain within nor to leave the family. Conditions that punish the member for remaining or reward the member for leaving appear in the right column.

The presentation in Table 10-1 is not developed to a point where it can be regarded as comprehensive. Rather, it is seen as a list that is probably partial and will gradually be supplemented and no doubt corrected.[3]

Table 10-1 makes the behavior of the individual the dependent variable. It seeks to answer the question: Under what conditions will an individual join, remain with, or leave a familial system? The conditions cited there can be regarded, however, as hypothetical answers to the reverse question: Under what conditions will the organization, the familial system, seek to recruit new members or to expel present members? This phrasing tends to make the state of the familial system the dependent variable.[4]

From a somewhat different point of view we are not turning our relationship around at all. Rather, what we are doing is viewing familial organization—the dependent variable of the entire book—from two different angles. One of these has to do with whether the individual is encouraged to join up or to leave, and the other is whether the system is encouraged to recruit or to expel. From either angle, causes hypothesized in these relationships occur in extrafamilial structures of the society and the consequences are felt in the familial system.

The sorts of things we have in mind here are exemplified by reports from the ethnographic literature. Linton (1939) has described the familial organization related to two different kinds of subsistence on the island of Madagascar. One community growing rice with a dry technique had a large family organization, but another community nearby and seemingly related to the first had recently adopted a wet-rice technique with the consequence that there needed to be a much more highly developed political organization to manage the irrigation of the fields. Along with this development there was a movement toward a nuclear family pattern.

Similarly, Sahlins (1957) reports on a pair of villages in Moala, Fiji. In this setting the extended family system was retained by the members of one village, who cultivated lands both near to and remote from that village. The second village had abandoned the cultivation of its more remote lands, changing to a

TABLE 10-1. Aspects of Functions That Appear to Reward, Leave Neutral, or Punish Members for Participating in the Familial System

Function	Rewarding Participation	Conditions	
		Neutral	Inducing Withdrawal
Economic	Family is unit of labor Family business Inheritance of property Subsistence agriculture with permanent settlement Wages of family members paid to family head Welfare paid to family head without respect to gender	Family is not unit of labor No property; no inheritance Individual employment Wages paid to worker	Migratory wage labor Categorical employment: Producers better off without dependents Welfare paid to head only if head is female
Political	External threat: family as unit of protection	State protects individual	Totalitarian state, e.g., Nazi Germany
Religious	Belief that behavior of living is beneficial to dead kin Ancestor worship, including belief that good will of ancestors is beneficial to living	Belief that deity rather than living humans affects post-mortem welfare; atheism	Beliefs that reward celibacy and/or disavowing family

Socializing educational	Much socializing in family Hereditary occupations	Little socializing in family Rapidly changing occupational system	Rapid social change plus professional teachers leading young to believe parents are ill informed, misguided
Replacement	Low perceived cost-benefit ratio, as among Asian Indians, where young children are useful and adult offspring give security		High perceived cost-benefit ratio, as in middle-class U.S., where children bring in little revenue and cost much to educate
Parental	Only family does		All done outside family, as in Israeli kibbutzim
Position-conferring	No positions outside kinship system	Valued positions conferred by economy, polity, etc.	Positions conferred by family negatively valued
Emotional gratification	Primarily within family	Primarily outside family	Family primarily source of frustration

nuclear family pattern. The ethnologist concluded that in the former village the extended family was needed to integrate the work assignments and to oversee the distribution of their crops.

Finally, Clignet (1970) concludes that among polygynous African societies that depend on subsistence agriculture in which the productive value of women is important, "each family group tends to use its surplus income to increase its labor force—and, more specifically, the number of its polygynous units as well as the number of its co-wives" (1970: 22-23; see also Chap. 8 above).

Suggestions for Needed Research

Exploitation of the Revised Model by Means of Data
from the Ethnographic Atlas

In Chapter 1, I stated that our task was to develop a theory of the familial system—that is, to discover those determinants that produce variation in the family with respect to its structure, functioning, and influence through space and time. Figure 10-1 represents our current formulation as to what those determinants are.

As implied in Figure 10-1, it is proposed that the two-stage analysis performed at the end of Chapter 7 be followed up with a four-stage analysis. The difference in results between the one-stage and two-stage analyses suggests that a further elaboration of stages will account for a higher proportion of variance. Perhaps it should be emphasized that such an elaboration of stages is in no way to be regarded as blind empiricism but, rather, as following the implications of the theoretical model set forth in Chapter 6.

The challenge to AID on the ground that it uses—indeed, overuses—degrees of freedom and is based on error in building up explained variance causes the researcher to seek ways to allow the data to speak freely. The data used in the AID analyses to this point have been indicators of variables that constitute the model. For this reason it has been expected that each of the indicators would make a contribution to the explained variance, and this is what we saw in the two-stage analysis when account was taken of splits resulting in small as well as large subsets. But how can the properly skeptical critic convince himself that the results shown in Table 7-4 are not based on a considerable amount of error?

One way to achieve this result is to create an additional set of variables known to be uncorrelated either with the predictors or with the dependent variable and to observe their performance in the AID. Thus, we might select from the EA variables thought to be unrelated to the variables of our problem. An example might use the codes developed by Murdock to measure "floor level" or "shape of roof" of dwelling. On reflection, however, it seems that such variables would not be satisfactory for the intended purpose, since variables pertaining to type of housing structure are no doubt related to the kind of environment and region. Both of these in turn would be related to the nature of the economy, the type of subsistence, the nature of work, and thus we can see from the model of Figures

6-1 and 10-1 that they could be expected to be related—even though indirectly—to our dependent variable.

Because of these considerations, it would appear that our purpose would be best served by creating some random variables and allowing them to work through the various stages of the AID. Hopefully they would show near zero associations at all stages, thereby increasing the plausibility of the variation accounted for by the indicators in our model as reflected in Tables 7-3 and 7-4.

Exploitation of the Revised Model by Means of Other Ethnographic Data

In Chapter 5 we noted that Murdock had developed a set of 186 societies that he regarded as constituting a rational sample of the universe of societies. We also noted that other samples had been created. Subsequently, Murdock and associates have published several papers of additional codes with ratings on this set of societies. Some of these codes have a bearing on our model and should be utilized in further analysis. Examples include societal complexity (Murdock and Provost, 1973b), patterns of settlement (Murdock and Wilson, 1972), political complexity (Tuden and Marshall, 1972), personnel involved in child care (Barry and Paxson, 1971), and familial structure (Murdock and Wilson, 1972).

We have noted that in our own empirical work to date we have lacked indicators for Boxes 1B, 3, and 4, and that we were quite dissatisfied with the two indicators for Box 2. A further line of research should take the direction of developing codes for these boxes. Such work is expensive, and it would seem prohibitive to try to assign ratings for all of the societies in the EA. To do so for Murdock's 186 societies, however, is a manageable undertaking. We have already made a beginning on this task with respect to a rationally selected subset of Murdock's 186 societies (see Reinhardt et al., 1975).

Because of the coding limitations of the EA, we have been able to use those data to investigate only one of the three components we have postulated for the familial system—structure, or more strictly, structure of the domestic family. In the work we have undertaken for the purpose of expanding our codes beyond those available in the EA and Murdock's subsequent work, we have tried to develop codes that will move into the context of familial function. Two functions have been explored: economic and socializing-educational. In the present context, suffice it to say that the code for economic functionality of the family does not appear to be very promising, but the code for the socializing-educational function looks better.

Exploration of the Revised Model over an Expanded Range of Societies

A shortcoming of the empirical work reported in Chapter 7 is that the range of data pertains only to preindustrial societies. It would be very desirable to pursue the exploration of our model through data on developing and developed societies, and to do so in a fashion such that the results could be related to our work on preindustrial societies. We have made one small effort in this direction with the use of data from the study by Adelman and Morris in connection with our test of the curvilinear hypothesis reported in Chapter 4. It would be desirable to look closely at other possible sources of data to see what may be available that would allow further tests at the industrial and near industrial levels.

Exploration of the Revised Model with Original Data

Because any study should involve considerable variation in the techno-environmental indicators, in the other variables of our model, and in familial organization, a satisfactory research design should call for the gathering of data in a variety of societies and/or societal categories.

In Chapter 1, I suggested a strategy for investigating the familial system in exotic societies. The suggestion involved two steps. One of these concerned the delineation of the familial structure through asking each of a set of respondents to list his/her living relatives and to specify the nature of the relationship to each. The second involved listing the basic societal functions, specifying a set of activities regarding each of these functions with respect to which the individual might be expected to engage, and then asking respondents with whom they carried out these various activities. I proposed that a cross-tabulation of the responses to these two different sets of inquiries would reveal the structure-function of the familial system.

There is nothing about this procedure that restricts it to an exotic context as its use in Chapter 2 illustrates. Indeed the strategy is an extension of the format of research used in our suburban study and abridged for our statewide study (cf. Chap. 2). The extension refers to the sample of respondents (since only housewives were interviewed in the suburban study) and to the sample of activities (in these studies, the activities centered on the management of the household).

In Chapter 5 and elsewhere I expressed vigorous objection to the disposition to interpret "household" as equivalent to "family," stating that the relationship between the two terms was problematic. We may now follow up on that observation by suggesting that a third line of inquiry be regarded as a supplement to both of the preceding steps. We should ask where each relative lives, with a view to determining both the composition of the respondent's household and the nearness-remoteness of the named relatives. Also, it would be desirable to learn where the important instrumental activities are carried out and the spatial relation of these activities to the household. Thus the problematic nature of the relationship between the household and the family would be illuminated.

From time to time writers suggest that it is useful to regard the life cycle of the family as an ingredient of a well designed family study. (See, e.g., Glick, 1957; Glick and Parke, 1965; Norton, 1974; Glick, 1977.) What is generally meant by this suggestion is that note should be taken of the fact that nuclear families are formed by marrying couples who expand the size of the family through procreation, and then that the family begins to dwindle as offspring mature and depart and the parents age and die. Where the familial organization is somewhat more elaborate—for example, stem or joint family occupying a single dwelling unit—it seems that after a generation or so the size of the unit exceeds the limitations of the dwelling space with the consequence that there comes a breaking up of the domestic unit. Typically this appears to occur at the death of the patriarch. Then there arises the empirical question as to whether the breaking up of the domestic unit signifies the simultaneous breaking up of the functional unit.

Multigenerational studies are useful to explore conditions under which large familial systems wax and wane (Corti, 1928a; Greven, 1970; see also Hill, 1970). Whitten (1970) has offered a five-generational model of upward mobility on the basis of his work in Latin America. Although the period of time embraced by such formulations may be so formidable that research would be feasible only by historical methods, still it is evident that a thoroughgoing study of the family in any setting would include the temporal dimension and thus allow for observations at various points in the development of the familial system.[5]

One other aspect of the study of the family that has not been mentioned here has to do with influence. By this is meant the degree to which and the ways in which each individual's daily behavior and lifelong activities are controlled, governed, regulated, influenced by considerations pertaining to the family as contrasted with control or influence on the part of extrafamilial considerations and structures.

Thus what I am proposing is that a complete diagramming of the familial system in a given setting would specify the structure, functioning, and influence of that system through space and time.

It should be noted that the procedure suggested above offers a way of avoiding the dilemma referred to in Chapter 5 about the difficulty in determining from ethnographic accounts whether it was the actual or the ideal familial system that was being reported. What is proposed here is that the functional familial system be regarded as consisting of those of ego's relatives whom he/she names as co-actors with himself/herself with respect to whatever functional activities the researcher may specify. Thus we are not asking respondents what the familial system *should* look like.

Other Topics

To this point the discussion has been oriented toward further exploration of our model. But are there other topics beyond the model that it would be fruitful to investigate? Our work to this point has suggested two such topics. One of these, as noted in Chapter 2, is that of ethnicity. Our investigation left us quite mystified about its nature. Although there has been a considerable amount of research on ethnicity, we are aware of none that serves to illuminate the ways in which it has affected, rather than merely reflected, familial organization.

A second topic raised by our own investigations—and again the context is Chapter 2—concerns trust. In the investigation into suburban families we learned that Jews reported they were much more disposed to place trust for rearing their children in relatives whereas Protestants were more disposed to rely on voluntary organizations. Why is this? Again, of course, we are being led back to ethnicity. However, there are other ideas related to trust that it would seem useful to investigate—for example, Fortes' notion of prescribed altruism, prosocial behavior, and congeniality.

Other Considerations

In our work we have made use of two types of data—surveys conducted in the United States by the Bureau of the Census and by ourselves (see Chaps. 2 and 3) and codes based on ethnographies of preindustrial societies (see Chaps. 4 and 7-8). What can we say about data for future studies?

As regards census data, we have indicated that the data required to illuminate familial systems involves relating a respondent's co-actors in functional activities to the set of that person's relatives wherever the relatives may reside. Since the Bureau of the Census shows no sign of accepting this kind of conceptualization, its relevance to students of the family seems confined to those who equate family with household. The reader should not construe these remarks as indicating the writer's belief that it would be easy to convert to the kind of inquiry advocated here. Having engaged in this sort of work ourselves, we are keenly aware of the difficulty and expense involved in collecting such data. It may be, moreover, that the present is a singularly inopportune time to advocate such a move because it would require census-takers to extend the range of questions that respondents might regard as personal, and the conduct of our government in recent years has not been such as to inspire confidence that such information might not be employed for malicious purposes. (While on the topic of the Census Bureau, it is relevant to point out that information on religious affiliation—one of the most useful indicators of ethnicity—has not been gathered since 1957.)

As regards the gathering of survey data on the part of independent researchers like ourselves, the picture seems almost as dismal. Three considerations seem to justify such pessimism. First is the obvious shrinkage of funds available for social research—especially for basic social science. A second difficulty that has become progressively inhibiting in recent years is the concern about the exploitation of respondents. Concerns that were generated out of widely publicized and regrettable events in the biomedical field have ramified into widespread restrictions on the use of "human subjects." And, finally, it appears that there is a progressive reluctance on the part of the general public to serve as participants in social science research for the understandable reason that they cannot be sure that information they give will not be used against them.

Perhaps the picture is rosier—or at least, less dismal—with respect to the secondary analysis of ethnographic data. (We should note, however, that the supply of "uncontaminated" primitive tribes is rapidly running out.) With respect to the three difficulties noted in the preceding paragraph, we can see that the second and third do not apply to ethnographies that are already published. Of course there is the omnipresent possibility that ethnographers may not have thought to include information codable for such categories. This can be determined only by conducting a systematic search.

Our quest for the determinants of familial organization has been wide-ranging.

We have demonstrated that familial organization—its structure, function, and influence—varies not only across cultures and across time but also within our own society. Many data are still needed. While the issues are complex, I have suggested some techniques and methods for addressing them. The topic is an important one and one which I believe bears further work.

Notes

1. For those disposed to make actuarial predictions, the consequence of the above statement is that we shall always have a familial system. The difficulty with actuarially based predictions is that frequently the actuary is unaware when the parameters of his predicting equation have changed values.

2. If the variables were ordinal and the relationships were known to be monotonic, we could use Harner's technique (1970) to infer direction of causation from synchronic data, but without these assumptions Harner's technique cannot help us.

3. Perhaps it is of interest—although I have not figured out how to make it theoretically relevant—to note that our language contains a number of terms to apply to people who have either left or been expelled from the familial system: orphan, divorcée, deserting husband, runaway child, runaway wife, widow, widower. All of these terms seem to carry—or at least seem at some time to have carried—negative connotations. Beyond the ruptured relationships denoted by the foregoing set of terms, there are other activities that denote the suspending or terminating of familial relationships. These include expulsion by the wife-mother of a husband-father when the latter fails to be economically productive, as reported by Rainwater for American black ghettos, leaving the aged to die of exposure by Eskimo tribes, abandoning aged parents in nursing homes, getting rid of the young through placing them for adoption, apprenticeship, boarding schools, and marriage.

4. In previous formulations (Winch, 1962; Winch and Gordon, 1974) I have postulated that the flow of influence is from system to individual rather than the reverse. Realizing that influence can flow in either direction, I sought thereby to avoid the loss of parsimony that occurs in the formulation that everything-is-related-to-everything-else because (1) it was and remains my judgment that more influence flows from societal systems to the individual than the reverse, and (2) in the works cited the behavior of the individual was the focus of research interest.

5. With time as the overarching concept of their discipline, it is interesting to note one historian chiding others for failing to take time into account in the study of the family (Hareven, 1974). Indeed, it is amusing to see some of these students of the past professing to constitute a wave of the future as they set about to show that Parsons was not only right in declaring the familial pattern of the United States to be isolated and nuclear, but also that such has been the universal pattern through time and space and over all cultures. It does appear that this wave will break up into minuscule droplets as the historians pursue their quest to estimate mean household size for every hamlet at every decade. Readers who regard this remark as hyperbole may consult Tables 4-1, 5-1, and 18-1 in Laslett (1972d), which constitute a giant stride in this direction.

Appendix A

Questions from a Survey in an Upper-Middle-Class Suburb Pertaining to the Study of Ethnicity and Extended Familism (Reported in Chapter 2)

Address (or description) of dwelling unit _____

_____

List all persons in dwelling unit 21 years of age or over (Total _____)
(FOR CODER)
(Total related by kinship _____)
(FOR CODER)

RELATION TO HEAD	SEX	AGE	MARITAL STATUS
Head			

List all minors in dwelling unit.   (Total _____)
(FOR CODER)

RELATION TO HEAD	SEX	AGE	MARITAL STATUS

(Total Household Members _____)
(FOR CODER)

19. One of the things we need to find out is the importance of different kinds
of kinfolks to people in the Chicago area. First, I'd like to ask you about
your relatives, in the Chicago area, then I want to ask about your husband's
relatives. I want to read through the card with you. You tell me when you
have any relatives of a given sort in the Chicago area. (SHOW CARD)
Just give me the number on this card.

1. Parents	7. Brothers and their Families
3. Grandparents	9. Sisters and their Families
5. Grandparents' Brother or Sister	

NOW, ON YOUR MOTHER'S SIDE ARE THERE ANY:
11. Mother's Brothers and their Families
13. Mother's Sisters and their Families
15. Male Cousins on your Mother's Side
17. Female Cousins on Your Mother's Side
19. Any other Kin on your Mother's Side (Nephews, Nieces, Married and
Living in Their Own Households, Second Cousins, and the Like?)

NOW, ON YOUR FATHER'S SIDE ARE THERE ANY:
21. Father's Brothers and their Families
23. Father's Sisters and their Families
25. Male Cousins on your Father's Side
27. Female Cousins on your Father's Side
29. Any other Kin on your Father's Side (Nephews and Nieces who are
Married and Living in Their Own Households, Second Cousins,
and the Like?)

31. An ex-husband of yours

Col. A	Col. B	Col. C	Col. D	(FOR CODER)	Col. E	Col. F
No. From Card	No. Sep. Hshlds.	No. in Hshld.	Where Live	Leave Blank	How Often See	How Often Phone

FOR EACH CATEGORY FROM #1 <u>THRU</u> #9 TO WHICH RESPONDENT CLAIMS KIN:

A. Record Code Number of Kin Relations from Card in Column A.

B. Ask: "How many separate households of (Relationship)?" Record by numbering one for each household in Column B. Then for each household ask Question C, D, E, F.

C. For each household ask "How many members are there in that household?" Record number in Column C.

D. Ask: "About where do they live? Is it this suburb, another Chicago suburb, North Chicago, Central Chicago, West Chicago, or South Chicago?" IF ANOTHER SUBURB, Ask: "What suburb is that?" Record by named place in Column D.

E. Ask: "About how often do you or some member of your family see one or more members of that household? Is it (1) Every day (2) At least once a week (3) Every few weeks (4) At least once in the past year (5) Not once in the past year?" Record number of response in Column E.

F. Ask: "And about how often are you or some member of your family in touch with them by telephone? Is it (1) Every day (2) At least once a week (3) Every few weeks (4) At least once in the past year (5) Not once in the past year?" Record in Column F.

FOR EACH CATEGORY FROM #11 to #31 TO WHICH RESPONDENT SAYS "YES" TO QUESTION 19:

A. Record Code Number of Kin Relation in Column A.

B. Ask: "How many separate households of (Relationship)?" RECORD TOTAL IN COLUMN B.

C. Ask: "Do you or anyone in your household see or phone anyone in any of these households at least once a month?" RECORD YES OR NO IN COLUMN F.

20. Now, I'd like to do the same thing for your husband's relatives who live in the Chicago area. Would you tell me when we come to a kind of relative he has living here?

1. Parents	7. Brothers and their Families
3. Grandparents	9. Sisters and their Families
5. Grandparents' Brother or Sister	

NOW, ON HIS <u>MOTHER'S SIDE</u> ARE THERE ANY:

11. Mother's Brothers and their Families

13. Mother's Sisters and their Families

15. Male Cousins on his Mother's Side

17. Female Cousins on his Mother's Side

19. Any other Kin on his Mother's Side (Nephews, Nieces, Married and Living in Their Own Households, Second Cousins, and the Like?)

NOW, ON HIS <u>FATHER'S SIDE</u> ARE THERE ANY:

21. Father's Brothers and their Families

23. Father's Sisters and their Families

25. Male Cousins on his Father's Side

27. Female Cousins on his Father's Side

29. Any other Kin on his Father's Side (Nephews and Nieces who are Married and Living in Their Own Households, Second Cousins, and the Like?)

31. An ex-wife of his

				(FOR CODER)		
Col. A	Col. B	Col. C	Col. D		Col. E	Col. F
No. From Card	No. Sep. Hshlds.	No. in Hshld.	Where Live	Leave Blank	How Often See	How Often Phone

FOR EACH CATEGORY FROM #1 <u>THRU</u> #9 TO WHICH RESPONDENT SAYS "YES" TO QUESTION 20:

A. Record Code Number of Kin Relations from Card in Column A.

B. Ask: "How many separate households of (Relationship)?" Record by numbering one for each household in Column B. Then for each household ask Question C, D, E, F.

C. For each household ask "How many members are there in that household?" Record number in Column C.

D. Ask: "About where do they live? Is it this suburb, another Chicago suburb, North Chicago, Central Chicago, West Chicago, or South Chicago?" IF ANOTHER SUBURB, Ask: "What suburb is that?" Record by named place in Column D.

E. Ask: "About how often do you or some member of your family see one or more members of that household? Is it (1) Every day (2) At least once a week (3) Every few weeks (4) At least once in the past year (5) Not once in the past year?" Record number of response in Column E.

F. Ask: "And about how often are you or some member of your family in touch with them by telephone? Is it (1) Every day (2) At least once a week (3) Every few weeks (4) At least once in the past year (5) Not once in the past year?" Record in Column F.

FOR EACH CATEGORY FROM #11 TO #31 TO WHICH RESPONDENT SAYS "YES" TO QUESTION 20:

A. Record Code Number of Kin Relation in Column A.

B. Ask: "How many separate households of (Relationship)?" RECORD TOTAL IN COLUMN B.

C. Ask: "Do you or anyone in your household see or phone anyone in any of these households at least once a month?" RECORD YES OR NO IN COLUMN F.

21. Do you or your husband have any children or stepchildren who are living outside your household now? That is, grown children with their own households?

    ☐ Yes　☐ No

    IF YES: RECORD "SON" OR "DAUGHTER" IN TABLE AND ASK QUESTIONS A-F ON PRECEDING PAGE.

    21a. Do you or your husband have any grandchildren with their own households?

    ☐ Yes　☐ No

    IF YES: RECORD "GRANDSON" OR "GRANDDAUGHTER" IN TABLE AND ASK QUESTIONS A-F ON PRECEDING PAGE.

22. In some families there is an organization called a "Cousin's Club." Is there one in yours?

    ☐ Yes　☐ No

    IF YES:
    22a. Which side of the family is that on?

    ☐ Yours　☐ Husband's　☐ Both　(IF BOTH, ASK Q 22c ABOUT WIFE'S)

    22b. Have you attended a meeting during the past year?

    ☐ Yes　☐ No

    22c. How many people were there last time it met? _____
    NUMBER

23. Have you attended a Family Reunion during the past couple of years?

    ☐ Yes　☐ No

    IF YES:
    23a. Which side of the family was that on?

    ☐ Yours　☐ Husband's　☐ Both　(IF BOTH, ASK Q 23b ABOUT WIFE'S)

    23b. How many people were there last time? _____
    NUMBER

24. Have you attended a funeral for someone in your family or your husband's family in the past couple of years?

    ☐ Yes　☐ No

    IF YES:
    24a. Which side of the family was that on?

    ☐ Yours　☐ Husband's　☐ Both　(IF BOTH, ASK Q 24b ABOUT WIFE'S)

    24b. How many relatives were there? _____
    NUMBER

25. Some people have a group of relatives with whom they are very close, called a Family Circle. Several couples visit and go out together regularly. Do you and your husband belong to such a Family Circle?

    ☐ Yes　☐ No

25a. Which side of the family is that on?

    ☐ Yours   ☐ Husband's   ☐ Both   (IF BOTH, ASK Q 25b ABOUT WIFE'S)

25b. How often do you meet as a group? Is it:

    ☐ Once a week   ☐ Once a month

IF YES: ☐ Several times a month   ☐ Several times a year

25c. How many people were there last time you met?_____
                                                 NUMBER

25d. Occasionally such groups elect officers and have a treasury. Does this group do that?

    ☐ Yes   ☐ No

26. Some people get together fairly regularly with several couples who are not their relatives, to visit, dine, go out together and the like. These are sometimes called Social Circles. Would you say you and your husband belong to a Social Circle?

    ☐ Yes   ☐ No

26a. How often do you meet as a group? Is it:

    ☐ Once a week   ☐ Once a month

IF YES: ☐ Several times a month   ☐ Several times a year

26b. How many people were there last time you got together?

                                                 NUMBER

27. How about your friends in the Chicago area, could you start with the one you feel closest to, and really trust, and tell me where they live? We don't want the exact address, but we do want the name of the suburb or the part of Chicago. (RECORD BELOW)

27a. Is this a single friend, a couple, or a family?

27b. What is the occupation of the head of the household?

27c. About how often do you or some member of your family see one or more members of the friend's household? Is it:

    1. Every day   3. Every few weeks

    2. At least once a week   4. At least once in the past year

           5. Not once in the past year

27d. About how often do you or some member of your family telephone one or more members of the friend's household? Is it:

    1. Every day   3. Every few weeks

    2. At least once a week   4. At least once in the past year

           5. Not once in the past year

LOCATION OF FRIEND'S HOME	S, C, F	OCCUPATION OF HEAD	FREQUENCY OF:	
			Seeing	Telephoning
1.				
2.				
3.				
4.				
5.				

CONTINUE: Now the one you feel next closest to, would you tell me where they live? S, C, F? Occupation of head? How often you see? How often you telephone? STOP WITH 5 FRIENDS.

28. In general, do you and your husband have mostly the same or separate friends?

    □ Mostly the same   □ Some in common, some separate

    □ Mostly separate

29. Do you ever spend an evening or afternoon with "the girls," that is, with other women friends?

    □ Yes   □ No

    IF YES: 29a. Is that: □ Often   □ Sometimes or □ Very seldom?

30. Whom do you generally spend a social evening or afternoon with? Is it:

    □ Your friends   □ Your husband's relatives

    □ Your own relatives   □ Other _____
                                       (SPECIFY)

31. In general, whom do you see most often socially? Is it:

    □ Your friends   □ Your husband's relatives

    □ Your own relatives   □ Other _____
                                       (SPECIFY)

32. Does your husband ever spend an evening or afternoon with "the boys," that is, other men friends?

    □ Yes   □ No

    IF YES: 32a. Is that: □ Often   □ Sometimes or □ Very seldom?

We have found that some people in Chicago depend quite a lot on their relatives, their friends, their neighbors, or all of them, while some people depend on other sources. In the following questions we'd like you to tell us which is the most important to you, in various kinds of situations.

33. First, if you need help in baby-sitting and caring for the children most generally, whom do you ask?

☐ Neighbors   ☐ Other agent _____

☐ Friend   (SPECIFY)

☐ Relative _____   ☐ Doesn't arise

      (SPECIFY)   ☐ Do it ourselves

34. And where have you usually borrowed equipment such as you might need for the house, extra dishes or glasses or a sewing machine?

☐ Neighbors   ☐ Other agent _____

☐ Friend   (SPECIFY)

☐ Relative _____   ☐ Doesn't arise

      (SPECIFY)

35. Where have you gotten the most help when there is serious illness in the immediate family?

☐ Neighbors   ☐ Other agent _____

☐ Friend   (SPECIFY)

☐ Relative _____   ☐ Hasn't arisen

      (SPECIFY)   ☐ Take care of it ourselves

36. Where have you gotten the most help with cooking, entertaining, and housework generally?

☐ Neighbor   ☐ Other agent _____

☐ Friend   (SPECIFY)

☐ Relative _____   ☐ Doesn't arise

      (SPECIFY)   ☐ Take care of it ourselves

37. Where have you gotten the most help with shopping and errands?

☐ Neighbors   ☐ Other _____

☐ Friend   (SPECIFY)

☐ Relative _____   ☐ Doesn't arise

      (SPECIFY)   ☐ Do it ourselves

38. Where did you get the most help getting settled, the last time you moved to a new house?

    ☐ Neighbors   ☐ Other _____

    ☐ Friend   (SPECIFY)

    ☐ Relative _____   ☐ Doesn't arise

              (SPECIFY)   ☐ Do it ourselves

39. Where do you and your husband go most frequently for advice and information?

    ☐ Neighbors   ☐ Other _____

    ☐ Friends   (SPECIFY)

    ☐ Relatives _____   ☐ Doesn't arise

              (SPECIFY)   ☐ Do it ourselves

40. Where do you go for advice and information on child-rearing?

    ☐ Neighbors   ☐ Other _____

    ☐ Friends   (SPECIFY)

    ☐ Relatives _____   ☐ Doesn't arise

              (SPECIFY)   ☐ Do it ourselves

41. Where does your husband go for advice and information on making major purchases?

    ☐ Neighbors   ☐ Other _____

    ☐ Friends   (SPECIFY)

    ☐ Relatives _____   ☐ Doesn't arise

              (SPECIFY)   ☐ Do it ourselves

42. Where have you gotten most help when you were looking for an apartment or a house?

    ☐ Neighbors   ☐ Other _____

    ☐ Friends   (SPECIFY)

    ☐ Relatives _____   ☐ Doesn't arise

              (SPECIFY)   ☐ Do it ourselves

43. Where do you and your husband usually go when you need financial assistance?

    ☐ Neighbors   ☐ Other _____

    ☐ Friends   (SPECIFY)

    ☐ Relatives _____   ☐ Doesn't arise

              (SPECIFY)   ☐ Do it ourselves

44. Suppose you had a serious emergency and needed more money than your credit would provide, where would you go?

☐ Neighbors   ☐ Other _____
                                      (SPECIFY)
☐ Friends
                     ☐ Do it ourselves
☐ Relatives _____
          (SPECIFY)

45. When your family goes on a vacation trip, do you ordinarily plan it so as to visit and stay with people?

☐ Yes   ☐ No

IF YES: 45a. Who have you usually visited with?

☐ Friends   ☐ Relatives _____
                                    (SPECIFY)

46. Where do you usually borrow equipment such as you might need for outdoor work, for example, lawnmower, hedge-trimmer, automobile tools and the like?

☐ Neighbors   ☐ Other _____
                                      (SPECIFY)
☐ Friends
                     ☐ Doesn't arise
☐ Relatives _____
          (SPECIFY)

47. When you last moved to a new house, where did you get help in the job of moving?

☐ Neighbors   ☐ Other _____
                                      (SPECIFY)
☐ Friends
                     ☐ Hasn't arisen
☐ Relatives _____
          (SPECIFY)   ☐ Do it ourselves

48. Where have you gotten help when you had to make repairs on your home or had trouble with your automobile?

☐ Neighbors   ☐ Other _____
                                      (SPECIFY)
☐ Friends
                     ☐ Hasn't arisen
☐ Relatives _____
          (SPECIFY)   ☐ Do it ourselves

49. Where has your husband obtained help when hunting for a job?

☐ Neighbor   ☐ Other _____
                                      (SPECIFY)
☐ Friend
                     ☐ Hasn't arisen
☐ Relative _____
          (SPECIFY)   ☐ Do it ourselves

50. Now we'd like to turn the questions around. For example, do you baby-sit for anyone or look after their children?

☐ Yes   ☐ No

IF YES: 50a. Whom do you help most?

☐ Neighbor   ☐ Relative_____
                              (SPECIFY)
☐ Friend

                ☐ Other_____
                              (SPECIFY)

51. Whom have you helped most in the way of loaning dishes, glasses, sewing machine, or other equipment used around the house?

☐ Neighbor   ☐ Other_____
                                          (SPECIFY)
☐ Friend

☐ Relative_____   ☐ Hasn't arisen
           (SPECIFY)

52. Whom have you helped most when there was serious illness in their immediate family?

☐ Neighbor   ☐ Other_____
                                          (SPECIFY)
☐ Friend

☐ Relative_____   ☐ Hasn't arisen
           (SPECIFY)

53. Whom have you helped most with cooking and housework?

☐ Neighbor   ☐ Other_____
                                          (SPECIFY)
☐ Friend

☐ Relative_____   ☐ Hasn't arisen
           (SPECIFY)

54. And whom have you helped most with shopping and errands?

☐ Neighbor   ☐ Other_____
                                          (SPECIFY)
☐ Friend

☐ Relative_____   ☐ Hasn't arisen
           (SPECIFY)

55. Whom have you helped most in getting settled into a new home?

☐ Neighbor   ☐ Other_____
                                          (SPECIFY)
☐ Friend

☐ Relative_____   ☐ Hasn't arisen
           (SPECIFY)

56. Who comes to you and your husband most often for advice or information?

    ☐ Neighbor   ☐ Other _____
                                                  (SPECIFY)
    ☐ Friend
                                    ☐ Hasn't arisen
    ☐ Relative _____
                  (SPECIFY)

57. Who comes to you most often for advice on child-rearing?

    ☐ Neighbor   ☐ Other _____
                                                  (SPECIFY)
    ☐ Friend
                                      ☐ Hasn't arisen
    ☐ Relative _____
                  (SPECIFY)

58. Who comes to your husband most often for advice and information on making major purchases?

    ☐ Neighbor   ☐ Other _____
                                                  (SPECIFY)
    ☐ Friend
                                      ☐ Hasn't arisen
    ☐ Relative _____
                  (SPECIFY)

59. Whom have you helped most in finding an apartment or a house?

    ☐ Neighbor   ☐ Other _____
                                                  (SPECIFY)
    ☐ Friend
                                      ☐ Hasn't arisen
    ☐ Relative _____
                  (SPECIFY)

60. Whom have you helped most by giving financial assistance?

    ☐ Neighbor   ☐ Other _____
                                                  (SPECIFY)
    ☐ Friend
                                      ☐ Hasn't arisen
    ☐ Relative _____
                  (SPECIFY)

61. Who has come most frequently to stay with your family?

    ☐ Neighbor   ☐ Other _____
                                                  (SPECIFY)
    ☐ Friend
                                      ☐ Hasn't arisen
    ☐ Relative _____
                  (SPECIFY)

62. Whom has your family helped most by lending equipment for outdoor work, such as lawnmower, hedge-trimmer, or automobile tools?

    □ Neighbor   □ Other _____
                                           (SPECIFY)

    □ Friend

    □ Relative _____   □ Hasn't arisen
               (SPECIFY)

63. Whom did your family last help in the job of moving into a new home?

    □ Neighbor   □ Other _____
                                           (SPECIFY)

    □ Friend

    □ Relative _____   □ Hasn't arisen
               (SPECIFY)

64. Whom has your family helped most through giving assistance with home or auto repairs?

    □ Neighbor   □ Other _____
                                           (SPECIFY)

    □ Friend

    □ Relative _____   □ Hasn't arisen
               (SPECIFY)

65. Whom have you and your husband helped most in looking for a job?

    □ Neighbor   □ Other _____
                                           (SPECIFY)

    □ Friend

    □ Relative _____   □ Hasn't arisen
               (SPECIFY)

66. Next we have a set of statements pertaining to family life. After I read each one, I want you to tell me whether you AGREE STRONGLY, AGREE, DON'T KNOW, DISAGREE or DISAGREE STRONGLY. Generally, I like the whole family—husband, wife, and children—to spend evenings together.

    □ SA   □ A   □ DK   □ D   □ SD

67. I want a house where family members can spend time together.

    □ SA   □ A   □ DK   □ D   □ SD

68. I want a location which would make it easy for relatives to get together.

    □ SA   □ A   □ DK   □ D   □ SD

69. I want a house with enough room for our parents to feel free to live with us.

    □ SA   □ A   □ DK   □ D   □ SD

70. Now we go back to another kind of question. With respect to such problems as raising children, getting along with relatives, and the like. Does it help you in deciding what to do to consider how your relatives might handle such problems?

☐ Yes   ☐ No   ☐ DK

71. Have you gotten any ideas about matters such as these recently from relatives?

☐ Yes   ☐ No   ☐ DK

72. If your relatives strongly disagree with you on such matters, would it bother you?

☐ Yes   ☐ No   ☐ DK

IF YES: 72a. How is that? _____

73. Would you talk over your differences with them?

☐ Yes   ☐ No   ☐ DK

IF YES: 73a. How is that? _____

74. If you did talk it over, would you reconsider your ideas or feelings on the matter?

☐ Yes   ☐ No   ☐ DK

IF YES: 74a. How is that? _____

75. In an emergency—like an earthquake, tornado, or flood—which relatives would be most likely to offer you help?

_____

_____

76. If in an emergency like we just talked about, you could make only one call, whom would you call?

☐ Neighbor   ☐ Relative _____
                                   (SPECIFY)
☐ Friend   ☐ Agency _____
                                   (SPECIFY)

IF RESPONDENT HAS CHILDREN, ASK QUESTIONS 77 and 78.

77. If your child at school came down with a bad cold but you were busy, which of these would you do:

☐ Bring the child home immediately

☐ Wait until you weren't so busy then get the child

☐ Rely on the school officials to do what was necessary

78. If something happened to you and your hsuband, who in the Chicago area would you want to see raising your children?

_____ Why is that? _____

_____

79. Outside your immediate family, is there anyone in this neighborhood you feel you could trust absolutely in an emergency?

☐ Yes   ☐ No

IF YES: Who is that?

☐ Neighbor   ☐ Relative _____

☐ Friend   (SPECIFY)

                                ☐ Agency _____

                                            (SPECIFY)

80. Outside this neighborhood, is there anyone in this suburb you feel you could trust absolutely?

☐ Yes   ☐ No

IF YES: Who is that?

☐ Friend   ☐ Relative _____

                                            (SPECIFY)

           ☐ Agency _____

                        (SPECIFY)

81. Outside this suburb, in the Chicago area, is there anyone you feel you could trust absolutely?

☐ Yes   ☐ No

IF YES: Who is that?

☐ Friend   ☐ Relative _____

                                            (SPECIFY)

           ☐ Agency _____

                        (SPECIFY)

82. Since you have been married, has your husband ever worked with relatives—including your relatives, his, or married children—as partner, employer, or employee?

☐ Yes   ☐ No   IF "NO" SKIP TO QUESTION 83.

IF YES, ASK FOLLOWING QUESTIONS ABOUT MOST RECENT BUSINESS CONNECTION:

82a. Was he: ☐ Partner   ☐ Employer   ☐ Employee

     IF PARTNER: Was there a formal agreement or contract?

                ☐ Yes   ☐ No

IF EMPLOYER OR EMPLOYEE: Was it a:

☐ Corporation   ☐ Partnership   or   ☐ Owned by one person?

82b. Is he still associated with this business?   ☐ Yes   ☐ No

IF
YES:
{
82c. How is it going financially?

☐ Well   ☐ So-so   ☐ Not so well

82d. How about relations with kinfolks? _____

_____
}

IF
NO:
{
82e. Why is he no longer with the business?

(DON'T READ) ☐ It dissolved   ☐ He was fired   ☐ He quit
}

82f. Which relatives were (are) in this business? LIST BY
SPECIFIC KIN RELATIONSHIP:

_____

82g. Who was head of the business? _____

82h. What kind of business was it? _____

82i. What was the largest number of people employed in this business
while your husband was (has been) associated with it? _____
(NUMBER)

82j. How were the financial records handled?

☐ Accountant   ☐ They did it themselves

☐ Bookkeeper   ☐ Other

☐ Cash

82k. From what you and your husband have seen, what are your and
his feelings about working with relatives? _____

_____

83. Since you and your husband have been married, have you ever lived
with relatives?

☐ Yes   ☐ No   IF YES: Which relatives were they?

_____

84. Since you and your husband have been married, have relatives ever
lived with you?

☐ Yes   ☐ No   IF YES: Which relatives were they?

_____

85. When you were first married, did you receive any financial support
from your family or your husband's family?

☐ Yes   ☐ No   IF YES: Which family was it from?

☐ Own   ☐ Husband's   ☐ Both

CENSUS DATA FOR THE HOUSEHOLD

1. How many years have you and your husband been married?

   _____ years

2. Have you ever been married before?   ☐ Yes   ☐ No

3. What was the highest grade
   in school you completed? _____
   (IF COLLEGE, SPECIFY COLLEGE)

4. Where were your parents
   living when you were born? _____
   (GET TOWN AND STATE)

   IF BORN OUTSIDE THE CHICAGO AREA
   4a. How long have you lived in the Chicago area? _____ years

5. How long have you lived in this suburb? _____

6. Where was your
   husband born? _____
   (GET TOWN AND STATE)

   IF HUSBAND BORN OUTSIDE THE CHICAGO AREA
   6a. For what reasons did he move?

   X IF MENTIONED RANK REASON

   _____ _____ Family moved when living with them

   _____ _____ Moved to be close to relatives

   _____ _____ Job transfer

   _____ _____ Chance for a job

   _____ _____ Health reasons

   Other reasons (SPECIFY AND RECORD RANK) _____

   _____

   IF MORE THAN ONE REASON MENTIONED IN QUESTION 6a,
   OBTAIN RANK ORDER OF IMPORTANCE AND RECORD ABOVE
   FOR EACH REASON, ASKING:

   Which would you say was the most important reason? . . .
   Second in importance? . . . etc.

7. What was the national origin of
   your family on your father's side? _____

   IF BORN IN U.S.: 7a. When did the family come from there—was
   it in your father's generation, your grandfather's, or before that?

   ☐ Father's   ☐ Grandfather's   ☐ Before that

8. Do you have a religious preference?   ☐ Yes   ☐ No

   IF YES: 8a. What is your preference? _____

   8b. How often do you attend religious services? Is it once a week or more, a few times a month, once a month, a few times a year or never?

   ☐ Once a week   ☐ A few times a year

   ☐ A few times a month ☐ Never

   ☐ Once a month

9. Are you employed outside the household?   ☐ Yes   ☐ No

   IF YES: 9a. What is your occupation?

   _____

   (E.G., TYPIST, SALESLADY, TEACHER)

10. Is your husband employed now? ☐ Yes ☐ No; unemployed ☐ Retired

11. What is his occupation? (IF UNEMPLOYED, RETIRED, GET LAST OCCUPATION)

    _____

    (E.G., ACCOUNTANT, SALESMAN, SUPERVISOR, JOURNALIST)

12. What business is that in?

    _____

    (E.G., GROCERY, FURNITURE FACTORY, INSURANCE)

    12a. Does your husband's firm have any branches outside the Chicago area to which people in jobs like your husband's might be transferred during their careers?

    ☐ Yes   ☐ No   ☐ Don't know

    12b. (SHOW CARD) Which of these categories best describes your husband's income from his work?

    1. Entire salary   3. Largely other, some salary
    2. Mostly salary, some other 4. Entire other than salary

    IF CATEGORIES 2, 3, OR 4 ASK:

    12c. Would you say his income varies depending upon how well <u>he does</u>, or how well the <u>business</u> does?

    ☐ How well he does   ☐ How well the business does

13. What was the last grade he completed in school? _____

    (IF COLLEGE, GET NAME OF COLLEGE)

14. What is his religious
    preference? _____

15. How long have you lived
    in your present dwelling? _____ years

16. Where did you live just
    before you moved here? _____

17. Do you get a local community
    paper or shopping news?   □ Yes   □ No

    IF YES: 17a. How many times
                  a month do you read it? _____

             17b. What do you like best in it?

                  _____
                  (IF "NEWS" ASK: WHAT KIND OF NEWS?"

18. (SHOW CARD) What was your total family income, <u>before</u> tax
    deduction in 1963—considering all sources such as rents, profits,
    wages, pensions, interest, and so on? We do not need the exact
    figure—all we need to have is the letter which comes closest to
    the total family income.

A. Under $5,000	G. $15,000-$16,999
B. $5,000-$6,999	H. $17,000-$18,999
C. $7,000-$8,999	I. $19,000-$20,999
D. $9,000-$10,999	J. $21,000-$25,000
E. $11,000-$12,999	K. Over $25,000
F. $13,000-$14,999	

Appendix B

Questions from a Statewide
Survey Pertaining to the
Study of Ethnicity and
Extended Familism
(Reported in Chapter 2)

1. This interview covers several subjects but we'd like to start out by asking some questions that will allow us to study how often Wisconsin residents get together with their relatives and others. First, how many—if any—brothers and sisters do you have?

☐ None   or   _____(# BROTHERS AND SISTERS)
(GO TO Q 2)

1a. Do any of your brothers or sisters live in or near your community here?

☐ Yes   ☐ No
(GO TO Q 1c)

1b. How many separate households is that? _____

1c. How often are you or some other member of your household here in touch by telephone or face-to-face with your brothers or sisters? (SHOW CARD 1)

CARD 1

☐ Every day	☐ Few times a year
☐ At least once a week	☐ Once a year
☐ Few times a month	☐ Less often
☐ Once a month	☐ Never

2. Are your parents living? ☐ Both ☐ Mother ☐ Father ☐ Neither
(GO TO Q 3)

2a. Do your parents (Does your _____) live in or near your community here?

☐ Yes   ☐ No   ☐ Parents live with R
(GO TO Q 3)

2b. How often are you or some other member of your household here in touch by telephone or face-to-face with your (parents; mother; father)? (SHOW CARD 1)

CARD 1

☐ Every day	☐ Few times a year
☐ At least once a week	☐ Once a year
☐ Few times a month	☐ Less often
☐ Once a month	☐ Never

3. Do any of your other relatives on your side live in or near your community here?

☐ Yes   ☐ No
(GO TO Q 4)

3a. How many separate households are there of relatives on your side who live around here?

_____(#)

4. How often are you or some other member of your household here in touch by telephone or face-to-face with any of your other relatives? (SHOW CARD 1)

_____(FROM CARD 1)

5. Do you (or does your SPOUSE) baby-sit for anyone or look after their children?

☐ Yes ☐ No
(GO TO Q 6)

5a. Whom do you usually help most this way ... would it be neighbors, other friends, or relatives?

☐ Neighbors ☐ Friends ☐ Relatives Other:_____
(GO TO Q 6) (GO TO Q 6)

5b. Which relatives have you helped this way?_____

6. Have you (and your SPOUSE) ever had the occasion to help anyone by giving financial assistance?

☐ Yes ☐ No
(GO TO Q 7)

6a. To whom have you given the most financial aid ... a neighbor, some other friend, or a relative?

☐ Neighbor ☐ Friend ☐ Relative Other:_____
(GO TO Q 7) (GO TO Q 7)

6b. Which relatives have you helped this way? _____

7. Outside of your immediate family, is there anyone in or quite near your community whom you feel you could trust absolutely?

☐ Yes ☐ No
(GO TO Q 8)

7a. Would that be a neighbor, a friend, a relative, or whom?

☐ Neighbor ☐ Friend ☐ Relative Other:_____
(GO TO Q 8) (GO TO Q 8)

7b. Which relative would that be? _____

8. Suppose you had a serious emergency and needed more money than your credit would raise. Where would you go first ... would it be to a neighbor, a friend, a relative, or where?

☐ Neighbor ☐ Friend ☐ Relative Other:_____
(GO TO Q 9) (GO TO Q 9)

8a. Which relative would this be?_____

9. In an emergency—like an earthquake, tornado, or flood—which of your (or your SPOUSE'S) relatives would be most likely to offer help?

_____

I'm going to read a series of statements you sometimes hear people make. For each one, I'd like to know if you strongly agree with it, agree, both agree and disagree, disagree, or strongly disagree. (SHOW CARD 2) Just give me the number on the card that comes closest to the way you feel about each statement.

CARD 2
---

1. Strongly agree	3. Agree-Disagree	5. Strongly disagree
2. Agree	4. Disagree	DK. Don't know

10. The first statement is: "Married couples should want a home with enough room for their parents to feel free to live with them." _____(#)

11. "Married children should live close to their parents." _____

12. "Children should take care of their parents in whatever way necessary when they are sick." _____

13. " Older couples should take care of their children in whatever way necessary when they are sick." _____

14. "Children should give their parents financial help." _____

15. "Older couples should give their children financial help." _____

16. "If children live nearby after they grow up, they should visit their parents at least once a week." _____

17. The last statement in this series is: "If children live nearby after they grow up, their parents should visit them at least once a week." _____

102. Are you employed now, looking for work, retired, or what?

☐ Employed   ☐ Looking ☐ Retired ☐ Housewife

(GO TO Q 103)

102a. What job are you now working at? (BE SPECIFIC)

Other: _____

102c. What kind of job did you have on the last regular job you had? (BE SPECIFIC)

_____

_____

_____

_____

_____

102b. Do you work for yourself or for someone else?

☐ Self   ☐ Else

☐ Both

102d. Did you work for yourself then or for someone else?

☐ Self   ☐ Else   ☐ Both

103. Here are a few questions about education. What is the highest grade of school or year of college that you finished?

_____(SCHOOL), or _____(COLLEGE)
(GO TO Q 104)

103a. What college did you attend? _____

103b. Why did you go there rather than to some other college?

_____

104. Did you get any of your education in a school that belonged to a church or religious group?

☐ Yes   ☐ No
                 (GO TO Q 105)

104a. What grades did you attend at this school?_____

104b. What religious group ran this school?_____

105. What is your religious preference now, if any?

☐ Protestant   ☐ Roman Catholic   ☐ Jewish   Other:_____
                        (GO TO Q 106)
                                                ☐ None
                                                (GO TO Q 106)

105a. What denomination is that?_____

106. Do you now belong to a church (synagogue)?   ☐ Yes   ☐ No

107. About how often do you usually attend religious services? (CARD 1)

CARD 1	
☐ Every day	☐ Few times a year
☐ At least once a week	☐ Once a year
☐ Few times a month	☐ Less often
☐ Once a month	☐ Never

108. How does your frequency of attendance at religious services <u>now</u> compare with five years ago? Would you say you are going to church (synagogue) more often now, about the same, or less often than five years ago?

☐ More   ☐ Same   ☐ Less
                (GO TO Q 109)

108a. What would you say are the reasons for this change?_____

_____

_____

127. Now, I have a few remaining background questions. What was your father's main job while you were growing up? (What sort of work did he do?) (BE SPECIFIC)

                  _____

128. While you were growing up, did your father consider himself a Republican, a Democrat, a Progressive, or what?

       ☐ Rep.   ☐ Dem.   ☐ Prog.   ☐ Independent

           ☐ Other   ☐ No pref.   ☐ DK

129. What do you estimate your total family income will be this year considering all sources such as rents, profits, wages, interest, and so on? (SHOW CARD 6)

CARD 6

A. Under $1,000	E. $4,000-$4,999	I. $8,000-$8,999
B. $1,000-$1,999	F. $5,000-$5,999	J. $9,000-$9,999
C. $2,000-$2,999	G. $6,000-$6,999	K. $10,000-$14,999
D. $3,000-$3,999	H. $7,000-$7,999	L. $15,000-$19,999
		M. $20,000 or over

130. How much of the total family income was earned by the head of the family? $_____ , or _____ %

131. What is your present age? _____ (AGE)

    (IF R IS NEGRO, DO NOT ASK NEXT Q; GO TO Q 133, BELOW)

132. What is the original nationality of your family on your father's side? (IF "AMERICAN," ASK: What country did his family come from originally?)

                  _____

133. Are you married, widowed, separated, divorced, or have you never married?

       ☐ Married   ☐ Widowed   ☐ Separated

       ☐ Divorced   ☐ Never married
                 (TERMINATE INTERVIEW)

134. When you were first married, did you receive any financial support from your family or your (SPOUSE'S) family?

       ☐ Yes   ☐ No
               (GO TO Q 135)

    134a. Was it your relatives or your (SPOUSE'S) relatives who gave this financial support?

        ☐ Own   ☐ Spouse's   ☐ Both

135. Since you've been married, have you (or has your husband) ever worked with relatives on either side of the family—including married children—as a partner, employer, or employee?

☐ Yes ☐ No
(GO TO Q 136)

135a. Are you still (Is he still)
associated with this business? ☐ Yes ☐ No

136. Since you've been married, have other people's children ever come to live with you for as long as a week?

☐ Yes ☐ No
(GO TO Q 137)

136a. Were these children of a neighbor, a friend, a relative, or what?

☐ Neighbor ☐ Friend ☐ Relative Other:_____
(GO TO Q 137) (GO TO Q 137)

136b. Which relatives? _____

137. Since you and your (SPOUSE) were married, have you ever lived with relatives?

☐ Yes ☐ No
(GO TO Q 138)

137a. Which relatives did you live with? _____

138. How many—if any—brothers and sisters of your (late; former) (SPOUSE) are living?

☐ None or _____(#)
(GO TO Q 139)

138a. Do any of your (SPOUSE'S) brothers and sisters live in or near your community here?

☐ Yes ☐ No
(GO TO Q 138c)

138b. How many separate households is that? _____

138c. How often are you or some other member of your household here in touch by telephone or face-to-face with your (SPOUSE'S) brothers and sisters? (SHOW CARD 1)

CARD 1	
☐ Every day	☐ Few times a year
☐ At least once a week	☐ Once a year
☐ Few times a month	☐ Less often
☐ Once a month	☐ Never

139. Are your (late; former) (SPOUSE'S) parents living?

□ Yes   □ No
(GO TO Q 140)

139a. Do your (SPOUSE'S) parents live in or near your community?

□ Yes   □ No   □ Parents live with R
(GO TO Q 140)

139b. How often are you or some other member of your household here in touch by telephone or face-to-face contact with your (SPOUSE'S) parents? (SHOW CARD 1)

CARD 1

□ Every day	□ Few times a year
□ At least once a week	□ Once a year
□ Few times a month	□ Less often
□ Once a month	□ Never

140. Do any of your (late; former) (SPOUSE'S) other relatives live in or near your community here?

□ Yes   □ No
(GO TO Q 141)

140a. How many separate households are there?   _____(#)

141. How often are you or some other member of your household here in touch by telephone or face-to-face with any other relatives on your (late; former) (SPOUSE'S) side? (SHOW CARD 1)

CARD 1

□ Every day	□ Few times a year
□ At least once a week	□ Once a year
□ Few times a month	□ Less often
□ Once a month	□ Never

142. How many children have you had, including any who may have died after birth?

□ None   _____ (# CHILDREN)
(SEE NOTE, BEFORE Q 148)

143. In the past when you needed help in baby-sitting and caring for your children generally, have you usually asked a neighbor, a friend, a relative, or whom?

□ Neighbor   □ Friend   □ Relative   Other:_____
(GO TO Q 144)   (GO TO Q 144)

143a. Which relative have you usually
asked to help you with the children? _____

144. Have your children ever lived with another household for as much
as a week?

      ☐ Yes   ☐ No
              (GO TO Q 145)

144a. With whom have your children stayed ... were they neighbors,
other friends, relatives, or whom? (CHECK ALL THAT APPLY)

☐ Neighbors ☐ Friends ☐ Relatives Other: _____
(GO TO Q 145)   (GO TO Q 145)

144b. Which relatives have your
children lived with?   _____

145. What is the sex and age of each of your living children?

SEX AGE	SEX AGE	SEX AGE	SEX AGE	SEX AGE
1. ___ ___	3. ___ ___	5. ___ ___	7. ___ ___	9. ___ ___
2. ___ ___	4. ___ ___	6. ___ ___	8. ___ ___	10. ___ ___

> IF R HAS ANY CHILDREN 18 OR UNDER, ASK Qs BELOW: IF R
> DOES NOT HAVE CHILDREN THIS AGE,
> SEE NOTE, BEFORE Q 148

146. Which, if any, of your children 18 or younger do you firmly expect
to go to college?

                                                     (USE
☐ None   ___, ___, ___, ___, ___, ___, ___, ___ ABOVE #)
(GO TO Q 147)

146a. What college do you think (they; he; she) will attend?

_____   ☐ Don't know

146b. What factors will be important to you in selecting one college
over others? _____

_____

_____

147. If something were to happen to you and your (SPOUSE) who in your
community or near it would you want to see raising your children
... would it be a neighbor, a friend, a relative, or whom?

☐ Neighbor ☐ Friend   ☐ Relative Other: _____
(SEE NOTE, BEFORE Q148)   (SEE NOTE, BEFORE Q 148)

147a. Which relative would this be? _____
                                (SEE NOTE, BEFORE Q148)

IF R IS <u>NOW</u> MARRIED, ASK REMAINING QUESTIONS ABOUT SPOUSE.
IF R IS <u>NOT</u> NOW MARRIED, TERMINATE INTERVIEW
---

148. Now I have a few questions about your (husband; wife). First, is your (SPOUSE) employed now, looking for work, retired, or what?

☐ Employed   ☐ Looking   ☐ Retired   ☐ Housewife
                                           (GO TO Q 149)
148a. What job is your   Other: _____
(SPOUSE) now
working at?   148c. What kind of work did your
(BE SPECIFIC)   (SPOUSE) do on the last regular
                         job (he; she) had?
                         (BE SPECIFIC)

_____   _____

_____   _____

_____   _____

148b. Does your (SPOUSE)   148d. Did your (SPOUSE) work for
work for (himself;   (himself; herself) then or for
herself) or for some-   someone else?
one else?
                               ☐ Self   ☐ Else   ☐ Both
☐ Self   ☐ Else

☐ Both

149. Where was your (SPOUSE'S) family living when (he; she) was born?

_____ (TOWN or CITY),

_____ (STATE or COUNTRY)

150. Where was your (SPOUSE) living when (he; she) turned 18?

_____ (TOWN or CITY),

_____ (STATE or COUNTRY)

151. Has (he; she) ever lived on a farm?   ☐ Yes   ☐ No
                                              (GO TO Q 152)

151a. How old was (he; she) when (he; she) lived on a farm?
                                              _____ to _____

151b. In what state did (he; she) live while on a farm? _____

152. What is your (SPOUSE'S) religious preference, if any?

☐ Protestant   ☐ Roman Catholic   ☐ Jewish   Other: _____
        | ☐ None
        ↓
152a. What denomination is that?   _____

153. About how often does (he; she) usually attend religious services?
(SHOW CARD 1)

CARD 1	
☐ Every day	☐ Few times a year
☐ At least once a week	☐ Once a year
☐ Few times a month	☐ Less often
☐ Once a month	☐ Never

154. What was the highest grade of school or year of college your
(SPOUSE) finished?

_____(SCHOOL), or _____(COLLEGE)

154a. What college did (he; she) attend? _____

Appendix C

An Interval Scale for Familial Structure

Robert F. Winch

I shall try to create a generally applicable interval scale of familial structure on the basis of the number of differentiated positions contained in familial systems.

In order that we may be sure what it is we want to measure, it is advisable to begin with a few nominal definitions:

A social structure is a social system viewed as a network of social roles and positions (Winch, 1971: 8).

A social system is a social group with two or more differentiated social positions (Winch, 1971: 8).

A social position is "a location in a social structure which is associated with a set of social norms" (Bates, 1956: 314).

A family (or familial system) is a social system in which the incumbents are related to each other by blood, marriage, or adoption, whose structure is specified by familial positions, and whose (basic societal) function is replacement (or reproduction) (Winch, 1971: 10-11).

Let us begin to develop our scale by considering the minimum set of familial positions that can fulfill the function of reproduction and produce evidence that the function has been fulfilled. This consists of a sexual dyad and the child resulting from the woman's impregnation. If the man and woman are married, this triad gives the nuclear family. If not, we have the mother-child family.[1]

This recalls two points raised in Chapter 9. First, we noted Richard Adams' argument that if we assume the nuclear family as our basic unit and building block for sociologizing about the family, we tend to regard the mother-child family as a degenerate form. Since the mother-child family has been found to be stable and functional in a number of places, he believes we should begin with the familial dyad, especially the mother-child dyad, as our building block. I am inclined to accept this view.

The second point is whether we are talking about the normative or the statistical family—the familial system as informants report it should be, or the familial association that censuses, surveys, and other such sources reveal as the average of actual day-to-day patterns. I gather that ethnographers are more disposed to report the normative than the statistical familial system. If we accept this view, then I believe that Adams' suggestions can be ignored because the husband-father seems normatively to be a universal participant (with the one widely noted exception of the Nayar).

Now let us begin to develop our scale by considering the nuclear family. After noting that the norms of all societies distinguish between the responsibilities of husbands-fathers and those of wives-mothers, we have here two differentiated familial positions.

Children, especially young children, are given responsibilities and rights that differ from those of either parent. This creates at least one more position. A question arises as to whether or not it is useful to distinguish more than one position for minor offspring. A case could be made for pointing to one additional distinction on the basis of gender and a further one on the basis of age. Where there is an expectation that an older child, especially a girl, will assume child-tending responsibilities, there is an argument for considering "senior daughter" as a differentiated position. Where there is an expectation that only one offspring, especially an oldest or youngest son, will inherit title, lands, and other property, there is justification for considering such a position as differentiated from that of other offspring. Whether more than one familial position should be designated for minor offspring, however, is a question each researcher may wish to settle for him- or herself. In the interest of keeping this exposition as simple as possible I shall use only one position for children. Then on the basis of one position each for husband-father, wife-mother, and offspring-sibling we shall conclude that the nuclear family rates three positions on the scale of complexity of familial structure.

Having located the nuclear family on our scale, we may think of more complex forms as elaborations of the nuclear family. Elaborations may occur along three dimensions: marital, lineal, and collateral. Marital elaboration involves one of the forms of polygamy: polygyny or polyandry.[2] Of these polygyny is the more widespread, and over four fifths of the societies in Murdock's Ethnographic Atlas practice (or at least permit) polygyny. Where polygyny exists, it appears that there is usually a distinction between the position of a man's first wife and that of subsequent wife or wives. Accordingly, we accord the polygynous marriage an additional familial position for the distinction between senior wife and other wife or wives, and where the family would otherwise be regarded as nuclear (i.e., independent in the sense of Nimkoff and Middleton, 1960, and of Murdock, 1967) we can assign the number four along the scale of number of familial positions. This implies, of course, that polygyny does not differentiate the position of the offspring of senior wife and those of other wives.

The stem family is a simple case of lineal extension. In this form, instances of which occur in traditional agricultural China and Ireland, the father designates one son to remain with him after the son reaches maturity. The familial system includes the wife and offspring of the designated son. Thus there are a husband and wife in each of two generations and a generation of offspring of the younger marital pair. Since we have not been differentiating positions among minors, we now have five positions. If the stem family should appear in a society favoring polygyny, then we should have two uxorial positions in each of the two older generations, and the additional two would give a total of seven positions for the stem-polygynous familial system.

We shall distinguish between a small extended and a large extended familial system. The former embraces a single marital couple in the senior generation and at least two in the next generation. The large extended family includes families of procreation of at least two siblings or cousins in each of at least two adjacent generations. Thus both forms of extended family involve both lineal and collateral extension, the difference being that the small version has collateral extension only in the second generation whereas the large version has collateral extension in both the senior generation and the following generation.

Accordingly, the small extended family has two familial positions in the senior generation, and it has four in the next when we distinguish between the senior son and his wife and the junior son and the latter's wife. A seventh position consists of the offspring of the second generation.

For the large extended family we add a junior male and his wife in the senior generation. This makes two positions (or a total of nine) beyond those in the small extended family. Polygynous versions of these extended families would add three wifely positions to the small and four to the large systems, for totals of 10 and 13, respectively.

What about polyandry? From the standpoint of counting the number of positions, I believe that the case is entirely parallel to that of polygyny and that we can merely substitute senior and junior husband for senior and junior wife. Practically, the matter looks a bit different in that the number of polyandrous societies appears to be so small that it is dubious whether they should be included in quantitative intersocietal studies. Murdock's 1,170 societies in the Ethnographic Atlas include 6 designated as polyandrous; his 186 include 2.

As long as we confine our analysis to data of the type that appear in the Ethnographic Atlas, it appears that we shall encounter no society with a mother-child familial system. It is our ambition, however, to expand our analysis to include subsocietal categories of complex societies. Here we shall encounter mother-child patterns statistically and perhaps normatively as well. Accordingly, we have included the mother-child system in our schema of the interval scale of complexity of familial structure. In Table C-1 we have also envisaged the matrilineal extension of the mother-child family with the particular addition of the mother's mother.[3]

These remarks are summarized in Table C-1 (see following page).

To date I have made use of this mode of indexing primarily with data from Murdock's Ethnographic Atlas. In Table C-2, I have cross-tabulated familial system by type of marriage for the societies in the Ethnographic Atlas and thus have indicated frequencies for the various degrees of familial complexity. Because it is not clear just how many positions should be assigned in societies having what Murdock calls "limited polygyny," I have not specified numbers of positions in column 2 of the table. Murdock uses that phrase to denote societies in which one fifth or less of the marriages are polygynous. One might argue that where the norm permits polygyny at all, it should be scored as polygynous. Or one might argue that where so few marriages are polygynous, the norm may be weak, and consequently it should be scored as monogamous. (Of course there may be other reasons for a low proportion of polygynous marriages.)

Table C-3 shows the frequency distributions resulting from assigning familial scores as shown in Table C-2 with the societies having "limited polygyny" treated as monogamous. Column 1 shows the distribution without grouping. Column 2 shows the data grouped into class intervals of two for the purpose of removing the gaps in the distribution created by the fact that no family-marriage combinations were assigned the scores of 6, 8, 11, or 12. It is seen that, as might be expected, the mean and standard deviation of the two distributions are virtually the same. The latter form was used in the AID analysis reported in Table 7-4.

Table C-4 demonstrates that there is virtually no improvement in the AID analysis when familial positions are grouped into class intervals of two as compared to the analysis performed without grouping.

Table C-1

Number of Differentiated Positions, by Type of Familial
System and Type of Marriage

Familial System	Differentiated Positions	Monogamy				Polygyny			
		Adults		Chil-dren	Total	Adults		Chil-dren	Total
		Male	Female			Male	Female		
Mother-child	Mo, Ch		1	1	2				
Mother-child matri-lineally extended	MoMo, Mo, Ch		2	1	3				
Nuclear	Fa, Mo, Ch	1	1	1	3	1	2	1	4
Stem	FaFa, FaMo, Fa, Mo, Ch	2	2	1	5	2	4	1	7
Small extended	FaFa, FaMo, SrFa, SrMo, JrFa, JrMo, Ch	3	3	1	7	3	6	1	10
Large extended	SrFaFa, SrFaMo, JrFaFa, JrFaMo, SrFa, SrMo, JrFa, JrMo, Ch	4	4	1	9	4	8	1	13

Note: The following simplifying assumptions are made:

1. No matter how many wives a man may have, a polygynous marriage provides just two positions for adult females: senior wife-mother, and junior wives-mothers. Thus the effect of introducing polygyny is to double the number of positions for adult females. The positions listed do not include those arising from polygynous marriages.
2. Polyandry is too rare to warrant inclusion, but it can be handled in the same manner as polygyny.
3. Stem and extended families are shown as patrilineal; the number of positions would be the same if they were matrilineal.

Legend: Fa = father; Mo = mother; Ch = child(ren); Sr = senior; Jr = junior;
FaFa = father's father.

Table C-2

Number of Societies in the Ethnographic Atlas by Type of Familial
System and Type of Marriage[a]

Type of Familial System	Type of Marriage			
	Monogamy	Limited Polygyny	Polygyny	Total
Independent nuclear	86 (3)	237	263 (4)	586
Stem	15 (5)	16	11 (7)	42
Small extended	35 (7)	110	150 (10)	295
Large extended	32 (9)	54	138 (13)	224
Total	168	417	562	1,147

Note: The tape from which this tabulation was made contains data on 1,170
societies. The 23 excluded societies are either polyandrous or else
the information about them is insufficient.

[a] Numbers in parentheses register number of familial positions for each
combination except those having limited polygyny; see text.

Table C-3

Frequency Distribution of 1,147 Societies in the Ethnographic Atlas,
by Number of Familial Positions

Number of Familial Positions	Number of Societies	
	Using Scoring Procedure of Table C-1	Using Class Interval of 2
2	0)	
	)	323
3	323)	
4	263)	
	)	294
5	31)	
6	0)	
	)	156
7	156)	
8	0)	
	)	86
9	86)	
10	150)	
	)	150
11	0)	
12	0)	
	)	138
13	138)	
Total	1,147	1,147
Mean	6.4	6.3
Standard deviation	3.5	3.5

Table C-4

Results of Two-Stage AID with Complexity of Familial Structure
as Dependent Variable

Predictor Variable	Proportion of Variance Explained	
	Index as Shown in Table C-1	Index in Interval of 2
Stage 1: Subsistence economy	.0347	.0517
Number of occupations	.0307	.0136
Gender differentiation in subsistence	.0292	.0209
Slavery	.1180	.1369
Caste	.0192	.0213
Stratification	.0206	.0418
Size of community	.0249	.0146
Type of settlement	.0560	.0437
Political complexity	.0382	.0316
Total for Stage 1	.3715	.3761
Stage 2: Mode of marriage	.0159	.0077
Marital residence	.0233	.0316
Inheritance: real property	.0372	.0459
Inheritance: movable	.0374	.0357
Descent	—	—
Total for Stage 2	.1138	.1209
Total for both stages	.4853	.4970

Note: Data from Ethnographic Atlas (Murdock, 1967). Requirement of
AID that each case have a value on every variable reduced N from
1,170 to 282. Bias is in the direction of well reported societies.

Notes

1. As Schneider points out (see discussion on p. 91), however, it is
not necessary for the child's genitor to be married to the mother in
order for the nuclear family to exist; it suffices for her to have a
husband who thereby becomes the child's pater.
2. Group marriage is another possible form of marital elaboration. I
know of no society in which it is normative, although the practice is
reported for some subsocietal categories (see Stephens, 1963 for a
review). Detailed ethnography should underlie assessment as to the
number of normatively differentiated positions in a specific context.
3. Another possibility is the pattern whereby the unmarried mother continues to live and function in her family of orientation. If that is a
nuclear family, then the result of her pregnancy would be to produce
a stem family with the male of the second generation removed (giving
four positions).

Appendix D

Some Observations on AID

Robert F. Winch

Two common tasks in multivariate analysis are prediction and the allocation of "explained variance" to predictor variables. The best known techniques, which involve data presented in interval scales, are regression analysis and correlation analysis. As is well known, such techniques call for assumptions concerning the distributions of observations, absence of error of measurement, and the linearity of relationships. Furthermore, consideration should be given to interaction among predictor variables. Where data appear in nominal scales, they are sometimes treated by these techniques either through dichotomization and treating the resulting proportions as interval scales or through an elaboration of the procedure that has come to be known as the dummy variable.

How the AID Works

Making no distributional assumptions and rendering the presence or absence of interaction problematic, the Automatic Interaction Detector (AID) technique seems better suited to multivariate analysis in the situation where predictor variables are largely attributional rather than quantitative, whether or not the categories be conceived as ordinal. As concerns the dependent variable, AID requires either that it be measured by an interval scale or that it be dichotomized.

In AID the computer calculates a mean and variance of the dependent variable for every category of every predictor variable. For each predictor, the researcher is asked to decide whether it should be regarded as ordinal or merely nominal. If the researcher decides that a given predictor is ordinal, the computer separates the first category from all others and computes the ratio of the "between" sum of squares to the total sum of squares. It then proceeds to do the same for the first two categories versus all others and so on until it has examined all possible dichotomies of that predictor variable. On the other hand, if the researcher has informed the computer that a variable is to be regarded as nominal rather than ordinal, the computer has the additonal task of first arranging the categories of that predictor variable in the order of the magnitudes of their means. Then it proceeds as before.

Thus for each predictor variable the computer finds the way of splitting the sample in such a fashion that the ratio of between sum of squares to total sum of squares (BSS/TSS) is a maximum. Next the computer examines the set of maximum BSS/TSS ratios for all predictors, locates the maximum one of these, and identifies the critical variable involved. On this basis the computer splits the original "parent" group of observations into two "children" groups. Then it repeats this operation on each of the children until certain limiting criteria are encountered.

The results of this procedure may be portrayed graphically as a tree with the original sample constituting the trunk and the successively fractionated subsamples constituting at first larger and then smaller branches. Tabular presentation can reveal the proportion of total variance of the dependent variable "explained" and the predictors "responsible" for fractions of this "explanation."

Some Problems Involved in Using AID: Masking Variables

The graphic and tabular modes of presentation may fail to reveal the importance of predictors that are highly correlated with the dependent variable but overshadowed by other predictors with still higher correlations. Of course the simplest technique is available when one variable is quite obviously doing the masking. We saw this situation in Chapter 8, where Region masked the explanatory power of other variables. The remedy, as was shown there, is to remove the masking variable from the set of predictors and then to rerun the AID. Table D-1 compares the explained variance of the two analyses from Chapter 8.

Table D-1

Variance Explained in Mother-Child Residence When Masking
Variable—Region—Is Present and Absent

Concept and Indicator	Region Included	Region Excluded
Region	.4753	
Mode of subsistence	.0180	.3689
Subsistence technology	(.0180)	(.3689)
Nature of work	.0583	.0577
Number of occupations	(.0378)	(.0412)[a]
Gender differentiation	(.0205)	(.0165)
Social inequality		.0167
Social classes		(.0167)[a]
Settlement		.0362
Type of settlement		
Political complexity		(.0362)
Inheritance	.0143	
Inheritance of movable property	(.0143)	
Residence and descent	.0139	.1017
Mode of marriage		(.0605)
Nuptial residence	(.0139)	(.0118)
Descent		(.0294)[a]
Total	.5798	.5812

[a] The splits resulting in these increments of explained variance do not appear in Figure 8-1. All increments of explained variance appearing in the "Region Included" column are represented by splits in Figure 8-2.

There are other techniques for assessing the contributions predictors would be able to make if it were not for the masking variable(s). The simplest of these involves merely the comparison of the maximum BSS/TSS ratios for all predictors in the first step of the analysis, that is, where the variance under analysis is that of the original set of observations. These ratios (eta squares) are the squared correlation ratios that would be obtained if all predictors were dichotomized at the point that maximizes their associations with the dependent variable. This comparison offers a rough index of the relative explanatory power of the predictors.

A somewhat more precise index of the relative explanatory power of the predictors can be obtained by computing the BSS of each predictor on the basis of the means of all of its categories and dividing this BSS by the TSS. This gives the true eta square of the predictor.

A third method is to compile a list of the "critical" variables (i.e., the variables responsible for the successive splits) and also of the "runner-up" variables (i.e., the variables that presented the second highest BSS/TSS ratios at the splits). (See Table D-2.) In my experience these runner-up variables tend to show up subsequently as critical variables.

Table D-2

Step-by-Step Results of AID Analysis, Showing Critical Variables, Proportion of Variance They "Explain," and Runner-Up Variables with Proportion They Could Have "Explained"

Step	Parent Group	Critical Variable		Runner-Up Variable	
		Indicator	Expl. Var.	Indicator	Expl. Var.
1	1	Inheritance—movable	.1129	Slavery	.0878
2	2	Inheritance—real	.0291	Inheritance—movable	.0260
3	4	Subsistence economy	.0213	Slavery	.0210
4	3	Subsistence economy	.0442	Nuptial residence	.0398
5	6	Slavery	.0195	Number of occupations	.0112
6	8	Subsistence economy	.0157	Nuptial residence	.0119
7	13	Slavery	.0136	Nuptial residence	.0128
8	9	Descent	.0345	Type of settlement	.0203
9	15	Inheritance—real	.0125	Nuptial residence	.0119
10	11	Subsistence economy	.0191	Inheritance—real) Inheritance—movable)	.0167
11	19	Type of settlement	.0103	Social classes) Gender differentiation)	.0094
12	7	Inheritance—movable	.0130	Nuptial residence	.0094
13	22	Size of settlement	.0155	Subsistence economy	.0086
14	21	Number of occupations	.0148	Social classes	.0134
15	10	Number of occupations	.0132	Type of settlement	.0078
16	17	Social classes	.0127	Type of settlement	.0084
		Total	.4019		

Note: The sum of the entries under "explained variance" of critical variables is the proportion accounted for by the AID analysis. The total of the values of the runner-up variables has no evident meaning.

Bernard Finifter (1975) has proposed a fourth method that he calls the PEP coefficient. Essentially, his coefficient looks at each predictor at each step of the analysis and notes how much of the variation in the dependent variable it can account for whether or not it becomes the critical variable. These values are summed across all steps and adjusted to become the PEP coefficient. Finifter then suggests that the variables be ranked with respect to their PEPs.

It should be emphasized that all four of these methods are crude, and the results they yield should be construed as providing rough cues. For the data of Chapter 7 these four methods have been worked out in Table D-3, and the degree of agreement of these four methods is reflected in a matrix of rank correlations in Table D-4.

Table D-3

"Explanatory" Power of Predictors of Dichotomized Familial Structure, by (A) "Best" Dichotomy, (B) Squared Correlation Ratio, (C) Finifter's PEP Coefficient, and (D) Variance "Explained" in AID, with Relative Ranks

Box	Indicator	(A) Dichotomy		(B$_2$)		(C) PEP		(D) AID	
		Rank	Expl. Var.	Rank	Expl. Var.	Rank	Expl. Var.	Rank	Expl. Var.
1A	Subsistence economy	4	.0627	4	.0837	2	.2263	2	.1002
2	Number of occupations	11	.0179	11	.0341	11	.1118	6	.0280
	Gender differentiation	13	.0011	13	.0013	12	.1098	11.5	—
5	Caste	12	.0118	12	.0126	13	.0798	11.5	—
	Slavery	2	.0878	3	.0933	1	.2833	5	.0332
	Social classes	5.5	.0520	7	.0589	6	.1954	8	.0127
6	Type of settlement	9	.0416	5	.0723	10	.1168	9	.0103
	Size of settlement	7	.0484	8	.0587	7	.1662	7	.0155
	Political complexity	8	.0449	9	.0487	9	.1301	11.5	—
7	Inheritance of real property	3	.0683	2	.0957	3	.2151	3	.0416
	Inheritance of movable property	1	.1129	1	.1189	4	.2096	1	.1259
8	Nuptial residence	5.5	.0520	6	.0682	5	.2064	11.5	—
	Descent	10	.0373	10	.0391	8	.1572	4	.0345
	Total								.4019
	Mean		.0491		.0604		.1698		.0309

Note: Explanation of the four columns. The first column reports the BSS/TSS ("between" sum of squares divided by total sum of squares) ratio in step 1 of the AID. Thus it is based on the dichotomy of categories in each predictor that maximizes the BSS/TSS ratio. It follows that the figures shown in the "explained variance" column of (A) register the eta square (square of the correlation ratio) derivable from the "best" dichotomy of each predictor.

Most predictors contain more than two categories. (In the present problem that is true of all predictors.) Since this is so, it follows that in most cases the eta square can be increased by taking all categories into account. This is done in column (B); every value in this column exceeds that in the same row of column (A). Sometimes the best predictor (the one having rank 1) is the same in columns (A) and (B), but it is not always so; here it is. Therefore the first split was on inheritance of movable property.

The entries in columns (A) and (B) reflect bivariate association with no account being taken of the simultaneous association with third or further variables. Bernard Finifter's PEP coefficient in column (C) tries to take account of the potentiality of each predictor in the light of the simultaneous functioning of the other predictors. Roughly speaking, the PEP coefficient is the maximum BSS/TSS ratio of each predictor totaled across all splits. Since the coefficient is affected by preceding steps and by the impact of other predictors that have been responsible for previous splits, it is in this sense "net."

Column (D) registers the amount of variance "explained" by each predictor during the course of the AID. It should be kept in mind that if one predictor is highly correlated with the dependent variable but another is correlated more highly, the effect of the former predictor may be masked by the latter predictor. (In the present problem, e.g., the inheritance of movable property masked the influence of the inheritance of real property.)

Table D-4

Intercorrelations (Spearman Rank Correlations) of Bivariate and Multivariate "Explanatory" Power of the 13 Predictors of Dichotomized Familial Structure

	A	B	C	D
A. "Best" dichotomy				
B. Squared correlation ratio	.94			
C. PEP coefficient	.94	.86		
D. Variance "explained" by AID	.64	.65	.66	
Average correlation for A-D	.84	.82	.82	.65

The Problem of Interpreting Explained Variance

The objection is frequently raised that since AID is a searching technique (in the sense that it looks for the way of dichotomizing a set of observations that maximizes the BSS/TSS ratio) some portion of the explained variance is based on sampling variation (or error). This is a serious problem, and the researcher should try to assess the stability of the obtained results in the face of this threat. In dealing with this threat to our analysis we have used two techniques in Chapter 7. One of these was to split the original sample randomly into two subsamples, rerun the AID, and note the similarity or diversity of the results. The second was to distinguish between splits resulting in subsamples of respectable size and splits resulting in subsamples of trivial size.

With respect to the first of these techniques, the sample of 289 societies that constitutes the base of the data for the first analysis in Chapter 7 was randomly split into two mutually exclusive subsamples of 139 and 150 societies. As expected, the means and variances of the dependent variable in the two subsamples do not differ significantly from each other. The AID program was run on each subsample. A comparison of the variance explained in the sample and two subsamples appears in Table D-5. It is seen that the same indicator is not highest or second

Table D-5

"Explained" Variance of Dichotomized Familial Structure by Concepts Shown in Figure 6-1 and Indicators from Table 7-1. Based on Sample of 289 Societies from Ethnographic Atlas Having Data on All Indicators and on Two Subsamples from That Sample

Box	Concept and Indicator	Sample N = 289	Subsample 1 N = 139	Subsample 2 N = 150
1A	Mode of subsistence	.1003	.1192	.0727
	Subsistence technology	(.1003)	(.1192)	(.0727)
2	Nature of work	.0280		.1042
	Number of occupations	(.0280)		(.1042)
	Gender differentiation			
5	Social inequality	.0458	.0388	.0311
	Caste			
	Slavery	(.0331)		
	Social classes	(.0127)	(.0388)	(.0311)
6	Settlement	.0258	.0659	.1011
	Type	(.0103)	(.0659)	(.0341)
	Size	(.0155)		
	Political complexity			(.0670)
7	Inheritance	.1675	.1657	.1164
	Real property	(.0416)		(.0172)
	Movable property	(.1259)	(.1657)	(.0992)
8	Residence and descent	.0345	.0632	
	Nuptial residence		(.0632)	
	Descent	(.0345)		
	Total	.4019	.4528	.4255
	Mean (proportion having large familial systems)	.6609	.6978	.6267
	Standard deviation	.4734	.4592	.4837

highest in all three distributions. Inheritance of movable property is the maximum index in the first two columns, but number of occupations is the largest in the third column. Subsistence economy is the second largest indicator in the first two columns but the inheritance of movable property is second in the third column. As remarked in Chapter 7, there is greater stability of concepts than of indicators. Inheritance is most important in all three samples. Mode of subsistence accounts for a respectable proportion in all three columns; it is in second place in columns 1 and 2 and in fourth place in column 3. Although they account for smaller proportions of variance, both social differentiation and settlement (each with three indicators) also appear in all three columns. Conversely, the nature of work and residence and descent (each with two indicators) appear in only one subsample plus the sample. Thus, system of inheritance and mode of subsistence seem established as stable predictors of size of familial structure.

With respect to the second technique mentioned above—size of each of the resulting children groups—we declared that a split resulting in two subsets, both of which contain at least 15 societies, would be acceptable; if one or both of the resulting subsets contained less than 15, we regarded that split as unsatisfactory for the purpose of this inquiry. We realize that some may think the number too low; others, too high; and still others may think the whole exercise quite unnecessary.

The results of this analysis appear in Tables D-6 through D-9, where again inheritance and subsistence economy show up as stable predictors of familial structure, with a fairly high degree of stability appearing, as before, in social differentiation and nature of settlement.

Table D-6

Analysis of Dichotomized Familial Structure of 289 Societies in Ethnographic Atlas: "Explained" Variance Contributed at Each Step of AID, by Size of Smaller Group Resulting from Split

Step	Indicator	$N \geqslant 15$	$N < 15$
1	Inheritance of movable property	.1129	
2	Inheritance of real property		.0291
3	Subsistence economy	.0213	
4	Subsistence economy	.0442	
5	Slavery	.0195	
6	Subsistence economy		.0157
7	Slavery		.0136
8	Descent		.0345
9	Inheritance of real property		.0125
10	Subsistence economy	.0191	
11	Type of settlement		.0103
12	Inheritance of movable property		.0130
13	Size of settlement		.0155
14	Number of occupations		.0148
15	Number of occupations		.0132
16	Social classes	.0127	
Total		.2297	.1722

Table D-7

Analysis of Dichotomized Familial Structure in Subsample 1 (N = 139)
of Sample of 289 Societies in Ethnographic Atlas: "Explained"
Variance Contributed at Each Step of AID, by Size
of Smaller Group Resulting from Split

Step	Indicator	N ⩾ 15	N < 15
1	Inheritance of movable property	.1657	
2	Nuptial residence		.0632
3	Subsistence economy		.0766
4	Subsistence economy	.0426	
5	Type of settlement		.0311
6	Type of settlement	.0348	
7	Social classes		.0221
8	Social classes		.0167
Total		.2431	.2097

Table D-8

Analysis of Dichotomized Familial Structure in Subsample 2 (N = 150)
of Sample of 289 Societies in Ethnographic Atlas: "Explained"
Variance Contributed at Each Step of AID, by Size
of Smaller Group Resulting from Split

Step	Indicator	N ⩾ 15	N < 15
1	Inheritance of real property	.0992	
2	Political complexity	.0670	
3	Subsistence economy	.0388	
4	Number of occupations		.0776
5	Inheritance of movable property		.0172
6	Type of settlement		.0341
7	Subsistence economy		.0339
8	Social classes		.0311
9	Number of occupations		.0266
Total		.2050	.2205

Table D-9

"Explained" Variance of Dichotomized Familial Structure by Concepts Shown in Figure 6-1 and Indicators from Table 7-1[a]

Box	Concept and Indicator	Sample (N = 289)			Subsample 1 (N = 139)			Subsample 2 (N = 150)		
		N ≥ 15	N < 15	Total	N ≥ 15	N < 15	Total	N ≥ 15	N < 15	Total
1A	Mode of subsistence	.0846	.0157	.1003	.0426	.0766	.1192	.0388	.0399	.0727
	Subsistence technology	(.0846)	(.0157)	(.1003)	(.0426)	(.0766)	(.1192)	(.0388)	(.0399)	(.0727)
2	Nature of work		.0280	.0280					.1042	.1042
	Number of occupations									
	Gender differentiation		(.0280)	(.0280)					(.1042)	(.1042)
5	Social inequality	.0322	.0136	.0458		.0388	.0388	.0311		.0311
	Caste	(.0195)	(.0136)	(.0331)				(.0311)		(.0311)
	Slavery	(.0127)		(.0127)						
	Social classes					(.0388)	(.0388)			
6	Settlement		.0258	.0258	.0348	.0311	.0659	.0670	.0341	.1011
	Type				(.0348)	(.0311)	(.0659)		(.0341)	(.0341)
	Size		(.0103)	(.0103)						
	Political complexity		(.0155)	(.0155)				(.0670)		(.0670)
7	Inheritance	.1129	.0546	.1675	.1657		.1657	.0992	.0172	.1164
	Real property	(.1129)	(.0130)	(.1259)	(.1657)		(.1657)	(.0992)		(.0992)
	Movable property		(.0416)	(.0416)					(.0172)	(.0172)
8	Residence and descent		.0345	.0345		.0632	.0632			
	Nuptial residence									
	Descent		(.0345)	(.0345)		(.0632)	(.0632)			
Total		.2297	.1722	.4019	.2431	.2097	.4528	.2050	.2205	.4255

[a] Based on sample of 289 societies from Ethnographic Atlas having data on all indicators and on two subsamples from that sample, by size of smaller group resulting from split.

Dividing the Analysis into Stages

For sociological problems where theory is just beginning to involve a number of concepts in simultaneous and/or processual interaction and where the data are in the form of nominal scales, I believe that AID is more appropriate than is the more elegant path analysis with its demand for specifying a multitude of generally unknown relationships. It should be noted, moreover, that AID can be set up for temporal—and thereby causal—hypotheses. Sonquist (1970) has proposed that where the researcher conceives of a sequence among the variables, it is in order to run two (or even more) AIDs sequentially with the residuals from the first constituting the dependent variable's input for the second AID, and so on. That is, the earliest predictors would be inserted in the first problem, and the residuals about the means of the terminal groups would then become the values for the dependent variable for a second AID, the predictors of which are the variables assumed by the researcher to be operative at a later stage in the causal sequence. We have followed this suggestion in Chapter 7 with results that showed each of our hypothesized predictors to have some relevance to familial structure.

Scrutinizing the Terminal Groups

One way of interpreting the AID is that it transforms an originally heterogeneous set of cases into progressively more homogeneous subsets. Every case is located in one or another of the terminal groups, which are the subsets eventuating from this homogenizing process. In a sense, then, these terminal groups may be regarded as heuristic or constructed types (Winch, 1947; McKinney, 1966). By this reasoning it is of interest to see which categories of the predictor variables are included in, and which are excluded from, terminal groups with varying values of the dependent variable. To follow this argument, it is useful to consider Tables D-10 and D-11 (see following pages).

Table D-10 lists the steps in the first AID analysis of Chapter 7, and for each step it shows:

1. the parent group (or set of observations being dichotomized)
2. the children groups (or pair of sets of observations resulting from the split)
3. the critical variable (the variable with respect to whose categories the maximum BSS/TSS ratio occurred)
4. the means of the high and low children groups
5. the categories of the critical variable falling into each of the dichotomous subsets of observations

Thus it is seen that the initial split of the 289 societies came from the indicator inheritance of movable property, with unequal inheritance favoring large families and equal or no inheritance favoring small familial organization.

Table D-10

Analysis of 289 EA Societies by AID, Showing Critical Variables, and Means of Their Categories: Dependent Variable—Dichotomized Familial Structure

Step	Parent Group Critical Variable				Children Groups					
	No.	Ȳ	N	Indicator	No.	Ȳ	N	Category	Ȳ	N
1	1	.6609	289	Inheritance—movable	2	.7865	178	6 Other patrilineal	.8261	23
								4 Children, daughters less	.8000	15
								7 Patrilineal	.7917	120
								3 Other matrilineal	.7714	14
								2 Matrilineal	.6667	6
					3	.4595	111	1 Absent	.4925	67
								5 Children equal	.4091	44
2	2	.7865	178	Inheritance—real	4	.8000	175	5 Children equal	1.0000	1
								6 Other patrilineal	.9000	20
								7 Patrilineal	.8202	89
								1 Absent	.7561	41
								4 Children, daughters less	.7500	12
								3 Other matrilineal	.6667	12
					5	.0000	3	2 Matrilineal	.0000	3
3	4	.8000	175	Subsistence economy	6	.8467	137	7 Intensive agriculture	.9167	36
								1 Gathering	.8750	8
								4 Pastoral	.8750	8
								6 Extensive agriculture	.8169	71
								3 Fishing	.7857	14
					7	.6316	38	2 Hunting	.7273	11
								8 Intensive agriculture-irrigation	.6316	19
								5 Incipient agriculture	.5000	8

Table D-10—(Continued)

Step	Parent Group Critical Variable				Children Groups					
	No.	Ȳ	N	Indicator	No.	Ȳ	N	Category	Ȳ	N
4	3	.4595	111	Subsistence economy	8	.6102	59	5 Incipient agriculture	1.0000	6
								2 Hunting	.5714	21
								6 Extensive agriculture	.5714	14
								3 Fishing	.5556	18
					9	.2885	52	8 Intensive agriculture-irrigation	.4000	15
								7 Intensive agriculture	.3333	9
								1 Gathering	.2222	27
								4 Pastoral	.0000	1
5	6	.8467	137	Slavery	10	.9195	87	2 Incipient; nonhereditary	1.0000	28
								3 Type not stated	.9333	15
								4 Hereditary—significant	.8636	44
					11	.7200	50	1 Absent or nearly	.7200	50
6	8	.6102	59	Subsistence economy	12	1.0000	6	5 Incipient agriculture	1.0000	6
					13	.5660	53	2 Hunting	.5714	21
								6 Extensive agriculture	.5714	14
								3 Fishing	.5556	18
7	13	.5660	53	Slavery	14	.8182	11	4 Hereditary—significant	.8333	6
								2 Incipient; nonhereditary	.8000	5
					15	.5000	42	1 Absent or nearly	.5000	42
8	9	.2885	52	Descent	16	.6667	12	2 Matrilineal	.7500	4
								1 Patrilineal	.6250	8
					17	.1750	40	3 Other	.1750	40

Table D-10—(Continued)

Step	Parent Group Critical Variable				Children Groups					
	No.	Ȳ	N	Indicator	No.	Ȳ	N	Category	Ȳ	N
9	15	.5000	42	Inheritance—real	18	1.0000	3	2 Matrilineal	1.0000	1
								4 Children, daughters less	1.0000	1
								6 Other patrilineal	1.0000	1
					19	.4615	39	5 Children equal	.5000	6
								7 Patrilineal	.5000	2
								1 Absent	.4516	31
10	11	.7200	50	Subsistence economy	20	.9048	21	7 Intensive agriculture	.9333	15
								1 Gathering	.8333	6
					21	.5862	29	4 Pastoral	.6667	3
								6 Extensive agriculture	.5789	19
								3 Fishing	.5714	7
11	19	.4615	39	Type of settlement	22	.5333	30	1 Nomadic	.3333	6
								2 Seminomadic	.5263	19
								3 Semisedentary	1.0000	1
								4 Compact, impermanent	1.0000	2
								5 Dispersed homesteads	.5000	2
					23	.2222	9	6 Hamlets	.0000	3
								7 Compact, permanent	.3333	6
12	7	.6316	38	Inheritance—movable	24	.6667	36	4 Children, daughters less	.8333	6
								7 Patrilineal	.6333	30
					25	.0000	2	6 Other patrilineal	.0000	2

Table D-10—(Continued)

Step	Parent Group Critical Variable				Children Groups					
	No.	Ȳ	N	Indicator	No.	Ȳ	N	Category	Ȳ	N
13	22	.5333	30	Size of settlement	26	.4615	26	1 Under 50	.4667	15
								2 50-99	.4545	11
					27	1.0000	4	3 100-199	1.0000	1
								4 More	1.0000	3
14	21	.5862	29	Number of occupations	28	.7500	16	0	.7500	16
					29	.3846	13	1	.2727	11
								2	1.0000	2
15	10	.9195	87	Number of occupations	30	.9302	86	0	.8824	17
								1	.9245	53
								2	1.0000	5
								3	1.0000	4
								4	1.0000	4
								5	1.0000	3
					31	.0000	1	7	.0000	1
16	17	.1750	40	Social classes	32	.3333	18	2 Wealth	.4286	7
								5 Classes	.2727	11
					33	.0455	22	1 Absent	.0476	21
								3 Elite	.0000	1

Table D-11

Terminal Groups Resulting from AID Analysis of 289 EA Societies in Order
of Means of Dependent Variable (Dichotomized Familial Structure), and with
Important Splits and Categories of Predictors Shown for Those with N ⩾ 15

No. of Terminal Group	Important Splits	Important Categories	N ⩾ 15		N < 15	
			N	Ȳ	N	Ȳ
12					6	1.0000
18					3	1.0000
27					4	1.0000
30	1, 3, 5	Unequal inheritance—movable Intermediate subsistence economy Slavery	86	.9302		
20	1, 3, 5, 10	Unequal inheritance—movable No slavery Intensive agriculture; gathering	21	.9048		
14					11	.8182
28	1, 3, 5	Unequal inheritance—movable No slavery Extensive agriculture; fishing; pastoral	16	.7500		
24	1	Unequal inheritance—movable	36	.6667		
16					12	.6667
26	1, 6, 7	No property or equal inheritance Hunting; fishing; extensive agriculture No slavery	26	.4615		
29					13	.3848
32	1, 4, 8, 16	No property or equal inheritance Gathering; irrigation agriculture	18	.3333		
23					9	.2222
33	1, 4, 8, 16	No property or equal inheritance Not unilineal descent	22	.0455		
31					1	.0000
25					2	.0000
5					3	.0000
Total			225		64	

Table D-11 lists all of the terminal groups from the foregoing analysis, the mean of each terminal group, and the number of societies in that group. Where the terminal group consists of at least 15 societies, Table D-11 also summarizes the more important categories of the critical variables (i.e., those containing relatively high proportions of the various subsets of observations) upon which the terminal group is based. Thus, for terminal group 30, Figure 7-1 tells us that the intermediate groups are 2, 4, 6, and 10, resulting from splits 1, 2, 3, and 5, respectively. Table D-11 shows that groups 2 and 3 were formed by split 1 with unequal inheritance going into group 2 and equal or no inheritance going into the lower branch (group 3). We see also that the split forming group 4 is trivial (only three matrilineal societies being excluded). Group 6 is formed of a considerable variety of subsistence categories, but 107 of the total 137 are extensively or intensively agricultural societies, which with respect to the range of types of subsistence under analysis are intermediate categories. Group 10 includes only societies with slavery, and the final split excluded only one society in setting up group 30. Thus we conclude that terminal group 30 has the properties ascribed to it in Table D-11.

At the other end of the range of values along the dependent variable is terminal group 33 with only 1 of 22 (or 5%) of its societies having the large familial system. Its branch involves intermediate groups 3, 9, and 17. Its properties include either equal inheritance of movable property or no inheritance at all and an absence of a unilineal descent system.

Table D-12 is included so that the reader may see what the distributions look like as the computer begins the AID analysis.

Table D-12

The Predictor Variables, Their Codes, Descriptions, Frequencies, and Means

Box	Indicator	Code	Description	N	$\bar{Y}$
1A	Subsistence	1	Gathering	35	.3714
	economy	2	Hunting	32	.6250
		3	Fishing	32	.6563
		4	Pastoral	10	.7000
		5	Incipient agriculture	15	.6667
		6	Extensive agriculture	86	.7674
		7	Intensive agriculture without irrigation	45	.8000
		8	Intensive agriculture with irrigation	34	.5294
2	Number of	0		147	.5986
	occupational	1		92	.7174
	specialties	2		22	.7273
		3		9	.7778
		4		6	1.0000
		5		9	.6667
		6		1	1.0000
		7		3	.3333

Table D-12 — (Continued)

Box	Indicator	Code	Description	N	$\overline{Y}$
	Gender	1	Males dominant	130	.6769
	differentiation	2	Indeterminate	68	.4300
		3	Females dominant	91	.6000
5	Caste	1	Absent or insignificant	247	.6397
		2	One or more despised occupational groups	26	.7692
		3	Ethnic stratification	7	.8571
		4	Complex caste stratification	9	.7778
	Slavery	1	Absent or nearly absent	165	.5394
		2	Incipient or nonhereditary	39	.8974
		3	Reported, type not identified	23	.8261
		4	Hereditary and socially significant	62	.7742
	Social classes	1	Absent among freemen	123	.5610
		2	Distinctions based on wealth	66	.7424
		3	Elite (based on control of resources)	6	.5000
		4	Dual (hereditary aristocracy)	53	.8491
		5	Complex (social classes)	41	.6098
6	Type of	1	Fully migratory or nomadic bands	22	.5000
	settlement	2	Seminomadic communities	59	.5085
		3	Semisedentary communities	28	.8571
		4	Compact but impermanent communities	8	.6250
		5	Neighborhoods of dispersed family homesteads	27	.8889
		6	Separate hamlets forming single communities	21	.6667
		7	Compact and relatively permanent settlements	116	.6810
		8	Complex settlements	8	.5000
	Size of	1	Fewer than 50 persons	65	.4769
	settlement	2	From 50 to 99 persons	48	.6042
		3	From 100 to 199 persons	47	.7872
		4	200 or more persons in absence of urban aggregations	77	.7532
		5	One or more indigenous settlements of more than 5,000 persons	52	.6931
	Political	1	No jurisdictional level beyond local community	146	.5614
	complexity	2	One level beyond local community	66	.7727
		3	Two levels beyond local community	33	.8182
		4	Three levels beyond local community	34	.7059
		5	Four levels beyond local community	10	.7000
7	Inheritance	1	No property rights or inheritance rules	109	.5780
	of real	2	Matrilineal (sister's sons)	4	.2500
	property	3	Other matrilineal	13	.6923
		4	Own children, daughters less	15	.6667
		5	Own children, equally to both sexes	26	.3846
		6	Other patrilineal	22	.9091
		7	Patrilineal (sons)	100	.7800

Table D-12 — (Continued)

Box	Indicator	Code	Description	N	$\bar{Y}$
	Inheritance	1	No property rights or inheritance rules	67	.4999
	of movable	2	Matrilineal (sister's sons)	6	.6667
	property	3	Other matrilineal	14	.7143
		4	Own children, daughters less	15	.8000
		5	Own children, equally to both sexes	44	.4091
		6	Other patrilineal	23	.8261
		7	Patrilineal (sons)	120	.7917
8	Nuptial	1	Neolocal	15	.2667
	residence	2	Ambilocal	31	.6129
		3	Matrilocal, avunculocal, or uxorilocal	45	.5111
		4	Patrilocal or virilocal	198	.7323
	Descent	1	Patrilineal	121	.7686
		2	Matrilineal	28	.6429
		3	Other	140	.5714

It can be seen from this table that the curvilinear relationship with the dependent variable, size of domestic familial structure, is present in virtually all predictors that may be regarded as ordinal, that is, those pertaining to boxes 1, 2, 5, and 6.

The reader may recall that a second AID analysis was reported in Chapter 7, wherein the dependent variable was an interval scale of familial organization, seven polyandrous societies were eliminated bringing the N down to 282, a new indicator—mode of marriage—was introduced, and the analysis was performed in two stages. For this analysis Tables D-13 through D-15 provide information parallel to that contained in Tables D-10 through D-12 for the first analysis of Figure 6-1.

Table D-13

Analysis of 282 EA Societies by Two-Stage AID, Showing Critical Variables, and Means of Their Categories: Dependent Variable is Interval Scale (2-13) of Familial Structure

Step	Parent Group Critical Variable				Children Groups					
	No.	Ȳ	N	Indicator	No.	Ȳ	N	Category	Ȳ	N
					Stage 1					
1	1	6.028	282	Slavery	2	7.333	120	3 Type not stated	7.652	23
								4 Hereditary—significant	7.441	59
								2 Incipient; nonhereditary	6.974	38
					3	5.062	162	1 Absent or nearly	5.062	162
2	2	7.333	120	Subsistence technology	4	7.776	98	3 Fishing	8.250	16
								7 Intensive agriculture	8.100	20
								6 Extensive agriculture	7.623	53
								2 Hunting	7.500	2
								1 Gathering	7.000	2
								4 Pastoral	7.000	5
					5	5.364	22	5 Incipient agriculture	5.500	4
								8 Intensive agriculture-irrigation	5.333	18
3	4	7.776	98	Type of settlement	6	9.684	19	6 Hamlets	10.222	9
								3 Semisedentary	9.200	10
					7	7.316	79	1 Nomadic	8.000	3
								5 Dispersed homesteads	7.857	14
								2 Seminomadic	7.273	11
								7 Compact, permanent	7.234	47
								8 Complex settlements	6.500	2
								4 Compact, impermanent	5.500	2

Table D-13—(Continued)

Step	Parent Group Critical Variable					Children Groups					
	No.	Ȳ	N	Indicator		No.	Ȳ	N	Category	Ȳ	N
4	3	5.062	162	Type of settlement		8	6.775	17	3 Semisedentary	6.923	13
									4 Compact, impermanent	6.000	4
						9	4.869	145	5 Dispersed homesteads	5.250	12
									7 Compact, permanent	5.240	50
									2 Seminomadic	4.875	48
									6 Hamlets	4.800	10
									1 Nomadic	4.053	19
									8 Complex settlements	3.667	6
5	7	7.316	79	Gender differentiation		10	8.120	50	1 Males dominant	8.343	35
									2 Indeterminate	7.600	15
						11	5.931	29	3 Females dominant	5.931	29
6	9	4.869	145	Size of settlement		12	5.214	98	6 1,001-4,999	7.000	3
									4 200-399	5.526	19
									5 400-1,000	5.400	10
									3 100-199	5.176	17
									2 50-99	5.000	28
									7 5,000-49,999	5.000	4
									8 50,000+	4.882	17
						13	4.149	47	1 Less than 50 persons	4.149	47
7	12	5.214	98	Number of occupations		14	5.796	54	7	7.000	1
									1	5.774	53
						15	4.500	44	4	5.000	4
									8	5.000	2
									3	4.889	9
									6	4.333	3
									2	4.269	26

Table D-13—(Continued)

Step	Parent Group No.	Ȳ	N	Critical Variable Indicator	Children Groups No.	Ȳ	N	Category	Ȳ	N
8	10	8.120	50	Social classes	16	9.107	28	1 Absent	9.800	10
								4 Dual	8.722	18
					17	6.864	22	5 Classes	7.250	8
								2 Wealth	6.923	13
								3 Elite	3.000	1
9	14	5.796	54	Size of settlement	18	8.000	7	6 1,001-4,999	9.000	2
								5 400-1,000	7.750	4
								8 50,000+	7.000	1
					19	5.468	47	4 200-399	6.143	14
								3 100-199	5.455	11
								2 50-99	5.000	22
10	19	5.468	47	Caste	20	13.000	1	4 Caste	13.000	1
					21	5.304	46	1 Absent	5.304	46
11	21	5.304	46	Type of settlement	22	6.250	20	6 Hamlets	9.000	2
								2 Seminomadic	5.944	18
					23	4.577	26	5 Dispersed homesteads	5.000	3
								1 Nomadic	4.857	7
								7 Compact, permanent	4.467	15
								8 Complex settlements	3.000	1
12	11	5.931	29	Number of occupations	24	13.000	1	3	13.000	1
					25	5.679	28	2	5.957	23
								1	5.000	2
								4	4.000	1
								5	4.000	1
								6	4.000	1

Table D-13—(Continued)

Step		Parent Group Critical Variable				Children Groups				
	No.	Ȳ	N	Indicator	No.	Ȳ	N	Category	Ȳ	N
13	16	9.107	28	Political complexity	26	9.783	23	2 One level	10.857	7
								3 Two levels	9.500	6
								1 Only local	9.200	10
					27	6.000	5	4 Three levels	6.000	5
14	25	5.679	28	Political complexity	28	7.000	15	2 One level	7.250	12
								1 Only local	6.000	3
					29	4.154	13	3 Two levels	4.286	7
								4 Three levels	4.000	6

Stage 2

Step		Parent Group Critical Variable				Children Groups				
	No.	Ȳ	N	Indicator	No.	Ȳ	N	Category	Ȳ	N
1	1	6.028	282	Nuptial residence	2	6.483	154	25 Ambi-patri-avunculocal	7.561	2
								31 Matrilocal	7.403	9
								11 Patrilocal	6.482	114
								24 Ambi-bi-utrolocal	6.128	29
					3	5.480	128	35 Ambi-uxori-avunculocal	5.874	1
								33 Uxorilocal	5.768	25
								13 Virilocal	5.576	79
								32 Avunculocal	4.841	9
								26 Neolocal	4.809	14
2	2	6.483	154	Inheritance of real property	4	7.810	24	2 Matrilineal (sons)	8.778	1
								6 Other patrilineal	7.818	18
								3 Other matrilineal	7.589	5
					5	6.238	130	5 Children equal	6.705	8
								4 Daughters less	6.352	9
								1 Absent	6.305	42
								7 Patrilineal	6.134	71

Table D-13—(Continued)

Step	Parent Group Critical Variable				Children Groups					
	No.	Ȳ	N	Indicator	No.	Ȳ	N	Category	Ȳ	N
3	5	6.238	130	Inheritance of movable property	6	8.978	5	6 Other patrilineal	9.767	3
								3 Other matrilineal	7.794	2
					7	6.129	125	5 Children equal	6.876	14
								4 Daughters less	6.293	9
								7 Patrilineal	6.041	79
								1 Absent	5.996	21
								2 Matrilineal (sons)	5.019	2
4	7	6.129	125	Mode of marriage	8	6.355	101	3 Token brideprice	7.079	8
								1 Brideprice	6.422	69
								6 No consideration	5.922	24
					9	5.176	24	2 Bride service	5.691	8
								5 Exchange	5.234	7
								4 Gift exchange	4.833	6
								7 Dowry	4.357	3
5	3	5.480	128	Inheritance of real property	10	5.916	92	1 Absent	5.949	65
								7 Patrilineal	5.835	27
					11	4.366	36	3 Other matrilineal	4.791	8
								4 Daughters less	4.740	5
								5 Children equal	4.324	17
								6 Other patrilineal	3.794	3
								2 Matrilineal (sons)	3.426	3

Table D-13—(Continued)

| | Parent Group Critical Variable | | | | Children Groups | | | | | |
Step	No.	Ȳ	N	Indicator	No.	Ȳ	N	Category	Ȳ	N
6	10	5.916	92	Inheritance of movable property	12	13.000	1	4 Daughters less	13.000	1
					13	5.822	91	3 Other matrilineal	7.609	2
								1 Absent	5.967	42
								7 Patrilineal	5.791	35
								6 Other matrilineal	5.523	3
								5 Children equal	4.972	9
7	13	5.822	91	Mode of marriage	14	7.635	6	5 Exchange	8.848	2
								7 Dowry	7.028	4
					15	5.694	85	2 Bride service	6.026	22
								6 No consideration	5.725	28
								4 Gift exchange	5.599	14
								1 Brideprice	5.434	13
								3 Token brideprice	5.262	8

Table D-14

Terminal Groups Resulting from Two-Stage AID Analysis of 282 EA Societies
in Order of Means of Dependent Variable (Interval Scale of Familial
Structure), and with Important Splits and Categories
of Predictors Shown for Those with N ≥ 15

No. of Terminal Group	Important Splits	Important Categories	N ≥ 15		N < 15	
			N	Ȳ	N	Ȳ
		Stage 1				
24					1	13.000
20					1	13.000
26	1, 2, 3, 5, 13	Slavery; fishing or intensive or extensive agriculture; permanent homesteads; male dominance in subsistence; low political complexity	23	9.783		
6	1, 2, 3	Slavery; fishing or intensive or extensive agriculture; hamlets or semisedentary settlements	19	9.684		
18					7	8.000
28	1, 2, 3, 5, 12, 14	Slavery; fishing or intensive or extensive agriculture; permanent homesteads; female dominance in subsistence; few occupations; low political complexity	15	7.000		
17	1, 2, 3, 5, 8	Slavery; fishing or intensive or extensive agriculture; permanent homesteads; male dominance in subsistence	22	6.864		
8	1, 4	No slavery; semisedentary settlements	17	6.775		
22	1, 6, 7, 9, 10	No slavery; 50-400 people; no occupations; no caste	20	6.250		
27					5	6.000
5	1, 2	Slavery; irrigated agriculture	22	5.364		
23	1, 6, 7, 9, 10	No slavery; 50-400 people; no occupations; no caste	26	4.577		
15	1, 6, 7	No slavery; over 50 people; few occupations	44	4.500		

Table D-14 — (Continued)

No. of Terminal Group	Important Splits	Important Categories	N ⩾ 15		N < 15	
			N	Ȳ	N	Ȳ
13	1	No slavery	47	4.149		
29					13	4.154
		Stage 2				
12					1	13.000
6					5	8.978
4	1, 2	Patrilocal residence; other patrilineal heirs than sons (e.g., younger brothers)	24	7.810		
14					6	7.635
8	1, 2, 3, 4	Patrilocal residence; no inheritance or patrilineal inheritance of both real and movable property	101	6.355		
15	1, 5, 6, 7	Virilocal or uxorilocal residence; no inheritance or patrilineal inheritance of both real and movable property	85	5.694		
9	1, 2, 3, 4	Patrilocal residence; patrilineal or no inheritance of movable and real property	24	5.176		
11	1, 5	Virilocal or uxorilocal residence; inheritance of real property equally for children of both sexes	36	4.366		

Table D-15

The Predictor Variables, Their Codes, Descriptions, Frequencies, and
Means with Respect to the Interval Scale (2-13) of Familial Structure for
282 Societies of the Ethnographic Atlas, by Stage of AID Analysis

Box	Indicator	Code	Description	N	$\bar{Y}$
			Stage 1		
1A	Subsistence	1	Gathering	35	4.629
	technology	2	Hunting	32	5.469
		3	Fishing	32	6.594
		4	Pastoral	8	5.625
		5	Incipient agriculture	14	6.429
		6	Extensive agriculture	84	6.631
		7	Intensive agriculture without irrigation	43	6.674
		8	Intensive agriculture with irrigation	34	5.088
2	Number of	0		144	5.868
	occupational	1		90	6.089
	specialties	2		20	6.000
		3		9	7.444
		4		6	8.500
		5		9	5.444
		6		1	7.000
		7		3	4.333
	Gender	1	Males dominant	126	6.516
	differentiation	2	Indeterminate	67	5.582
		3	Females dominant	89	5.674
5	Caste	1	Absent or insignificant	241	5.905
		2	One or more despised occupational groups	25	6.960
		3	Ethnic stratification	7	5.143
		4	Complex caste stratification	9	7.444
	Slavery	1	Absent or nearly absent	162	5.062
		2	Incipient or nonhereditary	38	6.974
		3	Reported, type not identified	23	7.652
		4	Hereditary and socially significant	59	7.441
	Social classes	1	Absent among freemen	122	5.467
		2	Distinctions based on wealth	63	6.937
		3	Elite (based on control of resources)	6	3.500
		4	Dual (hereditary aristocracy)	50	6.740
		5	Complex (social classes)	41	5.805

Table D-15—(Continued)

Box	Indicator	Code	Description	N	$\overline{Y}$
6	Type of settlement	1	Fully migratory or nomadic bands	22	4.591
		2	Seminomadic communities	60	5.300
		3	Semisedentary communities	24	7.708
		4	Compact but impermanent communities	7	5.429
		5	Neighborhoods of dispersed family homesteads	26	6.654
		6	Separate hamlets forming single communities	21	6.952
		7	Compact and relatively permanent settlements	114	6.175
		8	Complex settlements	8	4.375
	Size of settlement	1	Fewer than 50 persons	65	4.877
		2	From 50 to 99 persons	46	5.609
		3	From 100 to 199 persons	46	6.413
		4	From 200 to 399 persons	42	7.143
		5	From 400 to 999 persons	27	7.074
		6	1,000 or more persons; no town more than 5,000	4	6.000
		7	One or more towns of 5,000-50,000	19	6.526
		8	One or more cities of more than 50,000	33	5.788
	Political complexity	1	No jurisdictional level beyond local community	143	5.629
		2	One level beyond local community	65	6.985
		3	Two levels beyond local community	31	6.903
		4	Three levels beyond local community	33	5.273
		5	Four levels beyond local community	10	5.300

				N	Unadjusted $\overline{Y}$	Adjusted = Residual + $\overline{Y}$
			Stage 2[a]			
7	Inheritance of real property	1	No property rights or inheritance rules	107	5.850	6.089
		2	Matrilineal (sister's sons)	4	4.500	4.764
		3	Other matrilineal heirs (e.g., younger brothers)	13	6.077	5.867
		4	Own children, daughters less	14	5.786	5.776
		5	Own children, equally to both sexes	25	4.280	5.086
		6	Other patrilineal heirs (e.g., younger brothers)	21	9.000	7.243
		7	Patrilineal (sons)	98	6.122	6.050

Table D-15—(Continued)

Box	Indicator	Code	Description	N	Un- adjusted $\overline{Y}$	Adjusted = Residual + $\overline{Y}$
	Inheritance of movable property	1	No property rights or inheritance rules	65	5.523	6.113
		2	Matrilineal (sister's sons)	6	5.333	4.607
		3	Other matrilineal heirs (e.g., younger brothers)	14	6.286	5.740
		4	Own children, daughters less	14	7.429	6.797
		5	Own children, equally to both sexes	43	4.814	5.419
		6	Other patrilineal heirs (e.g., younger brothers)	22	8.545	7.229
		7	Patrilineal (sons)	118	6.119	5.994
8	Mode of marriage	1	Brideprice or bridewealth	115	6.878	6.458
		2	Brideservice	39	5.769	5.669
		3	Token brideprice	20	5.500	5.837
		4	Gift exchange	24	6.167	5.593
		5	Exchange	9	6.000	6.037
		6	Absence of any significant consideration	64	5.063	5.818
		7	Dowry	11	4.364	5.312
	Nuptial residence	11	Patrilocal	114	6.991	6.482
		13	Virilocal (without localized unilineal kin groups)	79	5.608	5.576
		24	Ambilocal, bilocal, or utrolocal (optionally with or near either parent)	29	5.310	6.128
		25	Ambilocal with option between patrilocal (or virilocal) and avunculocal	2	9.500	7.561
		26	Neolocal	14	3.429	4.809
		31	Matrilocal	9	7.667	7.403
		32	Avunculocal (with or near maternal uncle)	9	4.444	4.841
		33	Uxorilocal (without matrilocal and matrilineal kin groups)	25	5.040	5.768
		35	Ambilocal with option between uxorilocal and avunculocal	1	4.000	5.874
	Descent	1	Patrilineal	118	6.788	6.371
		2	Duolateral	10	8.100	6.493
		3	Matrilineal	27	5.741	5.853
		4	Quasi-lineages	6	6.000	6.046
		5	Ambilineal	7	4.857	4.418
		6	Bilateral	114	5.202	5.771

[a] As explained in the text, the input values of the dependent variable for the second stage of the AID consist of deviations from means of the terminal groups of the first stage. To transform these residuals from a distribution with a mean of zero back to the original scale, the original mean (= 6.028) has been added to each residual. These are the values in the right column under the second stage.

Appendix E

Bivariate Association of the Indicators from the Ethnographic Atlas

Robert F. Winch

The reader may be interested in knowing how the indicators used in our exploration of the model by means of the AID are related to each other. Our indicators are all in the form of nominal or ordinal scales. For this reason we are using the coefficient of contingency (C), which is appropriate for nominally scaled variables,[1] and gamma (G), which is appropriate for ordinally scaled variables. For the reason explained in note 13 of Chapter 4, we are also showing the "corrected" values of the coefficient of contingency ($\overline{C}$).

Table E-1 shows the bivariate association between the EA indicators as measured by C (below the diagonal) and by $\overline{C}$ (above the diagonal). Table E-2 reports the association of the same pairs by means of G.

The purpose of relating G to either C or $\overline{C}$ is to be able to draw some conclusion as to whether X and Y are related to each other in a monotonic manner, in a nonmonotonic (curvilinear) manner, or not at all. Where the data are in interval scales, we measure linear association by r^2 and departure from linearity by $\eta^2 - r^2$. Unfortunately, no analog for this procedure exists when the data are in nominal form.[2]

What inference can be drawn about monotonicity from the relationship between $\overline{C}$ and G? If both $\overline{C}$ and G are high, it is reasonable to infer that X and Y are associated monotonically. If they are both low, there is no association.[3] If $\overline{C}$ is high and G is low, it seems plausible that they are associated nonmonotonically. In the absence of any rational way to develop a statistic based on the difference between $\overline{C}$ and G (since they are not based on a common metric), we scrutinized the distributions of $\overline{C}$ and of G for some procedure that would yield plausible looking results. After considerable trial and error it was decided to regard a $\overline{C}$ as high if it was equal to or greater than .50, to regard a G as high if its absolute value was equal to or greater than .50, and to regard it as low if its absolute value was equal to or less than .25. Then, if both $\overline{C}$ and G are high, the relationship is interpreted as monotonic (M); if $\overline{C}$ is high and G is low, it is interpreted as nonmonotonic (O). (See Table E-3.) Vacant cells below the diagonal register situations where neither condition prevails and where, therefore, the data are interpreted as inconclusive on this point.

Table E-1

Coefficients of Contingency (below the Diagonal) and Corrected Coefficients (above the Diagonal) between Indicators Used in the AID Analysis

Box	Indicator	1	2	3	4	5	6	7	8	9	10	11	12	13	14	15	16	Md C̄
1A	Subsistence economy		.62	.71	.51	.53	.61	.72	.69	.58	.69	.69	.63	.58	.58	.31	.44	.61
2	Number of occupations	.58		.27	.59	.49	.62	.46	.66	.67	.54	.51	.44	.43	.52	.23	.34	.51
2	Gender differentiation	.58	.22		.23	.16	.24	.34	.34	.14	.33	.35	.34	.27	.27	.06	.31	.27
5	Caste	.44	.51	.18		.33	.55	.23	.51	.40	.40	.46	.21	.34	.36	.10	.27	.36
5	Slavery	.45	.42	.13	.29		.48	.36	.41	.42	.54	.57	.49	.42	.53	.40	.48	.48
5	Stratification	.55	.56	.19	.48	.42		.44	.74	.70	.47	.51	.35	.36	.54	.24	.36	.48
6	Type of settlement	.68	.43	.28	.20	.31	.39		.64	.38	.63	.58	.51	.47	.42	.32	.37	.44
6	Size of settlement	.65	.62	.28	.44	.36	.67	.60		.73	.63	.59	.51	.49	.57	.34	.46	.57
6	Political complexity	.52	.59	.11	.35	.37	.73	.34	.65		.52	.52	.43	.42	.48	.29	.36	.43
7	Inheritance of real property	.64	.50	.27	.35	.47	.42	.58	.58	.46		.95	.77	.78	.53	.40	.50	.54
7	Inheritance of movable property	.64	.47	.29	.40	.50	.45	.54	.55	.47	.88		.77	.77	.54	.44	.51	.54
8	Marital residence	.59	.42	.27	.19	.42	.31	.48	.48	.39	.72	.71		.85	.63	.44	.52	.51
8	Descent	.53	.39	.22	.29	.37	.33	.43	.45	.38	.71	.70	.78		.59	.35	.42	.43
8	Mode of marriage	.53	.48	.22	.31	.46	.48	.39	.52	.43	.49	.50	.58	.54		.35	.47	.53
9	Familial structure (0-1)	.22	.17	.05	.07	.28	.17	.23	.24	.21	.28	.31	.31	.25	.25		1.00	.33
9	Familial structure (2-13)	.41	.31	.26	.24	.42	.32	.34	.42	.32	.47	.47	.48	.38	.44	.71		.43
	Median C	.55	.47	.22	.31	.42	.42	.39	.52	.39	.49	.50	.48	.39	.48	.24	.40	

Note: Correction is that proposed by Cramér and consists of dividing the C by $\sqrt{\dfrac{k-1}{k}}$, where k is the number of rows or columns, whichever is the smaller.

Table E-2

Gammas between Indicators Used in the AID Analysis

Box	Indicator		1	2	3	4	5	6	7	8	9	10	11	12	13	14	15	16
1A	Subsistence economy	1																
2	Number of occupations	2	.68															
2	Gender differentiation	3	.04	-.01														
5	Caste	4	.46	.81	-.31													
5	Slavery	5	.29	.54	-.06	.47												
5	Stratification	6	.39	.63	-.13	.49	.43											
6	Type of settlement	7	.59	.43	.11	.14	.26	.33										
6	Size of settlement	8	.68	.60	-.12	.55	.32	.61	.59									
6	Political complexity	9	.49	.76	.01	.62	.44	.69	.33	.63								
7	Inheritance of real property	10	.52	.51	.12	.41	.25	.24	.41	.41	.33							
7	Inheritance of movable property	11	.34	.36	.01	.31	.14	.19	.23	.30	.24	.70						
8	Marital residence	12	-.31	-.47	-.08	-.69	-.32	-.19	-.18	-.25	-.32	-.56	-.53					
8	Descent	13	-.41	-.53	-.19	-.66	-.41	-.14	-.27	-.33	-.38	-.59	-.51	.76				
8	Mode of marriage	14	-.29	-.43	-.13	-.58	-.55	-.20	-.19	-.13	-.33	-.38	-.29	.53	.62			
9	Familial structure (0-1)	15	.21	.31	-.06	.22	.42	.14	.23	.24	.34	.30	.31	-.38	-.42	-.38		
9	Familial structure (2-13)	16	.09	.12	-.12	.11	.28	.07	.14	.17	.14	.11	.09	-.19	-.19	-.19	1.00	
	Median |G|		.39	.51	.11	.47	.32	.24	.26	.33	.34	.41	.30	.32	.41	.33	.30	.13

Table E-3

Monotonic (M) and Nonmonotonic (0) Relationships between
Indicators Used in the AID Analysis[a]

Box	Indicator		1	2	3	4	5	6	7	8	9	10	11	12	13	14	15	16
1A	Subsistence economy	1																
2	Number of occupations	2	M															
2	Gender differentiation	3	0															
5	Caste	4		M														
5	Slavery	5																
5	Stratification	6		M														
6	Type of settlement	7	M															
6	Type of settlement	8	M	M		M		M	M									
6	Political complexity	9		M				M		M								
7	Inheritance of real property	10	M	M		0												
7	Inheritance of movable property	11					0	0	0		0	M						
8	Marital residence	12							0	0		M	M					
8	Descent	13										M	M	M				
8	Mode of marriage	14					M	0		0					M	M		
9	Familial structure (0-1)	15																
9	Familial structure (2-13)	16										0	0	0				

[a] See text for explanation.

Notes

1. Goodman's lambda, a statistic for measuring association between pairs of nominally scaled variables, is more nearly parallel to G than is C. Lambda, however, blows up under certain conditions when one variable is a dichotomy. Since we were using a dichotomized scale of familial organization for our dependent variable, we chose C over lambda.
2. Citing a few of the relevant studies, Sheils (1975) has made the untenable proposal that the test involving the difference between the squared correlation ratio and the squared product-moment correlation be used to determine the curvilinearity of relationships among variables of the EA. The test, which has been known for many years (Fisher, 1944), involves the assumptions of those two coefficients: the dependent variable is to be measured by an interval scale for both coefficients and the independent variable is to be similarly measured in the case of the Pearsonian r. As Sheils indicates, the data are ordinal (he calls them rankings) at best.
3. Since the Ns in these computations are in the range 500-1,170, quite small values of C and G are statistically significant.

Appendix F

Supporting Tables for
Chapters 2 and 4

Table F-1

Subfamilies as a Percent of and Mean Number of Other Relatives of Head
Age 14 and Over Present in U.S. Domestic Families
by Age, Sex, and Race: 1970

Age and Sex	Subfamilies as a Percent of and Mean Number of Other Relatives of Head Age 14 and Over in Domestic Families by Race					
	Subfamilies as a Percent of Other Relatives of Head			Mean Number of Other Relatives of Head		
	All Races	Whites	Blacks	All Races	Whites	Blacks
Age 14-17						
Male	6	7	5	.03	.02	.09
Female	13	8	20	.04	.03	.11
Age 18-24						
Male	40	44	30	.07	.06	.16
Female	37	35	44	.08	.06	.19
Age 25-34						
Male	49	53	38	.03	.03	.08
Female	46	45	51	.03	.03	.08
Age 35-44						
Male	35	37	29	.02	.02	.05
Female	31	30	37	.02	.02	.05
Age 45-64						
Male	21	21	16	.03	.02	.06
Female	4	3	7	.05	.04	.09
Age 65-74						
Male	19	19	15	.05	.05	.08
Female	.2	.1	.9	.18	.18	.23
Age 75 and over						
Male	14	14	11	.14	.14	.17
Female	.2	.1	.3	.45	.45	.47

Source: U.S. Bureau of the Census. Census of the Population: 1970.
Subject Reports. Final Report PC(2)-4B, 1973. "Persons by
Family Characteristics." Table 2.

Table F-2

Mean Number of Other Relatives of Head Present in Domestic Families
by Family Income in 1969, Type of Domestic Family Used by the
U.S. Bureau of the Census and Race: 1970

Family Income in 1969	Mean Number of Other Relatives of Head Present by Type of Domestic Family and Race[a]				
	Total	White Husband-Wife Families	Black Husband-Wife Families	White Families with Female Heads	Black Families with Female Heads
Less than $1,000	.20	.05	.23	.19	.46
$1,000 to $1,999	.22	.05	.27	.33	.57
$2,000 to $2,999	.20	.05	.28	.34	.54
$3,000 to $3,999	.19	.06	.27	.33	.58
$4,000 to $4,999	.19	.07	.29	.36	.66
$5,000 to $6,999	.17	.07	.25	.40	.75
$7,000 to $9,999	.15	.07	.26	.49	1.00
$10,000 to $14,999	.15	.09	.29	.64	1.25
$15,000 to $24,999	.20	.13	.43	.84	1.51
$25,000 or more	.18	.13	.49	.86	1.62

Source: U.S. Bureau of the Census. Census of the Population: 1970.
Subject Reports Final Report PC(2)-4B, 1973. "Persons by Family
Characteristics." Table 6

[a] No breakdown by income and type of family members was provided for
families with other male heads.

Table F-3

Percentage Distribution of Ethnic Categories by Occupational Categories of Heads of Households*

| Occupational Category of Head of Household | Ethnicity | | | | | | Total |
| | Jewish | | Catholic | | Protestant | | |
	N	%	N	%	N	%	N
Entrepreneurial	53	48.2	25	43.9	23	31.5	101
Bureaucratic	57	51.8	32	56.1	50	68.5	139
Number of cases	110		57		73		240

* Gamma (.23) significant at the .05 level.

Table F-4

Percentage Distribution of Occupational Categories of Heads of Households by Couple's Migratory Status*

| Couple's Migratory Status | Entrepreneurial | | Bureaucratic | | Total |
	N	%	N	%	N
Neither spouse a migrant	66	64.7	76	53.9	142
One spouse a migrant	24	23.5	32	22.7	56
Both migrants	12	11.8	33	23.4	45
Number of cases	102		141		243

* Gamma (.24) significant at the .05 level.

Table F-5

Percentage Distribution of Ethnic Categories by Whether or Not the Head of Household Was Ever in a Family Business*

| Head of Household Ever in Family Business? | Ethnicity | | | | | | Total |
| | Jewish | | Catholic | | Protestant | | |
	N	%	N	%	N	%	N
Yes	47	42.7	20	35.1	18	24.7	85
No	63	57.3	37	64.9	55	75.3	155
Number of cases	110		57		73		240

* Gamma (.28) significant at the .01 level.

Table F-6

Percentage Distribution of Heads of Households Who Have Been and Have Not
Been in Family Businesses, by Couple's Migratory Status*

| Couple's Migratory Status | Ever in Family Business | | | | Total |
| | Yes | | No | | |
	N	%	N	%	N
Neither spouse a migrant	57	66.3	85	54.1	142
One spouse a migrant	18	20.9	38	24.2	56
Both migrants	11	12.8	34	21.7	45
Number of cases	86		157		243

* Gamma (.24) significant at the .05 level.

Table F-7

Percentage Distribution of Couple's Migratory Status by Level of Each
of Four Measures of Extended Familism

| Measure of Extended Familism | Migratory Status | | | | | | | |
| | Neither Migrant | | One Migrant | | Both Migrants | | Total | |
	N	%	N	%	N	%	N	Gamma
Extensity of presence (number of households of kin in metropolitan area):								
None	1	0.7	4	7.1	28	62.2	33	.85*
1-14	54	38.0	38	67.9	17	37.8	109	
15+	87	61.3	14	25.0	—	0.0	101	
Intensity of presence (classification of kin in area):								
None	1	0.7	4	7.1	28	62.2	33	.90*
Some	61	43.0	47	83.9	16	35.6	124	
Both have nuclear and extended	80	56.3	5	8.9	1	2.2	86	
Interaction (number of households of kin interacted with regularly):								
None	1	0.7	5	8.9	30	66.7	36	.86*
1-5	57	40.1	44	78.6	12	26.7	113	
6+	84	59.2	7	12.5	3	6.7	94	
Functionality (of interaction with households of kin):								
Low (0-5)	58	40.8	28	50.0	33	73.3	119	.39*
High (6+)	84	59.2	28	50.0	12	26.7	124	
Number of cases	142		56		45		243	

* Significant at the .001 level.

Table F-8

Percentage Distribution of Ethnic Categories by Couple's Migratory Status*

Couple's Migratory Status	Ethnicity						Total
	Jewish		Catholic		Protestant		
	N	%	N	%	N	%	N
Neither spouse a migrant	79	71.8	35	61.4	27	37.0	141
One spouse a migrant	24	21.8	10	17.5	20	27.4	54
Both migrants	7	6.4	12	21.1	26	35.6	45
Number of cases	110		57		73		240

* Gamma (.47) significant at the .001 level.

Table F-9

Percentage Distribution of Categories of Occupation of Heads of Households by Level of Each of Four Measures of Extended Familism

Measures of Extended Familism	Occupational Category					
	Entrepreneurial		Bureaucratic		Total	
	N	%	N	%	N	Gamma
Extensity of presence (number of households of kin in metropolitan area):						
None	6	5.9	27	19.1	33	.38***
1-14	43	43.2	66	46.8	109	
15+	53	52.0	48	34.0	101	
Intensity of presence (classification of kin in area):						
None	6	5.9	27	19.1	33	.26*
Some	55	53.9	69	48.9	124	
Both have nuclear and extended	41	40.2	45	31.9	86	
Interaction (number of households of kin interacted with regularly):						
None	7	6.9	29	20.6	36	.31**
1-5	48	47.1	65	46.1	113	
6+	7	46.1	47	33.3	94	
Functionality (of interaction with households of kin):						
Low (0-5)	47	46.1	72	51.1	119	.10
High (6+)	55	53.9	69	48.9	124	
Number of cases	102		141		243	

　* Significant at the .05 level.
　** Significant at the .01 level.
*** Significant at the .001 level.

Table F-10

Summary of Zero-Order Correlations (Gammas) among Measures of Ethnicity, Occupation, Migratory Status, and Extended Familism

| | 1 | 2 | 3 | 4 | 5 | 6 | 7 | 8 |
| | | Occupation | | | | Extended Familism | | |
	Ethnicity	Entrepreneur-Bureaucrat	Family Business	Migratory Status	Extensity	Intensity	Interaction	Functionality
1 Ethnicity								
2 Occupation: Entrepreneurial-Bureaucratic	.23*							
3 Occupation: Ever in Family Business	.28**	.44***						
4 Migratory Status	.47***	.24*	.24*					
5 Extended Familism: Extensity	.77***	.38***	.33***	.85***				
6 Extended Familism: Intensity	.66***	.26**	.33***	.90***	.93***			
7 Extended Familism: Interaction	.75***	.31**	.25*	.86***	.96***	.91***		
8 Extended Familism: Functionality	.33***	.10	.18	.39***	.56***	.58***	.56***	

* Significant at the .05 level.
** Significant at the .01 level.
*** Significant at the .001 level.

Table F-11

Estimated Jewish Population in the Four Largest U.S. Jewish Communities

Community[1]	Jewish Population[2]	Cumulative %
Greater New York[3]	2,381,000	41.2
Los Angeles Metropolitan Area	500,000	49.8
Philadelphia Metropolitan Area	330,000	55.6
Chicago Metropolitan Area	269,000	60.2[4]
	3,480,000	
Total U.S. Jewish Population (1967 est.)	5,779,845	

Source: Adapted from Table 3, pp. 285-289, of Alvin Chenkin, "Jewish Population in the United States, 1967," in Morris Fine and Milton Himmelfarb
(eds.), American Jewish Year Book, vol. 69 (New York: American Jewish
Committee, 1968).

[1] Chenkin notes that "individual community estimates were generally obtained
from member federations of the Council of Jewish Federations and Welfare
Funds and from the files of the National United Jewish Appeal" (p.281). Concerning the definitions of these communities, he states: "The areas covered
by [these] population estimates ... do not uniquely fit into any of [five stan-
dard] census definitions. The Jewish estimates are based upon the service
and campaign areas of Jewish federations, and these show wide variations.
Mostly, but with many exceptions, the areas in [this table] would be closest
in concept to urbanized area" (p.285). Examination of his table indicates
that these figures include only the Jewish population within the principal state
of a multistate metropolitan area. This is made explicit in the case of New
York (see note 3 below). In the cases of Chicago and Philadelphia, one notes
that Chenkin's table lists separate population estimates for the Indiana and
New Jersey communities included in each of these two cities' metropolitan
areas.

[2] Estimates are for 1967, with the exception of the figures for Greater New
York which are kept at 1962 levels. "The absence of more recent data for
this area," Chenkin notes, "represents the greatest potential for modification
of the national total, since approximately 40% of all United States Jews are
currently estimated to reside in New York City and [the] three suburban
counties (Nassau, Suffolk and Westchester Counties, New York)" (p.281).

[3] Greater New York figures are composed of the following:

New York City	1,836,000
Nassau County	372,000
Suffolk County	42,000
Westchester County	131,000
	2,381,000

[4] This 60.2% seems a serious underestimate of the proportion of the nation's
Jews who live in these four metropolitan areas, since, as noted, the New
Jersey and Connecticut suburban Jews are excluded from the New York esti-
mate (which is seven years old), New Jersey Jews are excluded from the
Philadelphia figures, and Jews from nearby Indiana are listed separately
from the Chicago totals.

Table F-12

Ten States Containing Most Jews vs. Ten Most Populated States in the United States: Cumulative Percentages

Ten States with Most Jews			Ten Most Populated U.S. States		
State	Total (7/1/67) Cumulative %	Jews (1967 est.) Cumulative %	State	Total Cumulative %	Jews Cumulative %
New York	9.3	43.6	California	9.7	11.3
California	19.0	54.9	New York	19.0	54.9
Pennsylvania	24.8	62.6	Pennsylvania	24.8	62.6
New Jersey	28.4	68.9	Illinois	30.3	67.5
Illinois	33.9	73.8	Texas	35.8	68.6
Massachusetts	36.6	78.2	Ohio	41.1	71.4
Maryland	38.5	81.3	Michigan	45.4	73.1
Florida	41.5	84.3	New Jersey	49.0	79.4
Ohio	46.8	87.1	Florida	52.0	82.4
Connecticut	48.3	88.9	Massachusetts	54.7	86.8
	95,495,000	5,138,075		108,341,000	5,019,455

Total U.S. Population[1] 197,863,000
Total U.S. Jewish Population[2] . . . 5,779,845

Source: Adapted from Table 1, pp.282-283, of Alvin Chenkin, "Jewish Population in the United States, 1967," in Morris Fine and Milton Himmelfarb (eds.), American Jewish Year Book, vol. 69 (New York: American Jewish Committee, 1968).

[1] Total U.S. population is as of July 1, 1967, and represents estimates of the total resident population of each state. Members of the armed forces abroad are excluded. Total United States population, including armed forces abroad, was 199,118,000. Source: U.S. Bureau of the Census, Current Population Reports, Series P-25, No. 384, February 13, 1968.

[2] Chenkin based his 1967 state estimates on community estimates (obtained from Jewish federations), after duplications were eliminated and adjustments made for "unlisted" Jews. This results in a total estimate of 5,779,845 Jews in 1967.

Table F-13

Percentage Distribution of Wisconsin Respondents by Income of Family and by Level of Extended Familism, for Four Measures of Extended Familism

Measure by Level of Extended Familism	Income of Family					Total	Gamma
	Under $3,000	$3,000-5,999	$6,000-7,999	$8,000-9,999	$10,000 and over		
	N = 48	N = 108	N = 148	N = 85	N = 94	N = 483	
Extensity of presence[1]							
None	8.3	12.0	10.8	16.5	20.2	13.7	.00
Some	66.7	50.9	35.8	38.8	43.6	44.3	
High	25.0	37.0	53.4	44.7	36.2	42.0	
Intensity of presence[2]							
None	8.3	12.0	10.8	16.5	20.2	13.7	-.15*
Some	64.6	69.4	59.5	61.2	68.1	64.2	
High	27.1	18.5	29.7	22.4	11.7	22.2	
Interaction[3]							
None	14.6	7.4	4.1	7.1	6.4	6.8	.07
Some	62.5	43.5	46.6	43.5	52.1	48.0	
High	22.9	49.1	49.3	49.4	41.5	45.1	
Functionality[4]							
None	6.3	13.0	10.8	14.1	17.0	12.6	-.05
Some	64.6	50.0	53.4	52.9	51.1	53.2	
High	29.2	37.0	35.8	32.9	31.9	34.2	

* Significant at the .05 level.

[1] Extensity of presence refers to the number of households of kin in the community: "some" = 1-8; "high" = 9+.

[2] Intensity of presence refers to the degree of kin present in the community; a nuclear kinsman is a member of the respondent's family of orientation or of procreation; "none" means neither the respondent nor spouse reports any household of kin in the community; "high" means both respondent and spouse report having households of both nuclear and extended kin in the community; "some" signifies the presence of kin but not satisfying the conditions of the "high" category.

[3] Interaction refers to the number of categories of households of kin with which some member of the respondent's household has been in contact (face-to-face, phone or mail) at least monthly; "some" = 1-3; "high" = 4+.

[4] Functionality refers to the number of categories of service either given and/or received from some kinsman; "some" = 1-2; "high" = 3+.

Table F-14

Percentage Distribution of Respondents by Ethnic Category and by Level
of Extended Familism, for Four Measures of Extended Familism

Measure and Level of Extended Familism[a]	Ethnicity				
	Catholic	Lutheran	Other Protestant	Total	Gamma
Extensity of presence	N = 197	N = 177	N = 138	N = 512	
None	9.1	13.0	21.7	13.9	−.26*
Some	40.6	45.8	48.6	44.5	
High	50.3	41.2	29.7	41.6	
Intensity of presence	N = 197	N = 177	N = 138	N = 512	
None	9.1	13.0	21.7	13.9	
Some	64.0	62.1	64.5	63.5	−.25*
High	26.9	24.9	13.8	22.7	
Interaction	N = 197	N = 177	N = 138	N = 512	
None	4.1	6.2	13.8	7.4	
Some	49.7	42.4	52.9	48.0	−.17*
High	46.2	51.4	33.3	44.5	
Functionality	N = 197	N = 177	N = 138	N = 512	
None	15.2	9.0	15.2	13.1	
Some	49.2	58.2	51.4	52.9	−.02
High	35.5	32.8	33.3	34.0	

[a] These indexes and categories are explained in notes 1-4 to Table F-13.

* Significant at the .01 level.

Table F-15

Measures of Association (Gammas) between Ethnicity and Three Measures
of Extended Familism, within Ecological Level

Measure of Extended Familism	Ecology			Total
	Metropolitan	Other	Rural	
	N = 115	N = 286	N = 112	N = 513
Extensity of presence	−.31*	−.30**	−.14	−.26**
Intensity of presence	−.35*	−.26**	−.15	−.25*
Interaction	−.24	−.23**	−.07	−.17*

* Significant at the .05 level.
** Significant at the .01 level.

Table F-16

Percentage Distribution of Domestic Family Structure in a
Riverside, California, Sample of Three Ethnic Groups

Domestic Family Structure	Ethnic Groups		
	Anglo	Mexican American	Black
Nuclear family	92	77	70
Father absent family	4	5	15
Nuclear family and extended kin	3	9	6
Other	1	9	9
Total	100	100	100
(N)	(556)	(254)	(164)

Source: Vivian Tong Nagy, "Family Characteristics, Attitudes and Values."
Pp.261-275 in Harold B. Gerard and Norman Miller, School Desegregation: A Long-Term Study. New York: Plenum, 1975, Table 12.1,
p.263.

Table F-17

Relationship between Mean Size of Local Community and Familial Complexity:
Ethnographic Atlas, excluding Fishing and Herding Societies

Familial Complexity	Mean Size of Local Community[a]				
	Fewer than 50 persons	50-99	100-199	200-399/ 400-1,000, but No Town of over 5,000	One or More Towns of 5,000-50,000; One or More Cities of over 50,000
High	39.5%	65.3%	77.5%	78.2%	69.0%
Low	60.5%	34.7%	22.5%	21.8%	31.0%
No. of cases (N = 458)*	(86)	(72)	(80)	(133)	(87)

[a] To eliminate categories with very small frequencies, we have reduced
Murdock's categories from eight to five. His categories are: (1) under 50;
(2) 50-99; (3) 100-199; (4) 200-399; (5) 400-1,000; (6) 1,000 or more, but no
town of more than 5,000; (7) one or more towns in range 5,000-50,000; (8)
one or more cities of 50,000 or more. Note that the first five categories
are classified with respect to mean size of community; category (6) intro-
duces the additional criterion of maximum size of city. Finally, in categories (7) and (8) there is no mention of average size of community but
merely size of largest city. Thus, although these categories are relevant
to our purpose, they are not unidimensional.

* $C = .29$, $\overline{C} = .41$, $P < .001$; $G = .30$, $P < .001$.

Table F-18

Relationship between Permanence of Settlement and Familial Complexity[a]

Familial Complexity	Permanence of Settlement	
	Nomadic	Non-nomadic
High	53.5%	75.1%
Low	46.5%	24.9%
No. of cases (N = 909)*	(157)	(752)

[a] We need not have been so hasty in believing that permanence of settlement would fail to discriminate medium- and higher-complexity societies suffi-ciently to show the curvilinear relationship with familial complexity. For our categories of permanence (nomadic or seminomadic, semisedentary, neighborhoods or hamlets, and compact or complex permanent settlements), the percentages of high complexity are: 54%, 71%, 80%, and 73%. Although not spectacular, the distribution does show an inflected curve.

* $C = .18$, $\overline{C} = .25$, $P < .001$; $G = .45$, $P < .001$.

Table F-19

Relationship between Stratification and Familial Complexity

Familial Complexity	Stratification			
	Absent among Freemen	Wealth and Elite Distinctions	Hereditary Aristocracy	Social Classes
High	66.4%	71.4%	79.1%	66.7%
Low	33.6%	28.6%	20.9%	33.3%
No. of cases (N = 851)*	(443)	(154)	(182)	(72)

* $C = .11$, $\overline{C} = .16$, $P < .05$; $G = .14$, $P < .05$.

Table F-20

Relationship between Political Complexity and Familial Complexity

Familial Complexity	Political Complexity (Levels of Jurisdictional Hierarchy beyond Local Community)			
	No Levels	One Level	Two Levels	Three or Four Levels
High	59.0%	82.5%	83.3%	74.1%
Low	41.0%	17.5%	16.7%	25.9%
No. of cases (N = 883)*	(398)	(274)	(126)	(85)

* $C = .24$, $\overline{C} = .34$, $P < .001$; $G = .38$, $P < .001$.

Table F-21

Relationship between Mean Size of Local Community and Familial
Complexity within Levels of Subsistence Economy

Subsistence Economy and Familial Complexity	Mean Size of Community				
	Under 50	50-99	100-199	200-399, 400-1,000, but No Town of over 5,000	One or More Towns of 5,000-50,000; One or More Cities of over 50,000
Hunting and gathering:					
High	38.5%	59.1%	85.7%	85.7%	—
Low	61.5%	40.9%	14.3%	14.3%	—
No. of cases					
(N = 108)*	(65)	(22)	(14)	(07)	—
Incipient Agriculture:					
High	35.7%	60.0%	87.5%	76.5%	100.0%
Low	64.3%	40.0%	12.5%	23.5%	—
No. of cases					
(N = 45)†	(14)	(05)	(08)	(17)	(01)
Extensive agriculture or horticulture:					
High	57.1%	69.2%	78.0%	83.0%	76.5%
Low	42.9%	30.8%	22.0%	17.0%	23.5%
No. of cases					
(N = 157)‡	(07)	(39)	(41)	(53)	(17)
Intensive agriculture on permanent fields:					
High	—	100.0%	81.8%	87.5%	84.6%
Low	—	0.0%	18.2%	12.5%	15.4%
No. of cases					
(N = 51)§	—	(03)	(11)	(24)	(13)
Intensive agriculture with irrigation:					
High	—	50.0%	33.3%	63.2%	50.0%
Low	—	50.0%	66.7%	36.8%	50.0%
No. of cases					
(N = 39)‖	—	(02)	(06)	(19)	(12)

* $C = .35$, $\overline{C} = .49$, $P < .01$; $G = .60$, $P < .001$.
† $C = .40$, $\overline{C} = .57$, N.S.; $G = .56$, $P < .01$.
‡ $C = .16$, $\overline{C} = .23$, N.S.; $G = .22$, N.S.
§ $C = .12$, $\overline{C} = .17$, N.S.; $G = .05$, N.S.
‖ $C = .21$, $\overline{C} = .30$, N.S.; $G = .08$, N.S.

Table F-22

Relationship between Permanence of Settlement and Familial
Complexity within Levels of Subsistence Economy

Subsistence Economy and Familial Complexity	Permanence of Settlement	
	Nomadic	Non-nomadic
Hunting and gathering:		
High	52.3%	62.1%
Low	47.7%	37.9%
No. of cases		
(N = 178)*	(149)	(29)
Incipient agriculture:		
High	100.0%	63.0%
Low	0.0%	37.0%
No. of cases		
(N = 85)†	(04)	(81)
Extensive agriculture or horticulture:		
High	50.0%	79.4%
Low	50.0%	20.6%
No. of cases		
(N = 396)‡	(02)	(394)
Intensive agriculture on permanent fields:		
High	0.0%	81.7%
Low	100.0%	18.3%
No. of cases		
(N = 154)§	(01)	(153)
Intensive agriculture with irrigation:		
High	100.0%	64.8%
Low	0.0%	35.2%
No. of cases		
(N = 89)‖	(01)	(88)

* $C = .07$, $\overline{C} = .10$, N.S.; $G = .20$, N.S.
† $C = .16$, $\overline{C} = .23$, N.S.; $G = -1.00$, N.S.
‡ $C = .05$, $\overline{C} = .07$, N.S.; $G = .59$, N.S.
§ $C = .17$, $\overline{C} = .24$, $P < .05$; $G = 1.00$, N.S.
‖ $C = .08$, $\overline{C} = .11$, N.S.; $G = 1.00$, N.S.

Table F-23

Relationship between Stratification and Familial Complexity
within Levels of Subsistence Economy

Subsistence Economy and Familial Complexity	Stratification			
	Absent among Freemen	Wealth and Elite Distinctions	Hereditary Aristocracy	Social Classes
Hunting and gathering:				
High	49.3%	73.5%	33.3%	—
Low	50.7%	26.5%	66.7%	—
No. of cases				
(N = 178)*	(138)	(34)	(06)	—
Incipient agriculture:				
High	57.4%	87.5%	75.0%	—
Low	42.6%	12.5%	25.0%	
No. of cases				—
(N = 81)†	(61)	(08)	(12)	—
Extensive agriculture or horticulture:				
High	78.6%	73.2%	79.4%	87.5%
Low	21.4%	26.8%	20.6%	12.5%
No. of cases				
(N = 354)‡	(173)	(71)	(102)	(08)
Intensive agriculture on permanent fields:				
High	85.4%	71.4%	88.9%	66.7%
Low	14.6%	28.6%	11.1%	33.3%
No. of cases				
(N = 137)§	(41)	(21)	(36)	(39)
Intensive agriculture with irrigation:				
High	69.6%	55.6%	76.2%	60.0%
Low	30.4%	44.4%	23.8%	40.0%
No. of cases				
(N = 87)‖	(23)	(18)	(21)	(25)

* $C = .20$, $\overline{C} = .28$, $P < .05$; $G = .32$, N.S.
† $C = .21$, $\overline{C} = .30$, N.S.; $G = .45$, N.S.
‡ $C = .06$, $\overline{C} = .08$, N.S.; $G = .01$, N.S.
§ $C = .23$, $\overline{C} = .33$, N.S.; $G = -.25$, N.S.
‖ $C = .16$, $\overline{C} = .23$, N.S.; $G = -.05$, N.S.

Table F-24

Relationship between Political Complexity and Familial Complexity
within Levels of Subsistence Economy

Subsistence Economy and Familial Complexity	Political Complexity			
	No Levels	One Level	Two Levels	Three or Four Levels
Hunting and gathering:				
High	48.3%	78.1%	100.0%	—
Low	51.7%	21.9%	0.0%	—
No. of cases				
(N = 178)*	(145)	(32)	(01)	—
Incipient agriculture:				
High	55.8%	72.0%	100.0%	100.0%
Low	44.2%	28.0%	0.0%	0.0%
No. of cases				
(N = 85)†	(52)	(25)	(07)	(01)
Extensive agriculture or horticulture:				
High	70.3%	83.8%	81.5%	100.0%
Low	29.7%	16.2%	18.5%	0.0%
No. of cases				
(N = 384)‡	(145)	(154)	(65)	(20)
Intensive agriculture on permanent fields:				
High	78.6%	95.3%	85.3%	68.4%
Low	21.4%	4.7%	14.7%	31.6%
No. of cases				
(N = 143)§	(28)	(43)	(34)	(38)
Intensive agriculture with irrigation:				
High	46.2%	75.0%	83.3%	61.5%
Low	53.8%	25.0%	16.7%	38.5%
No. of cases				
(N = 86)‖	(26)	(16)	(18)	(26)

* $C = .23$, $\overline{C} = .33$, $P < .01$; $G = .60$, $P < .001$.
† $C = .27$, $\overline{C} = .38$, N.S.; $G = .53$, $P < .01$.
‡ $C = .19$, $\overline{C} = .27$, $P < .01$; $G = .34$, $P < .001$.
§ $C = .26$, $\overline{C} = .37$, $P < .05$; $G = -.28$, N.S.
‖ $C = .28$, $\overline{C} = .40$, N.S.; $G = .21$, N.S.

Table F-25

Percentage Distribution of Large and Small Familial Systems by Level of Societal Complexity. Based on Ethnographic Atlas

Size of Familial System	Prevalent Form of Economic Organization							
	Hunting and Gathering	Incipient Agriculture	Pastoral	Fishing	Extensive Agriculture	Intensive Agriculture	Intensive Agriculture with Irrigation
Large	54%	65%	71%	73%	80%	80%	65%
Small	46%	35%	29%	27%	20%	20%	35%
No. of cases (N = 1,137)*	(180)	(86)	(86)	(116)	(415)	(163)	(89)

* C = .21, $\overline{C}$ = .30, P < .001; G = .21, P < .001.

Table F-26

Relationship between Socioeconomic Development and Familial
Complexity: 43 Developing Nations

Familial Complexity	Socioeconomic Development		
	Low	Intermediate	High
High	100.0%	60.0%	12.0%
Low	—	40.0%	88.0%
No. of cases (N = 43)*	(03)	(15)	(25)

Source: Adelman and Morris (1967: 170). Countries classified as having
low socioeconomic development are Cambodia, Laos, and South Viet-
nam (N = 3). Intermediate socioeconomic development includes Bolivia,
Burma, Ceylon, Ecuador, Guatemala, Honduras, India, Indonesia, Iran,
Iraq, Pakistan, Philippines, Surinam, Syria, Thailand (N = 15). Countries with high socioeconomic development include: Argentina, Brazil,
Chile, Colombia, Costa Rica, Cyprus, Dominican Republic, El Salvador,
Greece, Israel, Jamaica, Japan, Lebanon, Mexico, Nicaragua, Panama,
Paraguay, Peru, South Korea, Taiwan, Trinidad, Turkey, UAR, Uru-
guay, and Venezuela (N = 25). Excluded are countries in which the
"basic social organization" is reported as "tribal allegiance" (N = 31).

* $C = .52$, $\overline{C} = .74$, $P < .001$; $G = .88$, $P < .001$.

References

(Numbers in brackets represent the pages of this book on which the works listed below are cited.)

Aberle, David F.
  1961 "Matrilineal descent in cross-cultural perspective." Pp. 631–727 in David M. Schneider and Kathleen Gough (eds.), Matrilineal Kinship. Berkeley: University of California Press. [93]

Adams, Bert N.
  1968 Kinship in an Urban Setting. Chicago: Markham. [15]

  1968– "Kinship systems and adaptation to modernization." Studies in Com-
  1969   parative International Development 4: 47–60. [96]

Adams, Richard N.
  1960 "An inquiry into the nature of the family." Pp. 30–49 in Gertrude Dole and Robert L. Carneiro (eds.), Essays in the Science of Culture: In Honor of Leslie A. White. New York: Crowell. [146, 147, 177, 178]

Adelman, Irma, and George Dalton
  1971 "A factor analysis of modernization in village India." Pp. 492–517 in George Dalton (ed.), Economic Development and Social Change: The Modernization of Village Communities. Garden City, N.Y.: Natural History Press. [94, 104]

Adelman, Irma, and Cynthia Taft Morris
  1967 Society, Politics, and Economic Development. Baltimore: Johns Hopkins University Press. [66, 79, 80, 85, 86, 303]

Aginsky, B. W., and E. G. Aginsky

1947   "A resultant of intercultural relations." Social Forces 26: 84–87. [146]

1949   "The process of change in family types: a case study." American Anthropologist 51: 611–614. [146]

Aiken, Michael Thomas
1964   Kinship in an Urban Community. Unpublished Ph.D. dissertation, University of Michigan. [14]

Ainsworth, Mary D. S.
1973   "The development of infant-mother attachment." Pp. 1–94 in Bettye M. Caldwell and Henry N. Ricciuti (eds.), Review of Child Development Research, vol. 3. Chicago: University of Chicago Press. [177]

Anderson, Michael
1971   Family Structure in Nineteenth Century Lancashire. Cambridge: Cambridge University Press. [9]

Anspach, Donald F.
1976   "Kinship and divorce." Journal of Marriage and the Family 38: 323–330. [48]

Aschenbrenner, Joyce
1975   Lifelines: Black Families in Chicago. New York: Holt, Rinehart and Winston. [187]

Baerwaldt, Nancy A. and James N. Morgan
1973   "Trends in inter-family transfers." Pp. 205–232 in Lewis Mandell, George Katona, James N. Morgan and Jay Schmiedeskamp, Surveys of Consumers 1971–72: Contributions to Behavioral Economics. Ann Arbor, Mich.: Institute for Social Research. [18]

Bane, Mary Jo
1976   Here to Stay: American Families in the Twentieth Century. New York: Basic Books. [16]

Banfield, Edward C.
1970   The Unheavenly City. Boston: Little, Brown. [171]

Baran, Paul, and Paul Sweezy
1966   Monopoly Capital. New York: Monthly Review Press. [155]

Barnes, J. A.
1971   Three styles in the Study of Kinship. Berkeley: University of California Press. [178]

1973   "Genetrix: genitor: nature: culture?" Pp. 61–73 in Jack Goody (ed.), The Character of Kinship. Cambridge: Cambridge University Press. [177]

Barry, Herbert, III, Margaret K. Bacon, and Irvin L. Child
1957   "A cross-cultural survey of some sex differences in socialization." Journal of Abnormal and Social Psychology 55: 327–332. [101, 115, 116]

Barry, Herbert, III, Irvin L. Child, and Margaret K. Bacon
1959   "Relation of child training to subsistence economy." American Anthropologist 61: 51–63. [101]

Barry, Herbert, III, and Leonora M. Paxson
1971 "Infancy and early childhood: cross cultural codes 2." Ethnology 10: 466-508. [203]

Bart, Pauline B.
1974 Personal communication concerning unpublished study of divorced men in Cook County, Ill. [154]

Barth, Fredrik
1973 "Descent and marriage reconsidered." Pp. 3-19 in Jack Goody (ed.), The Character of Kinship. Cambridge: Cambridge University Press. [94]

Bascom, W. R.
1941 "Acculturation among the Gullah Negroes." American Anthropologist 43: 43-50. [146]

Bates, Frederick L.
1956 "Position, role, and status: a reformulation of concepts." Social Forces 34: 313-321. [242]

Bell, Norman W., and Ezra F. Vogel (eds.)
1960 A Modern Introduction to the Family. Glencoe, Ill.: Free Press. [147]

Benedict, Burton
1968 "Family firms and economic development." Southwestern Journal of Anthropology 24: 1-19. [94]

Berkner, Lutz K.
1973 "Recent research on the history of the family in Western Europe." Journal of Marriage and the Family 35: 395-405. [94]

Berry, Brian
1960 "An inductive approach to the regionalization of economic development." Pp. 78-107 in Norton S. Ginsburg (ed.), Essays on Geography and Economic Development. Chicago: University of Chicago Press. [111]

Bierstedt, Robert S.
1975 "Comment on Lenski's evolutionary perspective." Pp. 154-158 in Peter M. Blau (ed.), Approaches to the Study of Social Structure. New York: Free Press. [105]

Binford, Lewis R.
1971 "Post-pleistocene adaptations." Pp. 22-49 in Stuart Struever (ed.), Pre-historic Agriculture. Garden City, N.Y.: Natural History Press. [113]

Birmingham, Stephen
1967 "Our Crowd": The Great Jewish Families of New York. New York: Harper and Row. [43]

Blake, Judith
1961 Family Structure in Jamaica. New York: Free Press. [178, 179, 185]

Blau, Peter M.
1964 Exchange and Power in Social Life. New York: Wiley. [7]

Bloch, Maurice

1973   "The long term and the short term: the economic and political significance of the morality of kinship." Pp. 75–87 in Jack Goody (ed.), The Character of Kinship. Cambridge: Cambridge University Press. [99]

Blood, Robert O., Jr., and Donald M. Wolfe
1960   Husbands and Wives: The Dynamics of Married Living. New York: Free Press. [116]

Blumberg, Rae Lesser
1970   Societal Complexity and Familial Complexity: Inter- and Intra- societal Correlates of Family Structure, Functionality, and Influence. Unpublished Ph.D. dissertation, Northwestern University. [65, 73, 149]

1973   "Social structure, women, and fertility in Latin America." Paper presented at Latin American Population Conference (AID auspices), San José, Costa Rica. [156]

1974   "Structural factors affecting women's status: a cross-societal paradigm." Paper read at meeting of International Sociological Association, Toronto. [149, 161]

1976   "The erosion of sexual equality in the kibbutz: structural factors affecting the status of women." Pp. 320–339 in Joan I. Roberts (ed.), Beyond Intellectual Sexism: A New Woman, A New Reality. New York: David McKay. [149]

Blumberg, Rae Lesser, Donald E. Carns, and Robert F. Winch
1970   "High gods, virgin brides, and societal complexity." Paper presented at meeting of American Sociological Association, Washington, D.C. [9]

Blumberg, Rae Lesser with María-Pilar García
1974   "The political economy of the mother-child family; a cross-societal view." Paper read at meeting of International Sociological Association, Toronto. [144]

Blumberg, Rae Lesser, and Robert F. Winch
1972   "Societal complexity and familial complexity: evidence for the curvilinear hypothesis." American Journal of Sociology 77: 898–920. See also 78 (May 1973): 1522. [65, 162]

1973   "The rise and fall of the complex family: some implications for an evolutionary theory of societal development." Paper read at meeting of American Sociological Association, New York. [107, 120, 156, 162, 171]

Blumberg, Rae Lesser, Robert F. Winch, and Hazel H. Reinhardt
1974   "Family structure as adaptive strategy." Paper read at meeting of American Sociological Association, Montreal. [162, 171]

Bogue, Donald J.
1959   The Population of the United States. Glencoe, Ill.: Free Press. [26]

Boserup, Ester
1965   The Conditions of Agricultural Growth: The Economics of Agrarian Change under Population Pressure. Chicago: Aldine. [113]

1974 "Employment and education: keys to smaller families." Victor-Bostrum Fund Report, No. 18 (Spring). [171]

Boyer, Ruth M.
1964 "The matrifocal family among the Mescalero: additional data." American Anthropologist 66: 593–602. [146]

Brecht, Bertolt
1941 Mutter Courage und ihre Kinder. [184]

Brow, James
1972 "Marriage, inheritance, and the structure of Veeda villages." Paper read at meeting of American Anthropological Association, Toronto. [133]

Brown, Judith K.
1970 "A note on the division of labor by sex." American Anthropologist 72: 1073–1078. [149, 161, 181]

Browning, Harley L.
1967 "The demography of the city." Pp. 71–92 in Glenn H. Beyer (ed.), The Urban Explosion in Lation America. Ithaca, N.Y.: Cornell University Press. [156]

Buck J. L.
1937 Land Utilization in China: Statistics. Nanking, China: University of Nanking. [98, 133]

Burch, Thomas K.
1967 "The size and structure of families: a comparative analysis of census data." American Sociological Review 32: 347–363. [97]

Burgess, E. W., and J. J. Locke
1945 The Family: From Institution to Companionship. New York: American Book. [13]

Calley, M.
1956 "Economic life of mixed-blood communities in Northern New South Wales." Oceania 26: 200–213. [146, 152, 153]

Campbell, A. A.
1943 "St. Thomas Negroes: a study of personality and culture." Psychological Monograph, No. 55 (5). [146]

Campbell, Donald T.
1975 "On the conflicts between biological and social evolution and between psychology and moral tradition." American Psychologist 30: 1103–1126. [105]

Campbell, Donald T., and Julian C. Stanley
1963 "Experimental and quasi-experimental designs for research." Pp. 171–246 in N. L. Gage (ed.), Handbook of Research on Teaching. Chicago: Rand McNally. [64, 103]

Campisi, Paul J.
1948 "Ethnic family patterns: the Italian family in the United States." American Journal of Sociology 53: 443–449. [43]

Carroll, Vern (ed.)

1970   Adoption in Eastern Oceania. Honolulu: University of Hawaii Press.
        [189]

Chandler, Alfred D., Jr., and Stephen Salsbury
1971   Pierre S. Du Pont and the Making of the Modern Corporation. New
        York: Harper and Row. [43, 44]

Chapman, William
1974   "Report challenges war-on-poverty assumptions." Chicago Sun-Times,
        May 12: 32. [174]

Chenkin, Alvin
1968   "Jewish population in the United States, 1967." Pp. 271–290 in
        Morris Fine and Milton Himmelfarb (eds.), American Jewish Year
        Book, vol. 69. New York: American Jewish Committee. [292, 293]

Clarke, Edith
1957   My Mother Who Fathered Me: A Study of the Family in Three Se-
        lected Communities in Jamaica. London: Allen and Unwin. [178, 183,
        185]

Clignet, Remi
1970   Many Wives, Many Powers. Evanston, Ill.: Northwestern University
        Press. [202]

Comhaire, Jean L.
1956   "Economic change and the extended family." Annals 305: 45–52.
        [100]

Cooley, Charles Horton
1909   Social Organization. New York: Scribner's. [4]

Corry, John
1977   Golden Clan. Boston: Houghton Mifflin. [43]

Corti, Count Egon Caesar
1928a   The Rise of the House of Rothschild: 1770–1830. New York: Blue
        Ribbon Books. [44, 205]

1928b   The Reign of the House of Rothschild: 1830–1871. New York: Cos-
        mopolitan. [44]

Cruickshank, J. Graham
1916   Black Talk. Demerara, British Guiana: Argosy. [148]

D'Andrade, Roy G.
1966   "Sex differences and cultural institutions." Pp. 173-204 in Eleanor
        E. Maccoby (ed.), The Development of Sex Differences. Stanford,
        Calif.: Stanford University Press. [113]

Davis, James A.
1967   "A partial coefficient for Goodman and Kruskal's gamma." Journal
        of the American Statistical Association 62: 189–193. [85]

Despres, Leo A.
1970   "Differential adaptations and micro-cultural evolution in Guyana."
        Pp. 263–288 in Norman E. Whitten, Jr., and John F. Szwed (eds.),
        Afro-American Anthropology: Contemporary Perspectives. New York:
        Free Press. [149, 152]

Domhoff, G. William
1967 Who Rules America? Englewood Cliffs, N.J.: Prentice-Hall. [43]

Dotson, Floyd
1951 "Patterns of voluntary association among urban working-class families." American Sociological Review 16: 687–693. [13]

Driver, Harold E.
1966 "Geographical-historical *versus* psycho-functional explanations of kin avoidances." Current Anthropology 7: 131–148. [102]

Driver, Harold E., and Richard P. Chaney
1970 "Cross-cultural sampling and Galton's problem." Pp. 990–1003 in Raoul Naroll and Ronald Cohen (eds.), A Handbook of Method in Cultural Anthropology. Garden City, N.Y.: Natural History Press. [102]

Dumond, D. E.
1975 "Limitation of human population: a natural history." Science 187: 713–721. [192]

Duncan, Otis Dudley
1964 "Social organization and the ecosystem." Pp. 36–82 in Robert E. L. Faris (ed.), Handbook of Modern Sociology. Chicago: Rand McNally. [96, 110]

Durkheim, Emile
1933 The Division of Labor in Society. New York: Free Press [67]

Edgerton, Robert B.
1971 The Individual in Cultural Adaptation. Berkeley: University of California Press. [115]

Editors
1962 "Ethnographic atlas." Ethnology 1: 113–134. [101]

Edwards, R. C., M. Reich, and T. E. Weisskopf
1972 The Capitalist System. Englewood Cliffs, N.J.: Prentice-Hall. [171]

Einhorn, Hillel J.
1972 "Alchemy in the behavioral sciences." Public Opinion Quarterly 36: 367–378. [143]

Ekeh, Peter P.
1974 Social Exchange Theory: The Two Traditions. Cambridge, Mass.: Harvard University Press. [10]

Ember, Melvin
1971 "An empirical test of Galton's problem." Ethnology 10: 98–106. [102]

Engels, Frederick
1972 The Origin of the Family, Private Property and the State: In the Light of the Researches of Lewis H. Morgan. Introduction and Notes by Eleanor Burke Leacock. New York: International Publishers. [89, 90]

Epstein, Benjamin R., and Arnold Forster
1962 Some of My Best Friends . . . New York: Farrar, Straus and Cudahy. [26]

Erickson, Edwin E.
  1972   "Galton's worst: a further note on Ember's reflection." Paper presented at meeting of American Anthropological Association, Toronto. [102]

Fallers, Lloyd A.
  1965   "The range of variation in actual family size: a critique of Marion J. Levy, Jr.'s argument." Pp. 70–82 in Ansley J. Coale et al., Aspects of the Analysis of Family Structure. Princeton, N.J.: Princeton University Press. [97]

Farber, Bernard
  1974   Personal communication. [175]
  1976   "Kinship—now you see it, now you don't." Sociological Quarterly 17: 279–288. [9]

Farley, Reynolds
  1970   "Family types and family headship: a comparison of trends among blacks and whites." Paper read at meeting of American Sociological Association, Washington, D.C. [154]

Finifter, Bernard
  1975   Personal communication. [253]

Fisher, R. A.
  1944   Statistical Methods for Research Workers. London: Oliver and Boyd. [283]

Flannery, Kent V.
  1971   "Archeological systems theory and early mesoamerica. Pp. 80–100 in Stuart Struever (ed.), Prehistoric Agriculture. Garden City, N.Y.: Natural History Press. [113]

Ford, Clellan S. (ed.)
  1967   Cross-Cultural Approaches: Readings in Comparative Research. New Haven, Conn.: HRAF Press. [101]

Forde, Daryll
  1947   "The anthropological approach in social science." Advancement of Science 4: 213–224. [72, 92]

Fortes, Meyer
  1953   "The structure of unilineal descent groups." American Anthropologist 55: 17–41. [72, 92]
  1969   Kinship and the Social Order: The Legacy of Lewis Henry Morgan. Chicago: Aldine. [89, 92, 99, 179]

Frank, Andre
  1969   Latin America: Underdevelopment or Revolution. New York: Monthly Review Press. [68]

Frazier, E. Franklin
  1939   The Negro Family in the United States. Chicago: University of Chicago Press. [146, 178, 184]
  1950   "Problems and needs of Negro children and youth resulting from family disorganization." Journal of Negro Education 19: 269–277. [146]

Freed, Stanley A., and Ruth S. Freed
1971 "A technique for studying role behavior." Ethnology 9: 107–121. [10]

Freeman, Linton C.
1957 An Empirical Test of Folk-Urbanism. Unpublished Ph.D. dissertation, Northwestern University. [83]

Freeman, Linton C., and Robert F. Winch
1957 "Societal complexity: an empirical test of a typology of societies." American Journal of Sociology 62: 461–466. [81, 83]

Gans, Herbert
1962 The Urban Villagers. New York: Free Press. [43]
1968 "Urbanism and suburbanism as ways of life: a re-evaluation of definitions." Pp. 34–52 in Herbert J. Gans, People and Plans: Essays on Urban Problems and Solutions. New York: Basic Books. Pp. 625–648 reprinted from Arnold M. Rose (ed.), Human Behavior and Social Processes. Boston: Houghton Mifflin, 1962. [50]

Geertz, Hildred
1959 "The vocabulary of emotion." Journal for the Study of Interpersonal Processes 22: 225. [146]

Glick, Paul C.
1957 American Families. New York: Wiley. [204]
1975 "A demographer looks at American families." Journal of Marriage and the Family 37: 15–26. [48]
1977 "Updating the life cycle of the family." Journal of Marriage and the Family 39: 5-13. [204]

Glick, Paul C., and Robert Parke, Jr.
1965 "New approaches in studying the life cycle of the family." Demography 2: 187–202. [204]

Goffman, Erving
1961 Asylums: Essays on the Social Situation of Mental Patients and Other Inmates. New York: Doubleday. [53]

Goldschmidt, Walter
1959 Man's Way: A Preface to the Understanding of Human Society. New York: Holt. [74, 96]

Goldschmidt, Walter, and Evalyn Jacobson Kunkel
1971 "The structure of the peasant family." American Anthropologist 73: 1058–1076. [95, 117]

Gonzalez, Nancie L. Solien
1959 The Consanguineal Household among the Black Carib of Central America. Unpublished Ph.D. dissertation, University of Michigan. [145]
1969 Black Carib Household Structure. Seattle: University of Washington Press. [153, 178, 182, 186, 187]
1970 "Toward a definition of matrifocality." Pp. 231–243 in Norman E. Whitten, Jr., and John F. Szwed (eds.), Afro-American Anthropology: Contemporary Perspectives. New York: Free Press. [147, 153]

Goode, William J.
    1956   After Divorce. New York: Free Press. [16]

    1962   "Marital satisfaction and instability: a cross-cultural class analysis of divorce rates." International Social Science Journal 14: 507–526. [154]

    n.d.   "The role of the family in industrialization." Social Problems of Development, vol. 7 of U.S. papers prepared for United Nations Conference in 1963 on the Application of Science and Technology for the benefit of the less developed areas, pp. 32–38, United States Government Printing Office. Pp. 87–94 reprinted in Robert F. Winch and Graham B. Spanier (eds.), Selected Studies in Marriage and the Family. New York: Holt, Rinehart and Winston (4th ed.) (1971). [16, 66]

    1963   World Revolution and Family Patterns. New York: Free Press. [8, 11, 15, 66, 67, 83, 96, 116, 191]

Goody, Jack
    1969   "Inheritance, property, and marriage in Africa and Eurasia." Sociology 3: 55–76. [92]

    1971   "Part Three. The developmental cycle." P. 83 in Jack Goody (ed.), Kinship. Baltimore: Penguin Books. [9]

    1972   "The evolution of the family." Pp. 103–124 in Peter Laslett (ed.), Household and Family in Past Time. Cambridge: Cambridge University Press. [97]

    1973   "Strategies of heirship." Comparative Studies in Society and History 15: 3–20. [94]

Gordon, Daniel N.
    1970   "Societal complexity and kinship: family organization or rules of residence?" Pacific Sociological Review 13: 252–262. [143]

Gordon, David M.
    1972   Theories of Poverty and Underemployment. Lexington, Mass.: Heath. [173]

Gough, E. Kathleen
    1952   "A comparison of incest prohibitions and the rules of exogamy in three matrilineal groups of the Malabar Coast." International Archives of Ethnography 46: 82–105. [145]

    1960   "Is the family universal?" Pp. 76–92 in Norman W. Bell and Ezra F. Vogel (eds.), A Modern Introduction to the Family. New York: Free Press. [178]

    1961a "Variation in residence." Pp. 545–576 in David M. Schneider and Kathleen Gough (eds.), Matrilineal Kinship. Berkeley: University of California Press. [97]

    1961b "Variation in interpersonal kinship relationships." Pp. 577–613 in David M. Schneider and Kathleen Gough (eds.), Matrilineal Kinship. Berkeley: University of California Press. [93,94]

    1971   "The origin of the family." Journal of Marriage and Family 33: 760–771. [92, 177, 180]

Gouldner, Alvin W., and Richard A. Peterson
  1962 Notes on Technology and the Moral Order. Indianapolis: Bobbs-Merrill. [101, 111]

Greenbaum, Lenora
  1972 "Statistical probabilities, functional relationships and Galton's problem: a summary of ongoing research." Paper presented at meeting of American Anthropological Association, Toronto. [102]

Greenfield, Sidney M.
  1960 "Industrialization and the family in sociological theory." American Journal of Sociology 67: 312-322. [116]
  1966 English Rustics in Black Skin: A Study of Modern Family Forms in a Pre-Industrialized Society. New Haven, Conn.: College and University Press. [9, 147, 178, 185, 187, 192]

Greer, Scott
  1956 "Urbanism reconsidered: a comparative study of local areas in a metropolis." American Sociological Review 21: 19-25. [13]
  1958 "Individual participation in mass society." Pp. 329-342 in Roland Young (ed.), Approaches to the Study of Politics. Evanston, Ill.: Northwestern University Press. [13]

Greven, Philip J., Jr.
  1970 Four Generations: Population, Land, and Family in Colonial Andover, Massachusetts. Ithaca, N.Y.: Cornell University Press. [44, 94, 117, 205]

Grønseth, Erik
  1970 "Notes on the historical development of the relation between nuclear family, kinship system and the wider social structure in Norway." Pp. 225-247 in Reuben Hill and René König (eds.), Families in East and West: Socialization Process and Kinship Ties. Paris: Mouton. [94]

Habakkuk, H. J.
  1955 "Family structure and economic change in nineteenth-century Europe." Journal of Economic History 15: 1-12. [95]

Hall, Peter Dobkin
  1974 "Family structure and economic organization: Massachusetts merchants, 1700-1900." Paper presented at meeting of American Sociological Association, Montreal. [44]

Hammell, E. A.
  1972 "The zadruga as process." Pp. 335-373 in Peter Laslett (ed.), Household and Family in Past Time. Cambridge: Cambridge University Press. [94]

Handler, Joel F.
  1972 Reforming the Poor. New York: Basic Books. [173]

Handwerker, W. Penn
  1973 "Technology and household configuration in urban Africa: the Bassa of Monrovia." American Sociological Review 38: 182-197. [133, 148, 151]

Hareven, Tamara K.
   1974   "The family as process: the historical study of the family cycle."
          Journal of Social History 7: 322–329. [97, 207]

Harner, Michael J.
   1970   "Population pressure and the social evolution of agriculturalists."
          Southwestern Journal of Anthropology 26: 67–86. [207]

Harris, Marvin
   1968   The Rise of Anthropological Theory: A History of Theories of Culture.
          New York: Crowell. [89, 90, 100, 102, 103, 105]

Harvey, Edward
   1968   "Technology and structure of organization." American Sociological
          Review 33: 247–258. [152]

Hauser, Philip M.
   1963   "The social, economic and technological problems of rapid urbaniza-
          tion." Pp. 199–217 in Bert Hoselitz and Wilbert Moore (eds.), Industri-
          alization and Society. Paris: UNESCO. [156]

Heise, David, Gerhard Lenski, and John Wardwell
   1976   "Further notes on technology and the moral order." Social Forces
          55: 316–337. [95, 111]

Hempel, Carl G.
   1959   "The logic of functional analysis." Pp. 271–307 in Llewellyn Gross
          (ed.), Symposium on Sociological Theory. Evanston, Ill.: Row, Peter-
          son. [5]

Hendrix, Lewellyn
   1975   "Nuclear family universals: fact and faith in the acceptance of an
          idea." Journal of Comparative Family Studies 6: 125–138. [9]

Henriques, Fernando
   1953   Family and Colour in Jamaica. London: MacGibbon and Kee. [146,
          178, 179]

   1968   Family and Colour in Jamaica. London: MacGibbon and Kee (2nd
          ed.). [185]

Herskovits, Melville J.
   1937   Life in a Haitian Valley. New York: Knopf. [146]

   1941   The Myth of the Negro Past. New York: Harper. [146]

   1943   "The Negro in Bahia, Brazil: a problem in method." American Socio-
          logical Review 8: 394–404. [146]

Herskovits, Melville J., and Frances Herskovits
   1947   Trinidad Village. New York: Knopf. [146]

Hill, Reuben
   1970   Family Development in Three Generations. Cambridge, Mass.: Schenk-
          man. [18, 205]

Hobhouse, L. T., G. C. Wheeler, and M. Ginsberg
   1915   The Material Culture and Social Institutions of the Simpler Peoples.
          London: Chapman and Hall. (81, 100, 105]

Homans, George Caspar
  1961   Social Behavior: Its Elementary Forms. New York: Harcourt. [7]
  1974   Social Behavior: Its Elementary Forms. New York: Harcourt, Brace, Jovanovich (rev. ed.). [7]

Horowitz, Michael M.
  1967   Morne-Paysan, Peasant Village in Martinique. New York: Holt, Rinehart and Winston. [189]

Hsu, Francis L. K.
  1943   "The myth of Chinese family size." American Journal of Sociology 48: 555–562. [98, 116]
  1971   "A hypothesis on kinship and culture." Pp. 3–29 in Francis L. K. Hsu (ed.), Kinship and Culture. Chicago: Aldine. [191]

Hueckel, Glenn
  1975   "A historical approach to future economic growth." Science 187: 925–931. [96]

Human Relations Area Files
  1967   "The HRAF quality control sample universe." Behavior Science Notes 2: 81–88. [103]

Ianni, Francis A.
  1972   A Family Business: Kinship and Social Control in Organized Crime. New York: Russell Sage Foundation. [17, 43]

Jorgensen, Joseph G.
  1966   "Addendum: geographical clusterings and functional explanations of in-law avoidances: an analysis of comparative method." Current Anthropology 7: 161–169. [102]

Kaberry, Phyllis
  1953   Women of the Grassfields. London: Her Majesty's Stationery Office. [116, 162]

Kay, Paul
  1963   "Aspects of social structure in a Tahitian urban neighborhood." Journal of Polynesian Society 72: 325–371. [146]

King, C. E.
  1945   "The Negro maternal family: a product of an economic and a culture system." Social Forces 24: 100–104. [146]

Knudsen, Dean D.
  1969   "The declining status of women: popular myth and the failure of functionalist thought." Social Forces 48: 183–193. [154]

Köbben, André J.
  1952   "New ways of presenting an old idea: the statistical method in social anthropology." Journal of Royal Anthropological Institute 82: 129–146. [102]

Koyama, Takashi
  1965   "A rural-urban comparison of kinship relations in Japan." Paper presented at Ninth International Seminar on Family Research, Tokyo. [92]

Langman, Lauren
   1973   "Economic practices and socialization in three societies." Report to
          Office of Educational Research, Grant CRP 6-10-114. Paper pre-
          sented at meeting of American Sociological Association, New York.
          [115]

Laslett, Peter
   1972a "Preface." pp. ix–xii in Peter Laslett (ed.), with the assistance of
          Richard Wall, Household and Family in Past Time: Comparative
          Studies in the Size and Structure of the Domestic Group over the
          Last Three Centuries in England, France, Serbia, Japan and Colonial
          North America, with Further Materials from Western Europe. Cam-
          bridge: Cambridge University Press. [96]

   1972b "Introduction: the history of the family." Pp. 1–89 in Peter Laslett
          (ed.), Household and Family in Past Time. Cambridge: Cambridge
          University Press. [97]

   1972c "Mean household size in England since the sixteenth century." Pp.
          125–158 in Peter Laslett (ed.), Household and Family in Past Time.
          Cambridge: Cambridge University Press. [97]

   1972d Household and Family in Past Time. Cambridge: Cambridge University
          Press. [207]

Leach, E. R.
   1961   Pul Eliya, A Village in Ceylon: A Study of Land Tenure and Kinship.
          Cambridge: Cambridge University Press. [93]

Lee, Richard B.
   1968   "What hunters do for a living, or, how to make out on scarce re-
          sources." Pp. 30–48 in Richard B. Lee and Irven DeVore (eds.), Man
          the Hunter. Chicago: Aldine. [152, 153]

   1969   "Kung Bushman subsistence: an input-output analysis." Pp. 47–76
          in Andrew P. Vayda (ed.), Environment and Cultural Behavior. Garden
          City, N.Y.: Natural History Press. [152, 153]

Lee, Richard B., and Irven Devore
   1968   "Problems in the study of hunters and gatherers." Pp. 3–12 in Richard
          B. Lee and Irven Devore (eds.), Man the Hunter. Chicago: Aldine.
          [134]

Leichter, Hope Jensen, and William E. Mitchell
   1967   Kinship and Casework. New York: Russell Sage Foundation. [14, 17,
          25, 31, 43]

Lenski, Gerhard
   1963   The Religious Factor: A Sociological Study of Religion's Impact on
          Politics, Economics, and Family Life. Garden City, N.Y.: Anchor
          Books (rev. ed.). [50, 51]

   1966   Power and Privilege: A Theory of Social Stratification. New York:
          McGraw-Hill. [110, 116, 155]

   1970   Human Societies: A Macrolevel Introduction to Sociology. New York:
          McGraw-Hill. [67, 73, 78, 84, 110]

1975 "Social structure in evolutionary perspective." Pp. 135–153 in Peter M. Blau (ed.), Approaches to the Study of Social Structure. New York: Free Press. [105]

1976 "History and social change." American Journal of Sociology 82: 548–564. [105]

Lenski, Gerhard, and Jean Lenski
1974 Human Societies: An Introduction to Macrosociology. New York: McGraw-Hill (2nd ed.). [5, 6, 95, 96, 109]

Levin, Henry M.
1973 "Educational reform: its meaning?" Occasional Papers in the Economics and Politics of Education. School of Education, Stanford University. [157, 173]

Lévi-Strauss, Claude
1960 "The family." Pp. 261–285 in Harry L. Shapiro (ed.), Man, Culture, and Society. New York: Oxford University Press. [180, 181]

Levy, Marion J., Jr.
1965 "Aspects of the analysis of family structure." Pp. 1–63 in Ansley J. Coale et al., Aspects of the Analysis of Family Structure. Princeton, N.J.: Princeton University Press. [96]

Lewis, Oscar
1966 La Vida: A Puerto Rican Family in the Culture of Poverty. New York: Random House. [171]

Linton, Ralph
1939 "The Tanala of Madagascar." Pp. 251–290 in Abram Kardiner, The Individual and His Society. New York: Columbia University Press. [199]

Litwak, Eugene
1960 "Occupational mobility and extended family cohesion." American Sociological Review 25: 9–21. [13, 83]

Loftin, Colin
1972 "Galton's problem as spatial autocorrelation: comments on Ember's empirical test." Ethnology 11: 425–435. [102]

Lomax, Alan, with Norman Berkowitz
1972 "The evolutionary taxonomy of culture." Science 177: 228–239. [84]

Lombardi, John R.
1973 "Exchange and survival." Paper read at meeting of American Anthropological Association, New Orleans. [153]

Lopreato, Joseph
1965 "How would you like to be a peasant?" Human Organization 24: 298. [146]

1970 Italian Americans. New York: Random House. [43]

Lowie, Robert H.
1920 Primitive Society. New York. Boni and Liveright. [71, 92, 113]

Malinowski, Bronislaw

1929　"Marriage." Encyclopaedia Britannica 14: 940–950. [179]

Mamdani, Mahmood
1972　The Myth of Population Control: Family, Caste, and Class in an Indian Village. New York: Monthly Review Press. [155]

Marris, Peter
n.d.　"Individual achievement and family ties: some international comparisons." Manuscript. [100]

1962　Family and Social Change in an African City. Evanston, Ill.: Northwestern University Press. [100]

1970　"African families in the process of change." Pp. 397–409 in Reuben Hill and René König (eds.), Families in East and West: Socialization Process and Kinship Ties. Paris: Mouton. [100]

Marsh, Robert M.
1967　Comparative Sociology. New York: Harcourt, Brace and World. [72, 79, 80, 83, 86, 89]

Marx, Karl
1968　Karl Marx and Fredrick Engels: Selected Works. New York: International Publishers. [67]

McKinney, John C.
1966　Constructive Typology and Social Theory. New York: Appleton-Century-Crofts. [259]

Meyers, J. Thomas
1971　"The origin of agriculture: an evaluation of three hypotheses." Pp. 101–121 in Stuart Struever (ed.), Pre-historic Agriculture. Garden City, N.Y.: Natural History Press. [113]

Millar, John
1771　The Origin of the Distinction of Ranks. London: Murray. Third edition (1779). Pp. 165–322 reprinted in William C. Lehmann, John Millar of Glasgow, 1735–1801: His Life and Thought and His Contributions to Sociological Analysis. Cambridge: Cambridge University Press, 1960. [88]

Mindel, Charles H., and Robert W. Habenstein (eds.)
1976　Ethnic Families in America: Patterns and Variations. New York: Elsevier. [34]

Morgan, James M. et al.
1974　Five Thousand American Families: Patterns of Economic Progress: An Analysis of the First Five Years of the Panel Study of Income Dynamics. Ann Arbor, Mich.: Institute for Social Research. [174]

Morgan, Lewis Henry
1871　Systems of Consanguinity and Affinity in the Human Family. Washington, D.C.: Smithsonian Institution. [89]

1877　Ancient Society: or Researches in the Lines of Human Progress from Savagery through Barbarism to Civilization. Chicago: Kerr. [89, 90]

"Moynihan Report" (Moynihan, Daniel Patrick)
1965　The Negro Family: The Case for National Action. Washington, D.C.:

Office of Policy Planning and Research, U.S. Department of Labor. [146]

Murdock, George Peter
1937 "Correlations of matrilineal and patrilineal institutions." In G. P. Murdock (ed.), Studies in the Science of Society. New Haven, Conn.: Yale University Press. [91, 101]

1949 Social Structure. New York: Macmillan. [72, 85, 91, 101, 105, 106, 113, 147, 162, 176, 178, 180]

1957 "World ethnographic sample." American Anthropologist 59: 664–687. [68, 101]

1967 "Ethnographic atlas: a summary." Ethnology 6: 109–236. [66, 72, 73, 76, 102, 125, 127, 142, 145, 159, 168, 174, 243, 248]

1968 "World sampling provinces." Ethnology 7: 305–326. [125, 142]

Murdock, George P. et al.
1950 Outline of Cultural Materials. New Haven, Conn: Human Relations Area Files. [101]

Murdock, George P., and Caterina Provost
1973a "Factors in the division of labor by sex: a cross-cultural analysis." Ethnology 12: 203–225. [113, 149, 180]

1973b "Measurement of cultural complexity." Ethnology 12: 379–392. [203]

Murdock, George P., and Douglas R. White
1969 "Standard cross-cultural sample." Ethnology 8: 329–369. [84, 102, 103]

Murdock, George P., and Suzanne F. Wilson
1972 "Settlement patterns and community organization: cross-cultural codes 3." Ethnology 11: 254–295. [145, 161, 170, 203]

Myrdal, Gunnar
1944 An American Dilemma. New York: Harper. [146]

Nagy, Vivian Tong
1975 "Family characteristics, attitudes, and values." Pp. 261–275 in Harold B. Gerard and Norman Miller, School Desegregation: A Long-Term Study. New York: Plenum. [296]

Naroll, Raoul
1956 "A preliminary index of social development." American Anthropologist 72: 1227–1288. [81]

1964 "A fifth solution to Galton's problem." American Anthropologist 66: 863–867. [102]

1970a "The culture-bearing unit in cross-cultural surveys." Pp. 707–720 in Raoul Naroll and Ronald Cohen (eds.), A Handbook of Method in Cultural Anthropology. Garden City, N.Y.: Natural History Press. [102]

1970b "What have we learned from cross-cultural surveys?" American Anthropologist 72: 1227–1288. [84, 92, 102]

Naroll, Raoul et al.

1970   "A standard ethnographic sample: preliminary edition." Current Anthropology 11: 235–248. [103]

Naroll, Raoul, and Richard C. Sipes
1973   "A standard ethnographic sample: second edition." Current Anthropology 14: 111–140. [103, 142]

Nieboer, H. J.
1900   Slavery as an Industrial System: Ethnological Researcher. The Hague: Marinus Nihjoff. [100]

Nimkoff, M. F., and Russell Middleton
1960   "Types of family and types of economy." American Journal of Sociology 66: 215–225. (8, 68, 93, 101, 108, 129, 149, 243]

Nisbet, Robert
1969   Social Change and History. New York: Oxford Galaxy. [105]

Norton, Arthur J.
1974   "The family-life cycle updated: components and uses." Pp. 162–170 in Robert F. Winch and Graham B. Spanier (eds.), Selected Studies in Marriage and the Family. New York: Holt, Rinehart and Winston (4th ed.). [204]

Nutini, Hugo G.
1965   "Some considerations on the nature of social structure and model building: a critique of Claude Lévi-Strauss and Edmund Leach." American Anthropologist 67: 707–731. [95]

Ogburn, William Fielding
1922   Social Change: With Respect to Culture and Original Nature. New York: Viking Press. [6, 106]

1929   "The changing family." Publications of American Sociological Society 23: 124–133. [6, 13, 109]

Opler, Marvin K.
1943   "Woman's social status and the forms of marriage." American Journal of Sociology 49: 125–148. [148]

Oppenheimer, Valerie Kincaid
1973   "Demographic influence on female employment and the status of women." American Journal of Sociology 78: 946–961. [154]

Oppong, Christine
1974   Marriage among a Matrilineal Elite: A Family Study of Ghanaian Senior Civil Servants. Cambridge: Cambridge University Press. [187]

Osmond, Marie W.
1969   "A cross-cultural analysis of family organization." Journal of Marriage and the Family 31: 302–310. [72]

Otterbein, Keith F.
1965   "Caribbean family organization: a comparative analysis." American Anthropologist 67: 66–79. [178]

1966   The Andros Islanders. Lawrence: University of Kansas Press. [189]

Parish, William L., Jr., and Moshe Schwartz

1972 "Household complexity in nineteenth-century France." American Sociological Review 37: 154–173. [95]

Parsons, Talcott
1943 "The kinship system of the contemporary United States." American Anthropologist 45: 22–28. [12]
1949 "The social structure of the family." Pp. 173–201 in Ruth Nanda Anshen (ed.), The Family: Its Function and Destiny. New York: Harper and Row. [13]
1955 "The American family: its relations to personality and to the social structure." Pp. 3–33 in Talcott Parsons and Robert F. Bales, Family Socialization and Interaction Process. Glencoe, Ill.: Free Press. [147]
1966 Societies: Evolutionary and Comparative Perspectives. Englewood Cliffs, N.J.: Prentice-Hall. [106]

Parsons, Talcott, and Robert F. Bales
1955 Family, Socialization and Interaction Process. New York: Free Press. [13, 17, 147]

Pearlin, Leonard I., and Melvin Kohn
1966 "Social class, occupation and parents' values: a cross-national study." American Sociological Review 31: 466–479. [115]

Peattie, Lisa R.
1968 The View from the Barrio. Ann Arbor: University of Michigan Press. [133, 172]

Perrow, Charles
1967 "A framework for the comparative analysis of organizations." American Sociological Review 32: 194–208. [152]

Philpott, Stuart B.
1973 West Indian Migration: The Montserrat Case. New York: Humanities Press. [189]

Pitt-Rivers, Julian
1973 "The kith and the kin." Pp. 89–105 in Jack Goody (ed.), The Character of Kinship. Cambridge: Cambridge University Press. [99]

Piven, Frances Fox, and Richard A. Cloward
1971 Regulating the Poor: The Functions of Public Welfare. New York: Random House. [157]

Polgar, Steven
1972 "Population history and population policies from an anthropological perspective." Current Anthropology 13: 203–211. [155]

Powdermaker, Hortense
1939 After Freedom: A Cultural Study in the Deep South. New York: Viking Press. [146]

Radcliffe-Brown, A. R.
1950 "Introduction." Pp. 1–85 in A. R. Radcliffe-Brown and Daryll Forde (eds.), African Systems of Kinship and Marriage. London: Oxford University Press. [177, 191]

Rainwater, Lee
  1966   "Crucible of identity: the Negro lower-class family." Daedalus 95: 172–216. [178, 182]
  1970   Behind Ghetto Walls: Black Families in a Federal Slum. Chicago: Aldine. [185]

Redfield, Robert
  1947   "The folk society." American Journal of Sociology 52: 293–308. [67]

Reinhardt, Hazel H., Rae L. Blumberg, and Robert F. Winch
  1975   "Theory guided coding: a pilot study coding fertility and the economic function of the family." Paper presented at Cross-Cultural Society meeting, Chicago. [203]

Rodman, Hyman
  1971   Lower-Class Families: The Culture of Poverty in Negro Trinidad. New York: Oxford University Press. [186]
  1972   "Marital power and the theory of resources in cultural context." Journal of Comparative Family Studies 3: 50–69. [62, 63, 116]

Rosenberg, Ellen M.
  n.d.   "Linear and cultural evolution: toward a demographic hypothesis." Manuscript. [105]

Rosow, Irving
  1965   "Intergenerational relationships: problems and proposals." Pp. 341–378 in Ethel Shanas and Gordon F. Streib (eds.), Social Structure and the Family: Generational Relations. Englewood Cliffs, N.J.: Prentice-Hall. [15]
  1967   Social Integration of the Aged. New York: Free Press. [15]

Ross, Heather L., and Isabel V. Sawhill
  1975   Time of Transition: The Growth of Families Headed by Women. Washington, D.C.: Urban Institute. [188, 189]

Rubin, Lillian Breslow
  1976   Worlds of Pain: Life in the Working Class Family. New York: Basic Books. [52]

Sackrey, Charles
  1973   The Political Economy of Urban Poverty. New York: Norton. [155, 157, 172]

Safa, Helen L.
  1964   "From shantytown to public housing: a comparison of family structure in two urban neighborhoods in Puerto Rico." Caribbean Studies 4: 3–12. [156]

Sahlins, Marshall D.
  1957   "Land use and the extended family in Moala, Fiji." American Anthropologist 59: 449–462. [199]
  1965   "On the sociology of primitive exchange." Pp. 139–238 in Michael Banton (ed.), The Relevance of Models for Social Anthropology. New York: Praeger [153]

Sanford, Margaret

1974 "A socialization in ambiguity: childlending in a British West Indian society." Ethnology 13: 393–400. [189]

Sawyer, Jack
1967 "Dimensions of nations: size, wealth and politics." American Journal of Sociology 73: 145–172. [111]

Sawyer, Jack, and Robert LeVine
1966 "Cultural dimensions: a factor analysis of the World Ethnographic Sample." American Anthropologist 68: 708–731. [70, 101]

Scanzoni, John
1972 Sexual Bargaining: Power Politics in the American Marriage. Engle-wood Cliffs, N.J.: Prentice-Hall. [116, 172]

Schnaiberg, Allan, and Sheldon Goldenberg
1975 "Closing the circle: the impact of children on parental status." Journal of Marriage and the Family 37: 937–953. [15]

Schnaiberg, Allan, and David Reed
1974 "Risk, uncertainty, and family formation: the social context of pov-erty groups." Population Studies 28: 513–533. [156]

Schneider, David M.
1961 "Introduction: the distinctive features of matrilineal descent groups." Pp. 1–32 in David M. Schneider and Kathleen Gough (eds.), Matrilineal Kinship. Berkeley: University of California Press. [91]

Schneider, David M., and Raymond T. Smith
1973 Class Differences and Sex Roles in American Kinship and Family Structure. Englewood Cliffs, N.J.: Prentice-Hall. [183]

Schnore, Leo
1961 "The statistical measurement of urbanization and economic develop-ment." Land Economics 37: 228–245. [111]

Schuman, Howard
1971 "The religious factor in Detroit: review, replication, and reanalysis." American Sociological Review 36: 30–48. [51]

Shanas, Ethel
1973 "Family-kin networks and aging in cross-cultural perspective." Journal of Marriage and the Family 35: 505–511. [97]

Shanas, Ethel et al.
1968 Old People in Three Industrial Societies. New York: Atherton. [15]

Sharp, Harry, and Morris Axelrod
1956 "Mutual aid among relatives in an urban population." Pp. 433–439 in Ronald Freeman et al. (eds.), Principles of Sociology: A Text with Readings. New York: Holt, Rinehart, and Winston. [15]

Sheils, Howard Dean
1969 Agricultural Technology and Societal Evolution. Unpublished Ph.D. dissertation, University of Wisconsin. [111]
1975 "Statistical explanation in cross-cultural research: a comparison of the utility of linear and curvilinear correlation." Sociological Quarterly 16: 115–123. [283]

Simey, Thomas
  1946   Welfare Planning in the West Indies. Oxford: Clarendon Press. [146]

Simmons, Leo W.
  1937   "Statistical correlations in the science of society." Pp. 495–517 in George P. Murdock (ed.), Studies in the Science of Society. New Haven, Conn.: Yale University Press. [100]

Sjoberg, Gideon
  1960   The Pre-Industrial City. New York: Free Press. [116]

Smith, Adam
  1814   The Wealth of Nations. Edinburgh: Oliphant, Waugh, and Innes. [10]

Smith, M. G.
  1962   West Indian Family Structure. Seattle: University of Washington Press. [178, 186]

Smith, Raymond T.
  1956   The Negro Family in British Guiana: Family Structure and Social Status in the Villages. London: Routledge and Kegan Paul. [145, 147, 178, 183, 185, 186]
  1973   "The matrifocal family." Pp. 121–144 in Jack Goody (ed.), The Character of Kinship. Cambridge: Cambridge University Press. [96, 145, 183]

Sonquist, John A.
  1970   Multivariate Model Building: The Validation of a Search Strategy. Ann Arbor, Mich.: Institute for Social Research. [259]

Sonquist, John A., Elizabeth Lauh Baker, and James N. Morgan
  1973   Searching for Structure: An Approach to Analysis of Substantial Bodies of Micro-Data and Documentation for a Computer Program. Ann Arbor, Mich.: Institute for Social Research (rev. ed.). [124, 125]

Spencer, Herbert
  1910   The Principles of Sociology. New York: Appleton-Century-Crofts. [67]

Spicer, Jerry W., and Gary D. Hampe
  1975   "Kinship interaction after divorce." Journal of Marriage and the Family 37: 113–119. [48]

Spiro, Melford E.
  1956   Kibbutz: Venture in Utopia. Cambridge, Mass.: Harvard University Press. [4, 41, 178]

Stack, Carol B.
  1970   "The kindred of Viola Jackson: residence and family organization of an urban black American family." Pp. 303–312 in Norman E. Whitten, Jr., and John F. Szwed (eds.), Afro-American Anthropology: Contemporary Perspectives. New York: Free Press. [152, 153, 172]
  1974   All Our Kin: Strategies for Survival in a Black Community. New York: Harper and Row. [5, 43, 97, 99, 153, 172, 178, 183, 186, 187, 188, 189]

Stein, Robert L.
1970   "The economic status of families headed by women." Reprint 2703 from December Monthly Labor Review 93: 1-8 [158, 159, 173]

Steinmetz, S. R.
1930   Classification des Types Sociaux et Catalogue des Peuples. Gesammelte kleinere Schriften zur Ethnologie und Soziologie, vol. 2. Groningen: Noordhoff. [100]

Stephens, William N.
1963   The Family in Cross-Cultural Perspective. New York: Holt, Rinehart, and Winston. [163, 248]

Steward, Julian H.
1936   "The economic and social basis of primitive bands." Pp. 331-350 in Robert H. Lowie (ed.), Essays in Anthropology: Presented to A. L. Kroeber. Berkeley: University of California Press. [91]
1949   "Cultural causality and law: a trial formulation of early civilization." American Anthropologist 51: 1-27. [90]
1963   Theory of Culture Change: The Methodology of Multilinear Evolution. Urbana: University of Illinois Press. [105]

Stolte-Heiskanen, Veronica
1975   "Family needs and societal institutions: potential empirical linkage mechanisms." Journal of Marriage and the Family 37: 903-916. [80]

Sumner, William Graham
1906   Folkways: A Study of the Sociological Importance of Usages, Manners, Customs, Mores, and Morals. Boston: Ginn. [100, 103]

Sumner, William Graham, and Albert Galloway Keller
1927   The Science of Society. New Haven, Conn.: Yale University Press (4 vols.). [100, 180]

Survey Research Center
1956   A Social Profile of Detroit: 1955. Ann Arbor, Mich.: Institute for Social Research. [13]

Sussman, Marvin B.
1953   "The help pattern in the middle-class family." American Sociological Review 18: 231-240. [15]
1954   "Family continuity: selective factors which affect relationships between families at generational levels." Marriage and Family Living 16: 112-120. [13]
1959   "The isolated nuclear family: fact or fiction." Social Problems 6: 333-340. [13, 18]

Swanson, Guy E.
1960   The Birth of the Gods. Ann Arbor: University of Michigan Press. [101, 102]

Sweetser, Dorrian Apple
1966   "The effect of industrialization on intergenerational solidarity." Rural Sociology 31: 156-170. [92]

Tambiah, S. J.
  1965   "Kinship fact and fiction in relation to the Kandyan Sinhalese."
         Journal of Royal Anthropological Institute 95: 131–173. [93]

Tatje, Terrence A.
  1970   "Problems of concept definition for comparative studies." Pp. 689–
         696 in Raoul Naroll and Ronald Cohen (eds.), A Handbook of Method
         in Cultural Anthropology. Garden City, N.Y.: Natural History Press.
         [102]

Tatje, Terrence, and Raoul Naroll
  1970   "Two measures of sociological complexity: an empirical cross-cultural
         comparison." Pp. 766–833 in Raoul Naroll and Ronald Cohen (eds.),
         A Handbook of Method in Cultural Anthropology. Garden City,
         N.Y.: Natural History Press. [83]

Thibaut, John W., and Harold H. Kelley
  1959   The Social Psychology of Groups. New York: Wiley. [7]

Tönnies, Ferdinand
  1940   Fundamental Concepts in Society. New York: American Book. [67]

Tuden, Arthur, and Caterina Marshall
  1972   "Political organization: cross-cultural codes 4." Ethnology 11: 436–
         464. [203]

Turner, Jonathan H.
  1974   The Structure of Sociological Theory. Homewood, Ill.: Dorsey. [5]

Tylor, E. B.
  1889   "On a method of investigating the development of institutions: applied
         to laws of marriage and descent." Journal of Royal Anthropological
         Institute 18: 245–269. [89, 100]

Udy, Stanley H.
  1959   Organization of Work: A Comparative Analysis of Production among
         Nonindustrial Peoples. New Haven, Conn.: HRAF Press. [101]

U.S. Bureau of the Census
  1960   Historical Statistics of the United States: Colonial Times to 1957.
         Washington, D.C.: U.S. Government Printing Office. [33]

  1968   Current Population Reports—Population Estimates, Series P-25, No.
         384, February 13. Washington, D.C.: U.S. Government Printing Office.
         [293]

  1971   Statistical Abstract of the U.S. 1971 (92nd ed.). Washington, D.C.:
         U.S. Government Printing Office. [172]

  1972a Current Population Reports—Population Characteristics, Series P-20,
         No. 237, July. Washington, D.C.: U.S. Government Printing Office.
         [17]

  1972b 1970 Census of the Population: General Population Characteristics:
         United States Summary, PC (1)-B1. Washington, D.C.: U.S. Govern-
         ment Printing Office. [17]

  1973a Census of the Population: 1970. Vol. 1, Characteristics of Population.
         Part 1, United States Summary—Section 2. Washington, D.C.: U.S.
         Government Printing Office. [43, 158, 160]

1973b Census of the Population: 1970. Subject Reports. Final Report PC(2)-4B. Persons by Family Characteristics. Washington, D.C.: U.S. Government Printing Office. [286, 287]

1976a Current Population Reports—Population Characteristics. Series P-20, No. 291, February. "Household and Family Characteristics: March 1975." [19, 20, 21, 42]

1976b Statistical Abstract of U.S. 1976 (97th ed.). Washington, D.C.: U.S. Government Printing Office. [19]

1977 Current Population Reports—Population Characteristics. Series P-20, No. 306, January. "Marital Status and Living Arrangements: March 1976." [23, 24, 48]

U.S. Department of Labor
1973 "Facts about women heads of households and heads of families." [154, 173]

Valentine, Charles A.
1970 "Blackston: progress report on a community study in urban Afro-America." Mimeographed. St. Louis: Washington University. [153]

van den Berghe, Pierre L.
1973 Age and Sex in Human Societies: A Biosocial Perspective. Belmont, Calif.: Wadsworth. [177]

Vatuk, Sylvia
1973 Kinship and Urbanization: White-Collar Migrants in North India. Berkeley: University of California Press. [133]

Vermeulen, C. J. J., and A. de Ruijter
1975 "Dominant epistemological presuppositions in the use of the cross-cultural survey method." Current Anthropology 16: 29–52. [102]

Wallerstein, Immanuel
1974 The Modern-World System: Capitalist Agriculture and the Origin of the European World-Economy in the 16th Century. New York: Academic Press. [68]

Warner, W. Lloyd, and Paul S. Lunt
1941 The Social Life of a Modern Community. New Haven, Conn.: Yale University Press. [43]

Washburn, Sherwood L., and C. S. Lancaster
1972 "The evolution of hunting." Pp. 293–303 in Richard B. Lee and Irven DeVore (eds.), Man the Hunter. Chicago: Aldine. [98]

Westermarck, Edvard A.
1891 The History of Human Marriage. London: Macmillan. [90]

White, Leslie A.
1949 The Science of Culture: A Study of Man and Civilization. New York: Grove Press. [95]

Whiting, John W. M.
1959 "Sorcery, sin, and the superego: a cross-cultural study of some mechanisms of social control." Pp. 174–195 in Marshall R. Jones (ed.), Nebraska Symposium on Motivation. Lincoln: University of Nebraska Press. [101]

1960   "Resource mediation and learning by identification." Pp. 112–126 in I. Iscoe and M. Stevenson (eds.), Personality Development in Children. Austin: University of Texas Press. [101]

1961   "Socialization process and personality." Pp. 355–380 in Francis L. K. Hsu (ed.), Psychological Anthropology. Homewood, Ill.: Dorsey. [101]

Whiting, John W. M., and Irvin L. Child
1953   Child Training and Personality: A Cross-Cultural Study. New Haven, Conn.: Yale University Press. [101, 162]

Whitten, Norman E., Jr.
1970   "Strategies of adaptive mobility in the Colombian-Ecuadorian littoral." Pp. 329–343 in Norman E. Whitten, Jr., and John F. Szwed (eds.), Afro-American Anthropology: Contemporary Perspectives. New York: Free Press. [205]

Williams, Brett
1976   "Why migrant women make their husbands tamales." Paper presented at the meeting of National Council of Family Relations, New York. [52]

Wilson, C. S.
1953   The Family and Neighborhood in a British Community. M.Sc. thesis, Cambridge University. [146]

Wilson, Edward C.
1975   Sociobiology: The New Synthesis. Cambridge: Belknap Press of Harvard University Press. [100, 105]

Winch, Robert F.
1947   "Heuristic and empirical typologies: a job for factor analysis." American Sociological Review 12: 68–75. [259]

1958   Mate-Selection: A Study of Complementary Needs. New York: Harper. [7]

1962   Identification and Its Familial Determinants. Indianapolis: Bobbs-Merrill. [8, 55, 56, 61, 207]

1963   The Modern Family. New York: Holt, Rinehart, and Winston (rev. ed.). [xix, 177]

1970   "Determinants of interpersonal influence in the late adolescent male: theory and design of research." Pp. 578–601 in Reuben Hill and René König (eds.), Families in East and West: Socialization Process and Kinship Ties. Paris: Mouton. [8, 55]

1971   The Modern Family. New York: Holt, Rinehart, and Winston (3rd ed.). [1, 9, 177, 242]

1972   "Theorizing about the family." Journal of Comparative Family Studies 3 (Spring): 5–16. [1, 177]

1974a   "Some observations on extended familism in the United States." Pp. 147–160 in Robert F. Winch and Graham B. Spanier (eds.), Selected Studies in Marriage and the Family. New York: Holt, Rinehart and Winston (4th ed.). [11]

1974b "Permanence and change in the history of the American family and some speculations as to its future." Pp. 480–489 in Robert F. Winch and Graham B. Spanier (eds.), Selected Studies in Marriage and the Family. New York: Holt, Rinehart and Winston (4th ed.). [19]

1975 "Inferring minimum structure from function: or did the bureaucracy create the mother-child family?" Paper presented at Fourteenth Seminar of the Committee for Family Research, International Sociological Association, Curaçao. [176]

1976 "Typologizing the American Family." Paper presented at meeting of American Sociological Association, New York. [11]

Winch, Robert F., and Rae Lesser Blumberg
1968 "Societal complexity and familial organization." Pp. 70–92 in Robert F. Winch and Louis Wolf Goodman (eds.), Selected Studies in Marriage and the Family. New York: Holt, Rinehart and Winston (3rd ed.). [65, 149]

1972 "Preliminary investigation of a model of the familial system." Paper presented at meeting of American Sociological Association, New Orleans. [107, 120]

Winch, Robert F., and Donald T. Campbell
1969 "Proof? No. Evidence? Yes. The significance of tests of significance." American Sociologist 4: 140–143. [103]

Winch, Robert F., and Margaret T. Gordon
1974 Familial Structure and Function as Influence. Lexington, Mass.: Lexington Books. [8, 53, 55, 63, 64, 207]

Winch, Robert F., and Scott Greer
1968 "Urbanism, ethnicity, and extended familism." Journal of Marriage and the Family 30: 40–45. [11, 71]

Winch, Robert F., Scott Greer, and Rae Lesser Blumberg
1967 "Ethnicity and extended familism in an upper-middle-class suburb." American Sociological Review 32: 265–272. [11, 71]

Winch, Robert F., Scott Greer, Rae Lesser Blumberg, and Joyce Sween
1969 "Further observations on ethnicity and extended familism in an upper-middle-class suburb." Paper presented at meeting of American Sociological Association, San Francisco. [11]

Winch, Robert F., and Graham B. Spanier (eds.)
1974 Selected Studies in Marriage and the Family. New York: Holt, Rinehart and Winston (4th ed.). [64]

Wirth, Louis
1938 "Urbanism as a way of life." American Journal of Sociology 44: 1–24. [12, 13]

Wolf, Eric R.
1966 Peasants. Englewood Cliffs, N.J.: Prentice-Hall. [110, 113, 119, 156]

Woofter, T. J.
1930 Black Yeomanry. New York: Henry Holt. [146]

Worsley, P. M.
  1956   "The kinship system of the Tallensi: a reevaluation." Journal of Royal Anthropological Institute 86: 37–75. [93]

Yorburg, Betty
  1975   "The nuclear and the extended family: an area of conceptual confusion." Journal of Comparative Family Studies 6: 5–14. [9]

Young, Michael, and Peter Willmott
  1957   Family and Kinship in East London. Glencoe, Ill.: Free Press. [145, 146]

Zeitlin, Maurice
  1974   "Corporate ownership and control: the large corporation and the capitalist class." American Journal of Sociology 79: 1073–1119. [43]

Zimmerman, Carle C.
  1947   Family and Civilization. New York: Harper and Row. [12, 13, 50]

Index